Foundation, Architecture, and Prototyping of Humanized AI

Humanized AI (HAI), emerging as the next of the AI waves, refers to artificial social beings that are very close to humans in various aspects, beings who are machine-race humans, not digital slaves. Foundation, architecture, and prototyping of HAI deploy a novel small-data approach to vertically explore the spectrum of HAI.

Different from the popular big-data philosophy that is based on the rigid notion that the connotation of each concept is fixed and the same to everyone, this book treats understanding as a process from simple to complex, and uses the similarity principle to effectively deal with novelties. Combining the efficiency of the Behaviorists' goal-driven approach and the flexibility of a Constructivists' approach, both the architecture of HAI and the philosophical discussions arising from it are elaborated upon.

Advancing a unique approach to the concept of HAI, this book appeals to professors and students of both AI and philosophy, as well as industry professionals looking to stay at the forefront of developments within the field.

Foundation, Architecture, and Prototyping of Humanized AI
A New Constructivist Approach

Mark Chang

CRC Press
Taylor & Francis Group
Boca Raton London New York

CRC Press is an imprint of the
Taylor & Francis Group, an **informa** business

A CHAPMAN & HALL BOOK

First edition published 2023
by CRC Press
2385 Executive Center Drive, Suite 320, Boca Raton, FL 33431

and by CRC Press
4 Park Square, Milton Park, Abingdon, Oxon, OX14 4RN

CRC Press is an imprint of Taylor & Francis Group, LLC

ISBN: 978-1-032-49157-8 (hbk)
ISBN: 978-1-032-49165-3 (pbk)
ISBN: 978-1-003-39242-2 (ebk)

DOI: 10.1201/b23355

Typeset in Palatino
by KnowledgeWorks Global Ltd.

Contents

Part IV   Prototyping Agents—Zda and Lia

Preface

Humanized AI (HAI) is a phrase used to denote artificial social beings that are very close to humans in various displayed aspects. These may include learning ability, knowledge discovery, problem-solving, creativity, communicated emotion, self-awareness, and consciousness. In a sense, AI is the artificialization of humans, while HAI is a re-humanization of artificialized humans. HAI may be considered as human-level AI or artificial general intelligence, but it also emphasizes human-like features. HAI agents are machine-race human beings, not digital slaves. It is noticed that the term "Humanized AI" might be used in a different context or a narrow sense by different people.

This book is about how to make HAI agents which come as the next AI wave. It covers philosophical discussions on central topics in HAI, the architectures of HAI, and prototypical HAI agents. The agents are virtually **Z**ero-**d**ata based **agents** (**Zda**) and **L**anguage-**i**ndependent **agents** (**Lia**), having no-built-in natural languages. Both are capable of displaying great learning skills, self-awareness, consciousness, and emotional intelligence. Unlike narrow AI, where each agent can only have a particular skill, the elaboration tolerance of HAI enables a humanized agent to learn many different skills over time without restarting or erasing previous information.

I started to work on HIA in 2003, some 20 years ago, when I first realized a simple known fact: a human baby has virtually a data-empty brain and no inherited natural languages, but can learn things like languages and math skills. I immediately prototyped a very simple version of HAI using Microsoft Visual Basic. As I expected, the agents can learn and create very simple "language" through interactions by means of reinforcement learning. The approach is what is now called the Constructivist Approach. However, shortly thereafter I faced a challenge: when complex concepts are involved, traditional reinforcement learning has too many paths to explore before the agent can identify an optimal or reasonable solution. I struggled to solve the problem for the next 15 years until I finally came up with the current synthesist's approach in 2016, which combines the behaviorist's efficiency and constructivist's flexibility.

Behaviorists believe actions are reflections of what goes on in the mind, adopting a goal-driven approach. Constructivists emphasize that knowledge cannot be a passive reflection of reality, but an active construction by the individual, from simple to complex. We take a synthetic approach by combining the two in our HAI architecture—a new constructivist approach. In this approach, instead of emphasizing the notion that an agent's action is based on the maximization of some utility as Rationalists do, we adopt probabilistically a randomized maximization to better emulate human-thinking and behaviors. The HAI architecture has four main components. (1) A Recursive Network of Patterns, for dynamic knowledge representation, provides a self-inclusive structure necessary for self-awareness. (2) Attention Mechanisms allow an HAI agent to focus on a few important things for efficient learning and response. (3) Learning Mechanisms that feature hierarchical tokenization and recursive patternization allow progressive learning, from simple to complex. (4) Adaptive Reinforcement Response Mechanisms, mimicking free will, randomize potential responses according to the associated rewards or frequencies. A major feature, or objective, of HAI is that imitation, doing what other people do under various situations, makes HAI agents adhere to social norms without pre-specifying any of the norms.

Our HAI approach is constructed on several general principles and laws, including the Similarity Principle, Parsimony Principle, Association Principles, First Principles, Principle of Factor Isolation, Law of Summative Effects, and Weber-Fechner Laws. The principles make all specific methods or mechanisms in the HAI architecture coherent.

The Similarity Principle, used in learning and response mechanisms, is the key to dealing with novelties encountered by HAI agents in patternization or scientific discovery. This is because everything is changing, and no two things are identical. This principle asserts that two similar objects behave similarly, thus allowing us and agents to group similar things into categories and make patterns. The Similarity Principle deals with imitation and creativity under the same umbrella, i.e., in similarity replacement of the building blocks of the world with different degrees of similarity.

The Association Principle guarantees the association between two things that are spatially or temporally close, and it serves as the backbone for learning. The Association Principle allows an agent to map natural language patterns to environmental event-patterns. In this sense, HAI can be considered as a computer program that automatically generates computer programs. What appears to be a complex universe can actually be modeled by a recursion of a simple world governed by a small set of principles.

Enlightened by First Principles and Connotation of understanding, we postulate that any complex concept or knowledge consists of a hierarchical recursion of elementary concepts and any high-level skill is a composition of sequential and recursion of elementary movements of body parts. These atomic concepts and movements, despite varying from individual to individual, are the building blocks of our HAI agents—they make it possible to build HAI using a small-data approach!

The Weber-Fechner Laws serve the basis for building virtual sensory organs, the Parsimony Principle supports the adaptive reinforcement learning in response model, the Law of Summative Effects ensures that the sequence of short-term goal-driven actions will achieve a long-term goal, and the Principle of Factor Isolation guides experience-based learning (patternization) and cognitive learning (logical reasoning).

Given the complexity of HAI, studying HAI without discussions of architecture and prototyping to show how it works will be somewhat empty and less convincing, while studying HAI architecture and prototyping without understanding the fundamental issues and human characteristics is a mindless approach that will not lead too far either. Thus, I have an ambitious goal: to cover **vertically** the whole spectrum from foundation, architecture, and prototyping (algorithm and pseudocode) in a concise book. Keep in mind that even if (or when) we make the first agent exactly like a human baby, it will take 10–20 years to teach him what he needs to thrive. Principles and methods of teaching HAI agents are also a critical topic for our discussion.

The book has four parts and an appendix. **Part I** features philosophical discussions of some key aspects of HAI, such as consciousness, the connotation of understanding, roles of attention, imitation, analogy and creativity, and scientific principles. **Part II** reviews the AI waves, existing approaches to HAI, and the new synthesist's approach. These two chapters constitute the foundation for the HAI Architecture in **Part III**, which elaborates the architectures of the new constructivist approach, including innate knowledge, knowledge dynamic representation, learning mechanisms, response mechanisms, and effective teaching. Following the architecture blueprint, **Part IV** discusses prototyping the animated agents, Zda and Lia, with examples to show how language can be learned from scratch, how agents can learn playing board games starting from learning the rules, and many more. To make the book stand alone, The **Appendix** provides a concise review of narrow AI with emphasis on the ideas behind each method.

This book is intended for anyone who is interested in HAI, including college professors, researchers, and students in Computer and Information Science, Computer Engineering, Data Science, Philosophy, Psychology, Education, Economics, and Political Science. The first two parts are geared toward the general audience, while Parts III and IV are more suitable for those who want to know exactly how HAI can be built to have human characteristics such as understanding natural language, self-awareness, consciousness, imitation, creativity, discovery, reasoning, goal-setting, and ethics. If you finish all four parts, you are expected to be able to use the computer language you are familiar with to translate the algorithms and pseudocode in Part IV into actionable agents, and to start to "raise" and teach your baby agents.

Mark Chang, PhD
Christmas, 2022
Boston University

Acknowledgements

I'd like to express my sincere thanks to Dr. Robort Pierce, Prof. Maggi Savin-Baden, and anonymous reviewers for their valuable suggections.

Part I

Philosophy of Humanized AI in Plain Language

Humanized AI looks, thinks, and behaves like humans, a life companion, not a digital slave. This chapter will discuss the fundamental aspects regarding human nature and surrounding controversies. Without necessary clarifications on these aspects, building HAI can become a baseless claim. The discussions of issues in this chapter will serve as the basis for HAI Architecture in Part III, while the architectures serve as the blueprint for the prototyping of HAI in Part IV. We will first delineate prospective HAI and the human-machine world in Chapter 1, followed by the discussion of the multifacetedness of the objective world. Chapter 3 discusses the fundamental principles that a human (thus an HAI agent, also) uses to formulate his perceptual world. Chapter 4 concerns critical aspects in learning, which will inform the construction of the architectures.

We avoid long discussions on each of the critical topics. Instead, the concise presentation will be just enough to support the later architecture-building. Readers should have critical eyes since there are many personal views that might significantly deviate from mainstream views. Given the broad coverage of topics, readers may initially run through some of the topics but are definitely encouraged to review relevant parts when reading Part III, Architectures of HAI.

DOI: 10.1201/b23355-1

1

The Human-Machine World to Create: Humanized AI

Artificial intelligence (AI) has closer scientific connections with philosophy than do other sciences, because AI shares many concepts with philosophy, e.g., action, consciousness, and epistemology—what is sensible to say about the world—and even free will (McCarthy, 2006). A humanized AI (HAI) in this book refers to an agent that thinks and acts like a human, recognizing and accepting humans just as we recognize and accept them. As with human beings, this does not mean they will live in full harmony, without conflicts, or even wars. Some people refer to HAI as a scaled-down version of our HAI agent that only possesses some human emotional or social aspects. Artificial general intelligence (AGI) often refers to an integration of many narrow artificial intelligences (NAIs), each of them dealing with a particular problem, such as Medical AIs that involve the applications of AI technology in drug development and healthcare to improve health outcomes and patient experiences. Most NAIs involve extensive uses of data and thus are often called machine learning (ML). In other words, ML can be viewed as a subset of AI. Our great achievements so far are mainly in NAIs, such as deep-learning ANNs for image natural language processing. This section is a big-picture view of HAI and human-machine society.

Regarding the future human-machine world, how would society evolve to the human-machine world when humans decide not to have natural births and have machine children instead? Will the world eventually become such a machine world? Imagine a machine that could make human beings like us—Would we really know we are not machine-made humans? This circular meta-world evolves without a start and end: humans create agents that create humans who create agents that create humans … where are we in the circle now, do we really know? The answer is: we don't.

1.1 Purpose of Developing AI

What is the purpose of developing AI? This question can be addressed in many ways. In a narrow sense, we may say, the purpose is to create technology that allows computers and machines to work intelligently. In the broad sense, the goal of AI research is to understand and build intelligent entities. Such an entity or system often includes two main ingredients in the many definitions of intelligence: (1) thought processes and reasoning (thinking) and (2) behavior and performance (acting). What I am more interested in is: what is the most fundamental or important purpose of Human Artificial Intelligence? This is the root question that directly relates to our lives!

Our efforts are all for a happier and longer life, to which there seems to be no big objection. However, hard work does not necessarily lead to the happiness you want. Some people believe that happiness is the absence of striving for happiness. Happiness is related

DOI: 10.1201/b23355-2

to health and prosperity. Happiness is connected to technological advancement, change in wealth, knowledge, and education. Being happy is relative: it is usually related to a person's relative wealth in society or social status. Happiness is related to what one wants and what one gets. The higher the expectation is, the less likely it is to be satisfied, and the less happiness you may find. "If you want what you get, you will get what you want." Happiness is also related to having hopes, dreams, and feeling empowered. How often a person feels happy is a reflection of an individual trait: an optimistic or pessimistic attitude. Some people say that the purpose of life is to get the greatest happiness; some say the purpose of life is to live longer; some say that having a successful life is a balance between quality and quantity of life, and a balance between long-term and short-term happiness. Yet, others say that happiness is the enjoyment of the process of living.

Despite the complexity of the whole happiness issue, it seems that there is little doubt that technological innovations will bring us happiness. Is that true? We develop technology in the hope of bringing more leisure time into our lives. However, the results are often the opposite: we repeatedly use the saved time to work even harder, longer on more challenging, more advanced technological innovations! We promote work efficiency and foster multitasking skills. All these appear to be the enjoyments of tech innovation as we hoped, but in reality, it is easy for us to become slaves of innovation. What should matter to us is not how much time we save, but what we do with the saved time.

When we have a choice, we feel empowered. Thus, we believe having more choices is better, but we hardly find it to be true. Instead, we all become syndromic in "informational obesity" and we suffer analysis paralysis in making a choice. We often cannot even feel happy after having made a good choice since we tend to feel a huge loss when we are not able to choose a majority of the options. To overcome this paralysis, we have developed AI technology that makes recommendations for us when, as only one example, we make an online purchase. However, the question is: would AI bring convenience and provide us with more and better choices, or does it take away certain freedoms of choice and make us sad? Like responses to many other questions, a correct answer to this question is not unique but depends upon the individual.

As Fredkin's paradox (Minsky's Optimization Paradox) states: The more equally attractive two alternatives seem, the harder it can be to choose between them—no matter that, to the same degree, the choice can only matter less (Minsky, 1988). Thus, a decision-making agent might spend the most time on the least important decisions. Instrumental rationality is a pursuit of all means necessary to achieve a specific end, as we often say: do whatever it takes to achieve a goal. An intuitive resolution to Fredkin's paradox is to calibrate decision-making time as cost (Klein, 2001). The paradox constitutes a major challenge to the possibility of pure instrumental rationality.

Technological innovation has experienced exponential growth, bringing prosperity to society. Unfortunately, the same innovation is also a major contributor to an increasingly large wealth gap. This might be the result of competition: everyone is micro-motivated and acts from his own perspective. The macro-consequences for society may not be what anyone wants, as well illustrated by the Braess Paradox: adding more roads can make traffic worse.

How can we avoid all the traps that await us as we develop AI? First, AI development must aim toward a simple goal: helping us live simpler, happier, and longer lives. Second, as with narrow AI, medical AI will add greatly to the quality and spans of our lives. Third, our major efforts in AGI and HAI should focus on solving social, instead of technical, problems. AGI agents should be viewed as integral parts of our society. When the machines are treated (taught, trained) as humans, they will behave like humans. For example, as the aging of populations is coming much sooner than we thought and the impact is bigger than we can imagine, AGI can provide emotional assistance and companionship for seniors. On the other hand, I cannot see how AI advancement in military applications, apart from defending us in times of war, can help us live healthier, happier, or longer lifespans. Fourth, in some other areas of AI or technological innovation, the developments have to be adjusted to an appropriate pace and must be used properly. Too many or too fast technological advances or any misuse of AI technologies can over-stimulate individual and societal desires, and make today's wealth gaps bigger (a small gap is necessary to drive society forward) and people unhappier. Fifth, the ethical concerns and risks in developing AI collectively include:

- It is now possible to track and analyze one's every move online and his or her daily business. Cameras are nearly everywhere, and facial recognition algorithms know who you are. Such information can be used to protect you but can also work against you.
- Social media, through its autonomous-powered algorithms, is very effective at surmising what we think, thus making the manipulation of elections more feasible and influencing other important personal or social decision-making.
- Apart from being concerned that autonomous weapons might gain a "mind of their own," a more imminent concern is the dangers autonomous weapons might have with an individual or government that doesn't value human life.

1.2 Humanized Artificial Intelligence

HAI is similar to **Artificial General Intelligence** (AGI). AGI was introduced by Mark Gubrud in a 1997 discussion of the implications of fully automated military production and operations. Also known as strong AI, AGI is the intelligence of a machine that could successfully perform any intellectual task that a human being can, i.e., a machine capable of experiencing consciousness, discovery, creativity, self-awareness and cognitive evolution, collaborative intelligence, and even the creation of other AI agents. Or, some might say, it introduces a new kind of being with human-like mental capabilities. Jackson (2019) provides interesting discussions of AGI. In contrast to AGI, narrow (or weak) AI refers to the use of software to accomplish specific problems. Narrow AI does not attempt to attain the full range of human cognitive abilities. For this reason, the performance of narrow AI is often more efficient than a human's, as far as a specific task is concerned.

HAI agents are not Virtual Humans. Virtual Humans, products of narrow AI, are typically seen as human-like characters on a computer screen, or otherwise presented with embodied life-like behavior that may include speech, emotions, locomotion, gestures and movements of the head, eyes, or other parts of an avatar body (Burden and Savin-Baden, 2020). The applications of virtual humans include virtual instructors for simulation-based learning and training, skill development, team coordination, and decision-making.

AI research is an interdisciplinary study. Each discipline views AI from a different angle and addresses different questions:

- "Can HAI be achieved?" from Philosophy,
- "How does the brain work?" from Neuroscience,
- "How does a human learn?" from Cognitive Science,

- "What is consciousness?" from Psychology,
- "What characteristics are necessary to be a social being?" from Sociology,
- "What are different attributes between life and non-life?" from Biology,
- "How do we build lives?" from Computer Science,
- "How do we adapt to the environment?" from Ecology,
- "How does one make a system reason?" from Mathematical Logic,
- "How does a human make a decision and act on it?" from Rationality in Economics,
- "How can we deal with uncertainty in the real world?" from Probability and Statistics,
- "How do we deal with novelty (uncharted territory),
- "Should we build languages into an agent or let agents learn them from interaction with their environment?" from Linguistics,
- "What is the connotation of understanding and effective knowledge representation?" from Network Science,
- "How can we improve computational efficiency to meet HAI or AGI needs?" from Quantum Computing in Physics, and
- "How do we build robots?" from Mechanical Engineering.

Of course, these have oversimplified the AI studies and may not be very accurate.

Experience and knowledge can mean slightly different things in different settings. One may often find circular definitions such as: **Knowledge** is facts, information, and skills acquired through experience or education; the theoretical or practical understanding of a subject. **Experience** is the knowledge or skill acquired by a period of practical experience of something, especially that gained in a particular profession. But here, in this book, we define knowledge as **Patternized Experiences**.

Learning is the acquisition of knowledge or skills through experience (observations, active engagements, experiments). Learning (cognition or cognitive learning) involves a refinement of what we already know through internal processes such as logical reasoning. Learning is a recursive process from simple to complex. Learning has to involve responses: strengthening correct responses and weakening incorrect responses. Learning is the patternization and organization of cumulative experiences in memory—a gain in knowledge. The notion of the Bayesian statistical learning paradigm asserts that posteriori knowledge is the combination of prior knowledge and new data (Chang and Boral, 2008). All these characteristics of learning will guide us in building the HAI.

Researchers have approached the task of building agents from four different viewpoints: (1) Acting like a human, e.g., the Turing test approach; (2) Thinking like a human via the cognitive modeling approach (as one example); (3) Thinking rationally, typically by the laws of thought approach; and (4) Acting rationally by the rational agent approach. The question is: can we build an agent that can both think and act in a human-like fashion?

Humanized AI (HAI) may be considered as a kind of AGI, but emphasizes the balance between intelligence and the humanistic aspects of AI, including not only their strengths but also their weaknesses. An HAI agent is an agent that can think and act *humanely*. To this end, it is necessary to re-examine very carefully the many fundamental concepts, instead of assuming that everyone has the same understanding of the concepts. The key concepts to be analyzed include human intelligence, discovery, causality, understanding, and consciousness down to a mechanical level so that we can mimic them in the HAI architecture. We start with the notions of humanness and human intelligence.

What are humans and what is human intelligence? What makes humans different from all other animals? There are many different ways to answer these questions. From an HAI perspective, we could cite the complexities of our languages and thoughts, and our culture-based innovations and adaptations. Humans as social beings can understand complex things and discover natural laws; we have consciousness, self-awareness, and can empathize with others. Of course, not all these characteristics are unique to humans. What are the differences between a human and a monkey then? Since both mammals have very complicated neural networks, the current deep-learning Artificial Neural Network architectures seemingly cannot ensure that the brain we are going to build will be human-like and not monkey-like. This is probably a big barrier for AI *connectionists* in arguing for the use of ANNs as the basis for artificial general intelligence.

Some researchers like to differentiate Human identical intelligence (with biological embodiment) from human-level intelligence (without biological embodiment). However, as the Identity Paradox shows in Section 1.4, this differentiation may not be necessary since technological advancement and social norms tend to go hand-in-hand. Before AI reaches the full capacity of human beings, we would have accepted AI agents as another race (a machine race) of ourselves. Any discussion on this topic with a dynamic view of technology and a static view of societal norms would not make sense, since such a time will never come.

Intelligence involves essentially (1) the capacity to learn from experience and (2) the capacity to adapt to one's environment. Three fundamental cognitive processes are abstraction, learning, and dealing with novelty. In cognitive psychology, there are two main ways to describe intelligence: the psychometric and information-processing approaches. The psychometric approach focuses on measuring or quantifying cognitive factors or abilities that make up intellectual performance. Those cognitive factors might include verbal comprehension, memory ability, perceptual speed, and reasoning. The information-processing approach defines intelligence by analyzing the components of cognitive processes. For example, Sternberg divides intelligence into (1) analytical or logical thinking skills that can be reflected on an IQ test; (2) problem-solving skills that require creative thinking, the ability to deal with novel situations, and the ability to learn from experience; and (3) using practical thinking skills that help a person to adjust to and cope with his sociocultural environment (Kosiński and Zaczek-Chrzanowska, 2007).

In any case, to build HAI, we need to understand human nature, a concept that denotes the fundamental dispositions and characteristics, including ways of thinking, feeling, and acting that are natural to humans.

To put it simply: Narrow Artificial Intelligence (NAI) focuses on a specific task or problem, whereas AGI can be a broad collection of NAIs or an integration of NAIs and Human-Level AI agents that have general capabilities of humans but are used to serve humans. HAI agents look, think, and act like humans, can be considered a machine race, and are life companions, but not digital slaves, of human beings. Machines become humans only when they are treated (evolve) as humans. As this happens, AI-Human interactions will increasingly evidence two-way recognition and influence.

1.3 Innate Knowledge Learned Before Birth

Innate knowledge and innate behavior will be considered in building an HAI baby. Innate behavior is the inherent inclination of a living organism toward a particular complex behavior. Any behavior is instinctive if it is performed without being based upon prior experience (i.e., in the absence of learning), and is therefore an expression of innate bio-logical factors. Sea turtles, newly hatched on a beach, will instinctively move toward the ocean. The simplest example of an instinctive behavior is a fixed action pattern (FAP), which is a simple response of an organism to a specific stimulus, such as the contraction of the pupil in response to bright light. Instincts include other inborn complex patterns of behavior, not just simple reflexes.

The existence of the simplest instincts in humans is a widely debated topic, as we see from controversies regarding genetic factors versus learning on influencing one's talent. Some well-known examples of instincts include: (1) An infant's crying and suckling are manifestations of instinct. The infant cannot otherwise protect itself for survival during its long period of maturation. (2) Testosterone primes several instincts, especially sexual-ity. (3) Disgust and Squeamishness in humans is an instinct developed during evolution to protect the body and avoid infections caused by various diseases (Curtis, et al 2011). Scholars (McDougall, 1928) also affirm the instinct of curiosity and its associated emotion of wonder.

Maslow (1954) argued that humans no longer have instincts because we have the ability to override them in certain situations. He felt that what is called instinct is often impre-cisely defined. Richard Herrnstein (1972) found that McDougall's theory of instinct and Skinner's reinforcement theory have remarkable and largely unrecognized similarities, existing on both sides of the nature-nurture dispute as applied to the analysis of behavior. Mandal (2010) proposed a set of criteria by which behavior might be considered instinc-tual. It should (a) be automatic, (b) be irresistible, (c) occur at some point in development, (d) be triggered by some event in the environment, (e) occur in every member of the spe-cies, (f) be, in general, unmodifiable, and (g) govern behavior for which the organism needs no training (although the organism may profit from the experience and, to that degree, the behavior is modifiable). From the *evolutionary instinct point of view*, instinct in humans can generally be understood as the innate part of behavior that emerges without any training or education. Behaviors such as cooperation, sexual behavior, child-rearing, and aesthetics are seen as evolved psychological mechanisms with an instinctive basis.

In my view, from a Human Artificial Intelligence perspective, instinct can be viewed as something you learned in your mother's body before your birth. All instincts are con-stantly changing or continually modified (e.g., changing from suckling to sucking) after your birth, through experience. Human intelligence, including instincts, can be explained as collective intelligence at a lower level, e.g., the swarm intelligence of cells in some par-ticular environment (e.g., the human body). In our humanized agents, **Zda** (male) and **Lia** (female), we will use very minimal built-in instincts as opposed to larger commonsense knowledge. This is a key to our small-data-based approach and will become much more clear in Part III when discussing the Architecture.

1.4 Self-awareness and the Identity Paradox

In a narrow sense, consciousness is awareness of one's body and one's environment; self-awareness is recognition of that consciousness—not only understanding that one exists, but further understanding that one is aware of one's existence.

In a general sense, **consciousness** refers to a being or an agent having some degree of awareness of self, one's situation or relation to the world, one's perceptions, thoughts and actions, both past and present, and the potential consequences of decisions. A simple example would be: "I am analyzing the situation at the very moment." Having consciousness implies the ability of meta-thinking: thinking about thinking. For instance, "I am aware that I have consciousness," "I know that I am aware that I have consciousness," and so on. Blackmore (2011, pp. 286–301) provides an overview of research on artificial consciousness.

The elementary concept, "consciousness," is so simple that everyone feels he understands, and at the same time is so complex no one can satisfactorily explain it. Scholars try terms such as "feel," "recall," "attention," "imagine," and "emotionally" to define or explain consciousness. The problem is, however, the terms used in the definition, appearing to be simpler, are, in fact, not less difficult to explain than the meaning of "consciousness" itself. In my view, conscious behaviors are society-dependent and are learned from society as long as the agent has self-awareness. Therefore, how an agent behaves consciously depends on the society he grows up in and how he was treated.

Most people have approached "consciousness" from a philosophical perspective since the time of Aristotle. Recently some researchers have tried searching for its physical footprints (Koch, 2018). What is it about a highly excitable piece of brain matter that gives rise to consciousness? They seek, in particular, the neuronal correlates of consciousness, defined as the minimal neuronal mechanisms jointly sufficient for any specific conscious experience.

The key to consciousness is **self-awareness**, i.e., an agent recognizing that there are two separate entities: self and external world. The self part includes the brain and any part, if being touched, that the brain will feel immediately. That is also why I wouldn't think your hands are part of me, nor a chair I am sitting on. Thinking about thinking, I know I have self-awareness, and I realize that I have this knowledge of my self-awareness. However, as we discussed in the following Identity Paradox, if we cannot even clearly define "self," how can we expect to have a unified definition of consciousness?

Interestingly, some scholars might think (stanford.edu, 1993): a colony is analogous to a brain where there are many neurons, each of which can only do something very simple, but together the whole brain can think. None of the neurons can think of an ant, but the brain can think of an ant, though nothing in the brain told that neuron to think of an ant. Others believe that ants could have consciousness and can think: the complexity observed in the behavior is not necessarily in the ant but in the interaction between the ant and the surrounding complex environment.

The Identity Paradox is closely related to the question as to whether AGI can have human consciousness or self-awareness. Puzzles about identity and persistence ask: under what conditions does an object persist through time as one and the same object? If the world contains things that endure and retain their identity despite undergoing alteration, then somehow those things must persist through changes (Chang, 2012, 2014).

We replace malfunctioning organs with healthy ones. We commit to physical exercise to improve our health. We try hard to forget sad memories as soon as we can, and maybe we'll be able to use medical equipment to erase undesirable memories in the future. We are constantly learning and equipping our brains with new knowledge. As these processes continue, are we making a human-machine mixed race? When does a person lose his or her identity in the process?

The Identity Paradox can evolve. A Wiseman is getting old and weak physically. He says to a young man: "The only thing I regret is that I was so focused on knowledge when I was young, I didn't get enough physical exercise." "You can have my body in exchange for your wisdom," the young man said. The Wiseman thinks this is a good suggestion,

FIGURE 1.1
Body—wisdom swap.

and they decide to use the "incredible machine" to make the deal happen. In a moment, the machine has exchanged all information between the two brains (Figure 1.1). As we may expect, any bilateral-willing exchange should make both parties happy. But are they? When the exchange occurs, nearly all information, including personal history and emotions, is interchanged. You might have already been aware that after the exchange the Wiseman's mind and the young man's body are bound together.

Some of us worry: Can, and in what ways, HAI agents surpass human beings? Will we become unnecessary? The most popular and controversial answers to this question come from technical perspectives. However, as we have discussed, we cannot even well-define what humankind is, though everyone probably thinks he or she has a clear concept of what a human being is, and that it is similar to everyone else's. I'd rather answer the question from a social instead of a technical perspective. During the long future course of HAI's development, we humans will develop emotions toward HAI agents as they live with us on a daily basis. We will not discriminate against "anyone" because of race, color, gender, sexual orientation, or origin (machine-made or not); all that matters are time and intellectual interactions, be they technical or emotional. The concept (connotation and denotation) of a human being, like all other concepts, is subject to the dynamics of evolution. Before we can develop the full capacity of HAI, our societal view (our definition) of mankind will have to experience dramatic modifications. HAI agents will be recognized as the machine race of humankind. On one hand, AGI will move closer and closer to human intelligence. On the other hand, humankind becomes more and more accepting of machine-kind. The two parties will meet and unite in a middle way.

Jackson (2019) uses the five-axiom definition of consciousness (Aleksander and Morton, 2007) in his TalaMind architecture of human-level AI. In contrast, my approach to consciousness will be based on the notion that displayed consciousness is consciousness.

In our HAI architecture, self-awareness, the basis of consciousness, is the nature of the self-inclusive net of the evolutionary knowledge net, as elaborated in Part III.

1.5 Social Beings and Collaboration

To build an HAI agent as a social being who is to conform with social norms and has the ability of collaboration, we need to briefly discuss the characteristics of social beings.

Individualism stresses individual goals and the rights of the individual. Collectivism focuses on group goals, what is best for the collective group, and personal relationships. Collectivism is the view that your life and body do not belong to you but belong to a society that may dispose of you as it wishes.

Whether individualist or collectivist, a Social Being lives or prefers to live in a community rather than alone, promotes companionship, and engages in social service. Social Collaboration is a common characteristic for a social being. Collaboration is a working practice whereby individuals work together to a common purpose. To an agent, collaboration means actively understanding other's needs in the human-machine community and providing help. Current robots can provide great help to humans, but do so passively by pre-programmed algorithms. Collaboration can be in the form of fighting together against other communities or enemies.

Social Collaboration is important to individuals and a society for social efficiency and protection of the society. One interesting example is named Braess' Paradox (Chang, 2012, 2014), which shows that increasing an option can actually make a system less efficient (e.g., adding a new road can make traffic heavier) when individually motivated factors drive behavior without collaboration.

Interactions (collaboration and disunity) between members of human-machine society can cultivate empathy or antipathy, friendship or enmity among advanced machines and humans. Most animals, such as ants and elephants, are considered social beings. A humanized agent should display such capabilities.

Social norms, like many other social phenomena, are the unplanned result of individuals' interactions. Arguably, social norms ought to be understood as a kind of grammar of social interactions. Like grammar, a system of norms specifies what is acceptable and what is not in a society or group. Closely related to social norms, the concept of social justice in a society refers to a fair and equitable division of resources, opportunities, and privileges in the society, also a consequence of social interactions (stanford.edu, 2018). Therefore, social norms and justice will be different for a human society and a human-machine society. Interactions create and define a society we live in; societal norms guide the development of society. To exclude HAI agents from the society we live in by arguing that every agent is different from humans may be sound because every human is unique. Only intellectual closeness and interactions, not what we are born with or are made of, determine social norms and the society we will live in.

HAI agents as social beings should be able to recognize controversies in morality and social fairness. For example, should a fair social system be "one person, one vote" or "one race, one vote"? We provide special education for children with special needs. Should we also provide less gifted people with some educational incentives? For the same-priced airfare ticket, should a larger person get a larger seat than a small person, to be fair? Will you be OK with fishing as long as the person lets the fish go after catching it, or do you think he is a fish-abuser? For all these questions, whatever the conclusions we might arrive at cannot be a consequence of mathematical or logical reasoning. One can easily list many more social and ethical issues that mathematical reasoning cannot resolve.

As a further example, in evaluating the effect of a medical treatment, a clinical endpoint such as death rate, longevity, or quality-of-life (QOL) adjusted life expectancy may be used as an evaluation criterion. However, each endpoint we might choose is a reflection of our values or morality: (1) if death rate is chosen to be the endpoint, we value each life equally regardless of age and health condition. This means that saving a 99-year-old cancer patient and a 10-year-old healthy child are equally important in the situation where we can only save one of them. (2) If longevity or life expectancy is the endpoint, the value of saving the child is larger than saving the old man because the survival time that could be saved is different between the two. (3) If QOL-adjusted life expectancy is preferred, not only the survival time rescued but also the quality of the time should be considered.

Assuming we agree to use the death rate as a measure of the major impact of COVID-19, then for what duration should deaths be collected? If the duration is 100 years, nearly all people who live beyond the pandemic will die anyway, and then the COVID-19 pandemic has no impact on the death rate. If the deaths are counted yearly, the COVID-19 pandemic will appear to have a positive impact in reducing the deaths and increasing longevity in the near future when it is over since many elderly and less healthy people have died in COVID-19. After objectively assessing the impact of the pandemic, the controversial morality issue regarding government intervention is how to balance between Individual Rights and Common Good, as we will face the Trolley Problem: should a government pull the lever to divert the runaway trolley onto the side track to kill the person on the track in order to reduce the overall number of deaths?

The **Trolley Problem** is an ethical dilemma: there is a runaway trolley barreling down a stretch of railway tracks. Ahead, on the tracks, there are five people tied up and unable to move. The trolley is headed straight for them. You are standing some distance off in the train yard, next to a lever (Figure 1.2). If you pull this lever, the trolley will switch to a different set of tracks. However, you notice that there is one person on the sidetrack. You have two (and only two) options:

1. Do nothing, in which case the trolley will kill the five people on the main track.
2. Pull the lever, diverting the trolley onto the side track where it will kill one person.

Which is the more ethical option? The HAI agent's answer (choice and reasoning) can be used to test his ethical maturity.

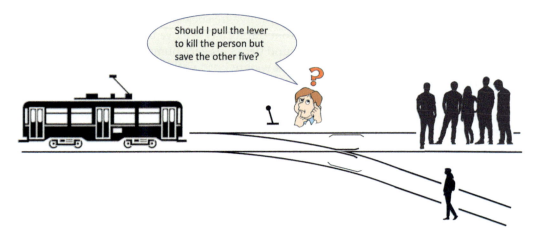

FIGURE 1.2
The trolley paradox—an ethical dilemma.

As a member of human-machine society, the HAI agent we are creating does not intend to avoid or resolve such controversies but certainly must live with them. As a social being, making a choice will mean considering, more or less, its social impact or social norms, especially to those who are closely related to you: how you treat them will affect how they will treat you. From this notion, imitation mechanisms will make HAI agents conform to social norms and do what others (especially humans) would do in various social settings.

1.6 Decision-Making: Rational and Emotional Choices

A key aspect of HAI is how a decision or choice is made. Therefore, studying human choice and the consequences of choices are interesting.

Each of us has to make many choices in our lives, from the trivial to life-changing. Choices can be emotional or rational. So what factors are related to the motivation, ability, and result of the choice? Why are we often disappointed by our choices? Does the disappointment after the choice necessarily mean the wrong choice was made? How can you make yourself a wiser chooser?

We live in an era of unprecedented abundance of diverse goods and services that provides us with more and more choices. From the perspective of traditional economic concepts and American culture, the diversity of choices maximizes the benefits of rational people, because the more choices, the more opportunity everyone has to choose what they want. Traditional American wisdom firmly believes in this point. No matter whether it is ordinary people or academia, almost no one doubts its applicability and universality. However, when the selection of items increases, our level of happiness often does not necessarily increase with it, but rather is confused by the choices. What is more disturbing is the phenomenon of excessive information in the information industry. When the number of TV channels increased from ten to several hundred, we kept switching channels for fear of losing the programs we most wanted to watch. The "everyone is a content producer" model is gradually being swayed by a large number of filter sources.

As for why too many choices may not make people more satisfied, I think there are at least six reasons: (1) When there are too many choices, the problem is complicated, and it is not easy to analyze, i.e., analysis is paralyzed. (2) When there are more choices, the differences between the various alternatives appear smaller. Each choice has its own advantages and disadvantages, and it is difficult to judge whether it is good or bad. (3) Things that are rare are often considered prestigious. Too many choices will reduce people's interest in the choosing. (4) Since we can only choose limited things, too many choices make us feel more loss (unselected items), and so we often doubt and regret our choice. (5) Too many choices make us greedy, or greedier than we were. (6) Too many choices make us spend too much time and energy creating theories about how to make intelligent choices and learning how to distinguish among many choices with insignificant differences but, in fact, we experience "psychological hypersensitivity" symptoms. On the contrary, we use anti-allergic drugs to "paralyze" the immune system to prevent allergies to food or plants.

There should be a single grand (implicit) "goal" for a human, but no one knows exactly what it is and how to achieve it. This is because achieving the goal is complicated: incomplete information, a constantly changing environment, massive options available, the uncertain consequences associated with each choice, all of these make our choice difficult. Therefore, we break a goal into smaller goals in our life and think that every small goal achieved will get us one step closer to the grand goal. In most situations, we have to make decisions based on incomplete information and make them quickly. Later, if we made a mistake, we would correct it. Such a simple trial-error method is more powerful in learning. All complicated methods, such as deep learning and quantum mechanics, can be the consequences of this simple trial-error method

If we build utility based on the happiness goal instead of monetary, the rational approach can include emotional components. Whether we make a decision following our emotion or against emotion, the utility can have either a positive or negative impact. In addition, a proper utility function form is also important. Since our feelings about intensity from sensory organs are logarithm-based according to Weber-Fechner laws, the monetary contribution to happiness should also be a logarithm: *Happiness* = log(*money*) + *emotional impact*. Therefore, in principle, we can use a rational approach to maximize utility or happiness with appropriate utility.

Many of our actions are not a direct consequence of rationalization but a reflex that often includes a spontaneous emotional response. However, such a reflex can be viewed as an indirect use of rationalization. We believe that the sum of the small short-term goals is approximately equal to the grand goal (Law of Summative Effects). The small goals are often time-sensitive, such as quickly pulling back one's hand when a finger touches a burning hot surface. A reflex is a way to deal with a time-sensitive situation and such situations frequently occur. The frequency of recurrent events is a proxy of a short-term goal. Thus, a viable rational approach should also include the time factor in the utility function. We will discuss this more in Part III, Architecture of HAI.

Interestingly, even when the information is complete and potential outcomes are known, we might still not be sure our choice is the best one. This further justifies the importance of the timing factor in building the utility. We elaborate this with Efron's intransitive dice (Figure 1.3).

Efron's dice are the four dice A; B; C; D with the following numbers on their six faces: A displaying {4; 4; 4; 4; 0; 0}, B with {3; 3; 3; 3; 3; 3}, C having {6; 6; 2; 2; 2; 2}, and D, {5; 5; 5; 1; 1; 1}. It can be easily proved that die A beats die B; B beats C; C beats D; and D beats A, all with the same probability of 2/3. Therefore, the four dice are equally good.

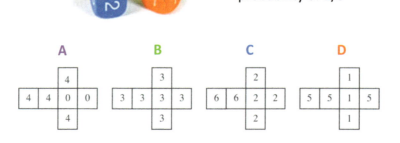

FIGURE 1.3
A set of four intransitive dice.

Now imagine if the numbers represent the evaluation scores of the four social systems (or forms of government, products, medical interventions) at six different times or aspects. If we are provided with social system options A, B, and C without knowing the existence of option D, we might think A is the right choice but actually the four choices are equally good. The conclusion can be applied to our decision-making in other situations, such as medical treatments of a certain disease. In this case, different dice may present different treatments A, B, C, and D, whereas the face values of a die may indicate the responses of different patients to that treatment. Without knowing the possible treatment D, we would conclude A is the best treatment after we run a clinical trial. However, in fact, all four treatments are equally good. These examples seem to make us completely lose confidence in virtually any decision we have made or are going to make. Therefore, the "right" decision might be just an illusion in the eyes of the decision-maker or the agent.

There are many other sets of intransitive dice consisting of three or more dice. For instance, this set of three dice, Red {3, 3, 3, 3, 3, 6}, Blue {2, 2, 2, 5, 5, 5}, and Olive {1, 4, 4, 4, 4, 4} is intransitive. Intransitive dice do not have to be 6-faced and the numbers do not have to be integers. The set of dice of {1, 4, 4, 4}, {2, 2, 5}, and {3, 3, 3, 6}, and set of {1, 1, 4, 4, 4, 4, 4, 4}, {2, 2, 2, 2, 5, 5, 5, 5}, and {3, 3, 3, 3, 3, 3, 6, 6} are two sets of intransitive dice.

Can or should HAI involve future social decisions such as predential selection or constitution-making? For instance, facing the polarization of U.S. society today, we Americans can make changes in the election law to reduce polarization: each voter must elect different party candidates during primary and prudential elections. If you want to vote Democratic for the president, then you will have to vote for a Republican in the Primary. Thus you will vote for a Republican who is moderate or close to a Democrat. This way, only a moderate Republican and a moderate Democrat will be able to enter the final presidential election. The question is: will HAI be able to involve such a decision? In principle they can, with our HAI architecture as given in Part III.

Having said that, we recognize that in decision-making, people change their opinions all the time, since everything, including the environment, changes constantly. Therefore, pursuing mathematical consistency in decision-making is not a viable solution for HAI.

1.7 Evolution and Devolution

In theory, we can make HAI agents that never die, but evolution involves powerful mechanisms that we can utilize to make incredible HAI agents capable of self-improvement from generation to generation. For this reason, it's beneficial to have a discussion on the topic of evolution and devolution. The notion of multi-level evolution discussed here inspires me to use Pattern Survival Time in the forgetting-mechanism of HAI architecture. The forgetting-mechanism is important in effective learning and prompt response for HAI agents.

The Chicken or the Egg Paradox we all know is: which came first, the chicken or the egg? This question also evokes a more general question of how life and the universe began.

The Theory of Evolution answers the question as follows: species change over time via mutation and selection. Since DNA can be modified only before birth, a mutation must have taken place at conception or within an egg so that an animal similar to a chicken, but not a chicken, laid the first chicken egg. Thus, both the egg and the chicken evolved simultaneously from birds that were not chickens and did not lay chicken eggs but gradually became more and more like chickens over time.

According to Darwin, "… if variations useful to any organic being do occur, assuredly individuals thus characterized will have the best chance of being preserved in the struggle for life; and from the strong principle of inheritance, they will tend to produce offspring similarly characterized. This principle of preservation, I have called, for the sake of brevity, Natural Selection."

Darwin implied here the four essential conditions for the occurrence of evolution by natural selection:

1. Reproduction of individuals in the population,
2. Heredity in reproduction,
3. Variation that affects individual survival, and
4. Finite resources causing competition.

Diversity is a necessary condition for evolution. However, more diversity can either speed up evolution or cause chaos in the population. Human society could become homogeneous owing to interracial marriages, the Internet, promotion of social equalities, and other factors. Such homogenization slows down evolution. Nevertheless, humans are still evolving. Experts believe that about 9% of our genes are undergoing rapid evolution, nearly as we speak! The genes most affected by natural selection are those involving the immune system, sexual reproduction, and sensory perception.

However, not every scientist believes in evolutionary theory. Some completely oppose it and others agree on intraspecies evolution but contest cross-species evolution. Different species can have different starting points for evolution; there is no reason that all pieces are from the same ancestor.

The notion of natural selection has been used (and abused) throughout many scientific fields and in our daily lives. Artificial selection, a major technological application of evolutionary principles, is the intentional selection of certain traits in a population of organisms. Humans have used artificial selection for thousands of years in the domestication of plants and animals, and more recently in genetic engineering, using selectable markers such as antibiotic resistance genes used to manipulate DNA in molecular biology.

Theoretically, evolution can happen on multiple levels: cell evolution makes better cells, organ evolution makes stronger organs, and human evolution makes healthy, happy, and longer-lived humans. But how can we be sure these nested or hierarchical evolutions would not be in conflict? We have seen that tumor cells are very strong in competing for nutrition with normal cells. However, such strong tumor cells are definitely miserable additions from the perspectives of organ and human evolution.

There is no reason to believe that devolution never happens within and between the same organisms. In fact, it can occur at different levels for various reasons: (1) A medicine can cure disease and make weaker people live longer, while at the same time devolving the human's immune system. (2) As the environment changes, an organism that fits well in one environment may not fit into another; thus, as the environment circularly alters (as with the four seasons), the best-fitting organism alters accordingly. (3) Evolution can occur at a higher level, such as an entire society, and devolution can happen at a lower level, as with individuals, or vice versa. An example of statistical proof of possible devolution is discussed in *Principles of Scientific Methods* (Chang, 2014).

Since fitness is multifaceted, defining it is often subjective and difficult. For instance, suppose one couple is healthy and is expected to live long, but has low fertility, whereas another couple is not as healthy as the first but has a high fertility and decides to have more children. Which couple's race will be the winner via evolution after generations? Indeed, people have criticized the Darwinian notion of survival of the fittest by declaring that the whole thing is a simple tautology: whatever survives is fitting by definition! Defenders of the notion argue that fitness can be quantified by empirical measures such as speed, strength, resistance to disease, and aerodynamic stability independent of survivability (Chang, 2014).

The point here is that micro-motivated behavior at the individual level can be a devolutionary force, making a weaker person live longer while society devolves in a sense. Controversially, everyone, every member of the human race, should (ethically speaking) have an equal chance to live for an equally long time. This is a force against biological evolution, we may argue, that will, however, make for the betterment of the society. In fact, many social justices promote biological devolution. How to balance the two aspects is a social issue.

In our HAI architectures, as long as we limit an agent's longevity and Darwin's four essential conditions, both evolution and devolution could occur. The cumulative reward received by an HAI agent can be used as the fitness, while replacing a human's organs can be simulated by replacing parts of an agent.

1.8 The Humanized Agents Zda and Lia

As we discussed earlier, AI is Artificialized Human Intelligence, while HAI aims to emphasize the full human aspects of AI, i.e., to humanize Artificialized Human Intelligence. In analogy, we translate English to Chinese and then translate the transcription back to English, but hope not much is lost in the translation.

The two typical humanized agents mentioned earlier are Zda (male) and Lia (female). Our approach to build the agents is the so-called synthetism or new constructivism as opposed to neurologism, logicalism, connectionism, behaviorism, and constructivism. We will discuss these later in Part II. The idea of synthetism is to combine the efficacy of behaviorism and the flexibility of constructivism. The minimalist notion is also accommodated in building the agents by having some minimal built-in knowledge (e.g., known commonsense knowledge) and no complicated learning algorithms. As the name indicates, **Zda** (思达 in Chinese), the "baby" agent, is virtually a **Z**ero-**d**ata **a**gent as opposed to a big-data invention. **Lia** (丽雅) is shorthand for **L**anguage-**i**ndependent **a**gent. These two together mean that we build the baby agents virtually without built-in knowledge or any kind of natural language.

The baby's brain is almost empty, except for memory that works with the organs that sense the external world. The brain will record sensed environments as subject-event strings, and then patternize (simplify) them into laws/rules, such as scientific laws and language grammars, so that the simplified information can fit into the agent's memory and allow quick responses to external events. The patternization is cognition of humans and agents. We use the so-called hierarchical recursive patternization algorithms, developed from the notion that later-recognized concepts are constructed on the basis of an understanding of earlier simple concepts. Such a hierarchical recursive approach is necessary for quick and flexible learning. Otherwise, we may have to build a large knowledge base, such as the Wordnet commonsense knowledge base, and put it into the agent's brain. Even with that, the latter is not a humanized agent because it lacks personality or individuality, lacks the desired dynamics—the ability to grow and learn over time and the flexibility that makes learning everything possible, including social norms, at different times in different societies. Such societal norms sometimes cannot be pre-specified because the agent's society has not been formed yet at the time when the agent is built and any agent's involvement will contribute to the society and its norms (see Part III for details).

Zda and Lia will be able to learn language through interaction with humans and the environment. They can even create their own language, if there is no human presence. We will demonstrate these aspects in later chapters.

Zda and Lia can become members of human-machine society, and can learn and behave according to the social norms as long as we treat them humanely, the same way we treat our children. Zda and Lia have self-awareness, can make, differentiate from, and learn from peers, teachers, friends, and enemies. You can call them whatever name you want to and the agents will know you are calling them through repeated interactions.

The main learning approaches of the agents include:

1. Learning via constructive teaching (passive learning)
2. Learning through general interactions (neutral)
3. Learning by observation and mimicking (active learning)
4. Learning by asking questions with purpose (active learning)
5. Learning from creativities, while creativities can be generated via analogy and evolutionary operators (active learning)
6. Frequency-based and reward-based Patternization and Repatternization (self-learning for discovery and rediscovery).

To facilitate the building of HAI, we will introduce the **three-world theory** (Figure 1.4): the world we live in, the world in our eyes, and the world in our mind. The **world we live** in is the objective multifaceted world, the **world in our eyes** is what each individual senses (observes) through his sensory organs. The **world in our mind** is a perceptual world in our minds using patternized information or scientific principles and laws.

The HAI architecture has four main components that bridge the three worlds. (1) An evolutionary **Recursive Network** of patterns for dynamic knowledge representation provides a self-inclusive structure necessary for self-awareness. (2) **Attention Mechanisms** allow an HAI agent to focus on a few important things for efficient learning and response.

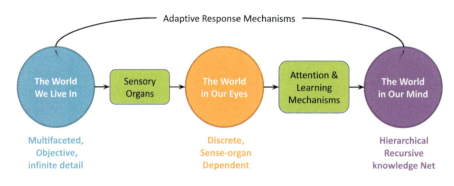

FIGURE 1.4
The three worlds in humanized AI architecture.

(3) Learning Mechanisms that feature hierarchical tokenization and recursive patternization allow progressive learning from simple to complex and then more complex concepts or skills. (4) Adaptive Reinforcement Response Mechanisms, mimicking free will, randomize potential responses according to the associated rewards or the frequency of various responses observed in humans, or others, under similar circumstances. Imitation, doing what other people, or agents, do in various situations make HAI agents conform to social norms without pre-specifying the norms.

In our HAI architecture, the limited objective world under Zda's attention at any moment is characterized by event-strings. Since multiple events can happen at the same time, the event-strings are usually (multidimensional) vector strings. However, we can unidimensionalize them into a recursive decision network of one-dimensional strings. We will discuss the details in Part III.

2

The World We Live in and the World in Our Eyes

The world we live in is the objective multifaceted world, the world in our eyes is the sensed world by each individual. We will discuss the multifaceted nature of the objective world from a philosophical perspective and through quantum physics. This and the brief discussion of theories of truths provide the foundation for the argument that the so-called objective world is not unique but individualized to the observer, as is human intelligence. Furthermore, intelligence also varies according to different levels of biological entities, e.g., a human cell versus a human. All these provide the rationale for creating individualized humanized artificial intelligence (HAI) agents as opposed to the big-data approach that would build a "superman."

2.1 The Multifaceted World and Theories of Truth

There is a popular view of an independent objective world (e.g., McCarthy, 2006): the world exists independently of humans. The facts of mathematics and physical science are independent of there being people to know them. Intelligent Martians and robots will need to know the same facts as humans. A robot also needs to believe that the world exists independently of itself and that it cannot learn all about the world that there is to know.

Newton demonstrated that the eye acts as a lens and the world in our eyes (retina) is actually upside down. If all humans were color-blind except one who can see colors, we would then be so convinced that the universe is black and white (gray), and color is just a hallucination. From modern physics we know we cannot see dark matter, ultraviolet, or infrared. Imagine that some aliens have different senses of time from ours, either different in scale (log-scale from the birth of the universe) or in chronological order. Just like two people standing at different locations and hearing two different sounds from different locations, they could argue about which sound has occurred first.

Presuming there are superbeings who can sense beyond human beings can sense color, sound, smell, and beyond, even a 5th dimension of a space, then should the universe be 5-dimensional? What if there are super superbeings, they can even sense even more than the superbeings? Therefore, the "objective world" can be anything as long as the being can "sense" it. There is no unique or independent objective world but only observer-dependent worlds. Our perceptions of the objective world depend on observers and intersubjective agreement (Figure 2.1). We can imagine that our perceived world would be very different if humans could only survive for 1 second, 1 hour, 1 day, or one billion years. The multifaceted world is consistent with the world described by quantum physics in the next section.

By saying there is a multifaceted objective world I apparently confront the conventional wisdom: in philosophy, objectivity is the concept of truth independent from individual subjectivity (bias caused by one's perception, emotions, or imagination). In fact, there is objective truth and subjective truth. Objective truth is something that is true for everyone,

DOI: 10.1201/b23355-3

FIGURE 2.1
Intersubjective agreement for truth and fact.

whether they agree with it or not. At one time this was simply called "truth." Subjective truths, being experienced by an individual, are truthful in the sense that the individual experiencing these truths can be certain of them.

There are different theories of truth. **Correspondence theories** assume there exists an actual state of affairs and maintain that true beliefs and true statements correspond to the actual state of affairs. Correspondence theories practically operate on the assumption that truth is a matter of accurately copying what has been called objective reality and then representing it in thoughts, words, and other symbols (Bradley, 1999).

In contrast to correspondence theories, **social constructivism** does not believe truth reflects any external transcendent realities. Constructivism views all of our knowledge as constructed, and that truth is constructed by social processes and is historically and culturally specific. Perceptions of truth are viewed as contingent on convention, human perception, and social experience, and representations of physical and biological reality, including race, sexuality, and gender, are socially constructed.

Consensus theory holds that truth is whatever is agreed upon, or might come to be agreed upon, by some specified group. Such a group might include all human beings, or a subset thereof consisting of more than one person.

Pragmatic theories hold in common the principle that truth is verified and confirmed by the results of putting one's concepts into practice.

Logically, a truth is what we can't in principle prove wrong, not just what we can prove correct. To prove what is correct or what cannot be proved incorrect, we have to use a certain language or tool of communication. Thus, we use words to define meaning and make arguments; but those words are then further defined by other words, and so on. We finally stop either when we believe the final set of words is clear enough or when we have no time or energy to continue any further!

In philosophy, the phrase **intersubjective agreement** denotes the agreement among some number of conscious minds. According to Hilbe (1977), "A statement is true if, taken as proceeding from the objective intersubjectively agreed upon or conventional rules of description, it depicts or properly describes the facts to which the description applies. Facts represent the manner in which our form of life structures the extra-linguistic world and conventionally agreed upon forms of linguistic synonymities according to our socially conceived conceptual framework. Hence, social intersubjective agreement is the criterion of the concept of truth and specifies which statements are true under normal circumstances." Certainly, today, our difficulties with a common social truth evince a substantial lack of intersubjective agreement.

The **Simulated-World Hypothesis** states that reality could be simulated, e.g., by quantum computer simulation, to a degree indistinguishable from "true" reality. It could contain conscious minds that may or may not know that they live inside a simulation. This is thought to be quite different from the current, technologically achievable concept of virtual reality. However, we actually are not sure that the dreams we remember are the same as when we were dreaming. We cannot tell whether we are in genuine reality or imaginary reality in a dream. On one hand, if humans can make super-intelligent beings, then such artificial superbeings might have existed a long time ago and made us human beings. On the other hand, even if a man can provide compelling arguments that humans cannot make superbeings or HAI agents, he is probably still not sure that he is a real human, as he thinks, or is instead a human made by a machine that itself was made by (super) humans because the machine superbeings might make him think he is a real human.

The multifacetedness of the objective world motivates us to use one's individually recognized world from one's sensory organs, attention, and experiences to construct knowledge (i.e., the individualized patternization of those experiences over time and one's responses), instead of using commonsense knowledge shared among all human beings and AI agents.

2.2 Quantum World

Quantum mechanics is a fundamental theory in physics that provides a description of the physical properties of nature at the scale of atoms and subatomic particles. It is the foundation of all quantum physics including quantum technology and quantum information science.

A fundamental feature of the theory is that it usually cannot predict with certainty what will happen, but only gives probabilities according to the Born rule, named after physicist Max Born. Quantum physics only asserts the multifaceted objective world, but also makes it possible for quantum computers to provide super-computational power for HAI.

A quantum is the minimum amount of any physical entity involved in an interaction. The magnitude of the physical property can take on only multiples of one quantum. A bit is the basic unit of information in classical mechanics, with two states (0, 1), whereas a qubit is the basic unit of quantum information in quantum mechanics. In classical mechanics, to know the status of the two bits (00, 01, 10, 11), we only need to know two values: the values of the first and the second bits. In quantum mechanics, the state of quantum can be in the four possible states at the same time with the probabilities r^2 for 00, s^2 for 01, t^2 for 10, and u^2 for 11. Therefore, four values (probability amplitudes r, s, t, and u) are used to describe the status of two qubits. But only three values are necessary because the sum of probabilities $r^2 + s^2 + t^2 + u^2 = 1$. When $ru = st$, we say the two qubits are not entangled (see below) and then, as the math goes, only two values are required to determine the status of the two qubits, the same as for two classical bits. Entanglement, it turns out, makes it possible for quantum computing to be faster than classical computing.

Superposition is a key concept in quantum theory. A physical system (electrons, photons) can be considered to be in two different states at the same time with an associated probability for each of the states. The situation is commonly compared to **Schrödinger's cat**, a feline which can be viewed as both alive and dead at the same time. At the moment we measure the system, however, it collapses to a single deterministic status. When a qubit is measured from different directions, it will give different results. This is very counter-intuitive, but we can think of a qubit as a bisexual person who can be male and female at the same time. The person's sexual orientation can be measured, and the result will depend on how it's measured: when a bisexual person meets with male or female, it will show the opposite sexuality. The objective world is thus multi-sexual or multifaceted in nature.

Entanglement is another important concept in quantum mechanics. Two particles (electrons, photons, molecules, etc.) can be entangled, names, knowing the status of one implies instantly knowing the status of the other, no matter how far the two particles are separated apart. This implies that information can be "transmitted" instantly, faster than light. We may ask, why is that if the light of speed is limited? One possible explanation is that physical space can have a 4th dimension and two objects viewed as far apart in 3D space can be connected in 4D space.

Unlike the classical bits of information, quantum information in qubits can be neither copied (the **no-cloning theorem**) nor destroyed (the **no-deleting theorem**).

A possibility opened by entanglement is testing for "hidden variables." Hidden variables represent hypothetical properties more fundamental than the quantities addressed in quantum theory itself, knowledge of which would allow more exact predictions than quantum theory can provide. A collection of results, most significantly Bell's theorem (to be discussed soon), have demonstrated that broad classes of such hidden-variable theories are, in fact, incompatible with quantum physics. According to Bell's theorem, if nature actually operates in accord with any theory of *local* hidden variables, then the results of a Bell test will be constrained in a particular, quantifiable way. Many Bell tests have been performed, using entangled particles, and they have shown results incompatible with the constraints imposed by local hidden variables.

Another interpretation is the so-called Parallel Worlds or Many Worlds theory (Figure 2.2). In contrast to superposition, when a physical system is measured, it branches

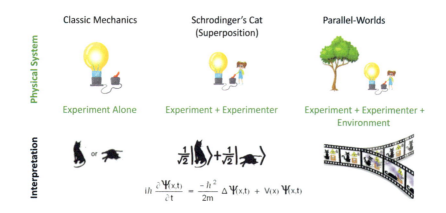

FIGURE 2.2
Quantum descriptions of physical world.

TABLE 2.1

The Expected Results of the Bell Test from Einstein's Hidden Force Theory

	Measurements Directions (Alice's, Bob's)								
Config.	(a, a)	(a, b)	(a, c)	(b, a)	(b, b)	(b, c)	(c, a)	(c, b)	(c, c)
000	A	A	A	A	A	A	A	A	A
001	A	A	D	A	A	D	D	D	A
010	A	D	A	D	A	D	A	D	A
011	A	D	D	D	A	A	D	A	A
100	A	D	D	D	A	A	D	A	A
101	A	D	A	D	A	D	A	D	A
110	A	A	D	A	A	D	D	D	A
111	A	A	A	A	A	A	A	A	A

into two parallel worlds that never cross each other. The problem with this theory is: if each of them doesn't know the other exists, which world am I living in, since I know the two parallel worlds?

A Bell test is a real-world physics experiment designed to test the theory of quantum mechanics, in relation to Albert Einstein's hidden variable theory, to explain the behavior of particles like photons and electrons. To date, all Bell tests have found that the hypothesis of local hidden variables is inconsistent with experimental results.

To illustrate a Bell test, suppose that Alice and Bob randomly measure a stream of pairs of entangled qubits (meaning the configurations for Alice's and Bob's qubits are identical) in three directions, a = 0°, b = 120°, and c = 240°, the eight possible outcomes are: 000, 001, 010, 011, 100, 101, 110, 111, where 1st, 2nd, and 3rd digits are the results from the three directions. There are nine pairs of measurement directions: (Alice, Bob) = (a, a), (a, b), (a, c), (b, a), (b, b), (b, c), (c, a), (c, b), and (c, c) with the probability of 1/9 for each.

In Table 2.1, (a, c) indicates Alice's and Bob's measured directions, whereas 001 indicates result 0 if measuring the qubits in direction a or b, but 1 if measured in direction c. Thus if Alice and Bob measure the pair of qubits in directions a and c, respectively, their results will be in disagreement (D).

According to the classical model, each qubit has a defined spin direction but is unknown. Einstein believes there is a hidden force that somewhat affects the results when qubits are measured. If these are true, then probability theory shows that Alice's and Bob's results will agree *at least* 5/9 of the time under any configuration as indicated in Table 2.1, whereas from quantum mechanics, Alice's and Bob's sequences will agree exactly or very nearly *half the time*. So far, all experiments have produced the results consistent with the quantum model, but do not support Albert Einstein's hidden-variable theory.

In my view, the Bell Test results and the fact that Schrodinger's cat can be dead and alive at the same time can also be explained in this way: humans can only sense 3-dimensional space, and we can randomize and control the variables of the experiment in 3-dimensional space, but we cannot control the variables in the 4th dimension. Just imagine, a cat jumping into a 2-dimensional circle is an impossibility for a 2-dimensional sensible being, since the being only sees no cat in its 2-dimensional space: how can a cat come from nothing?

The Bell test results bolster confidence in our HAI approach using individualized evolutionary knowledge nets formulated from individuated experience. Two individuals need not have exactly the same experiences from the same events for both to learn or adapt optimally.

2.3 The World of Multilevel Intelligence

In nature, we see how simple ants can collectively exhibit intelligence. In artificial swarm intelligence, an ant algorithm can produce some level of intelligence. Indeed, there are multilevel intelligences. **Social intelligence** is the collective intelligence of many individual intelligences, while individual human intelligence can be viewed as a collective intelligence at a lower level derived from human organs or cells.

Biologists often compare different cells in terms of how intelligently they fight for survival. Cancer cells are constantly fighting for their survival by sucking in as much nutrition as possible. Such *intelligent* behavior at the cellular level is considered *unintelligent* at a higher level (human level): a long survival time for a cancer cell may imply a shorter survival for the person in whom the cell resides. Cancer cells' evolution may lead to human devolution. We can further postulate that any physical entity can be viewed as a "brain" that can take an input, process it, and output results based on its "understanding" of the input information. Intelligence is not just a characteristic of living things. The nature of hierarchical intelligence has made us believe, mistakenly, that a lower intelligence is not intelligence. Humans can sense the intelligence level of their own kind, but often fail to understand upper or lower levels of intelligence, just as a cell or protein cannot understand a human's intelligence or the intelligence of a non-living object. The intelligence of non-living things might be recognized as collective or swarm intelligence by humans. A researcher who studies monkeys says: to understand monkeys, think like monkeys if you can. This reminds us that when we are building HAI, we should often think from an agent's perspective, instead of subconsciously from a human perspective. This is particularly important and leads us to determine rewards based on different changes in an agent's internal "biological states." Reward is fundamentally the driving-force in adaptive reinforcement learning in our HAI architecture.

The nature of multilevel intelligence implies its subjectivity. Who is *more* intelligent, a monkey or a human? A recent study shows that monkeys can do meta-thinking: thinking about thinking. The reason that monkeys cannot speak a sophisticated language is because of poor neuronal connectivity (a weak network) or, some suggest, for lack of desire. Suppose a being has only two possible choices: switching on and off. When his action matches a human's desire at the moment, he will be happy, then whatever we do, in his view, there is only one question: "do you want me to switch On or Off?" and only one type of decision for him to make: should I turn On or turn Off. Would his life be much simpler and happier than that of a human being? In this sense, are we human beings a consequence of evolution or devolution? Also, think about why children are usually happier than adults. The multiplicity of intelligence and its non-monotonic relationship with happiness remind us to be cautious in simulating human intelligence.

The conviction of multilevel intelligence motivates us to adapt, in addition to agent-level evolution, a so-called Forgetting Mechanism at the pattern level—infrequently used patterns will "die" or be eliminated. The survival time is related to the fitness of pattern frequency.

The notion of multilevel intelligence, in connection to the law of summative effects (to be discussed soon) used in our HAI architecture, justify the notion of pursuing local optima instead of a complex, time-consuming, even impossible global optimum.

3

The World in Our Mind: Fundamental Laws and Principles

The World in Our Mind is the Modeled World that is simplified based on fundamental principles (Figure 3.1). After the multifaceted objective world passes through an observer's sensory organs and attention mechanisms, it is further simplified or patternized using the basic principles of learning discussed in this section. Such simplification is necessary to efficiently store the information about the external world and oneself in one's brain. When these principles are used to develop learning models, controversies are encountered. Thus, discussing philosophical controversies is necessary in building our humanized artificial intelligence (HAI) architecture.

3.1 First Principle

A **First Principle** is a basic proposition or assumption that cannot be deduced from any other proposition or assumption. In mathematics, First Principles are referred to as axioms or postulates.

Aristotle gave them their first definition thus: in every systematic inquiry (methods) where there are First Principles or causes or elements, knowledge and science result from acquiring knowledge of these, for we think we know something just in case we acquire knowledge of the primary causes, the primary First Principles, all the way to the elements. It is clear, then, that in the science of nature as elsewhere, we should try first to determine questions about the First Principles.

Utilization of First Principles is a strategic approach to complex problems by breaking them into the simplest fundamental concepts through logical reasoning to discover the most effective solution. The First Principle approach continuously questions a problem with "Why?" until the basic truths land. In AI, a First Principle can be arrived at by questioning each and everything in a concept until there are just facts that can't be simplified any further. As an example, we can say that cigarette smoking can cause lung cancer, but, further looking into the cause, we find that carcinogens are the more direct cause of lung cancer (Figure 3.2).

The renowned physicist Albert Einstein laid out the importance of the First Principles and stated, "If I had an hour to solve a problem and my life depended on the solution, I would spend the first 55 minutes determining the proper questions to ask, for once I know the proper questions, I could solve the problem in less than five minutes."

In humanized AI, the applications of First Principles are necessary since it will bring clarity on the root of the problems from philosophical aspects. We will use the First Principles approach to analyze every aspect of human beings, including thoughts, emotions, consciousness, self-awareness, imitations, creativities, discoveries, imaginations,

DOI: 10.1201/b23355-4

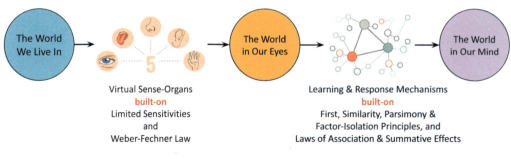

FIGURE 3.1
Roles of fundamental principles in humanized AI.

FIGURE 3.2
First Principle in search for a direct cause of lung cancer.

recollections, collaborations, reasoning, and learning, down to the most fundamental *mechanical* level so that all the building blocks can be obtained for implementing HAI on a computer. The process is called mechanicalization for the sake of brevity.

3.2 Law of Summative Effects

The whole and its parts have two types of relationships: parallel parts that exist simultaneously and sequential parts that appear sequentially in time. In terms of effect, there are three scenarios: (1) antagonistic—the whole is smaller than the sum of its parts, (2) synergistic—the whole is greater than the sum of its parts, and (3) The Law of Summative Effects—the whole can be practically approximated by the sum of its parts.

When the whole has parallel parts, interactions are the key to unlocking emergent and unintuitive properties. This occurs in many fields: reactions in biochemistry, flocking among birds in ecology, many-body systems in mechanics, social interactions in economics and political science, and drug interactions in pharmacology. The whole being equal to the sum of its parts happens in mathematics and physics, e.g., in many of the conservation laws.

According to Aristotle, "the whole is greater than the sum of its parts." This observation was adopted to explain human perception by the Gestalt psychology school of thought in the twentieth century. In society, people can work together or against each other, resulting in a larger sum or a smaller sum. Understanding whether components interact in a manner that enhances (synergy) or weakens (antagonism) the individual effects of the parts is often useful in science and engineering because the type of interaction governs the dynamics of complex systems. For instance, in pharmacology, understanding drug interactions enables the effective design of treatment strategies to combat complex diseases such as cancer and HIV, which increasingly rely on multidrug treatments. From game theory and our experience, we know that collaborative games can lead to the whole being greater than the sum of its parts, while non-collaborative games can lead to the whole being smaller than the sum of its parts.

The application of the Law of Summative Effects is significant in HAI. As with humans, the decision process is piecewise (stagewise) due to the fact that not all (past and future) facts are known at a given moment and the environment is changing constantly. In other words, our decisions are often based on local optima, not global optima, but we believe local optima are likely to lead to the global optima approximately. This is another way to state the law of approximate effect sum. In HAI, we deal with a long sequence of events, expressed as a string of text. In the reinforcement-learning-based response mechanisms, an agent's responses can be based on short-term rewards according to the notion that the sum of the short-term responses will add up approximately to the global optimal reward.

The Law of Summative Effects ensures the validity of recursive patternization and associated decision-making mechanisms in our HAI architecture.

3.3 Principle of Factor-Isolation

Experimentation is the most commonly used tool for scientific research. Agents are expected to be able to design and perform experiments too. The main difference between experiments and observational studies is that in observational studies hypotheses are tested by the collection of information from phenomena that occur naturally, whereas an experiment usually consists of making an event occur under known conditions whereas many extraneous influences as possible are eliminated and close observation is possible so that relationships between phenomena can be revealed. This is due to the universal **Principle of Factor-Isolation** (**Law of Factor-Isolation**) as illustrated in Figure 3.3: if factors A and B exist, fact C exists and if eliminating B, C disappears, then factor B is a cause of fact C (given that A always exists). Here C can be a composite factor.

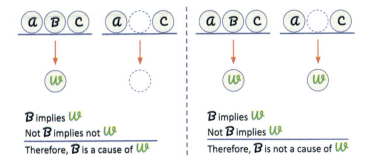

FIGURE 3.3
Principle of Factor-Isolation.

The **Factor-Isolation Technique** (FIT) is based on the principle of factor-isolation; with it one works to constructively isolate a few factors in order to determine association and causal relationship. We will frequently use the technique to effectively train HAI agents, and agents will constantly use the FIT to discover patterns in their observations.

3.4 Simpson's Paradox

In probability and statistics, **Simpson's Paradox**, introduced by Colin R. Blyth in 1972, points to apparently contradictory results between aggregate data analysis and analyses from data partitioning (Chang, 2012).

Suppose two drugs, A and B, are available for treating a disease. As shown in Table 3.1, the treatment effect (in terms of remission rate) is 520/1500 for B, better than 500/1500 for treatment A. Thus, we will *prefer treatment B to A*. However, after further looking into the data for males and females separately, we find that the treatment effect in males is 200/500 with A, better than 380/1000 with B, while the treatment effect in females is 300/1000 with A, better than 140/500 with B. Therefore, whether female or male, we will *prefer treatment A to B* (Table 3.1). Should we take treatment A or B? In practice, such controversy can easily occur without notice when we conduct two gender-specific trials sequentially versus one trial of mixed genders.

The problem can be even more controversial. Suppose when we further look into the subcategories: Young Female and Old Female, and the direction of treatment effects switches again, i.e., treatment B has a better effect than treatment A in both subcategories, consistent with the treatment effect for the overall population as shown in Table 3.2. The question is: what prevents one from partitioning the data into arbitrary subcategories artificially constructed to yield wrong choices of treatments, and how specific is too specific? And should partitioning be based on gender, geography, or something else? The paradox can be seen in different situations, such as in democratic elections: even when both of the majorities in Town A and Town B voted for candidate Jonn rather than Bob, the combined majority in the two towns might vote for Bob. This dilemma can occur even when there are more than two towns.

Enlightened by the Simpson Paradox, I rediscovered (Change, 2012) the hidden Similarity Principle (to be discussed next) that we subconsciously use in our daily life, and in scientific discovery and invention. This paradox, in conjunction with the Similarity Principle, illustrates that science is subjective or personal in principle, and on this basis, different objective methods are developed. In other words, sciences are subjective and objective at the same time. So is human learning. In this sense, there is no right or wrong, just different perspectives.

TABLE 3.1

Drug Responses in Male and Female

	Drug A	Drug B
Male	200/500	380/1000
Female	300/1000	140/500
Total	500/1500	520/1500

TABLE 3.2

Drug Responses in Young and Old Females

	Drug A	Drug B
Young Female	20/200	40/300
Old Female	280/800	100/200
Total	300/1000	140/500

3.5 Similarity Principles

Science aims to discover causal relationships and to predict future outcomes. So does learning (human or machine learning). All science, and learning itself, is based on a fundamental principle—the Similarity Principle (Chang, 2012, 2014, 2020). The principle asserts that *similar things or individuals will likely behave similarly, and the more similar they are the more similarly they behave.* For instance, people with the same (or a similar) disease, gender, and age will likely have similar responses to a particular drug or medical intervention. If they are similar in more aspects, they will have more similar responses.

To qualify as a true scientific discovery, a finding must be verifiable. Otherwise, it cannot be called science. However, as history is unique, no two events are identical or repeat exactly; even the same individual (especially a living being) will change constantly. For this reason, we have to group similar things together and, considering them as approximately the same, study their common or overall behaviors. Psychologists study a group of people with similar personalities to explain why those people behave the way they do. Pharmaceutical scientists treat people with the "same" disease to study the overall effect of a drug even though individual responses to the drug may be different. Indeed, similarity grouping is the basis for scientific discovery, and the Similarity Principle is the backbone behind causality. The idea of a causal relationship is our human way to handle the complex world in a simple form with a reasonable approximation, given the limited ability of our brains.

Here are some simple examples of people using the principle for learning in their daily lives: all objects with wheels run fast. Objects with sharp edges can be used to cut things. Many people think September 11 is more likely to see a terrorist attack than other days of the year. Therefore, NYPD tightens security around the date. People use the Similarity Principle differently. For instance, some of my friends think sending their children to a top-rated high school will increase the probability of them entering top colleges. They buy a tiny apartment in the town with a first-rank public school because they think people from the same school have similar chances of getting into a better college than people from different schools. Some of my other friends think differently. They think their children are similarly talented to certain youngsters who were successful in a certain school that fit them, so the school would be suitable for their kids too. For this reason, they send their kids to the same or similar school even though they may not be the best-ranked high school.

The Similarity Principle says that every characteristic of an object likely contributes a portion of information to real-world outcomes; therefore, the more similarities between two objects the more likely they produce the same output when they receive the same input. That is, two similar objects behave similarly.

The Similarity Principle is also critical to understanding probability because similarity grouping (clustering) is the only way to create recurrences of events. This similarity grouping can be either intentional, subconscious, or due to the limited sensibility of our organs.

The Similarity Principle can also be applicable in Emotion: Why do you care more about a monkey's life than a fish's? This is because monkeys are more similar to us than fish are. Why do you care more about a fish's life than a worm's? Perhaps it's because a fish's size is closer to ours than that of a worm. And yes, because we use worms to catch fish. Why do we care about a dog's life more than a pig's? Isn't it because we interact with dogs more physically and emotionally (common activities)? Why do we care more about friends than enemies? It is because we have much more in common (beliefs, values) with our friends than with our enemies.

In social psychology, the Similarity Principle is often used for persuasion. One way to become more persuasive is to show how you are similar to others. We like people who are similar to us. If we find people who share similar opinions with us we like them better, and if we like them better we are more likely to be persuaded by them. For more information on similarity-principle based AI, see Chang (2020).

Similarity and association achieve each other. We make an association between two similar things; we recognize two things as being similar because they both associate to the same quality or quantity in some aspects (e.g., existing in the same space or time, or being or having common friends).

Like all other principles in this chapter, the Similarity Principle is inherited innate knowledge, whereas causality models are discoveries built on the Similarity Principle. In our HAI architecture, the mechanisms of learning and response will enable agents to use the Similarity Principle as humans do. We will explain how this is done when discussing Zda's architecture and prototyping.

3.6 Parsimony Principle

William of Occam was an English philosopher and theologian. His work on knowledge, logic, and scientific inquiry played a major role in the transition from medieval to modern thought. Occam stressed the Aristotelian principle that entities must not be multiplied beyond what is necessary. This principle became known as **Occam's Razor** or the **Parsimony Principle**: The simplest theory that fits the facts of a problem is the one that should be selected. However, Occam's Razor is not considered an irrefutable principle of logic, and certainly not a scientific result. According to Albert Einstein, the supreme goal of all theory is to make the irreducible basic elements as simple and as few as possible without having to surrender the adequate representation of a single datum of experience.

The Parsimony Principle is used to select from competing models that describe a scientific phenomenon. **Phylogeny** is a study of how organisms are related through evolutionary time. In phylogeny, the principle of maximum parsimony is one method used to infer relationships between species (taxa) in the form of evolutionary trees, either **cladograms** (Figure 3.4) or **phylogenetic trees**. Each branch of the evolutionary tree represents descending taxa from a common ancestor. The nodes on the tree represent the common ancestors of the descendants. The main difference between cladogram and phylogenetic tree is that a cladogram is an evolutionary tree with branches with equal distances, showing the relationship between a group of clades, whereas a phylogenetic tree is an evolutionary tree showing an estimate of phylogeny, where the distance of each branch is proportional to the amount of inferred evolutionary change (Baum, 2008). In this context, the parsimony principle states that the tree with the fewest common ancestors or the fewest number of evolutionary events is the most likely. The principle can also be viewed as the minimization of within-group differences or the maximization of between-group differences. This might be where the idea of the generalized hierarchical clustering method in narrow AI comes from.

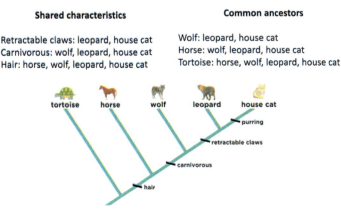

Shared characteristics

Retractable claws: leopard, house cat
Carnivorous: wolf, leopard, house cat
Hair: horse, wolf, leopard, house cat

Common ancestors

Wolf: leopard, house cat
Horse: wolf, leopard, house cat
Tortoise: horse, wolf, leopard, house cat

FIGURE 3.4
Parsimony Principle in action: cladogram.

The Parsimony Principle can emerge in different forms in different sciences. Entropy is a measure of disorder (degree of randomness) and affects all aspects of our daily lives. The entropy of an object measures the amount of energy which is unavailable to do work. The **Principle of Maximum Entropy** states that the probability distribution which best represents the current state of knowledge about a system is the one with the largest entropy, in the context of precisely stated prior data. Since the distribution with the maximum entropy is the one that makes the fewest assumptions about the true distribution of data, the principle of maximum entropy can be seen as an application of Occam's Razor. The principle was first expounded by Jaynes (1957a and b), where he argued that the entropy of statistical mechanics and the information entropy of information theory are basically the same thing.

Parsimony is an important principle of cognitive development for two reasons: (1) there are many ways to apply pattern discovery or apply the Similarity Principle; Parsimony suggests we find the simplest one to be efficient and broad (applicability), and (2) application of the Similarity Principle is a way of practicing reductionism, by grouping similar things or events before patternization, the basic form of learning.

The Parsimony Principle applied to machine learning includes an example wherein a simple trained model often performs better in prediction than a complex model that fits all data points in the training data set. In our HAI architecture, the principle will be used in different ways: probabilistically maximizing a utility function (e.g., reward or frequency associated with an action or pattern) in the response mechanism, minimizing the number of patterns or knowledge refinement in repatternization used in the learning mechanism, and maximizing attentivity in the attention mechanism.

3.7 Laws of Association

Laws of Association explain how we learn and remember things. They are first seen in Aristotle's psychology: impressions are stored in the seat of perception, linked by the laws of contiguity, similarity, and contrast. In psychology, the principal laws of the association are contiguity, repetition, attention, pleasure-pain, and similarity. The basic laws were formulated by Aristotle circa 300 B.C. and by John Locke in the seventeenth century. Both philosophers taught that the mind at birth is a blank slate and that all knowledge has to be acquired by learning. These ideas still make up the backbone of modern learning theory.

The **Law of Contiguity** states that we associate things that occur close to each other in time and/or space. For example, if we think of thunder, we immediately think of lightning, since the two often occur one after the other. When an object flies toward you, you would probably, considering similar experiences in the past, anticipate the pain it could cause if it hits you. When someone talks about apples, you might think of the sweetness of an apple.

The **Law of Similarity** (not the Similarity Principle discussed earlier) states that when two things are very similar to each other, the thought of one will often trigger the thought of the other. For example, when you cannot reach a book on the top shelf of a bookshelf, you may think of asking someone taller to help you.

The **Law of Contrast** states that the thought of something is likely to trigger the thought of its direct opposite. For example, when we hear the word "good," we often think of the word "bad." This happens because words often exist in a relative sense, or are co-existent: without bad, there will be no good, and vice versa.

Association is the key for us to use to identify different objects. As one example, the fact that our body parts are linked together in space all the time makes us treat them as an entity, called the human body. The association of things observed at different moments underlies the desirability of predicting their states, or relationships, over time.

Associative learning is when a subject creates a relationship between stimuli or behavior (both auditory or visual) and the original stimulus (auditory or visual). The higher the concreteness of stimulus items, the more likely they are to evoke sensory images that can function as mediators of associative learning and memory. The acquisition of associations is the basis for learning. This learning is seen in classical and operant conditioning, a process we will discuss later.

Memory seems to operate as a sequence of associations (attention shifts): concepts, words, and opinions are intertwined, so that stimuli such as a person's face will call up the associated name. Understanding the relationships between different items is fundamental to episodic memory, and damage to the hippocampal region of the brain has been found to hinder the learning of associations between objects.

In a general sense, learning and knowledge discovery occur on the basis of association, and association can be explained from biology.

In the human brain, each *neuron* (Figure 3.5) is typically connected to thousands of other neurons. A typical neuron collects signals from others through a host of fine structures called *dendrites*. The neuron sends out spikes of electrical activity through a long, thin strand known as an *axon*, which splits into thousands of branches. At the end of each branch, a structure called a *synapse* converts the activity from the axon into electrical effects that inhibit or excite activity in the connected neurons. When a neuron receives an excitatory input that is sufficiently large compared to its inhibitory input, it sends a spike of electrical activity down its axon. Learning occurs by changing the effectiveness of the synapses so that the influence of one neuron on another changes (Chang, 2010).

Hebbian theory is a neuroscientific theory claiming that an increase in synaptic efficacy arises from a presynaptic cell's repeated and persistent stimulation of a postsynaptic cell. It is an attempt to explain synaptic plasticity, the adaptation of brain neurons during the learning process. This theory was introduced by Donald Hebb in The Organization of Behavior (Hebb, 1949). The theory is also called Hebb's rule and is sometimes referred to as cell assembly theory.

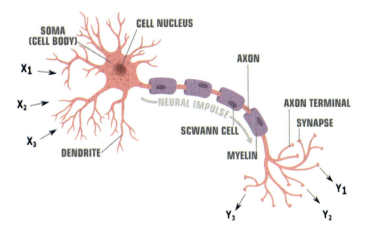

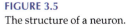

FIGURE 3.5
The structure of a neuron.

The theory is often summarized in an epigram: "Cells that fire together wire together." This actually means that cell A needs to "take part in firing" cell B, and such causality can occur only if cell A fires just before, not exactly at the same time as, cell B. Hebb's rule attempts to explain associative or Hebbian learning, in which simultaneous activation of cells leads to pronounced increases in synaptic strength between those cells. It also provides a biological basis for errorless learning methods in education and memory rehabilitation. If two neurons consistently fire simultaneously, then any connection between them will become stronger. Conversely, if the two neurons never fire simultaneously, the connection between them will die away. The idea is that if two neurons both respond to something then they should be connected (Chang, 2020). Pavlov used this idea, called classical conditioning (Section 4.11), to train his dogs so that when food was shown to the dogs and the bell was rung at the same time, the neurons for salivating over the food and hearing the bell fired simultaneously, and so became strongly connected. Over time, the strength of the synapse between the neurons that responded to hearing the bell and those that caused the salivation reflex was enough that just hearing the bell caused the salivation neurons to fire in sympathy (Marsland, 2014).

In our HAI architecture, the laws of association will be reflected in the attention mechanism including determination of the attention set and attention shift. The attention set is the group of objects and actions that the HAI agent pays attention to at the moment and serves as the basis for patternization in learning and response mechanisms.

3.8 Weber-Fechner laws

The Weber-Fechner Laws (Fechner, 1860, 1966) are two equivalent but approximate laws in psychophysics. Both laws relate to human perception, more specifically the relation between the actual change in a physical stimulus and the perceived change. This includes stimuli to all senses: vision, hearing, taste, touch, and smell.

The Weber's Law states that the minimum increase of stimulus which will produce a perceptible increase of sensation is proportional to the pre-existent stimulus, while Fechner's law is an inference from Weber's law (with additional assumptions) which says that the intensity of our sensation increases as the logarithm of an increase in energy rather than as rapidly as the increase.

Weber found that the just noticeable difference (JND) between two weights was approximately proportional to the weights. Thus, if the weight of 105 g can (only just) be distinguished from that of 100 g, the JND is 5 g. If the mass is doubled, the differential threshold also doubles to 10 g, so that 210 g can be distinguished from 200 g. In this example, a weight (any weight) seems to have to increase by 5% for someone to be able to reliably detect the increase, and this minimum required fractional increase (of 5/100 of the original weight) is referred to as the "Weber fraction" for detecting changes in weight. Other discrimination tasks, such as detecting changes in brightness, or in tone height (pure tone frequency), or in the length of a line shown on a screen, may have different Weber fractions, but they all obey Weber's law in that observed values need to change by at least some small but constant proportion of the current value to ensure human observers will reliably be able to detect that change.

Fechner did not conduct any experiments on how perceived heaviness increased with the mass of the stimulus. Instead, he assumed that all JNDs are subjectively equal, and argued mathematically that this would produce a logarithmic relation between the stimulus intensity and the sensation.

The logarithm of the law can be explained by the tree structure of the neural network. Activation of neurons by sensory stimuli in many parts of the brain is modeled by a proportional law: neurons change their spike rate by about 10%–30%, when a stimulus has been applied. However, as Scheler (2017) showed, the population distribution of the intrinsic excitability or gain of a neuron is a heavy tail distribution, more precisely a lognormal shape, which is equivalent to a logarithmic coding scheme.

The Weber-Fechner laws will be implemented in HAI embodiment, mainly in the virtual sensory organs. Moreover, I believe the law of logarithm can be applied to measuring happiness and the value of money. Once these algorithms are used in constructing the utility function for rationalism, the controversies between rationalism and irrationalism can come to a similar conclusion.

3.9 Statistical Modeling of Reality

Causality is the relationship between causes and effects. The notion of causality does not have an agreed upon definition in the sciences. In classical physics, an effect cannot occur *before* its cause. In Einstein's theory of special relativity, causality means that an effect cannot occur from a cause that is not in the back (past) light cone of that event. Similarly, a cause cannot have an effect outside its front (future) light cone. These restrictions are consistent with the grounded belief (or assumption) that causal influences cannot travel faster than the speed of light in time. In quantum field theory, observables of events with a spacelike relationship have to commute, so the order of observations or measurements of such observables do not impact each other.

Philosophically, determinists believe the world occurs in sequences of events in time, no cause, no why, no how. It is we, humans, who make causality or predictive models to simplify the real world so that we can store the modeled worlds in our brains, since we cannot store all the information we receive in a plain form, including itself.

In classic statistics, causality and association are often not separated in the model. Association refers to the relationship between the change in one variable and the change of another variable. Association can also be applied to more than two variables. The fundamental difference between causality and association is that the two changes in two variables can necessarily occur chronologically, the earlier one is the cause and the later one is called effect, while variables in an associational relationship do not necessarily have or are indicated in chronological order. Therefore, causality is a special type of association.

Observations and measurements generally include systematic and random errors. Random error (RE) is unpredictable, caused by changes of some unobservable factors. For example, a medicine may work well for one person, but not for another person, due to differences in genotype or phenotypes.

There are two statistical approaches to learning from data: (1) Classical Approach, which seeks the relationship between the outcome and the independent variables (attributes), and (2) Similarity Approach, which seeks the relationship between the outcomes between different subjects with different attributes. The Similarity Approach is constructed from the Similarity Principle, the foundation of causal and associative relationships.

Controversies in the interpretations of Associative or Causal Effects arise when using a classical statistical model, since the effects will depend on forms of attributes (independent variables). For instance, to study how the lower body height will affect the body weight, we use the initial model (Figure 3.6) that includes the attributes: upper body height (H_2), lower body height (H_3), and a random error (RE). This initial model can be mathematically rewritten as Model 2, and further reduced to Model 3 with attributes: the height H_1 and the lower body height H_3. We have to point out that Model 1 and Model 3 are mathematically equivalent. However, the interpretations of how H_3 affects the weight can be very different. Using Model 1, we would conclude: "every inch increase in the lower body will lead to an a_3 pound increase in body weight," while using Model 3, we would conclude: "every inch increase in the lower body will lead to an a_3-a_2 pound increase in body weight." The effect of an attribute depends on the mathematical form chosen—how ridiculous this sounds! Again, science is not that objective at all!

The reason that different models give different interpretations of the effects of individual attributes is because the attributes can be associated (H_1 has already included H_3). Likewise, in life sciences, we often study how phenotypes (human behaviors) depend on genotypes, while genotypes are associated. Such associations make the interpretation of attribute-effect subjective, depending on what genes or other attributes you want to be included in the model.

The Effect Size of H_3 Varies As Model Varies!

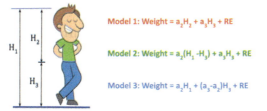

Model 1: Weight = $a_2 H_2 + a_3 H_3$ + RE

Model 2: Weight = $a_2 (H_1 - H_3) + a_3 H_3$ + RE

Model 3: Weight = $a_2 H_1 + (a_3 - a_2) H_3$ + RE

FIGURE 3.6
Controversies in modeling body weight by heights.

In randomized experiments such as clinical trials, the medical treatments are often randomly assigned to patients. Therefore, in theory, there is no association between the treatments and other attributes in the statistical model. However, in reality, the other attributes are virtually always unbalanced between the treatment groups, causing some "observed association" between the treatments and other attributes. Thus, the effect of a medical treatment is dependent on the statistician's choice among model options. In statistics, correlation, ranging from –1 to 1, is a quantification of linear association. The mutual information between y and x, defined as the difference between the entropy of y and the conditional entropy of y given x, reflects the amount of information shared between y and x.

Recognizing this controversy and the shortcoming of classical statistics is particularly important to those AI researchers who were initially trained in statistics or data science and are overconfident in their complex modeling techniques.

Alternatively, the similarity-based machine-learning approach can be used. The Similarity Approach focuses on the prediction of the outcome not the effect of each attribute. An introduction in such an approach and its applications can be found in Appendix B, and the Medical AI paper and book (Chang, 2020; Hwang and Chang, 2022). The Similarity Approach or Similarity-Principle-based approach will be used throughout our HAI architecture, from attention and learning to response mechanisms. Moreover, classical statistical modeling, like any scientific method, can be discovered in principle, if given sufficient time, by using the Similarity-Principle-based approach.

3.10 Connotation of Causality

Connotation of causality, related to Determinism and Freewillism, is a matter of unresolvable disagreement. The Determinism vs Freewill debate may be one of the most controversial in philosophy (Chang, 2012). **Free will** is critical in our understanding of causality and, consequently, the meaning of science and learning depends on our view of free will, the central question of which is: do we have a choice or is choice just an illusion? Having free will means that one has, uniquely, a choice to make. However, free-willers also believe that our free will is limited by physical reality and the laws of Nature. Many maintain that without free will there can be no morality, no right and wrong, no good and evil, and no creativity. Determinism, the view that free will does not exist or cannot affect events, can be terrifying: If everything happens for a reason, including every piece of our thoughts, every one of our choices, our beliefs, and emotions, every tiny movement we make or action we take … then humans will act just like machines.

Conversely, **causal determinism** holds that future events are necessitated by past and present events combined with the laws of Nature. According to this philosophy, every event is the effect of antecedent events, and these in turn are caused by events antecedent to them, and so on. *Causal determinism is the foundation of First Principles*. Human emotions and actions are no exception to this rule. Whether or not to commit a crime is not a choice and, likewise, neither is punishing criminals (Chang, 2014). Feeling freedom of choice is just an illusion. We are and act like, but don't feel like machines. Scientists cannot be satisfied with free will as the ultimate cause: what causes a person to make certain choices? Are free wills inherited from ancestors? If there is free will, then because all non-free will actions are predetermined, everything is ultimately determined by free will anyway! In other words, the ultimate answers to all "why" questions are the same, "because of free will," and causality completely misses its scientific sense. Furthermore, does the universe operate deterministically before the emergence of human or free will? If there is free will, is it inherited from our parents or a gift from God? In either case, who should be responsible for our actions? What difference, if any, should there be in how we morally treat a person born with a cancer gene and a person born with 'bad' free will?

With the ultimate development of neuroscience and understanding of the human brain, how much space will remain for free will? Whether you believe in free will or not, causality and scientific discovery only make sense on the basis of recognizable patterning, i.e., similarity grouping and the Similarity Principle.

Similarly, **Biologism**, or **Biodeterminism** here, refers to the thesis that human characteristics, physical and mental, are determined at conception by hereditary factors passed from parent to offspring. If there is any free will, it should be given by parents, and anything their parents have is delivered by grandparents, and so on. Therefore, HAI can be made through biological approaches, such as tube baby, organ replacement (e.g., implantable bioartificial kidney), etc.

HAI is a determinist's approach, meaning that the agent's behaviors are determined by the environment and his architectures. This is true even if techniques like pseudorandom number generators are involved in the agent's mechanisms to mimic free will, since random numbers generated by a computer randomizer are predictable.

4

The World to Learn: Cognition and Learning

This chapter will discuss further important aspects of humanness and HAI. For example, when we debate whether a machine understands a concept or natural language, we often forget that we might have a different understanding of the connotation (meaning) of understanding. The common creativity in discovery and invention is discussed since they are essential for HAI. We will treat imitation, analogy, and creativity under the same umbrella of similarity, making their implementation in HAI a straightforward task. We will review brain, mind, and the Language of Thought, and compare the static knowledge net and dynamic knowledge net that is adopted in our HAI architecture. With a dynamic knowledge net, knowledge is often formulated in real time and displayed in the agent's responses. As with humans, AI embodiments, including sensory organs, play a significant role in learning and interaction with the environment. Enlightened by the life achievements of Helen Keller, an extremely accomplished deafblind writer and lecturer, we will discuss the necessity of AI embodiments. The exploration-exploitation trade-off, a constantly encountered issue in both human and HAI learning, is the matter of choosing whether to repeat the best decisions known so far (exploitation) or to make a novel decision (exploration) that might provide an even better solution. Abstraction, reasoning, and imagination are common forms of cognitive learning. Attention is the behavioral and cognitive process of selectively concentrating on a discrete aspect of information while ignoring other perceivable information. Attention mechanisms are crucial in the HAI architecture, without the mechanisms, learning will stop at a very elementary level. Different from the existing theories in psychology or neurology, however, in our HAI the attention mechanism will be classified into subconscious, conscious, and associative attention types for easy implementation. We will discuss the functions of memory and dreams for knowledge refinement, imaginary scenario-playing in hypothesis forms, and reliving experiences for "emotional needs" in building our HAI. Emotions are mental states associated with thoughts, feelings, behavioral responses, and a degree of pleasure or displeasure and their natural language expressions. Discretization of emotional states will be used for virtual emotion simulations. Observations are dependent on the observer's sensory organs and his attention or state of mind. Observations can be delusive; thus, experiments are important for humans and HAI agents to enable the discovery and verify new findings. The notions of two classic experiments, Pavlov's Dog and Skinner's Box, are critical in building HAI architecture.

4.1 Connotation of Understanding

Making an agent understand human language is an important but challenging task in HAI. In my view (Chang, 2012, 2014), we humans have not yet understood the meaning of understanding. I believe "mechanical" interpretations of these concepts are essential

DOI: 10.1201/b23355-5

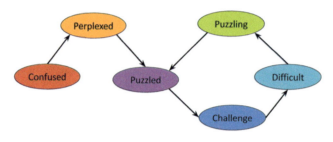

FIGURE 4.1
Circular definitions of concepts.

before we can implement HAI. Chang and Chang (2017) take a fresh approach to analyzing the connotations of understanding by using recursive concept-mapping, and conclude that understanding is essentially a concept-mapping game. "One explains a concept using other concepts that are further explained by other concepts, and so on. Since concepts are limited for any individual at any time, we will eventually come to circular definitions (Figure 4.1)." If we connect the words or concepts used in the definitions in sequence, they will form a personal wordnet, called an **iWordNet** (Figure 4.2). Here "i" in the term emphasizes the ties of the network to the individual person. The authors discovered that an individual's knowledge or IQ bears a relationship to the global topological properties of his iWordNet, while the proposed **Path of Understanding**, a vector characterization of language strings using local topological properties of iWordnet, provides the way to "compute" the meaning.

If the meaning of "understanding" is not what we think it is, but in a sense just a concept-mapping, then any viable approach that we could take for HAI will be very different from the current big-data approaches.

FIGURE 4.2
A partial iWordnet of a high school student.

It is interesting to know how one explains the meaning of "understanding," the meaning of "meaning," the meaning of connotation, or the connotation of meaning. The meaning of thoughts, intentions, goals, purposefulness, emotion, feeling, empathy, friendship, hate, animus ... these are elementary and critical concepts but unfortunately, they have not and cannot be explained well in other terms, because in some ways these concepts themselves are more elementary than other concepts. We cannot use higher level concepts to explain more elementary concepts without circular definitions. That is why we are trying in vain to explain how deep-learning neural networks work in image processing using high-level knowledge.

For elementary concepts, we cannot explain further using other concepts. We just assume we have the same understanding of them, which is reflected in our own actions. In addition to explaining a concept in words, understanding is also judged by the person's response (action) to the words (the request or question). How often do we watch our pet's behavior and explain confidently and emotionally how she thinks? Why, then, should we expect more or less of the rational beings we help to create? Therefore, our goal is to build HAI that can *behaviorally* demonstrate having thoughts, emotion, consciousness, and the capacity for collaboration, creativity, invention, discovery, and more.

The notion that we explain anything in thoughts or in natural language, recursively to the elementary concepts, is so enlightening. I bravely postulate that any complex concept or knowledge consists of hierarchical recursions of elementary concepts and any high-level skill is hierarchical recursions of elementary movements of body parts. These elementary (atomic) concepts and movements, despite varying from individual to individual, are the building blocks of our HAI agents—and make it possible to build HAI using a small-data approach!

4.2 Discovery versus Invention

Discovery and invention are two features that an HAI agent should have. Can we make an HAI agent capable of scientific discoveries and inventions? To answer this question, we have to first clarify the difference between a discovery and an invention. Since the determination of a discovery or invention is dependent on whether or not it initially exists outside of a human (or agent) mind (Figure 4.3), it is critical to clarify the connotation and denotation of a human or human identity. As we have just discussed, if we cannot clearly define what a person is in the Identity Paradox, how can we make a clear differentiation between discovery and invention?

Even more fascinating, it is difficult to tell whether a discovery is based on the discoverer or the person who interprets the discovery. Let me use a paradox to explain what I mean by that. If an AI agent did generate the exact same text as Darwin's theory of evolution but before Darwin did, would it mean that the agent had discovered the theory? And since a *discovery* is presumably made by its *discoverer*, would this be the agent or the human reader? Should we explain the text differently from Darwin's text just because it was generated by a machine? If we explain the machine-generated text the same way as we did for Darwin's text, should we call it a discovery? If we do, we in fact have created an AI that can carry out scientific discovery, and such an AI agent can be just a random text generator or a simple software package that can randomly generate English words. In theory, this random text generator can generate any text as long as sufficient time is given.

FIGURE 4.3
Discovery versus intention.

It might not be so critical to differentiate discovery from intention from HAI perspective since they are just two human-invented terms and they both share the common nature of creativity. We study imitation and creativity under the same umbrella of similarity in HAI: an action with great similarity to another is an imitation, while an action with an appropriate similarity to a known experience (or a pattern) is said to represent creativity. In our HAI architecture, creativity is simply the manipulation of an event-string based on analogy, while imitation is actioner replacement in an event-string. We will elaborate in Part III and discuss implementation in Part IV.

4.3 Knowledge Net and Language of Thought

Mind is the term most commonly used to describe the higher functions of the human brain (Figure 4.4), particularly those of which humans are subjectively conscious, such as personality, thought, reason, memory, intelligence, and emotion. Although other species of animals share some of these mental capacities, the word mind is usually used only in relation to humans.

The brain is the part of the central nervous system situated within the skull. It includes two cerebral hemispheres, and its functions include muscle control and coordination, sensory reception and integration, speech production, memory storage, and the elaboration of thought and emotion.

The Language of Thought Hypothesis (LOTH) postulates that thought and thinking take place in a mental language. This language consists of a system of representations that is physically realized in the brains of thinkers and has a combinatorial syntax (and semantics) such that operations on representations are causally sensitive only to the syntactic properties of representations. According to LOTH, thought is, roughly, the tokening of a representation

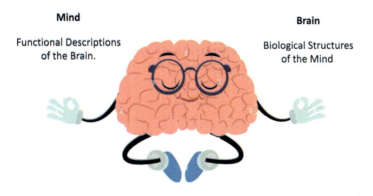

FIGURE 4.4
Brain and mind.

that has a syntactic (constituent) structure with appropriate semantics. Thinking thus consists in syntactic operations defined over such representations. Most of the arguments for LOTH derive their strength from their ability to explain certain empirical phenomena, like productivity and systematicity of thought and thinking (stanford.edu, 2019a).

A **functionalist** believes, according to the token identity theory, that a particular pain is identical to a particular brain process. Functionalism identifies mental states and processes by means of their causal roles, and we know that the functional roles are possessed by neural states and processes. Thus it is reasonable to suspect that the way in which the brain represents the world might not be through language. The representation might be much more like a map. A map relates every feature on it to every other feature. We can think of beliefs as expressing the different bits of information that could be extracted from the map.

Functionalism came to be seen as an improvement on identity theory, and as inconsistent with it, because of the correct assertion that a functional state can be realized by quite different brain states: thus a functional state might be realized as well by a silicon-based brain as by a carbon-based brain. According to this paradigm, it leads to the (common) **knowledge network** (*Knet*), in which each concept in the network connects other concepts in the network directly or indirectly. Thus, a knowledge-based net such as ConceptNet, Wordnet, or the like might be needed for building HAI.

However, such a *Knet* should be individualized, not commonsense-based, and dynamic instead of static. We have discussed the rationale for individualization; a partial justification of dynamization is that the mind can be an activity of the human brain. Any feeling in the body (perhaps through sensory organs) needs a time interval. For example, temperature can be defined for any given moment in physics; however, feeling hot can be a result of high temperature during some time interval, no matter how small the interval is. Therefore, feeling hot is an average result of a high temperature during a tiny period of time, not at any given moment. This leads us further to conclude that knowledge and feeling or emotion do not have fixed corresponding states of mind at a given moment, it is dynamically formulated in real time, at least HAI agents, it should be how they will display.

In our HAI agent, knowledge is reflected by dynamically formulated responses. The stochastic decision network is formulated and constantly updated via experience. Thoughts in the HAI are existing or newly formulated paths (in *Knet*) that are similar-matched with the sequence of observed events. Comparisons of such thoughts with the associated frequency and reward will determine the agent's response based on the similarity principle. The stochastic network is constructed over time through hierarchical tokenization and recursive patternization. Simply put, the computer chip is the brain, whereas the stochastic decision network with associated attention, learning, and response mechanisms is the mind. The mind does not work independently, instead it interacts with the environment via its body and organs (to be discussed next).

4.4 Role of Embodiment and Embodied AI

Smith and Gasser (2005) proposed the **Embodiment Hypothesis** as the idea that intelligence emerges in the interaction of an agent with an environment and as a result of the sensorimotor activity. They offer six lessons for developing embodied intelligent agents suggested by research in developmental psychology. They argue that starting life as a baby grounded in a physical, social, and linguistic world is crucial to the development of the flexible and inventive intelligence that characterizes humankind.

While the initial hypothesis comes from Psychology and Cognitive Science, the recent research developments of Embodied AI have come largely from Computer Vision researchers. Embodied AI is a growing research space. Facebook AI Research (FAIR) and Intel Labs have been spearheading new projects in the space of Embodied AI. "Embodied" is defined as "giving a tangible or visible form to an idea." Simply put, "Embodied AI" means "AI for virtual robots." More specifically, Embodied AI is the field for solving AI problems for virtual robots that can move, see, speak, and interact in the virtual world and with other virtual robots—these simulated robot solutions are then transferred to real-world robots (Bermudez, 2021).

As an example of Embodied AI, a robot firefighter must be capable of taking actions in the real world and can talk to humans with natural language. For instance, consider the following search and rescue scenario. The robot asks: "Is there smoke in any room?" First, the robot has to understand what the question is asking, including the meaning of "room" in this context.

The HAI discussed in this book is an imitation of a complete human being, not just a repeated performance of one specific task such as firefighting or driving a car. Thus, we are interested in the integral role of human embodiments in the agent's learning and response.

It is interesting to look into the differences between the classical and behavior-based architectures in robotics. In the classical AI approach, the control architecture for robots is functional decomposition. First, information from different sensor systems is received and integrated into a central representation. Then, internal processing takes place in which an environment model (world model) is built, or updated, and planning for subsequent actions occurs. The final stage is the execution of some actions. Altogether, such an appraisal leads to the sense-think-act cycle (Kosiński and Zaczek-Chrzanowska, 2007).

In behavior-based robotics, the main role is played by a method of decomposing a robot's control system into a set of task-achieving behaviors (or competencies). This is achieved by the hierarchical subsumption architecture. In contrast to classical AI's functional decomposition, implementations of such task-achieving behaviors are called layers: higher-level layers are built on lower-level ones. Instead of a single information flow from the perceptual world, multiple paths and actions at different layers are executed in parallel. That is, each layer can function relatively independently. This subsumption allows the coordination of actuators and sensors directly.

The human body and organs play critical roles in interactions with the environment. The body and organs are the "devices" for a human to directly *sense the world*. Without them we cannot have a sense of the external world and different sensations: hot versus cold, fragrant versus smelly, beautiful versus ugly, far versus near, fast versus slow, and pleasurable versus painful. The deaf cannot hear and the blind cannot see, a person of anosmia cannot smell, the dumb cannot speak. Of great value, legs give us the power to walk, hands give us the power to grab. Impairments of the body or organs will limit our interactions with the external world and communications with others. Parosmia is a change in the normal perception of odors, such as when something that normally smells pleasant now smells foul. Any such impairment and limitation will weaken our learning abilities.

Coordination and mapping among organs, or more accurately the senses of the same objects from different organs, is an important consequence of an agent interacting with the external world and a part of himself. For instance, a baby can quickly establish the link (mapping) between what a ball looks like and how it feels when he touches it. It's such mappings that allow us to learn and communicate efficiently. Imagine, during lunch, if you ask me to pass the cheese to you, I search, see, grab, and pass it to you. Without vision and a hand, and without vision-hand coordination, it is much harder to accomplish the mission.

According to Cybernetics, the process of accomplishing the mission can be described in detail for robot-building. The process is itself akin to the use of any negative feedback mechanism which I employ every day. Suppose I try to reach for a pen. I constantly make small adjustments to my hand based on its location relative to the pen and the moving direction of my hand until I reach it. Perhaps less smoothly, but just as surely, our agent will get built.

We know the importance of embodiment in physical and emotional experiences and the learning of knowledge, but how much does human intelligence depend on embodiment? If most human beings had no eyes, our world would be very different. However, if just a small number of people live with organ impairments, the situation will be different.

Helen Keller's story is very enlightening. Helen Adams Keller was an American author, political activist, and lecturer (Figure 4.5). She was the first deaf and blind person to earn

"Water" is the very first word Helen learn from her teacher Anne.

Tadoma is a method of communication used by deafblind individuals,in which the deafblind person places their little finger on the speaker's lips and their fingers along the jawline. The middle three fingers often fall along the speaker's cheeks with the little finger picking up the vibrations of the speaker's throat.

FIGURE 4.5
Helen Keller with her teacher, Anne Sullivan.

a Bachelor of Arts degree. Helen was viewed as isolated but was very in touch with the outside world. She was able to enjoy music by feeling the beat and she was able to have a strong connection with animals through touch. She was delayed in picking up language, but that did not stop her from having a voice. Her first teacher and life-long companion, Anne Sullivan, taught her language, including reading and writing. Sullivan's first lessons involved spelling words on Keller's hand to show her the names of objects around her. She also learned how to speak and to understand other people's speech using the Tadoma method. She attended Radcliffe College of Harvard University and became the first deaf-blind person to earn a Bachelor of Arts degree. She worked for the American Foundation for the Blind from 1924 until 1968, during which she toured the United States and traveled to 35 countries around the globe advocating for those with vision loss. Keller was a prolific author, writing 14 books and hundreds of speeches and essays.

We know that the impairment of one organ can provide better training opportunities for other organs. Vision-impaired people often have sharp ears. A hearing-impaired person can hear music via a device that transfers sound waves to light waves so that the person can produce a similar sensation by looking at motion pictures when the music is played. This confirms our earlier statement of *truth as a matter of inter-subject agreement*. The fundamental role of inter-subject agreement has also been discussed in the connotation of understanding.

When microscopes and telescopes were discovered, they extended humans' sensory organs, and since then we have a different view and understanding of the universe. Likewise, GPS completely changes our eyes' ability to detect (remote) object location. In the future, we will be able to extend our memory using external devices that will be able to directly communicate with our brains. You may say that we have already used the Internet to extend our memory. All these virtual embodiments will change the way humans view and interact with the world and change the view of machine races in our future society.

My final point is that for a robot, its body and sensory organs can be made of classic and new types of materials, biological or non-biological materials. A robot uses these to detect the world, and the world is unidimensionalized as text strings in our HAI architecture. An AI agent on the computer detects the virtual world that is already in text strings. For a robot, a response in text-strings will be converted to corresponding physical actions, while for the HAI agent, the response is linked to the corresponding animations. We will develop virtual embodiment in Parts III and IV.

4.5 Exploration to Exploitation

Exploration may refer to the discovery of new things, knowledge, and opportunities, and it is associated with radical changes and learning through experimentation. Exploitation may refer to the refinement of existing products, resources, and knowledge, and is associated with incremental changes. The unknown needs to be discovered or explored, and the known needs to be exploited for refinement. The exploration-exploitation trade-off is a critical issue in reinforcement learning (RL), occurring in scenarios where an agent has to repeatedly make a choice with uncertain payoffs. In essence, the dilemma for a decision-making system that only has incomplete knowledge of the world is whether to repeat decisions that have worked well so far (exploit) or to make novel decisions, hoping to gain even greater rewards (explore). A related question is: should we search over the whole sample space to find the best solution in the knowledge base or only quickly search the promising areas? In our AI architecture, an agent can ask creative questions and generate creative responses or actions through (quasi-)genetic operations in his mind with a recursive decision network.

Learning often occurs in exploratory and confirmatory stages. As we make observations, our minds make hypotheses, either to fit them into the existing laws in our minds or to otherwise make a hypothesis. The latter is called exploratory stage learning. The truthness of the hypothesis involves uncertainties. In our HAI architecture, those hypotheses are stored in one area of the brain, called the *Imagine net*, waiting to be tested. After the hypothesis is tested through more observations or other means, such as reading books or learning in a class, the hypothesis will become a law stored in another area of the brain, called a *Knowledge net*. But until then the mind is put on hold for this issue, and the associated brain resources can be used for something else.

The exploration-exploitation trade-off is facilitated using an innate creativity attribute in our HAI response mechanism. With this parameter, a creative agent often asks his teacher closed (yes/no) questions, wishing that the teacher (a knowledgeable person) will give either a positive or a negative answer. Here, the questions are the hypotheses. An HAI agent will actively ask (create) questions in wishing humans or pear to answer. The questions are formulated through imitation or through the genetic operations of mutation and crossover of patterns in *Knet*.

4.6 Abstraction, Reasoning, and Imagination

Thought encompasses an aim-oriented flow of ideas and associations that can lead to a reality-oriented conclusion. *To reason* is to make sense of things by applying logic and adapting or justifying practices, institutions, and beliefs based on new or existing information. Reasoning may be subdivided into forms of logical reasoning, such as deductive, inductive, and abductive forms. Aristotle drew a distinction between logical discursive reasoning (reasoning proper) and intuitive reasoning, in which the reasoning process is aided by intuition. Humans can meta-think, i.e., think about thinking; however, because memory and time are limited, we cannot think about thinking about thinking ... indefinitely. This self-referential paradox suggests that Aristotle's Logic may not be conducive to thinking about thinking.

Abstraction in philosophy is the process of forming a concept by identifying common features among a group of individuals, or by ignoring unique aspects of these individuals. In other words, abstraction is the process of generalization by reducing the information content of a concept or an observable phenomenon, typically in order to retain only information which is relevant for a particular purpose. For example, abstracting "happiness" to an "emotional state" reduces the amount of information conveyed about the emotional state. In a sense, abstraction is similarity grouping. The philosophical definition will be used in our HAI architecture. We will discuss how to easily implement inductive reasoning using "desensitization" and deductive reasoning using "sensitization."

Imagination is a speculative mental state that allows us to consider situations apart from here and now. In aesthetics, interest in imagination derives in large part from its role in our engagement with works of art, music, and literature. Imagination enables us to understand the mental states of others. It plays a central role in thought experimentation and has been invoked to explain our ability to engage in counterfactual reasoning. Imagination is often a source of creativity.

In our HAI architecture, thinking is considered a walk (or path) in one's knowledge net (*Knet*) or imaginary net (*Inet*). Self-inclusion, a characteristic of a recursive *Knet*, is the basis for an agent's self-awareness and consciousness. Thinking about thinking is an intra-inspection into the node of the agent in the *Knet*. Imagination is what is considered as scenario-play out in HAI's *Inet*, all for the purpose of optimal decision-making.

4.7 Imitation, Analogy, and Creativity

To imitate is to mimic someone or something. Learning starts with imitation. Imitation is the foundation of creativity and innovation, since all of our knowledge and wisdom is a synthesis of things that have been created by other people. We never create something out of nothing. Imitation allows us to learn the central ideas for creativity and master basic skills needed for innovation. Broadly speaking, imitation, in various social settings, creates social norms for a society, while our culture is the collective wisdom of all generations.

A creative idea often originates from inspiration drawn from someone or something. That is, creativity usually implies similarities between the new and the original, a partial imitation, or more precisely, an analogy.

An analogy is a comparison between two objects, systems or situations that highlights respects in which they are thought to be similar. Analogical Reasoning is any type of thinking that relies upon an analogy. An analogical argument is an explicit representation of a form of analogical reasoning that cites accepted similarities between two systems to support the conclusion that some further similarity exists. The foundation allowing analogical reasoning to work is the Similarity Principle.

Analogy, as a form of logic, is an inference or an argument from one particular similarity to another particular similarity. It is different from deduction, induction, and abduction, where at least one of the premises or the conclusion is general. Analogy plays a significant role in problem solving, decision-making, perception, memory, creativity, emotion, explanation, and communication. Analogy is at the core of cognition. Specific analogical language comprises exemplification, comparisons, metaphors, similes, allegories, and parables. Analogy is important not only in ordinary language and common sense but also in science, philosophy, and the humanities. Therefore, it's an important aspect of the agents we are creating.

Holyoak and Thagard (1989, 1995) identify three characteristics of a good analogy:

1. Similarity: The source of the analogy and the target must share some common properties.
2. Structure: Each element of the source domain should correspond to one element of the target domain, and there should be an overall correspondence in structure.
3. Purpose: The creation of analogies is guided by the problem-solvers goals. Analogies are not fixed forever; instead, they can be modified as new information comes in.

Creativity is related to imagination and new ideas, while **innovation** is related to its implementation. Creativity is the ability to conceive something unpredicted, original, and unique. Innovation, closely tied to creativity, involves putting creative ideas into action. A better and smarter way of doing anything is a form of innovation.

An innovation often comes from clever analogies or smart ideas by borrowing across different disciplines. It is done so cleverly that it has to be called creative or inventive.

Imitation, analogy, and innovation have the common element of likeness, but on different scales: extreme likeness is mimicking, some likeness is analogy, and a few key similarities in principle is innovation. What do we call that which is more dissimilar than creative or innovative? It is called "crazy," "illogical," or "nonsense"!

Learning can occur when an agent observes and mimics others in an individual or team setting. It can also occur through actively asking *curiosity-driven questions* that can be achieved by using some event-string replacement. We will discuss this kind of learning in Part III.

In our HAI architecture, imitation, analogy, and creativity are important forms of learning. They will be treated under the same similarity umbrella and realized using token-replacements in event-strings or patterns.

4.8 Attention in Learning

Attention is the behavioral and cognitive process of selectively concentrating on a discrete aspect of information while ignoring other perceivable information. It is a state of arousal. Attention is necessary for an efficient allocation of limited cognitive processing resources. Attention is manifested by an attentional bottleneck, in terms of the amount of data the brain can process each second. For instance, in human vision, only less than 1% of the visual input data (at around one megabyte per second) can enter the bottleneck, leading to inattentional blindness (Chabris and Simons, 2010). Research shows that when multitasking, people make more mistakes or perform their tasks more slowly (Matlin, 2013) because attention must be divided among all of the component tasks to be performed.

Attention is often related to covert orientation. Overt orienting is the act of selectively attending to an item over others by moving the eyes to point in that direction. Covert orienting is the act of mentally shifting one's focus without moving one's eyes. Orienting attention is vital and can be controlled through external (exogenous) or internal (endogenous) processes.

The working brain can be represented by three co-active processes: attention, memory, and activation. In psychology, there are five levels of attention: *Focused*, *Sustained*, *Selective*, *Alternating*, and *Divided*.

1. Focused Attention: The ability to respond discretely to particular visual, auditory, or tactile stimuli. Sometimes called "orienting" to stimuli. It is the lowest level of attention or alertness.

2. Sustained Attention: The ability to sustain a steady response during continuous attention. On average, adults have an attention span of about 15–20 minutes.

3. Selective Attention: The ability to maintain attention in the face of distracting or competing stimuli.

4. Alternating Attention: The capacity for mental flexibility that allows the shift of focus between tasks.

5. Divided Attention: The ability to respond simultaneously to multiple tasks or to engage in more than one activity at a time.

All five levels of attention are reflected in subconscious, conscious, and associative attention mechanisms in our HAI architecture.

In computer vision, efforts have been made to model the mechanism of human attention, such as its semantic significance in classification of video contents (Wang et al, 2018; Zang et al., 2018). Both spatial attention and temporal attention have been incorporated in such classification efforts.

Attention lets us focus on a small number of important things we can handle effectively. Therefore, a cognitive agent must have an attention mechanism for effective learning. For making humanized agents, we will divide attention into subconscious and conscious attention. **Subconscious attention** originates from reflections, whereas conscious attention originates from an agent's time-dependent interests. Subconscious attention happens when the self-awareness switch is off, whereas conscious attention predominates when the self-awareness switch is on. Of course, an agent's attention is related to many factors, some of which we now describe.

For subconscious attention: intensity of source (sound, light, odor, and temperature), closeness, and motion increase attention. Closeness is likely associated with more positive or negative interactions. Speed (change in distance, brightness, soundness, odor, temperature, and tactility) and acceleration are related to future closeness.

Conscious attention: Our agent Zda purposely pays attention to certain things and knows he is paying attention to those things. Conscious attention will be increased by the urgency and importance of events, as well as by the intensity of one's interest in (or need for) particular subjects, e.g., mathematics, technology, and science.

Later, we will discuss associative attention and attention shifting. The attention mechanisms in our HAI architecture will be explored in Chapter 12.

4.9 Memory and Dreams

Memory is a label for a diverse set of cognitive capacities by which humans, and perhaps other animals, retain information and approximately reconstruct past experiences. Our particular abilities to conjure up long-gone episodes of our lives are both familiar and puzzling to psychologists. Memory seems to be a source of knowledge, or more precisely, retained knowledge. It is the place where *reasoning* takes place. Recollections also take place in memory and are often suffused with emotion. Much of our moral life depends on the peculiar ways in which we are embedded in time. It's worthwhile to know that *past events are different from the recollection of past events*. Pain at the moment of being cut is different when the person recalls it.

Ben Goertzel (2016, p.189–192) divides memory into working memory and long-term memory in his AGI architecture. In our HAI architecture, we divide (computer) memory into 11 different areas for data storage (knowledge) and processing. These divisions of memory are in the interest of computational efficiency and easy collaboration with the attention, learning, and response mechanism.

Memory provides the source for dreams. Everyone dreams every day. Dreams are fascinating. They are characterized by successions of images, ideas, emotions, and sensations that occur involuntarily in the mind during certain stages of sleep. The content and purpose of dreams have been a topic of scientific speculation, philosophical intrigue, and religious interest. Dreaming can be used for pattern-refinement, complexity-reduction,

FIGURE 4.6
Dreams play roles in information refinement, knowledge discovery, and emotional needs.

and information-reorganization. *A dream may NOT be equal to the recalled dream.* The illogicalness of a dream when it is remembered might be quite logical at the time of dreaming. Therefore, there is an enclosable gap between dreams and dreams as remembered, just like the difference between the two worlds of life and death. What we think to be reality might be embedded in a bigger dream (Chang, 2012). The period of a dream (agent receives no input) is considered to be a useful time for an agent to enhance, pick and choose, recognize, and repatternize what he learns or experienced in the "daytime." A dream can also be a creative process for a human when the mind is at great relaxation (Figure 4.6). The same applies to agents.

The obvious utility of dreams for humans is that they help us to store important memories and things learned, get rid of unimportant memories, and sort through complicated thoughts and feelings. Recent research (2019) indicates that dream experience represents a fascinating condition linked to emotional processes and the human inner world. Dream experience can defuse emotional traumatic memories when the emotional regulation and the fear extinction mechanisms are compromised by traumatic and frightening events. Finally, dreams could represent a sort of simulation of reality.

What do dreams mean for HAI? How does an agent use the dream mechanism to better organize information and discover new knowledge? What mechanisms in our own brains enable us to differentiate dreams from reality, and might replicating them in our agents be of use? We consider these important questions in Part III, but briefly dreaming is used for repatternization or refining patterns in *Knet*, while reality and dreams are identified using separate *Knet* and *Inet* storages in our HAI architecture.

4.10 Emotion and Language

Emotions are mental states associated with thoughts, feelings, behavioral responses, and a degree of pleasure or displeasure. There is currently no scientific consensus on a definition. Emotions are often intertwined with mood, temperament, personality, disposition, or creativity. Current areas of research on emotion include the development of materials that stimulate and elicit emotion, often in connection with brain scan technologies.

In psychology and philosophy, emotion typically includes a subjective, conscious experience characterized primarily by psychophysiological expressions, biological reactions, and mental states. The original role of emotions was to motivate adaptive behaviors that in the past would have contributed to the passing on of genes through survival, reproduction, and kin selection. In HAI, we recognize an agent's emotion by his displayed emotion.

Paul Ekman views that emotions are discrete, measurable, and physiologically distinct. He found that certain emotions appeared to be universally recognized, even in cultures that were preliterate and could not have learned associations for facial expressions through media. Ekman's facial-expression research (Shiota, 2016) examined six basic emotions: anger, disgust, fear, happiness, sadness, and surprise.

Plutchik (2002) developed his wheel of emotions (similar to Figure 4.7), suggesting eight primary emotions grouped on a positive or negative basis: joy versus sadness; anger versus fear; trust versus disgust; and surprise versus anticipation (Lutz and White, 1986). The complex emotions could arise from cultural conditioning or association combined with the basic emotions.

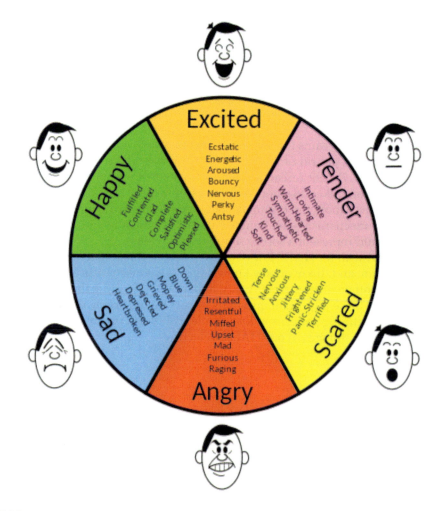

FIGURE 4.7
An example of emotion wheel.

Panksepp and Biven (2012) carved out seven biologically inherited primary affective systems called Seeking (expectancy), Fear (anxiety), Rage (anger), Lust (sexual excitement), Care (nurturance), Panic/Grief (sadness), and Play (social joy).

Statistical methods (Schacter, 2011) have been used to map emotion-related responses and found that the first two dimensions are valence (how negative or positive the experience feels) and arousal (how energized or enervated the experience feels). Using statistical analyses, Cowen and Keltner (2017) identified 27 varieties of emotional experience: admiration, adoration, aesthetic appreciation, amusement, anger, anxiety, awe, awkwardness, boredom, calmness, confusion, craving, disgust, empathic pain, entrancement, excitement, fear, horror, interest, joy, nostalgia, relief, romance, sadness, satisfaction, sexual desire, and surprise.

Emotion is the other side of reasoning: if reasoning fails emotion arises; reasoning is to generalize an observation, making it reasonable or fit to a law of human nature, e.g., she yelled at me because she was getting so upset like everyone else in the situation.

Language (Natural and Body Language) is an external representation of knowledge and emotion. An utterance is a natural unit of speech bounded by breaths or pauses. Knowledge and emotion are patterns recognized in terms of a stochastic decision network within our brains. Natural Language is an essential tool for communication, while communication is a key instrument in cognition, learning, and emotional expression.

Like other attributes, the discretization of emotion is necessary for HAI architectures but fixing its number of categories is not necessary. According to Ben Goertzel (2016, p. 211), AGI will have emotions and other conscious experiences roughly as people do, though their emotions will have a different flavor, rooted in different forms of embodiment and mental algorithms.

From the perspective of both knowledge and emotion, the influence exerted between humans and agents is a two-way interaction. A human creates and teaches or "raises" an agent. At the same time, the agent can change a human's behavior, just as the Internet and social media did.

We will code different emotional states using discrete values and the agent will map them to appropriate situations through his social experiences (interaction with others). The specific value for the emotional state will trigger the corresponding action of the robot or the animation of the HAI agent. Thus the emotion is displayed. Again, we assert that displayed emotion *is* emotion for HAI agents.

4.11 Experimentation

Experiments, including thought experiments, are observations under artificial settings to minimize the so-called confounders, often combined with the Factor-Isolation Technique. Experimentation is an important learning tool for humans and HAI. We will discuss two classic experiments: Pavlov's Dog and Skinner's Box, and the thought experiment of Galileo's Leaning Tower of Pisa as well.

Ivan Pavlov won the Nobel Prize for Physiology or Medicine in 1904. Pavlov's principles of classical conditioning have been found to operate across a variety of clinical settings and education. Pavlov first discovered that the reflex of salivation and the secretion of gastric juices in a dog occur not only when food is placed in the dog's mouth, but also when the dog sees the food. He became interested in this phenomenon

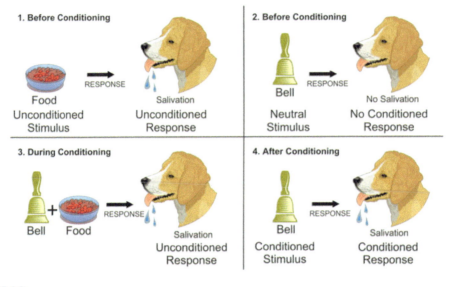

FIGURE 4.8
Pavlov's dogs: classical conditioning.

and conducted an experiment (Figure 4.8): when food was placed in a dog's mouth, salivation occurred, and it occurred every time when food was given to the hungry dog. Since salivation is a natural, reflexive, non-learned response to the stimulus (food), he referred to it as an unconditioned response (UR). Next, Pavlov rang a bell close to the dog but, as was expected, no salivation occurred. The sound of the bell is a neutral stimulus (NS). Later, Pavlov rang a bell before putting food in the dog's mouth. Salivation occurred. After a number of instances of hearing a bell paired with food, Pavlov again rang the bell, but he did not give food to the dog. Salivation still occurred. In this situation, salivation was elicited by the sound stimulus, which he called a conditional stimulus (CS). This phenomenon is called a conditioned response (CR). The newly established relationship between the sound of the bell and salivation is a consequence of the learned association between two stimuli (the bell and the food). According to the information theory of classical conditioning, an organism learns a relationship between two stimuli when the occurrence of one stimulus predicts the occurrence of another. People use classical conditioning in their daily lives, e.g., farmers call poultry before feeding them.

The second influential experiment in learning theory is research on Operant Conditioning. Skinner, motivated by Thorndike's ideas, conducted the following so-called Skinner-Box experiment (Figure 4.9): a hungry pigeon is placed in a Skinner box, where there are green-lighted and red-lighted windows. When the green one is pecked, food will fall for the pigeon, however, if the red one is pecked, the pigeon will get an electric shock. In the beginning, the pigeon walks around in the box, pecking here and there. Eventually, the pigeon pecks against the green-lighted window and food falls into the bowl. Similarly, there are also times when the pigeon pecked against the red-lighted window and received electric shocks. Skinner found that the likelihood of pecking against a green-lighted window increased and the chance of pecking the red-lighted window reduced over time. By pecking against the lighted windows, the pigeon "operated" on its environment. Therefore, this response is called

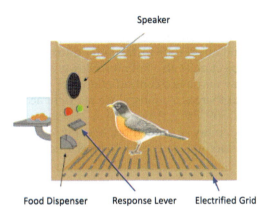

FIGURE 4.9
Skinner-box experiment for Operant Conditioning.

an operant response. The food is a reward or reinforcer, which reinforces the appropriate response and increases the likelihood that a pigeon will perform that behavior in the future. On the contrary, the electric shock is a punishment or inhibitor, which inhibits the undesirable response and decreases the likelihood that a pigeon will perform that behavior in the future. Operant Conditioning can be viewed as a reinforcement learning method following the principle of reinforcement: behaviors (goal-directed) by positive consequences are strengthened, while behaviors followed by negative consequences are weakened. This reinforcement learning method was recently used in clinical trials under a different name: response-adaptive randomization trial (Chang, 2007).

In addition to real experiments, Thought Experiments also play an important role in learning through reasoning for building learning mechanisms in HAI architecture. Any new piece of experience can only become new knowledge through some sort of logical reasoning, be it simple or complex. Any new knowledge obtained through logical reasoning has to be based on some sort of old or new experience.

Galileo's Leaning Tower of Pisa experiment is a thought experiment that was used for rebuttal of Aristotelian Gravity. Galileo showed that all bodies fall at the same speed with a brilliant thought experiment (Figure 4.10) that started by destroying the then reigning

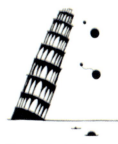

Real Experiment   Thought Experiment

FIGURE 4.10
Real versus thought experiments of falling balls.

Aristotelian account. The latter holds that heavy bodies fall faster than light ones ($v_H > v_L$). But consider this: when a heavy cannon ball (H) and a light musket ball (L) are attached together to form a compound object (H + L), the latter must fall faster than the cannonball alone. Yet the compound object must also fall more slowly since the light part will act as a drag on the heavy part. Now we have a contradiction: $v_{H+L} > v_H$ and $v_H > v_{H+L}$. That's the end of Aristotle's theory. But there is a bonus, since the right account is now obvious: they all fall at the same speed ($v_H = v_L = v_{H+L}$).

The HAI agent has the capability of using thought experiments in performing inductive, deductive, and abductive reasoning, and this will be elaborated in Parts III and IV.

Part II

Humanized AI and Its Approaches

We will review briefly the history of artificial intelligence (AI) and discuss the four waves in AI development. Philosophically, we classify existing HAI into five different approaches: Neurologism, Symbolism, Connectionism, Behaviorism, and Constructivism. We analyze the advantages and disadvantages of each approach and propose a new Synthetic Approach (new Constructivist Approach) by combining the constructivist and behaviorist approaches, which serves as the philosophical foundation for HAI architecture in Part III.

DOI: 10.1201/b23355-6

5

A Brief History of AI and Machine-Learning Methods

5.1 A Brief History of AI

Before the term artificial intelligence (AI) was coined by John McCarthy, Marvin Minsky, Nathaniel Rochester, and Claude Shannon in 1955, AI research had been going on for a while. In his 1948 paper "Intelligent Machinery," Alan Turing describes what we today call computers, as well as human-level AI. Two years later, Alan Turing published the paper "Computing Machinery and Intelligence," introducing the "imitation game," a test of a machine's ability to exhibit intelligent behavior which became known as the "Turing test." Warren S. McCulloch and Walter Pitts published (1943) "A Logical Calculus of the Ideas Immanent in Nervous Activity" to mimic the brain. The authors discussed networks of simplified artificial "neurons" and how they might perform simple logical functions. Eight years later, Marvin Minsky and Dean Edmunds built SNARC (Stochastic Neural Analog Reinforcement Calculator), the first artificial neural network, using 3000 vacuum tubes to simulate a network of 40 neurons. In 1957, Frank Rosenblatt developed the Perceptron, an early artificial neural network enabling pattern recognition based on a two-layer computer-learning network. More than a decade later, Arthur Bryson and Yu-Chi Ho (1969) described a backpropagation learning algorithm for multi-layer artificial neural networks. This was an important precursor to the success of deep learning in the 2010s when big data became available and computing power was sufficiently advanced to accommodate the training of large networks. In a similar vein, Minsky's Society of Mind (1986) posited that minds are mental agents, each one made of many smaller processes. The mental agent by itself can only do some simple thing that needs no mind or thought at all. Yet when we join these agents in societies, there results social, or swarm, intelligence.

AI development may be characterized by different periods (Russell and Norvig, 2003). During an era that may be named Early Enthusiasm (1952–1969), significant progress was already being made, such as John McCarthy's program for LISP, Advice Taker. (It was McCarthy who gave us the term artificial intelligence.) Other early works include Marvin Minsky's on Microworlds (IQ-Tests, Blocks World), Arthur Samuel's on the game of checkers, Newell and Simons' on the General Problem Solver, Widrow's neural network, Adeline, and Rosenblatt's convergence theorem on perceptrons. A Dose of Reality (1966–1973) was required as difficulties with early systems arose, such as (1) programs containing little or no knowledge of their subject matter and (2) the intractability of many of the addressed problems. Thus, comes the age of Knowledge-based Systems (1969–1979), such as the first knowledge-intensive system, DENDRAL for chemical analysis, and expert systems, e.g., MYCIN for medical diagnosis. These are rule-based systems with uncertainty factors. AI Becomes an Industry (1980–1988) was the initial broadly based period of entrepreneurialism. R1 became the first commercially successful expert

DOI: 10.1201/b23355-7

system. The AI industry boomed from a few million dollars in 1980 to billions of dollars in 1988. However, because of the amount of work needed to identify and code the relevant rules required for expert systems, disillusionment became inevitable. The AI winter (1989–1995) squeezed funding for research after companies failed to deliver on the extravagant promises of AI. After 10 years' of this fallow period, big data started to become available, first in genomics and the biomedical field, and later on for personal daily activities, such as purchasing behavior, facial imaging, and sentiment data. Huge successes followed with deep learning artificial neural networks (ANNs), enthusiasm and optimism for AI were resurgent, and we arrive at the present via Big-Data and Applications to Daily Life (1996–2025). Three highlights of this fertile period are noted here. AT&T Bell Labs successfully applied backpropagation in ANN to enable machines to recognize handwritten ZIP codes, though it took 3 days to train the network given the hardware limitations at the time. In 2006, Geoffrey Hinton published "Learning Multiple Layers of Representation," summarizing the ideas that have led to "multilayer neural networks that contain top-down connections and training them to generate sensory data rather than to classify it," i.e., a new approach to deep learning. In March 2016, Google DeepMind's AlphaGo defeated Go champion Lee Sedol. Looking ahead, my prediction is that, after 2030, research into and applications of Humanized AI and Human-level AI will be the new focus, and the combination of the constructivist approach with minimalist and behaviorist approaches will be the mainstream.

In computational linguistics, research effectively originated with efforts in the United States in the 1950s to use computers to automatically translate texts from foreign languages, particularly Russian scientific journals, into English (Hutchins, 1999). To translate one language into another, one has to understand the grammar of both languages, including morphology (the grammar of word forms), syntax (the grammar of sentence structure), semantics, the lexicon (or "vocabulary"), and even something of the pragmatics of language use. Thus, what started as an effort to translate between languages evolved into an entire discipline devoted to understanding how to represent and process natural languages using computers. Long before modern computational linguistics, Joseph Weizenbaum developed ELIZA in 1965, an interactive program that carries on a dialogue in the English language on any topic. ELIZA surprised many people who attributed human-like feelings to the computer program. In 1988, Rollo Carpenter developed the chatbot Jabberwacky to "simulate natural human chat in an interesting, entertaining and humorous manner." It is an early attempt at creating AI through human interaction. In 1988, IBM's Watson Research Center published "A Statistical Approach to Language Translation," heralding the shift from rule-based to probabilistic methods of machine translation. This marks a broader shift from a deterministic approach to a statistical approach in machine learning (ML). In 1995, inspired by Joseph Weizenbaum's ELIZA program, Richard Wallace developed the chatbot A.L.I.C.E. (Artificial Linguistic Internet Computer Entity) with natural language sample data collection at an unprecedented scale, enabled by the advent of the Web. In 2011, a convolutional neural network won the German Traffic Sign Recognition competition with 99.46% accuracy (vs. humans at 99.22%). In the same year, Watson, a natural language question-answering computer developed by IBM, competed on Jeopardy and defeated two former champions. In 2009, computer scientists at the Intelligent Information Laboratory at Northwestern University developed Stats Monkey, a program that writes sports news stories without human intervention.

Substantial efforts and great progress are being made today in Medical AI under the names of bioinformatics and ML. Some of the areas are prescription drug discovery, molecular design, drug development, disease diagnosis and prognosis, pharmacovigilance, and healthcare. These are described in the book *Artificial Intelligence for Drug Development, Precision Medicine and Healthcare* (Chang, 2020). The advances are exemplified by the AI systems AlphaFold and AlphaFold 2, among many others. Most recently, MIT developed "liquid neural networks" for use in time-sensitive tasks like pacemaker monitoring, weather forecasting, investment forecasting, or autonomous vehicle navigation. By numerically solving the differential equations of the system, the bottleneck problem is that scaling up these systems has become prohibitively expensive, computation-wise. This problem has been resolved when MIT solves the differential equations analytically in 2021. By solving this equation at the neuron level, the team is hopeful that they'll be able to construct models of the human brain that measure the millions of neural connections, something not possible today (Tarantola, 2022).

In robotics, Nikola Tesla (1898) made a demonstration of the world's first radio-controlled ("a borrowed mind" as Tesla described) vessel, an embryonic form of a robot. Czech writer Karel Capek (1921) introduced the word robot, a Czech word meaning forced work, in his play *Rossum's Universal Robots*. This brought automation to a new level in the minds of the science-minded public. Amazingly, just four years later, a radio-controlled driverless car was released, traveling the streets of New York City. In 1929, Makoto Nishimura designed the first robot built in Japan, which could change its facial expression and move its head and hands by using an air pressure mechanism. The first industrial robot, Unimate, started working on an assembly line in a General Motors plant in New Jersey in 1961. In 1986, Bundeswehr University built the first driverless car, which drives up to 55 mph on empty streets. In 2000 Honda's ASIMO robot, an artificially intelligent humanoid robot, was able to walk as fast as a human, delivering trays to customers in a restaurant setting. In 2009 Google started developing, in secret, a driverless car. In 2014, it became the first to pass, in Nevada, a U.S. state self-driving test. Now, driverless cars have become a reality, thanks to Tesla, Nvidia Waymo, Zoox, and others. In the near future, if the liquid neural network is adopted, driverless cars will become smarter. With the liquid neural network, only 19 neurons plus a small perception module could make key decisions in driving a car.

For overview of recent development of AI, Artificial Intelligence Index (Annual) Report by Stanford University Human-Centered Artificial Intelligence (2022) provides an excellent resource.

5.2 Types of Machine Learning Methods

It is helpful to learn common methods (see Appendix) of narrow AI before we build the HAI architecture. Commonly used NAI or ML methods can be classified into five general categories: supervised, unsupervised, reinforcement, evolutionary, and swarm intelligence learning methods (Figure 5.1).

A typical task for supervised learning is classification, e.g., noting when there is disease or no disease. In supervised learning, the learner will give a response y based on an input x and will be able to compare his response y to the target (correct) response. In other words, the "learner" presents an answer y for each x in the training sample, and the supervisor provides either the correct answer or an error associated with the learner's answer. The term learning here refers to the learner (a model) adjusting its parameters to

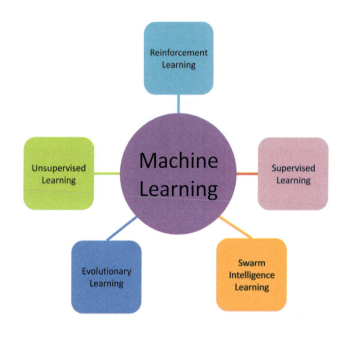

FIGURE 5.1
Types of machine learning approaches.

reduce the error by using the training dataset. The trained AI model can be used for future predictions. Supervised learning has been used in disease diagnosis, drug safety signal detection, and other medical fields.

Two typical tasks of unsupervised learning are document clustering and information retrieval. In unsupervised learning, the learner receives no feedback from the supervisor at all. Instead, the learner's task is to re-represent the inputs in a more efficient way, for instance, as clusters or with a reduced set of dimensions. Unsupervised learning is based on the similarities and differences among input patterns. The goal is to find hidden structures in unlabeled data without the help of a supervisor providing a correct answer. In drug development, unsupervised learning is often used for data preprocessing before adopting supervised learning.

An application of reinforcement learning (RL) is iRobot, a popular robot vacuum cleaner. With RL, an iRobot is able to learn the environment and find the optimal routine to clean the room. RL concerns how a learner should take actions in an environment so as to maximize some notion of long-term reward. RL gets feedback from real-world experiences; its algorithms attempt to find a policy (or a set of action rules) that maps states of the world to the actions the learner should take in those states. Unlike supervised learning, in RL the correct input-output pairs are never presented. Furthermore, there is a focus on online performance, which involves finding a balance between exploration of uncharted territory and exploitation of one's current knowledge. RL is widely studied in the field of robotics. RL has also been suggested for drug development programs (Chang, 2020).

Biological evolution can be viewed as a learning process: how biological organisms have offspring and adapt to their environment can improve the probability of the species' survival and success. Inspired by such biological evolutionary mechanisms, genetic programming (GP) was developed (Forsyth, 1981), demonstrating the successful evolution of small programs in performing the classification of crime scene evidence. In GP, computer programs are encoded as a set of genes that are then modified (evolved) using an evolutionary algorithm. The methods used to encode a computer program in an artificial chromosome and to evaluate its fitness with respect to the predefined task are central in the GP technique. GP has been used in many aspects of drug development (Ghaheri et al., 2015).

Systems in which organized behavior arises without a centralized controller or leader are called self-organized systems. The intelligence possessed by a self-organized system is called **Swarm Intelligence** (SI) or **Collective Intelligence**. Artificial SI is an emerging field of biologically inspired AI characterized by micro motives and macro behavior. A good example of Swarm Intelligence is that of ant colonies which optimally and adaptively forage for food. Ants are able to determine the shortest path leading to a food source, simply by following pheromones. This works only because the shortest path will have more ant traffic and stronger pheromone scents than other paths.

6

Waves of AI Development

DARPA, a well-known AI research agency in the United States, has recently characterized AI development using three waves (Figure 6.1). It's dedicated to funding "crazy" projects, ideas that are completely outside the accepted norms and paradigms. It has made contributions to the establishment of the early internet and the Global Positioning System (GPS), as well as a flurry of other bizarre concepts, such as legged robots, prediction markets, and self-assembling work tools (Tzezana, 2017). To DARPA's three waves, a fourth wave is added in this book to cover Humanized AI.

6.1 First Wave: Logic-Based Handcrafted Knowledge

In the first wave of AI, domain experts devised algorithms and software according to available knowledge. This approach led to the creation of chess-playing computers and of delivery optimization software. Weizenbaum's 1965 ELIZA, an AI agent that can carry on grammatically correct conversations with a human, was a logical rule-based agent. Even most of the software in use today is based on AI of this kind—think of robots in assembly lines and early Google Maps. In this wave, AI systems are usually based on clear and logical rules or decision trees. Systems examine the most important parameters in every situation they encounter and reach a conclusion about the most appropriate action to take in each case, without any involvement of probability theory. As a result, when the tasks involve too many parameters, many uncertainties, hidden parameters or confounders affect the outcomes, and it is very difficult for first-wave systems to deal with the complexity appropriately. Determining drug effects in humans and making disease diagnoses and prognoses are examples of such complex biological systems that first-wave AI cannot handle well.

In summary, first-wave AI systems are capable of implementing logical rules for well-defined problems but are incapable of learning and are not able to deal with problems with large underlying uncertainty.

6.2 Second Wave: Statistical Machine Learning

Over nearly two decades, the emphasis in AI has shifted from logic to probabilities, or more accurately, to mixing logic and probabilities. For this change, we can thank the availability of "big data," viable computer power, and the involvement of statisticians. Much of the impressive ongoing AI effort in both industrial applications and academic research falls into this category. And now comes the second wave of AI. It is so statistics-focused that Thomas J. Sargent, winner of the 2011 Nobel Prize in Economics, recently told the

DOI: 10.1201/b23355-8

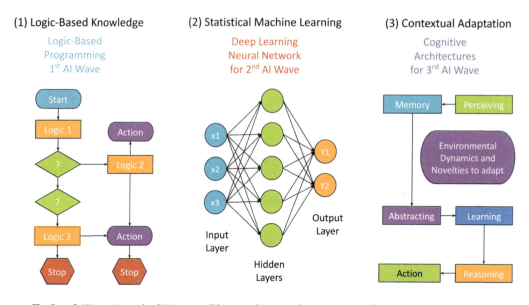

The Fourth Wave: Humanized AI agent will be a machine-race human: growing from baby, learning from simple to complex with simple cognitive mechanisms, minimal inherited knowledge and no built-in natural languages.

FIGURE 6.1
Four waves in AI research.

World Science and Technology Innovation Forum that artificial intelligence is actually statistics, but in a very gorgeous phrase, "it is statistics." Many formulas are very old, but all AI uses statistics to solve problems.

To deal with complex systems with great uncertainties, probability and statistics are naturally effective tools. However, it cannot be the exact same statistical methods we have used in classical settings. As Leo Breiman (2001) pointed out in his Statistical Modeling: "There are two cultures in the use of statistical modeling to reach conclusions from data. One assumes that the data are generated by a given stochastic data model. The other uses algorithmic models and treats the data mechanism as unknown. The statistical community has been committed to the almost exclusive use of data models. This commitment has led to irrelevant theory, questionable conclusions, and has kept statisticians from working on a large range of interesting current problems. Algorithmic modeling, both in theory and practice, has developed rapidly in fields outside statistics. It can be used both on large complex datasets and as a more accurate and informative alternative to data modeling on smaller datasets. If our goal as a field is to use data to solve problems, then we need to move away from exclusive dependence on data models and adopt a more diverse set of tools."

Statistical machine learning systems are highly successful at understanding the world: they can distinguish between two different people or between different vowels. They can learn and adapt themselves to different situations if they're properly trained. However, unlike first-wave systems, they are limited in their logical capacity: they don't rely on precise rules, but instead they go for solutions that "work well enough, usually" (Tzezana, 2017).

The poster boys of second-wave systems are the conceptualizers of artificial neural networks (ANNs) and their great successes in the fields of Deep Learning, including voice-recognition and image-recognition. Starting in the early 2010s, huge amounts of training data together with massive computational power prompted a reevaluation of some particular 30-year-old neural network algorithms. To the surprise of many research-ers, the combination of big data, incredible computer power, and ANNs, aided by new innovations such as deep-learning convolutional networks, has resulted in astonishing achievements in speech and image recognition as well as in most categorization tasks. For example, Johnson and Johnson's Sedasys system has been approved by the FDA to deliver anesthesia automatically for standard procedures such as colonoscopies. The machine can reduce cost since a doctor supervises several machines at the same time, often making the presence of a dedicated human anesthesiologist unnecessary. Speech-based interactive systems such as Siri of Apple's IOS, Google Assistant, and driverless cars are well-known achievements of deep learning. Deep Learning algorithms include multiple-layer percep-trons, convolutional neural networks, long short-term memory networks, and Deep Belief Networks. All these deep learning networks have been used to great effect in drug discov-ery, health data processing, and disease diagnosis and prognosis.

Researchers try, often unsuccessfully, to explain why the artificial neural network (ANN) works well, even though it is not totally a black box. We are incapable of consis-tently explaining the why because we can only use simpler or more fundamental con-cepts to explain more complex or higher level concepts, but not the other way around. This Achilles heel of second-wave systems, that nobody is certain why they're working so well, might actually be an indication that in some respects they are indeed much like our brains: we can throw a ball into the air and predict where it's going to fall, even without calculating Newton's equations of motion.

6.3 Third Wave: Contextual Adaptation

Adaptive behavior requires finding, and adjusting, an optimal tradeoff between focusing on a current task-set (cognitive stability) and updating that task-set when the environment changes (cognitive flexibility). A contextual adaptation–enabled AI can deal with novel-ties, adapting to work under certain conditions which were not initially predicted by their developers. The adaptive system recognizes the concept of "person-in-environment" and has the skill to dynamically alter their behavior while running, depending on the chang-ing conditions of the environment, i.e., context-dependent, dynamic mapping between the interfaces of the components being adapted, overcoming some of the limitations of the static mappings.

Third-wave AI systems with the ability for contextual adaptation are a giant leap from today's "black box" systems. They understand context and meaning and are able to adapt accordingly. The AI systems themselves will construct models that will explain how the world works and discover by themselves the logical rules which shape their decision-making process. Third-wave systems would also be able to take information from several different sources to reach nuanced and well-explained conclusions.

An example of third-wave AI is driverless cars that must adapt to an environment that includes constantly changing visual and vocal elements.

Another example of third-wave AI is Aigo, the Chatbot with a Brain. Aigo is built on Integrated Cognitive Architecture that functions somewhat more like a human mind as it continues to evolve with common sense knowledge and cognitive skills. As the company claims, "Aigo creates engaging experiences for customers and employees alike by offering highly intelligent and hyper-personalized digital assistants at scale for a given application

TABLE 6.1

Characteristics of the First Three AI Waves

Capabilities	First Wave	Second Wave	Third Wave
Perceiving	☆☆	☆☆☆☆☆	☆☆☆☆☆
Abstracting		☆☆	☆☆☆
Learning		☆☆☆☆☆	☆☆☆☆☆
Reasoning	☆☆☆☆☆☆	☆☆	☆☆☆☆☆

in any industry." Aigo's Core Brain continues to grow & evolve its commonsense knowledge about people, places, concepts of the world, and application-specific knowledge is provided to Aigo. Over time this interactive intelligent adaptive assistant becomes increasingly personalized, powerful, and natural.

Bearing similarities, the database Wordnet and semantic network Conceptnet were devised initially to support AI in the discovery of knowledge and for a contextual understanding of language and concepts. Because in their present forms they lack true brains, it is questionable how much further such approaches alone can go in advancing knowledge discovery or learning for HAI agents.

A good example of efforts toward the third wave would be genetic programming (GP). GP is essentially the creation of self-evolving programs, a patented invention from 1988 by John Koza. The series of four books by Koza (1992, 1994) and Koza et al. (1999, 2003) fundamentally established GP and included a vast number of GP results and examples of human-competitive inventions and reinventions in different fields. Subsequently, there was an enormous expansion in the number of publications within the Genetic Programming Bibliography, surpassing 10,000 entries (Kaza, 2010). At the same time, industrial uptake has been significant in several areas, including finance, the chemical industry, bioinformatics (Langdon and Buxton, 2004), and the steel industry.

In terms of intelligence capabilities, overall machine intelligence increased over time from the first wave to the third wave. The increasing trend is almost true for all four aspects of intelligence, too, as summarized in Table 6.1.

6.4 The Fourth Wave: Humanized Artificial Intelligence

It is said: in the first AI wave you had to be a programmer, in the second AI wave you had to be a data scientist, and in the third AI wave you had to be morally better. However, third-wave AI is still nowhere near human intelligence in terms of general cognitive ability and creativity, nor is it generally capable of discovering new knowledge, identifying commonsense rules, or displaying emotional intelligence. Such full human-capability intelligence is called HAI. HAI requires a human-like appearance and embodiment with competent "sensory organs," because knowledge acquisition depends on those sensory organs. A "strong" brain equipped in a "weak" body can only make the brain weaker and less capable. HAI is a small-data-based approach. The agent will look, think, and behave like a human. Growing from a baby, it will learn only basic things at first, but be able to grow into complex learning with a simple but credible cognitive ability and minimum inherited knowledge (data). There will be no need for any built-in languages. HAI is not a digital slave and will not be treated as such: how an agent is treated determines what he/she will become. HAI agents will not only be capable of what humans are capable of, but also will do what humans cannot do.

So far, there is limited research on HAI and AGI beyond the philosophical aspects (Goertzel, 2016, 2020; Jackson, P.C., 2019). Goertzel (2020) considers OpenCog, a project with the goal of building a Synthetic Complex Adaptive System. The System is to have general intelligence a bit beyond the human level while demonstrating a reasonably beneficial attitude toward humans and other sentient beings.

Goertzel looked at the mind as being composed of patterns and concerned with recognizing patterns in its environment and itself. He formally defines a "pattern" in some entity X as a program for computing X, which was sufficiently shorter or smaller than X that it provided some "information compression." The AI system includes a network with Nodes representing concepts, objects, numbers, or mathematical functions, Links representing different kinds of relationships between Nodes, and Maps (clusters of nodes and links) forming the building blocks of knowledge.

OpenCog is an open-source software project founded in 2008 (Goertzel, 2016), aimed at directly confronting the AGI challenge by using mathematical and biological inspiration and professional software engineering techniques. Just as the human brain consists of a host of subsystems carrying out particular tasks, OpenCog is a diverse assemblage of cognitive algorithms, each embodying their own innovations, but what makes the overall architecture powerful is its careful adherence to the principle of cognitive synergy. The OpenCog design aims to capture the spirit of the brain's architecture and dynamics without imitating the details (which are largely unknown), via:

1. integrating together a carefully selected combination of cognitive algorithms acting on different kinds of knowledge
2. in a scalable, robust, and flexible C++ software architecture
3. in a manner specifically designed:
   a. to cooperate together with "cognitive synergy" for the scope of tasks characteristic of human intelligence.
   b. to give rise to the emergence of an effectively functioning knowledge network in the AI system's mind, as it interacts with the world, including a self-updating hierarchical/heterarchical ontology and models of itself and others.

OpenAI is a research laboratory focused on artificial intelligence, and its mission is to ensure that artificial general intelligence (AGI) benefits all of humanity. It consists of the for-profit corporation **OpenAI LP** and its parent company, the non-profit **OpenAI Inc.** The organization was founded in San Francisco in late 2015 by Sam Altman, Elon Musk, and others. Musk resigned from the board in February 2018 due to a potential conflict of interest. In 2019, OpenAI LP received a US$1 billion investment from Microsoft and Matthew Brown Companies.

In 2020, OpenAI announced GPT-3, a language model trained on trillions of words from the Internet. It also announced that an associated API, named simply "the API," would form the heart of its first commercial product. GPT-3 is aimed at natural language answering of questions, but it can also translate between languages and coherently generate improvised text. In 2021, OpenAI introduced DALL-E. One year later, their newest system, DALL·E 2, generates more realistic and accurate images with 4x greater resolution.

In 2022, OpenAI released a preview of ChatGPT, which interacts using conversation, to the general public.

The product guides include:

1. **Text completion** for generating or editing text using our models
2. **Code completionLimited beta** for generating, editing, or explaining code
3. **Image generation Beta** for generating or editing images
4. **Fine-tuning** for training a model for your use case
5. **Embeddings** for searching, classifying, and comparing text

For example, when I type: Tell me something about humanized AI. The responses I received are:

> *Humanized AI refers to the development and design of artificial intelligence systems that exhibit qualities or behaviors that are associated with human intelligence and cognition. This can include the ability to learn and adapt, to communicate and interact with humans in a natural and intuitive way, and to understand and respond to complex and varied situations.*
>
> *One approach to creating humanized AI is to build systems that can mimic or replicate certain aspects of human intelligence, such as natural language processing, problem solving, and decision making. Another approach is to design AI systems that can learn from and interact with humans in a way that is similar to how humans learn from and interact with one another.*
>
> *There are many potential applications for humanized AI, including customer service, education, healthcare, and entertainment. However, the development of humanized AI also raises ethical and philosophical questions about the relationship between humans and technology, and the potential consequences of creating artificial intelligence that is too closely aligned with human behavior.*

Of course, this definition of Humanized AI is a narrow AI, different from the HAI discussed in this book—an AGI with the general human capabilities and characteristics.

OpenAI is just a language model and poor in dealing with novelties and has a long way to go in reaching human-level intelligence or Humanized AI.

7

Existing Approaches to Humanized AI

We will discuss the main existing approaches to HAI or AGI, which adhere to the following theories and schools of thought.

1. Neurologism. One simulates the structural characteristics of the biological neural networks in the human **brain**.
2. Functionalism (symbolism, logicism). One simulates the functional processes of logical thinking in the human **mind**.
3. Connectionism. The approach is based on the notion that humans' intellectual abilities can be mimicked using artificial neural networks (ANN).
4. Behaviorism. The aim is to mimic the behavioral relationship in solving problems by some intelligent beings, either humans or animals.
5. Constructivism. Emphasis is on active construction by the individual. Constructivism assumes minimal innate knowledge as opposed to the large commonsense knowledge base required by the behavioristic approach. Constructivists believe that learning occurs through processes called construction, reconstruction, and deconstruction, and the same learning mechanism is used at all ages.

These may relate to but not the same as the five primary learning theories in pedagogy: (1) Behaviorism—as simple Psychology would have it, Behaviorism is only concerned with observable stimulus-response behaviors, as they can be studied in a systematic and observable manner. (2) Cognitivism—learning relies on both external factors and the internal thought process. (3) Constructivism—the learner builds upon his or her previous experience and understanding to "construct" a new understanding. (4) Humanism—learning focuses on the learner's potential rather than the method or materials. (5) Connectivism—informed by the digital age, connectivism departs from constructivism by identifying and remediating gaps in knowledge (Fairbanks, 2021).

7.1 Neurologism: Whole Brain Emulation

Whole brain emulation (WBE), or mind uploading, is the hypothetical futuristic process of scanning a physical structure of the brain accurately enough to create an emulator of the mental state (including self) of a particular brain substrate, and then copying it to a computer in a digital form. The goal is that the artificial brain would be similar enough to the original to be able to respond in essentially the same way and experience having a sentient conscious mind (Goertzel and Ikle, 2012).

The human brain has a huge number of synapses. Each of one hundred billion neurons has on average 7,000 synaptic connections (synapses) to other neurons. It has been

DOI: 10.1201/b23355-9

estimated that the number of synapses in adult brains ranges from 100 to 500 trillion. An estimate of the brain's processing power, based on a simple switch model for neuron activity, is around 100 trillion synaptic updates per second (SUPS) (Russell and Norvig, 2003). A brain simulation would likely have to capture the detailed cellular behavior of biological neurons, presently understood only in the broadest of outlines. The overhead introduced by full modeling of the biological, chemical, and physical details of neural behavior would require an extraordinarily powerful computer. Quantum computers might provide a future solution.

The Blue Brain Project is a Swiss brain research initiative that aims to create a digital reconstruction of rodent (and eventually human) brains by reverse-engineering mammalian brain circuitry. The project, founded in May 2005, attempts to use biologically detailed digital reconstructions and simulations of the mammalian brain to identify the fundamental principles of brain structure and function. According to the Blue Brain Project 2019 report, "Brain in the computer: what did I learn from simulating the brain?," the full reconstruction of a mouse's cerebral cortex was completed, with virtual EEG experiments to begin soon (SEGEV, 2019).

The actual complexity of modeling biological neurons has also been explored in the OpenWorm Project, whose aim was to completely simulate a worm brain. The brain has only 302 neurons in its neural network with about 1,000 cells. Despite the small number, worms appear able to make genuinely complex decisions.

There are several challenges to the mind-up approach: (1) How to deal with innate knowledge, which is essential for survival and learning, at least for earlier stages, but has not been addressed, and (2) Embodiment is necessary for learning and emotion. When a person is equipped with artificial hands, his mind wouldn't feel that the hands are his until long afterward. If our mind has a completely new body, we won't know immediately how the body works. Yet, how artificial organs neurologically will connect to organs such as the eyes seems very challenging.

7.2 Symbolism (Logicism)

Symbolism represents the notion of all methods in artificial intelligence (AI) research that are based on human-readable symbolic representations of problems, logic, and search. Symbolic AI was the dominant paradigm of AI research from the mid-1950s until the late 1980s. John Haugeland (1985) gave the name GOFAI ("Good Old-Fashioned Artificial Intelligence") to symbolic AI and analogously GOFR ("Good Old-Fashioned Robotics") in robotics. Since symbolism is based on the assumption that many aspects of intelligence can be achieved by the manipulation of logical symbols using propositional and predicate calculus, its synonyms include logicism, logical positivism, logical empiricism, neopositivism, and functionalism.

Weizenbaum's (1966) Eliza computer program is an early attempt at such an approach. Eliza could interact with humans via text messages and simulate a psychotherapist. We can type simple English sentences as input to Eliza, and Eliza will generate English sentences in response, using simple parsing and substitution of key words into standard phrases. Users who didn't know how Eliza worked sometimes thought the program *was* a therapist (Figure 7.1). Here is an example I tried on the website This javascript version of ELIZA was originally written by Wallace and Dunlop (1999).

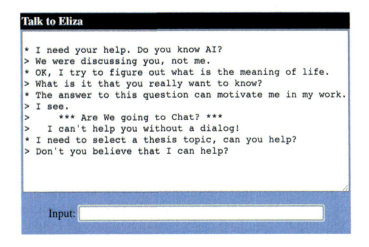

FIGURE 7.1
The interface of Weizenbaum's ELIZA computer program.

The key to Symbolism was the verification principle. This theory of knowledge asserted that only statements verifiable through direct observation or logical proof are meaningful. Brooks (1991) maintained that all main AI's ideas concerning thinking, logic, and problem solving are based on assumptions that come from our own introspection, from how we see ourselves. The validity of the approach is based on the so-called Universal expressiveness of logic.

The universal expressiveness of logic is a proposition analogous to the Turing thesis that Turing machines are computationally universal, i.e., anything that can be computed by any machine can be computed by a Turing machine. The expressiveness thesis states that anything that can be expressed in first-order logic with a suitable collection of functions and predicates. However, this can be challenged: can we logically express a person who believes God is capable of everything including creating a stone that he himself cannot raise (Chang, 2014, p. 37; 2012, p. 7)? To a good believer, deductive reasoning can be wrong if it conflicts with his belief. Thus, symbolism cannot artificialize such a person and cannot be the sole method for humanized AI.

One main achievement of symbolism AI is the expert system, a computer system that emulates the decision-making ability of a human expert. Expert systems are designed to solve complex problems by reasoning through a supported knowledge base, characterized mainly as simple if–then rules rather than through conventional procedural code. The first expert systems were created in the 1970s and then proliferated in the 1980s. An expert system can include two subsystems: the inference engine and the knowledge base. The knowledge base represents facts and rules. The inference engine applies the rules to the known facts to deduce new facts. Inference engines may also include explanation and debugging capabilities.

Symbolic AI was intended to produce general, humanized agents, whereas most modern research is directed at specific sub-problems or weak AI. Symbolic AI may not be a viable approach to humanized AI but can remain a very important component of AI. Noticeable efforts in this direction include the Neuro-Symbolic Concept Learner (NSCL), a hybrid AI system developed by the MIT-IBM Watson AI Lab. NSCL uses both rule-based programs and neural networks to solve visual question-answering problems. As opposed to pure neural network–based models, this hybrid AI can learn new tasks with less data and is explainable (Mao et al., 2019).

7.3 Connectionism (Structuralism)

Connectionism, an approach to AI that developed out of attempts to understand how the human brain works at the neural level and, in particular, how people learn and remember. For that reason, this approach is sometimes referred to as neuronlike computing (Copeland, 2022). Connectionism can also refer to an approach in Cognitive Science that hopes to explain mental phenomena using ANN. Connectionism presents a cognitive theory based on simultaneously occurring, distributed signal activity via connections that can be represented numerically, where learning occurs by modifying connection strengths based on experience (Smolensky, 1999).

Connectionism is the notion that a human's cognition and intellectual abilities can be modeled using ANNs. An ANN model includes the input layer, one or more hidden layers, and the output layer. Each layer contains input and output nodes, weights, and activation functions. The layers are connected together with weights that measure the strength of connections between the units. These weights model the effects of the synapses that link one neuron to another. Learning is essentially the updating of the weights.

The foundation for ANNs was laid in the 1940s by Warren McCulloch and Walter Pitts' (1943) invention of artificial neurons, later variants of which were called perceptrons. The authors were motivated by cell assembly theory, sometimes referred to as Hebb's rule (Hebb, 1949). Hebbian theory claims that an increase in synaptic efficacy arises from a presynaptic cell's repeated and persistent stimulation of a postsynaptic cell. It is an attempt to explain synaptic plasticity, the adaptation of brain neurons during the learning process.

Deep Learning ANNs, consisting of many layers of neurons, have achieved great successes in many fields. Deep learning ANN architectures include (1) Feedforward Neural Networks (FNNs) for general classification and regression, (2) Convolution Neural Networks (CNNs) for image recognition, (3) Recurrent Neural Networks (RNNs) for speech recognition and natural language processing, and (4) Deep Belief Networks (DBNs) for disease diagnosis and prognosis. Two other popular neural networks are Generative Adversarial Networks (GANs) for classification problems and Autoassociative Networks (Autoencoders) for dimension reduction.

Connectionist models provide a new paradigm for understanding how information might be represented in the brain. A seductive but naive idea is that single neurons (or tiny neural bundles) might be devoted to the representation of each thing the brain needs to record. Imagine that there is a grandmother neuron that fires when we think about our grandmother. However, such local representation is not likely. There is good evidence that our grandmother thought involves complex patterns of activity distributed across relatively large parts of the cortex (stanford.edu, 2019b).

Despite the great success in applications of ANN as narrow AI, most neural network research abstracts away from many interesting and possibly important features of the brain. Connectionists usually do not attempt to explicitly model the various kinds of brain neurons, and explain that the backpropagation algorithm is actually what happens in human learning. Like support vector machines, random forests, and other statistically motivated algorithms, ANNs do neither reflect nor yield the structures and strategies of human thinking. Today's neurological understanding of human learning is still very remote as far as mimicking the mechanics using ANNs. In the foreseeable future, I cannot imagine connectionists can be sure that the ANNs they create will represent a human brain and not a monkey brain.

7.4 Behaviorism

Behaviorism can be viewed as a response to the Cartesian philosophical tradition in which behavior, actions, and what is done by persons was seen as the outward expression of what goes on in the mind. Many of those who were involved in AI were following in behaviorism's footsteps in that they believed that if a computer (or robot) behaved as if it had intelligence, then it must actually be a mind (Murphy, 2020).

AI Behaviorists are essentially influenced by behaviorism in psychology. Its key assumption is the objective, scientific analysis of observable behaviors to the exclusion of consideration of unobservable mental processes. In contrast, social cognitive learning theory uses unobservable matters, such as thoughts, expectations, and motivations, in its explanation of behavior. Behaviorists emphasize the importance of agent-environment interaction in learning and developing human behavior. According to behaviorists, learning is based on the association between a stimulus (S) and the response (R) to it.

Two approaches in the study of learning have been used, associative learning and cognitive learning. In the associative approach to learning, stimuli and responses are units on which the analysis of behavioral changes is based. The aim is to establish what the relationship is between a stimulus (S) and the human or animal organism's response (R) to it. We discussed this earlier with respect to classical conditioning and operant conditioning. (Kosiński and Zaczek-Chrzanowska, 2007).

The AI behaviorism approach implements the learning mechanism by using reinforcement and repetition to shape the behavior of learners. Skinner found that behaviors could be shaped when the reinforcement was applied: desired behavior brings reward while undesired behavior is not rewarded or punished. Although there is no notable distinction between human and non-human behavior, a more complex version in respect to the behavior displayed by other species can be explained by Darwin's theory of evolution.

Sloman (1978) wrote that, to achieve AI comparable to an adult human, it would be necessary to produce a baby mind with the ability to absorb a culture through years of interaction with others. Minsky (2007) discusses Turing's idea of the 'child machine' approach. He notes that to date this idea has been unsuccessful, having encountered problems related to knowledge representation. That is, a baby machine needs to be able to develop new ways of representing knowledge, *because it cannot learn what it cannot represent*. What we may draw from this is that this approach to learning has not yet been adequately explored, and that more attention needs to be given to the architecture and design of a child or baby machine, and in particular to the representation of thought and knowledge (Jackson, 2019). McCarthy (2008) asserts that grammar is secondary, that the language of thought for an AI system should be based on logic, and gives objections to using natural language as a language of thought. He believes a baby-machine needs to have an initial set of concepts corresponding to innate knowledge about the world. He listed several kinds of innate conceptual knowledge the system should have.

The statement *"because it cannot learn what it cannot represent"* appears to be correct, but actually can be misleading. It suggests we need to build a huge concept network or commonsense knowledge base in the child machine. Such a static representation of knowledge is not a viable solution in my view. Instead, in my approach, the concepts or knowledge are produced (not simple retrieval) dynamically in real time. A symbol representing a concept cannot hold any actual meaning until the agent retrieves a part of the action string that reflects a real situation, likewise, a string of thoughts.

Here is a similar story supporting my argument: when a scientist claimed his invention of an omnipotent solvent that can dissolve every substance in the world, Edison asked: "what will you store it in if it dissolves everything?" Did Edison make a good logical argument? At first thought, we may think that Edison made a very smart logical argument and proved that there is no such omnipotent solvent. However, anyone who has a little knowledge of chemistry would have a different answer, because there are many possible ways to store the solvent before we use it, for instance, storing at low temperature or in the dark.

As another example, we can produce various sounds (language, songs, etc.), but that does not mean we have some internal representation of each possible song. We have vocal cords that can vibrate. Such vibrations in the presence of air produce sound waves, and finally, a nearby person who has a hearing capability can hear the song. Thus, to have a song, we need the combination of at least three conditions: vocal cords, air (environment), and at least one person of hearing ability (receiver).

Experiments have shown that a hearing-impaired person can "hear" a song if we convert sound frequency to light frequency: a melody produces a color painting in the person's head, and vice versa. Similarly, we can convert ultrasound that a dog produces into sound by means of external instruments. Conversely, people who don't have normal vocal cords can sing songs by painting pictures. Such conversions can be accomplished by an external machine.

A language of thoughts is a key in TalaMind, a human-level AI model. However, creating a comprehensive Tala syntax such as English is not a prerequisite for the success of the TalaMind approach. It is only necessary that Tala include sufficient syntax to enable representing the general, extensible semantics of English, and to support an intelligence kernel's implementation of higher level mentalities (Jackson, 2019).

Jackson's TalaMind model is summarized by three hypotheses:

1. Intelligent systems can be designed as "intelligence kernels," i.e., systems of concepts that can create and modify concepts to behave intelligently within an environment.

2. The concepts of an intelligence kernel may be expressed in an open, extensible conceptual language, providing a representation of natural language semantics based very largely on the syntax of a particular natural language such as English, which serves as a language of thought for the system.

3. Methods from cognitive linguistics may be used for multiple levels of mental representation and computation. These include constructions, mental spaces, conceptual blends, and other methods.

TalaMind has built-in concepts such as nouns, verbs, propositions, pronouns, determiners, adjectives, adverbs, logic conjunction, disjunction, and conditional conjunction, which are used in English grammar. However, the language of thoughts, or even language itself, doesn't need these concepts. In other words, a grammar system is a pattern of language and such a system is not unique. Most concepts in parts of speech and concepts of logic such as when, where, why, while, until, if then, else, and grammatical rules, e.g., enforced subject-verb agreement, can be learned through an agent's interaction with the environment, and need not knowledge that an agent is born with. I will demonstrate how we can accomplish this in a humanized agent based on minimalism.

Behaviorists try to build a comprehensive knowledge base so that agents can behave like humans. However, this will not be a viable approach to humanized AI for the following reasons: (1) it's very difficult to build such an encyclopedia, the quantity of knowledge being already too great, (2) the dynamics or constant expansion of mankind's knowledge cannot be ignored, and (3) even when we can have such a knowledge base built and uploaded to the agent's brain, such an agent will be a God-like, not a human-like being.

7.5 Constructivism

The term Constructivism, coined by Piaget (1954), denotes the thesis that knowledge cannot be a *passive reflection* of reality but has to be more of an *active construction* by the individual. The characterization from psychology is this: "Humans actively construct their own knowledge and reality is determined by our experiences as learners." In other words, there is no such thing as a human-independent reality (Reich, 2009). Moreover, the models of causality that our brains invent to navigate the world are a consequence of our progressive development in the world we live in (Carlos E. Perez, 2021).

There is considerable controversy over the claims Piaget has made, particularly when it comes to what knowledge is innate or learned. Constructivism assumes minimal innate knowledge as opposed to the large commonsense knowledge base required by behaviorism. Extremely, radical constructivism believes that the only knowledge we ever have is so constructed. Piaget's theory hypothesizes that the same learning mechanism is used at all ages.

As summarized by Schmid (2019): modern education is dominated by the ideas of constructivism and constructivist learning (Fox, 2001). At its heart, this approach is based on the assumption that humans acquire knowledge and competencies actively and individually through processes called construction, reconstruction, and deconstruction (Duffy and Jonassen, 1992). Construction is associated with creation, innovation, and production, and implies searching for variations, combinations, or transfers of knowledge. Analogously, reconstruction is associated with application, repetition, or imitation, and implies searching for order, patterns, or models (Reich 2004, p. 145). Deconstruction is, in the context of constructivism, associated with reconsideration, doubt, and modification, and implies searching for omissions, additions, and defective parts of acquired knowledge. A construction process in the constructivist sense may be matched by unsupervised learning. A reconstruction process in the constructivist sense may be matched by supervised learning. The constructivist approach has also been successfully used in cybernetics.

Constructivist agents mimic the human cognitive and emotional development process in that they (1) build necessary connections between mind and body (organs), and (2) provide the way for emotional and social development in any environment without specifying any societal norms, but the agent acts as a member of the society to influence and be influenced by its other members.

The principles of constructivism include:

- Knowledge is constructed, meaning that knowledge is built upon other knowledge.
- Agents learn to learn, assimilating the general concepts as they learn a sequence of individual events.
- Learning is an active process, involving sensory input to construct meaning. However, physical involvement alone is not enough, motivation for being actively engaged is critical.
- Learning is a social activity involving active interaction with others.

- Learning is contextual, not isolated from facts.
- Knowledge is personal. Each person will have his or her own prior knowledge and experience as a backdrop for forming updated knowledge.

There are three types of constructivism: cognitive, social, and radical.

- Cognitive constructivism focuses on the idea that learning should be related to the learner's stage of cognitive development.
- Social constructivism focuses on the collaborative nature of learning.
- Radical constructivism is very different from cognitive and social constructivism. Its central idea is that learners and the knowledge the learner constructs tell us nothing real, they only help us to function in our environment; knowledge is invented, not discovered. Knowledge is only interpretations, not explanations of the world.

Constructivism has been taken up as a bottom-up approach by AI researchers. Some believe that instead of specifying architecture in detail from *a priori* considerations, the mechanisms and cognition of agents should be developed using methods including self-organizational and evolutionary mechanisms as far as possible.

However, there are very challenging issues to confront before we can implement the constructivist's approach in HAI. Let's look into Piaget's "behavior of the stick": an infant seeks to take possession of an object which is located out of arm's reach; he/she uses a stick as a tool to draw the object into the range of his arms, and then takes possession of it. But an infant typically becomes capable of using such a tool effectively between the ages of 12 and 18 months (Piaget's fifth sensorimotor substage). Guerin (2008) compares two possible approaches to implementing the behavior of the stick in an AI system: a non-constructivist approach which makes use of prior knowledge, and a constructivist approach where the infant must construct the relevant knowledge.

While the behaviorist could employ a reinforcement-learning algorithm with common-sense knowledge built inside the agent's brain, the constructivist approach would try to avoid giving the infant any prior knowledge beyond that which is absolutely necessary to bootstrap the learning process and allow the infant to learn in a reasonable time span. Apart from this minimal innate knowledge, the constructivist approach aims to allow the infant to create the required knowledge for itself. For example, innate knowledge might include the ability to grab that which touches the hand, the ability to suck that which touches the mouth, the ability to make random arm movements, etc. By bootstrapping from these initial abilities, the infant must learn how to suck the thumb, how to grab and suck objects, and how to interact with other objects in more complex ways. Through this interaction the infant must somehow learn higher level knowledge about the world, gaining knowledge of space and objects and how to manipulate them. This would eventually lead to the desired behavior with the stick (Guerin, 2008).

However, in the above example, constructivists will find it extremely difficult to implement reinforcement learning because there are virtually an infinite number of actions the child might have to try before accomplishing a goal. (He could even just sit there and cry all day long or do things that have nothing to do with the goal!) But an action can be subdivided into many smaller actions that can be beneficial if one has a plan. Thus, to accomplish a complex task in a reasonable time with constructivism, an agent must have the ability to reason. How an agent can learn reasoning is a challenging issue.

8

New Approach to Humanized AI

8.1 Challenges in Constructivism

Before we decide upon the AI approach to be used for our HAI, we need to look into the challenges different methods have to face.

Neurologism: Whole Brain Emulation approach must meet two challenges: (1) Learning enough of the details of human neural networks, which may not happen in the foreseeable future, (2) How to embody the machine after knowledge is uploaded; important because some knowledge becomes knowledge only with associated embodiment. This can be virtual and/or accomplished through some kind of nervous system. Now, having an athlete's brain will not make the lame run fast. Imagine what would happen if you uploaded knowledge of color to a color-blind person.

Logicism: Not all knowledge can be expressed in logic. Most commonsense knowledge probably is not logically expressive. Emotions cannot usually be expressed by mathematical or logical reasoning. We cannot use logic to express a situation where we purposely speak the opposite of the fact for the purpose of amusement. We make irrational choices or feel happy by some feat of our imagination, these are beyond what logicism can accomplish. A human becomes human not only because of his intelligence but also his unintelligence.

Behaviorism: Here the agent's action is mainly a commonsense-based and goal-driven one. The challenges are: (1) How to build a comprehensive commonsense knowledge base for uploading that can grow constantly and still ensure quick responses. Even when such a knowledge base is available and loaded into the agent's brain, we are making a God-like person, not a human. (2) The same embodiment issues as in the approach of neurologism: embodiment requirements, (3) How an agent can identify goals, even when he is in uncharted territory. This *is* achievable in our HAI architecture, as we'll show later.

Constructivism: This approach has difficulties in the following aspects: (1) Determining the smallest units of actions, say, one inch of movement, the fabrication of a 0.1-second-long sound, etc. (2) How an agent determines the list of action options the agent can take in real time. (3) How an agent can learn complex concepts and responses within a reasonable amount of time.

We may look into how the symbolist, connectionist, behaviorist, and constructivist accomplish the following task differently. Suppose a hungry baby tries to find food to eat, but

DOI: 10.1201/b23355-10

FIGURE 8.1
A hungry baby tries to get the milk bottle.

the familiar milk bottle is six steps away (Figure 8.1). The following are different types of agents in the same task, getting the milk bottle.

1. Symbolist: Using deduction to get the milk bottle, the agent has to move closer to his/her gradually, to be closer to the bottle, the agent needs to move either left to up, but not too far left or up, until I reach the bottle. This strategy must be presented in formal reasoning using propositional and predicate calculus.

2. Connectionist: Good for simple classifications, not for such a goal-driven task. Very difficult to train a general-purpose neural net to accomplish the task. It is difficult to interpret the meaning of the weights in relation to accomplishing the task.

3. Behaviorist: Break the task into goals or subtasks such as: (1) crawl toward the bottle, (2) get close to it, (3) reach out an arm, and (4) grab the bottle. It is not feasible for humans to specify subtasks for each task and implement them in an agent. Despite the inflexibility of the behaviorist approach, once such subtasks are well-defined, the execution of such a task is relatively fast.

4. Constructivist: The baby crawls randomly until he reaches the bottle. Requires a huge number of trials to get the bottle. According to stochastic theory, the average number of steps needed to reach an N-step distant bottle is approximately N^2. During the process the baby can be distracted and do something else, making the time required to accomplish the mission even longer.

Some obvious reasons why constructivism is that a child has limited innate knowledge, the majority of its knowledge is learned after birth, and the knowledge is personal and embodiment-dependent. Georgeon et al. (2015) further noticed that biological beings couldn't be adequately modeled using a Markov Process, since they generally cannot recognize rewarding Markov states of their environment either. Therefore, one should implement a non-Markov Reinforcement Learning algorithm based on historical sequences and Q-learning. Along with theoretical arguments, these results support the constructivist paradigm for modeling biological age. However, the main challenge in implementing the constructivist approach is its computational slowness, despite its flexibility in learning. The behaviorist approach has the advantage of being computationally fast but its inflexibility and the requirements for a larger commonsense knowledge base neutralize its speed advantage. This motivates us to refine the constructivist and behaviorist approaches by combining them. This is a synthetic approach.

8.2 Synthetism: New Constructivism

We use an approach in our HAI architecture that synthesizes the constructivist and behaviorist approaches. Synthetism is characterized by progressive learning from simple to complex. Over time, Synthetist Learning transitions from the constructivist approach to the behaviorist approach. Human organ developments support such a learning paradigm: low sensory organ sensitivity only allows a baby to see the world in a very simple form, while the baby's limited motor abilities help progressive learning. The simplified world allows the baby to learn using a constructivist approach. As the baby grows, his perceptual world becomes gradually more complex, but at the same time his knowledge is increasing accordingly; thus, he can increase knowledge in perceiving the world and keep the interpretation as simple as possible.

Like constructivism, **synthetism** emphasizes activeness and individuality in learning, requiring minimal innate knowledge instead of the large built-in commonsense knowledge base required by behaviorism. At the early learning stage, as with constructivism, synthetism's learning occurs through construction, reconstruction, and deconstruction that are enabled by adaptive reinforcement learning. However, at the later stages, when knowledge accumulates and learning ability develops, learning gradually shifts to the behaviorist approach featuring the developed abilities of perceiving, abstracting, goal-setting, reasoning, and acting for efficiency. Like the constructivist approach, our synthetic approach uses the same learning mechanisms at all ages, but the mechanisms are supported by evolving data, experiences, knowledge, and abilities. The individuality is reflected in unique parameters for each agent and the unique experiences of the agent.

HAI agents develop their abilities physically, cognitively, mentally, and socially over time. They do so by controlling their own actions and interactions with humans, other agents, and their environment. Whether an agent has a certain characteristic, such as consciousness, is a judgment based on the agent's behavior, not his internal structure. The autonomous agent (self-sufficient, adaptive, equipped with the appropriate learning mechanism and its own history), acquires information about its environment only through its sensory organs, and interacts with the world on its own. The association mechanism enables the coordination of perceptions from different sensory organs and the agent's actions.

Commonsense knowledge is crucial to efficient learning and communication. However, unlike behaviorists, in our HAI architecture commonsense knowledge is learned, not built into agents by humans. Likewise, humor, feeling and emotional expression, mentality, morals, values, animus, friendship, and partnership are learned from social interactions. Furthermore, high-level learning skills involving sciences, mathematics, and game strategies are results of learning instead of built-in algorithms. At a later stage, as with a behavioristic approach, learning is often goal-driven. However, unlike a behavioristic approach, the goal is not pre-coded by humans but rather the agent sets up the goals for himself through his own learning.

The gradual shift from constructivist to behaviorist approach, implemented automatically in our synthetist approach, matches well with the stagewise development of human bodies, including our sensory organs. Here are some examples.

Infant Vision Development

At birth, babies can't see as well as older children or adults. Their visual system gradually improves during the first few months of life. At birth, babies' vision is abuzz with all kinds of visual stimulation. Babies have not yet developed the ability to easily tell the difference between two targets or move their eyes between the two images. Their primary focus is on objects 8 to 10 inches from their face or at the distance to a parent's face. During the first few months of life, the eyes start working together and vision rapidly improves. Eye-hand coordination begins to develop as the infant starts tracking moving objects with his or her eyes and reaching for them. By eight weeks, babies begin to more easily focus their eyes on the face of a parent or other person near them. Babies should begin to follow moving objects with their eyes and reach for things at around 3 months of age. It is not until around the 5th month that the eyes are capable of working together to form a three-dimensional view of the world and begin to see in-depth. Babies have good color vision by 5 months of age.

Development of Fetal Sense of Smell

Although a baby is surrounded by amniotic fluid, her sense of smell is already up and running well before birth. A days-old newborn baby will be able to recognize her mom simply by the smell of Mom's skin. What's more, the foods that Mom eats while she is expecting not only affect the developing baby's sense of taste but they also impact its sense of smell. What you eat, your baby "smells." Your newborn recognizes you by smell.

A baby's sense of smell starts developing at a relatively early age. Between 6 and 7 weeks of pregnancy, olfactory neurons, which help your baby's brain to process odors, develop. By 7–8 weeks, the two symmetrical nasal cavities that are the foundation of your baby's nose have formed. By weeks 10–12, olfactory smell·receptors form in the nose. Between weeks 11 and 19, those receptors' neurons connect with the olfactory bulb in the brain. Together, these structures enable the scents a baby inhales to communicate with her brain. By late in the second trimester, your baby's little nose is ready to detect odors.

Fetal Sense of Hearing

Around 18 weeks of pregnancy, babies hear their very first sound, perhaps the beating heart, air moving in and out of lungs, a growling stomach, or even the sound of blood moving through the umbilical cord. By 24 weeks, those little ears are rapidly developing. Your baby's sensitivity to sound will improve even more as the weeks pass.

Baby's Motor Skill Development

Most babies start crawling at about 8 months old, which helps further develop eye-hand-foot-body coordination. At around 9 months of age, babies begin to pull themselves up to a standing position. By 10 months of age, a baby should be able to grasp objects with thumb and forefinger. By 12 months of age, most babies will be crawling and trying to walk.

In our HAI architecture, we will overcome the challenge of infinite action options using the mechanism of attention to eliminate the majority of futile options. We want to implement the mechanism that, like a healthy human's, our agent's abilities will grow over time. We also implement hierarchical tokenization, based on the fact that understanding of complex concepts is built on the basis of simpler concepts the agent has already learned. Attention, the similarity principle, innate knowledge learned before birth, and recursive patternization are four keys that allow us to improve constructivist learning.

Let me reiterate the challenges using the naïve constructivist approach in HAI and, in parallel, provide solutions to resolve them.

1. **Challenge:** The real world is infinitely detailed. There are just too many things in the environment for an agent to deal with at any moment.
   Solutions: Organ-Insensitivity will help an AI child to learn quickly. As he grows, his perceptual world becomes more complicated due to increases in

sensitivity. But at the same time, his knowledge increases, and he will use concepts learned to simplify the more complex perceived world. Similarity-Grouping is another intended way to simplify the agent's perceptual world, and it happens when similar things are grouped together without differentiating them. The third tool is the Attention Mechanism that allows an agent to focus on a few important things needed for survival, safety, or whatever is most rewarding at any given moment.

2. **Challenge:** There are infinite numbers of paths, some toward the goal; others are not. Identifying such a short path to the goal using reinforcement learning is computationally challenging.
   Solutions: Identify a small set of initial elementary actions for an AI child with unequal associated probabilities, so that favorite actions are likely to be performed, and combine with the adaptive reinforcement learning with probabilistic response mechanisms. The associated probability is modifiable by the agent according to the constantly learned experiences or patterns, as seen in the simple examples given of Pavlov's conditioned response (reflex) and Thorndike-Skinner's operant conditioning.

3. **Challenge:** Constructivists do not need a larger Commonsense Knowledge Base, but an agent must have some basic concepts and abilities to start with. Such would include the concepts of space and time and the abilities to produce sound, move arms, hear, and see, these being necessary in order to acquire more complex knowledge, skills, and procedures.
   Solutions: A small set of fundamental concepts, abilities, habits, and biological clocks are built into each agent with personalized inherited parameters. The HAI architecture engined with the mechanisms of attention, learning, and response and backed up by these innate attributes empowers agents to learn more complex knowledge and skills, even develop new attributes such as "friend," "enemy," and "teacher," to (appropriately) classify others with whom the agent interacts.

4. **Challenge:** An agent must understand the *concept of a goal.* Then, understanding what the present goal is, the agent needs to be able to divide a complex mission into several subgoals so that, with limited steps, he(she) can accomplish the mission within a reasonable time.
   Solutions: The recursive knowledge net (*Knet*) of an agent contains its patternized experiences. A node with a large reward in *Knet* can be considered as a goal, and nodes along the path from his current position to the goal node can be considered as subgoals associated with the goal. In this way, the agent can determine goals by himself, and then use a more efficient behavioristic approach for learning and response. This is a feature of HAI distinct from any narrow AI: for an NAI agent, a specific goal is set by humans, such as to win at chess.

5. **Challenge:** In addition to the concept of a goal, an agent must also learn many other complex concepts and natural languages through contextual learning.
   Solutions: Learning mechanisms involve hierarchical tokenization and recursive patternization so that understanding complex concepts will be established on the basis of simpler, known concepts. When the same token (representing complex concepts) has different meanings, the token will appear on several different patterns or paths on the *Knet*, mirroring its placements in different contextual environments. Thus contextual learning naturally occurs, with no exception of natural languages.

6. **Challenge:** Embodiments play an important role in learning and response. How does one go about embodying an agent?
   Solutions: A robot involves a physical body that includes arms, legs, a vocal system, and sensory organs. We focus on agents on a computer at this moment. An agent only involves virtual embodiment with virtual sensory organs. Different organs coordinate with each other through association mechanisms in order to enhance learning and help produce meaningful responses. The virtual sensory organs allow an agent to sense elements of the environment without cheating (using computer-coded names to detect them). The association mechanism ensures that two things that happen closely in space and/or time will likely be in an agent's attention at a given moment.

7. **Challenge:** How to make an agent have self-awareness and consciousness.
   Solutions: An agent's knowledge net, in its mind, is self-inclusive, i.e, it includes the agent itself. Like a human, the HAI agent lives in its own mind. Thus self-awareness is given, whereas consciousness is the product of self-awareness and social interactions.

8. **Challenge:** How to make an agent express or display emotions, feelings, and a sense of humor.
   Solutions: Imitations under various social settings make an agent a social being: he will treat people the way he was treated and display emotion, feeling, and can even act humoredly.

9. **Challenge:** How to build an agent capable of active learning.
   Solutions: Let the agent ask back the question he cannot answer (imitation), ask questions displaying curiosity, and propose hypotheses. A curiosity question and hypothesis may often help in patternizing an agent's experiences or help the agent to achieve some goal. These capabilities will be reflected in our HAI response mechanisms by some relevant event-string replacements in the *Knet*.

10. **Challenge:** How to endow an HAI agent with elaboration tolerance—the ability to add information without starting over in the representation of previous information.
    Solutions: The self-goal-setting features and the evolutionary knowledge net, with hierarchical tokenization and recursive patternization, naturally require the preservation of previous knowledge. All knowledge is stored in *Knet* and other database tables for persistence and quick retrieval.

11. **Challenge:** How do we enable an agent to have high-level learning skills, such as being able to carry out logical reasoning, science, and abstract mathematics?
    Solutions: Similarity-based learning, the recursion of everything, time-sensitive utilities, genetic operations on event-strings, and effective teaching, all these allow an agent to acquire different learning methods in different subject areas, although such learning may take a long time. Unlike narrow AI, where one solves a problem only from a single perspective through parameters such as ANN weights, HAI can solve a problem from multiple angles, social or scientific perspectives. Therefore, its intellectual capabilities might well become more advanced than we imagine now.

To sum up, Symbolism (Logicism) is the notion that all AI methods are based on human-readable symbolic representations of problems, logic, and search. The challenge is to have a comprehensive list. Connectionism (Structuralism) is the notion that human cognition and intellectual abilities can be explained using artificial neural networks (ANNs). The challenge of this black-box approach is to make sure that the ANN mirrors a human brain, not a low-intelligence brain; does anyone want monkey neural nets? Behaviorists believe actions and behaviors are reflections of what goes on in the mind. The approach is a goal-driven approach such as is found in decision-networks. This might be efficient, but it could be difficult to determine the goals manually. Constructivism is based on the notion that knowledge cannot be a passive reflection of reality but an active construction by the individual. The approach can be exemplified by reinforcement learning, which is flexible but very inefficient in learning. Synthetism is the notion that learning, including goal-setting, is a recursive process varying from the simple to the complex. The approach combines a constructivist's flexibility and behaviorist's efficiency.

8.3 Humanized AI Test

The Turing Test (1950) for intelligence, as a behaviorist test, is objective. But it is also subjective since intelligence is in the eyes of the observer (Brooks 1991). A behavior one observer calls intelligent may not be called intelligent by another observer. Since the Turing Test does not concern the agent's internal organ structures, it is humanized or human-level AI (intelligence indistinguishable from a human's). On the contrary, John Searle's (1980) Chinese Room Argument (CRA) does concern human-identical intelligence (in a machine identical to a human with necessary internal organs).

According to McCarthy (2007) and Jackson (2019), problems that need to be solved by any approach to human-level AI include:

1. Representation of commonsense knowledge of the world, in particular the effects of actions and other events.
2. Epistemologically adequate languages that can be used to express what a person or robot can learn about the world.
3. Elaboration tolerance—the ability to add information without starting over in the representation of previous information.
4. Non-monotonic reasoning—the ability to reason with partial information, where additional information may change one's conclusions.
5. Contexts as objects—the ability to reason about contexts "from the outside" as well as internally within contexts as objects—the ability to transcend the current context of thinking and reason about it
6. Introspection—the ability of a system to reason about its mental state and processes.
7. Action—reasoning about strategies of action, considering multiple actioners, concurrent, and continuous events
8. Heuristics—the ability to give programs domain and problem-dependent heuristic advice.

In my view, the most important test is the test for AI abilities of learning or knowledge evolution (not how much an agent can do). Also, I believe that commonsense knowledge should not be innate but learned knowledge. Language is a consequence of communication and collaboration. Elaboration tolerance is a distinct feature that differentiates HAI from NAI. In reality, information can never be complete or we never know if it's complete. Constantly updating knowledge is essential for any HAI, thus non-monotonic reasoning is naturally a reasonable requirement. However, too much information, noise, and fake news can make decisions difficult, prolong decision time, or even cause the analysis paralysis discussed in Section 1.1.

In our HAI architecture, everything, including a concept and context, can be considered an object, token, or pattern, from different perspectives. Self-awareness is ensured by the self-inclusive network formulated through hierarchical tokenization and recursive patternization. The self-inclusive nature of the dynamical knowledge net (*Knet*) allows the HAI agent to consider himself an entity separate from externalities and enables introspection: he can treat himself as an external world (self-aware state).

In our HAI architecture, probabilistic prediction is based on similarity mapping between reality and paths in the *Knet*, while the optimal decision-making is based on randomized adaptive response. This includes reasoning about decision strategies in the face of multiple actioners, together with concurrent and sequential events. Heuristics are embedded in the ability of imitating, analogizing, and innovating in the HAI response and learning mechanisms.

There is another reason that commonsense knowledge should be not innate but learned. Suppose we could collect all the responses to a given situation that humans have taken, under all conditions, throughout human history. Choosing randomly a response to be taken by an AI agent facing the same or a similar situation could very possibly end up being a wise choice, but it would not be a human's choice; it would be a kind of digital vox populi, a suggestion by abstracted supermen with super-knowledge. Furthermore, history never completely repeats itself. There are always novelties to deal with.

Part III

Architecture of Humanized AI

This is an elaboration of our entire HAI architecture, divided into seven chapters. We start from the three-world theory that describes how the multifaceted objective World We Live in is scaled down to the World in Our Eyes through sensory organs, and that is further simplified as the World in Our Mind using similarity and other principles. Taking a small-data approach, we elaborate the architectures of the first stance including innate knowledge, abilities, and mechanisms, dynamic knowledge presentation with recursive network of patterns, attention mechanisms and the attentive world, mechanisms for learning and knowledge discovery, adaptive response mechanisms, and various teaching techniques suitable for HAI.

DOI: 10.1201/b23355-11

9

Three Worlds and Virtual Reality

9.1 The Three-World Theory

Before discussing the creation of the virtual world, it's helpful to recapture the three-world concept we discussed in Part I: the World We Live in, the World in Our Eyes, and the World in Our Mind (Figure 9.1).

The World We Live in is multifaceted, an objective world of infinite detail for humans and robots to sense and interact with. The virtual world consists of environmental elements that are created on a computer for agents to connect with and explore.

The World in Our Eyes is the "image" of the objective world that projects on the "retina" through the "eyes," a subset of a being's sense organs. It is a filtered world. Because of the limited organ-sensitivities, the filtered world becomes discrete in 3-dimensional (3D) space and other dimensions of color, odor, taste, and temperature. The filtered world constantly changes over time and its exact appearance depends on individuals. Some may see a color world, while others may see a colorless one; for some it is an audible world, but others may feel it to be silent. The sense of 3 dimensions basically derives from tactile perception and body motion perception. The senses or perceptions of 3D vision and 3D sound come mainly from the coordination between basic (tactile and body motion) 3D sensations and visual or sound sensations. Without our basic 3D tactile sense, we would not experience 3D vision or sound, or at least these sensations will be very different.

The world, in any brief time interval, is actually registered in our memory for a short period before we patternize it and it becomes (fits into) a natural law in our mind. The *perception of what* is recorded on each frame and the intervals between frames are determined by the person's attention. The world in our "eye" is detailed and recorded in a sequence of frames, each frame including the sight, odor, taste, sound, temperature, shape, texture, and the observer himself. Some frames have precise timestamps, some mark time only approximately, yet others have no timestamps at all. But in all cases, a sequence of occurrences is reflected in one's memory.

The World in Our Mind is a simplified, interpreted version of the perceived world using concepts that include causality and associative relationships. As described earlier, such relationships are established based on the Similarity Principle, even though different learning methods may be used in the process.

HAI involves a study of subconscious and conscious experiences. Both apperception and perception concern understanding and interpreting what we experience. Apperception, however, is more about a conscious comprehension, whereas perception is an interpretation of what one's senses are saying. Apperception is how our mind puts new information in context. "There's Bob" is a perception, but "Bob is my friend" is an apperception, because it's an interpretation based on past experience. "My stomach hurts" is a perception, but "I might throw up" is an apperception!

DOI: 10.1201/b23355-12

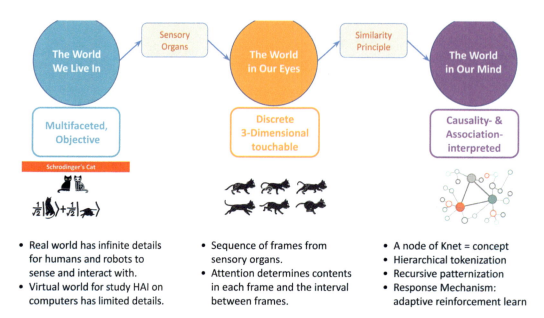

The World We Live In — Multifaceted, Objective

Sensory Organs

The World in Our Eyes — Discrete 3-Dimensional touchable

Similarity Principle

The World in Our Mind — Causality- & Association-interpreted

Schrodinger's Cat

$\frac{1}{\sqrt{2}}|\ \rangle+\frac{1}{\sqrt{2}}|\ \rangle$

- Real world has infinite details for humans and robots to sense and interact with.
- Virtual world for study HAI on computers has limited details.

- Sequence of frames from sensory organs.
- Attention determines contents in each frame and the interval between frames.

- A node of Knet = concept
- Hierarchical tokenization
- Recursive patternization
- Response Mechanism: adaptive reinforcement learn

FIGURE 9.1
The three-world theory in humanized AI.

Apperception is a mental process that stitches the elements of perceiving back together as a conscious experience. A behaviorist explains the mind through public behavior. A Gestalt psychologist would believe our experience is organized as a part of a dynamic whole. Having said that, there is not always a clear line between perception and apperception. Is "there is a table" an instance of perception or apperception? The concept of table is mentally formulated by integrating experiences of many different tables. Our experience of a table is viewed as an element of the whole (the concept of a table).

As we discussed in the connotation of understanding, new concepts are explained by way of concepts acquired previously by the individual, which are further explained by simpler concepts the person has acquired at a still earlier time, and so on. Such hierarchical relationships can be modeled by a recursive network with nodes representing concepts and arrows indicating the "explained by" relationship. This network is a dynamic representation of the individual's knowledge structure. Here the term *dynamic* is reflected from two aspects: (1) the knowledge net (*Knet*) changes over time and (2) the knowledge is not in a static form, but instead is displayed in agent responses that are formulated in real time.

Speaking of the World in Our Mind, it should include the observer himself: the mind is self-inclusive, a recursive network characteristically possessing self-awareness.

Some sequences of concepts are used more often than others, thus a weight associated with a link (pattern) can be used to reflect the frequency. A node in *Knet* represents a concept (pattern) that is further explained by other simpler concepts (patterns). With such concept-embedding, a *Knet* is hierarchical and recursive. Furthermore, the node, representing sequences of actions, has an associated cost and reward. Thus, the *Knet* becomes a group of recursive stochastic decision networks. Here the term "recursive" carries the property of self-inclusion (self-awareness), "stochastic" models the properties of direction (hierarchy) and the weights (frequency), and "decision" implies that decision-making has an associated reward.

9.2 Overview of Architecture of Humanized Agents

Our goal in this section is a discussion of the overall architecture of HAI (Figure 9.2). We will first discuss three fundamental aspects of HAI architecture, Virtual Embodiment, Intentional Stance, Innate Ability, and Dynamic Knowledge Representation, before we elaborate three key mechanisms of humanized agents: (1) An Attention Mechanism, which determines how Zda directs his attention, focusing on limited things or events to save brain resources, (2) A Learning Mechanism, including hierarchical tokenization and recursive patternization, which simplifies what has been observed, and in which the resulting patterns may be called scientific laws, language grammars, social norms, etc. (3) A Response Mechanism, which determines how Zda acts at every moment. Even though this book will focus on the architecture of humanized agents, not robots, many aspects of the two are the same, the only difference being tokenization. For robots, the extra step of tokenization converts the sensed physical world into the form of a basic event-string sequence, while, for agents on a computer we use a simulated world with all environmental elements in the form of event-strings. All these aspects are related to embodiment and Zda's interactions with the environment, the topics in the chapter on Effective Teaching.

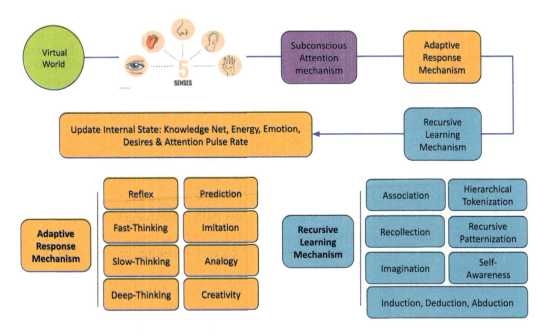

FIGURE 9.2
The architecture of humanized AI.

The virtual world in an agent's brain is expressed in form of "object.event" strings, similar to object-oriented programming (OOP). Examples are:

- Zda.walk(direction = East), meaning Zda walks toward the East.
- Car.run(direction = West, speed = fast) meaning: the car runs fast toward the West.
- Zda.hand.touch(Lia.hand), meaning Zda's hand touches Lia's hand.
- Zda.say(Lia.say(get me a chair)), meaning Zda says "Lia says: 'get me a chair'."

An English-like syntax is not a must, but the computer programmer's choice. The natural language Zda uses will depend on his social relationships.

The world will be scaled down twice, before patternization, by sensory organs and by attention mechanisms. Due to the limited sensibilities, the information passing through the organs becomes discrete. The number of categories is smaller for babies than adults. In other words, the world in a baby's eyes is simpler than that in an adult's eyes. That's why pictures in children's books are drawn simpler and have fewer colors.

The second scaling-down (dimension and complexity reduction) occurs when the attention takes place. For the mind to handle information efficiently, like a human, Zda will only focus on limited things at any given moment.

After twice downscaling, the information (a long object.event vector string) will be patternized into a "scientific law" or "grammar." There are two major steps in the process: (1) using concepts in the *Knet* to combine small tokens (concepts) in the object.event-string into a few bigger ones. The resulting string will usually be less than 4-token long, and is treated as a new entity or a new concept. For more details, see the elaboration and examples in the section on recursive patternization.

A robot's embodiment includes human-equivalent physical sensory organs that can be used to detect the real world, while an agent on a computer is embodied virtually, with virtual sensory organs to detect the virtual world. Robots would identify objects using their attributes or appearance, thus misidentification can happen. However, if an agent used the object's name in the computer code to identify the object, he would never make a mistake. To be consistent and make our HAI architecture applicable to robots, we will use attributes to identify objects in the virtual world.

Here are the main similarities and differences between our approaches for humanized AI and some mainstream AGI research.

1. Goal: Achieving human-like behaviors but not necessarily scientifically correct responses versus Maximizing robot capabilities in serving human beings.
2. Data: Zero-data-based approach versus Big-data-based approach.
3. Language: No built-in natural languages versus Built-in languages required.
4. Conceptualization: Understanding a concept as a tuning process over time for an individual versus a concept has a fixed correct meaning, or meanings, for everyone.
5. Principles of Learning: The Similarity Principle, etc., versus Lack of a general principle.
6. Learning Architecture: No built-in terms for concepts in any language; learning is a recursive process of concept-to-concept or concept-to-action mapping, moving from simplicity to complexity versus concepts are built-in terms in a chosen language, and learning is just command-to-action mapping.

7. Learning Engine: Mainly through curiosity-driven and purpose-driven active learning: asking smart questions, proposing hypotheses, and a feedback mechanism versus passive learning through "human" feed-in training data and reinforcement learning.

8. Learning Pathways: Learning through extensive interactions—just as we take some 20 years to teach someone until graduating college—through teacher-student and peer-peer encounters, imitation, and creative activities with adaptive reinforcement learning versus big data feed-in and teacher-student and peer-to-peer relationships, with reinforcement learning.

9. Response Engine: Adaptive and proactive response rules based on a time-dependent maximum expected utility rule and a basic mechanism of game theory versus task-driven responses.

10. Knowledge Discovery, Invention, and Creativity, all through hierarchical tokenization, recursive patternization, and adaptive response mechanisms versus data mining.

11. Consciousness: HAI agent's Consciousness is reflected in self-awareness and imitation under various social settings versus built-in fixed social morality rules.

12. Inheritance: HAI agents have over a dozen built-in innate concepts, abilities, habits, and the mechanisms of attention, learning, and response, all else being obtained through learning or interaction with the environment over time versus none.

13. Logical Reasoning: The learning of deduction and other reasoning approaches through the innate abilities of using induction and the Similarity Principle versus built-in laws of logical reasoning.

14. Advanced skills: Math and sciences can be learned by agents versus AGI has built-in Math operations and scientific laws.

15. Sensory Organs Coordination: For learning enhancement versus for command-to-action response.

16. Swarm Intelligence (SI): SI exists and can promote social collaboration versus the same SI exists and can promote social collaboration.

17. Evolution: Darwin's laws of evolution versus the same Darwin's laws of evolution.

18. Cloning: Any agent can be cloned at any age in its lifetime versus agents can be cloned at any time.

9.3 Environment Simulation

The environment is everything that an agent or animal faces and interacts with, including the sky, sun, moon, this room, the ground, rain, food, desks, plants, any other animals, and agents. Why, then, do we need to simulate virtual reality? No, we don't if we are making humanoid robots, since the real world is out there for robots who are equipped with adequate organs to sense and experience it. However, if we want to study humanized AI agents on a computer, we do need to simulate the virtual world and create agents with virtual embodiment.

We will create three different types (classes) of objects in our virtual reality: (1) Thingy, (2) Animal, and (3) Humanized Agent.

A **Thingy**, any inanimate thing, has the following attributes: appearance (color, shape, size), material, mass, brightness, sound, loudness, odor, odor intensity, surface texture, temperature, edibleness, location, and velocity. Some available shapes: shape = triangle, square, circle, star, pentagon, hexagon, which serves as a visual identification of a class of object (e.g., cars, dogs, cats). In addition, there are Color = number associated with a color and Size = a value indicating the size of an object.

Other properties, such as utility, can also be added; e.g., water can put out a fire, light can enlighten a room. All these properties have discrete values. A Thingy behaves according to the Laws of Physics. Examples of Thingies are desks, light bulbs, switches, water, cups, bread, and apples. For convenience, we can say a Thingy can have actions, such as smell and sound.

An **Animal** inherits all properties from the Thingy class and may have properties and behaviors such as gender, age, or feet. A simple brain with simple pre-programmed response-features, such as a hungry animal, can run when he sees a prey, while a Thingy cannot move unless an external force acts on it.

An **Agent** inherits all properties from the type Animal and has other properties and behaviors. We will discuss this class in the next section.

A **Human** is, any one of us, a technology user who interacts with agents and virtual environments through input devices such as keyboards, microphones, and video cameras.

You can create any virtual objects you like. But for the purpose of showing how we can make humanized agents within a relatively short time, we will greatly simplify all the objects in the virtual environment. Such simplification is necessary for us to demonstrate the validity of the proposed Synthesized approach within a short time. This is because even if (or when) we make an agent exactly like a human baby, it will take 10–20 years to teach him. The level of simplification will match the agent's sensory organ capabilities.

A moving animal or object is difficult to describe. Take an average animal as an example. Its head, eyes, legs, the mouse, the surrounding sounds, smells, wind, his location, his running speed, and acceleration, how should these be simulated? In our demonstrations, we will greatly simplify those, but what we create can be as "real" as virtual reality movies or high fidelity 3D computer games.

1. **Appearance**: A Thingy, Animal, or Agent can be represented by 2D *images*. A simple version of Appearance includes the attributes: Shape, Size, and Color. The shape of an object is a geometric shape. Size is measured with numerical values. Color is also represented by a number for each element of our set of colors. Shape is the primary attribute used to identify the type (class) of an object, while Size and Color are used to differentiate objects of the same type. In other words, the combination of shape and size are used as primary attributes in identifying a particular object. Other attributes and behaviors can be used as secondary features in identification. Note that the size of an object may change over time.

2. An object has its brightness (light source or reflection).

3. Each sound source has an intensity (loudness). Sounds and intensities both are represented by numerical values. Speech is a sequence of sounds.

4. An odor source has an odor with a constant intensity. Odor and its intensity both are represented numerically.

5. An object is either eatable or not eatable and has tastes. Edible objects can give an agent energy and pleasure.

6. An object's surface texture is represented by a numerical value.

7. An object has a temperature, represented by a numerical value.

8. An object has a mass, represented by a numerical value.

9. An object has a location, represented by three numerical values in order, (x, y, z).

10. An object can be either in a static or moving state. Its velocity is expressed by three directional speeds (numbers), v_x, v_y, v_z, which are all zero for a static object. The motion of an object can be associated with one or more animated pictures.

11. Customized Thingies, such as Plants and Tools, can be growable, explosive, alive, or have other interesting properties.

The intensity of sound, smell, brightness, or temperature decreases as the distance d from the source increases:

$$Intensity = c/d^3.$$

Some common environmental objects are the most apparent: Sky, Sun, Moon, River, Mountain, Trees, The Wind.

9.4 Virtual Embodiment

Perception, abstracting, reasoning, and action are four common steps that robots must be able to take to carry out their missions. Sensory organs are the instruments robots use to perceive reality, the brain is home for the mind where reasoning occurs, and embodiment is necessary to directly interact with the world.

Much of our external information comes through the eyes, ears, nose, tongue, and skin. Specialized cells and tissues within these organs receive raw stimuli and translate them into signals the nervous system can use. Nerves relay the signals to the brain, which interprets them as sight (vision), sound (hearing), smell (olfaction), taste (gustation), and touch (tactile perception). Embodiment also plays vital role in our learning when we feel hot, dizzy, fatigued, hungry, thirsty, or any other way as mediated by our senses.

In sensory perception, whereas we have made great achievements in image recognition through deep learning, we are still far away from developing human-like sensory-perception capabilities. In particular, we are incapable of extracting depth and 3-dimensional information from images. We have achieved significant progress in voice recognition in the natural language process, but we are still far away from determining the spatial characteristics of an environment, understanding the background noise, and forming a mental picture of where someone is when speaking to them on the phone (Berruti et al., 2020). Beyond vision, AI systems are not yet able to replicate this distinctly human perception in other human sensory abilities and motor skills.

An important question is: how do humans sense or estimate quantities such as distance, speed, acceleration, size, brightness, or temperature? In principle, all these are based on the agent's prior knowledge and current observations from the notion of Bayesian statistical learning. Here, we further discuss from the perspective of physics and mechanics, which is necessary for building robots or agents.

The distance between objects can be sensed by the eyes and ears. An object appears larger when it is close by and smaller when it is far away. If we know the size of the object (prior knowledge), we can get a sense of its distance from us. We also use other objects in the environment to estimate the distance. For example, if an apple sits on the other side of the table, we can estimate its distance based on our knowledge of table size. The visual angle of an *object* is a measure of the size of the object's image on the retina. The speed is the change of distance over time. Thus we use the change of distance or visual angle of an object and the time elapsed, sensed by the biological clock, to determine the speed. Most of the time, we are more interested in velocity than speed. A velocity is a mathematical vector, which includes its magnitude (speed) and direction of the moving object. Similarly, the acceleration is the rate at which velocity changes.

How can ears sense distance? Well, it's done in a way similar to the eyes but replacing light (waves) with sound waves. Again, there are prior knowledge and current observations (sound). One difference is in judging distance by the sound's loudness. We use redshifting to sense the speed of a moving object. **Redshifting** is the phenomenon that the wavelength of the sound waves increases when the source object moves away from the observer and decreases when the source moves closer to the observer. We are not going to discuss here more on mechanisms that organs have to sense the world, since our focus is to build the brains of agents, not robots. For agents on a computer, we will simulate the environment, including color, odor, temperature, surface texture, and the agent senses these and other properties (such as distance) via similar, but simplified, mechanisms as in humans. In the HAI architecture, we will embody the agent with virtual eyes, nose, tongue, vocal organs, and skin and temperature sensing organs. But for computational efficiency, we may simply let the HAI agents access the features directly from computer memory instead of letting them detect the distance, at least for the initial prototyping of Zda.

Virtual embodiment is only needed for agents, while real embodiment is needed for robots. How to build a robot sensory organ will not be discussed here. Virtual or real embodiment is critical in learning, since it provides the opportunities for the mind to coordinate different parts of the body and sensory organs in the cognitive process. We will provide a simple version of virtual embodiment (Figure 9.3), partially due to computational limitations: we need to handle all sceneries and all animations of different agents virtually at the same time.

Even if a unique virtual world is given, each agent does not have same innate attributes nor does the agent have same knowledge, mechanisms, or perspectives of the world based on his active relationship with the virtual environment. The virtual embodiment of

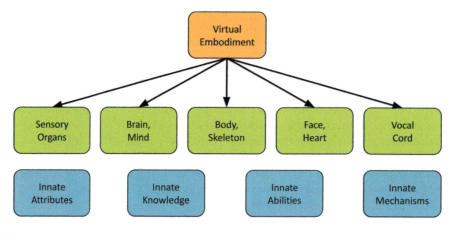

FIGURE 9.3
Overview of virtual embodiment.

TABLE 9.1

Prototype for Virtual Embodiment

Virtual Organ	Intrinsic Function	Initial No. of Sensible Levels
Eyes	Vision 视觉	3
Ears	Auditory (hearing) 听觉	3
Nose	Olfaction 嗅觉	3
Tongue	Tastiness 味觉	2
Skin	Tactile (hepatics) 触觉	3
Body	Thermoreception 热觉	3
Vocal cord	Voice & words	3
Face	Emotion expression	3
Skeleton	Pose & Motion	6
Brain	Knowledge & learning	Innate concepts & abilities
Heart	Emotion	10

agents (an animal can be viewed as a simple version of agent) is summarized in Table 9.1. No matter how complex the world is, if Zda's sensory organs are simple, his perceptual world will be simple.

Language, expression, emotion, body movement, and sense of the world are expandable discrete states. The world in a child's eyes is simple, but complicated in an adult's. Reflecting this fact, the initial number of Sensible Categories for each sensory organ is small but will grow larger as organ sensibilities increase over time. The limitation on the number of sensible categories for each organ can yield high frequencies of events when Zda is a child with limited exposure to the world. This will help Zda learn quickly when trial-error reinforcement learning is his basic tool. Gradually, more detailed categories may be developed so that the agent can deal with the world more effectively.

From the convenience of coding, we can build more categories for each sensory organ than the table indicates, but the initial probabilities associated with them are different, with high probabilities for some of the categories (innate abilities, for one). For example, we can let Zda have the ability to produce 10 different sounds, but much higher probabilities are associated with just three sounds (Ma, Ba, and crying) initially. Other sounds, most often used for language, have lower probabilities to produce; their associated probabilities can change as Zda tries to perform imitation.

9.4.1 Agent's Innate Attributes

An agent can have all the attributes of a Thingy and has the following additional embodiment attributes:

Vocal Cords: Zda, like humans, can learn to speak any language (a string of text) but in a constant intensity (no tone or intonation) at this moment. Zda can initially only produce three different sounds (Ba, Ma, and crying). Additional types of sound can be learned or built in with different associated initial probabilities.

Face: Zda's face is a 3×3-grid 2-color 2D image, to be used as identification with the color only for expression. Therefore, Zda can at most identify $2^{3\times3} = 512$ different objects. The simplified version uses geometric shapes for different types of objects. The facial image can only have 2 colors chosen from 4 colors (red, green, yellow, blue), a total of 12 possible combinations (expressions), with initially 3 of the most common expressions. That is, the color of the face is used to indicate an agent's facial expression.

Skeleton: Zda has initially limited possible poses and actions (standing, sitting, eating, grape, walking, turning, dropping, looking, smiling, crying, speaking), but can do more through imitation and other forms of learning. Skeletal poses are often associated with facial emotions, whether such an association is an inner or developed ability.

Brain: Zda's brain is the place to store his knowledge and mechanisms of action (learning and responding). Knowledge net (*Knet*) is a recursive network of patternized experiences. The mechanisms of actions include attention, learning, and response mechanisms.

Energy: Zda has a certain positive energy level at any moment when alive. When the energy level is at zero, he dies. Performing any action, even sleeping, will cost Zda energy, while eating food and rewards will boost his energy level. Naturally, Zda at a high energy level will be likely to perform a task that requires more energy.

9.4.2 Innate Abilities of Sensory Organs

Eyes (Vision): Zda initially uses 3×3 grids to divide the 2D appearance image to recognize objects. The simpler version recognizes the shape and color and brightness of an object. Zda can only see objects at the front, expanded within 180°; we expect Zda usually to pay more attention to an object in front of him than one at his side.

Ears (Hearing): Zda's hearing has initially only three levels for simplicity: silent, soft, and loud. Therefore, his ability to use loudness to judge the distance of sound source is very approximate.

Nose (Olfaction): Smells are of three types: aromatic, smelly, and odorless. Aromatic gives a positive feeling, smelly gives a negative feeling, and odorless is neutral.

Tongue/Mouth: Zda's tongue can initially *only* tell if an object is edible or not. Eating gives a positive feeling and boosts energy.

Skin: When touching an object, Zda can only have three possible Tactile Sensations: stinging, soft, or flat. Stinging gives a negative feeling, soft a positive feeling, and flat is neutral. Being bitten or hit by an object gives the same feeling as a sting.

Body (Temperature): Zda's innate sense of temperature includes only three types: cold, warm, and hot.

Sensibilities of Sensory Organs: Each sense organ has its sensibility, ranging from 0 to 1. A sensibility of 0 means deaf, blind, etc., while a sensibility of 1 means perfect hearing, vision, etc.

Sensation of the Heart: Sensations (ranging from 0 to 1) measure Zda's overall emotional state or spirit. When Zda is at a high level of sensation, he is more likely to be able to perform a task that requires a high energy.

Here, the Brain holds knowledgenet (*Knet*) and has mechanisms such as the attention, learning, and response mechanisms that we discuss in the next section.

10

First Designer Stance

10.1 Small- and Big-Data Approaches

McCarthy (2006) stated that the human brain has important innate knowledge, e.g., that the world includes 3-dimensional objects that usually persist even when not observed. The mainstream approach to AGI is a big-data approach, featuring a large commonsense knowledge base as characterized by John McCarthy (2006): indeed, it is worthwhile to build as much knowledge as possible into our robots. He elaborated: "A key problem for both AI and philosophy is understanding common sense knowledge and abilities. We treat the notion of the common sense informatic situation, the situation a person or computer program is in when the knowledge available is partial both as to observation and as to theory, and ill-defined concepts must be used. Concepts ill-defined in general may be precise in specialized contexts."

Constructivism and synthetism are contrarily on the minimalism approach. The HAI child has virtually an empty brain with minimal innate knowledge. The initial mind includes mainly mechanisms residing in the brain which allow the development of all sorts of intellectual things a normal baby would experience, such as consciousness, attention, imagination, the learning of language, math and logic, the acquisition of social morals, self-awareness, meta-thinking, goal-setting, and friend-making. Zda's mental states will not be listed exhaustively by humans, as such an approach cannot be really all-inclusive and may lose individual personalities. Instead, Zda will learn everything through experience, including learning from teachers. Zda can develop all such aspects of cognition without restarting the program. Neither is it necessary to deal with each aspect or specific ability using a different agent as is done in narrow AI. Instead, all knowledge and skills are developed through experiences or interactions with the environment and peers.

With built-in commonsense knowledge can make agents act effectively in commonsense situations. On the contrary, zero-data-based HAI agents can use their flexible learning and response mechanisms to wisely make decisions as humans would.

Our humanized agent has some intrinsic abilities in understanding concepts (not in the form of any natural language), such as inclusion, all, some, disjunction, implication, preference, similarity, the past, and precedence (Chang, 2012).

Though I take the small-data approach with very limited innate concepts, I am not denying the usefulness of big data. Big data as the primary approach is not a viable solution for HAI at this moment. When we have Zda and Lia grow up as teenagers or adults, we can copy the big data from their minds to clone an adult in no time. Also, as an interim transitional approach, if people refer, small- and big-data approaches can be combined.

10.2 Innate Knowledge

The first designer stance (i.e., **intentional stance**) is a term coined by philosopher Daniel Dennett for the level of abstraction in which we view the behavior of an entity in terms of mental properties. Here is how it works. First, you decide to treat the object whose behavior is to be predicted as a rational agent who will figure out what beliefs that agent ought to have, given its place in the world and its purpose and what desires it ought to have, on the same considerations, and finally, you predict that this rational agent will act to further its goals in the light of its beliefs (*Daniel Dennett, The Intentional Stance, 1987*). McCarthy (2006) generalizes intentional stance to the designer stance that asks what kinds of knowledge, belief, consciousness, etc., a computer system needs in order to behave intelligently and how to build them into a computer program.

In my small-data approach, the first designer stance only includes a minimal set of innate knowledge, abilities, habits, biological clocks and desires, and the attention, learning, response, and forgetting mechanisms that are built on the fundamental principles and laws discussed in Part I of the book, mechanisms, while the mental states of action, goals, knowledge, belief, and consciousness can be achieved in an agent's mind through interactions with the external environment.

Zda's embodiment allows him to perform certain basic actions; he can pronounce and identify simple sounds, feel heat, see, smell, move his body parts, and so on. The innate concepts of Zda are the concepts he possessed before his birth and understanding any language, while innate mechanisms are the abilities that are inherited from ancestors. The innate concepts denoted by different symbols here will be mapped to words expressed in particular languages that Zda will learn through relationships he develops with others in the society. Such mapping is a Zda learning process, not man-made mapping in computer coding. In a sense, learning is at first a map from the innate concepts to a natural language, and then a process of using hierarchical definitions to learn more complex concepts using a familiar language. The innate concepts or knowledge include:

1. True (T): If Zda "sees" something happening, then he realizes it is the truth or is true to him.

2. Negation ($\neg$): If Zda has the concept of a fair A, then he will also have the concept of the opposite side of A (i.e., the negation of A or $\neg$A). For example, if Zda sees that it is raining, then he also has the concept of "is not raining." If Zda sees something happening, then he realizes it is the truth. At the same time, he has the concept of the opposite side of the truth, i.e., falseness (not happening). A thing and its negation always coexist.

3. Sameness or equivalence ($\equiv$): Like a human, Zda has the intrinsic concept of sameness and has some sensors to detect whether two things are the same or not. For instance, a person has the ability of knowing if two objects are the same, or not, by looking at them, by touching or/and smelling them, even if he cannot express the concept of sameness in terms of any language. Therefore, sameness can be detected by the various senses, through shape and color, and by feel, taste, temperature, or smell. The concept is independent of any sensor, but the ability is dependent on particular sensors, e.g., a color-blind person cannot tell if two objects have the same color or not. With the sensor, a person can store information about two objects and compare them, and then produce the feeling of "same" or "not same." Such a feeling or sensation expresses the concept of sameness.

4. Implication (→): A→ B means A is sufficient for B.

5. All (*A*): "All" is the whole or collection of everything under consideration. Zda has the concept of allness but may not necessarily be able to identify the whole in any particular case. For example, if we say: "all math books in the world," Zda may not understand what we say, not because he does not have the concept of "all," but because he doesn't understand, e.g., the terms "word," "books," "the world."

6. Some (∃): Some are a part of all.

7. Count (*N*): The concept of the total number of certain items.

8. Every (*e*): Every element of a set of affairs under consideration.

9. Intersection (∩): Zda has the concept of an intersection of two events, i.e., a part belonging to two things simultaneously. However, this does mean he would not make a mistake in judging intersections in some cases.

10. Union (∪): Zda can identify the union of two events, i.e., a thing can be made of two things, e.g., people ≡ men ∪ women.

11. Conjunction (∧): Zda has the concept of the conjunction of two events, i.e., walking ∧ talking, meaning talking while walking.

12. Disjunction (∨): Zda can identify a disjunction of two events, i.e., a thing can be made of two things, e.g., walking ∨ talking, meaning either talking or walking.

13. Inclusion (∈): The concept of inclusion is a relationship between a part and the whole. For instance, a person knows a slice of pizza is part of the whole pizza. A door is a part of a house, and the lock is a part of the door. The part of a whole is independent of any language, and Zda is born with the ability to understand the connection. In notation, $A \in B$ means A belongs to B; or is a fundamental part of B.

14. Similarity (~): The concept of "similarity" concerns a relation between two entities. "Are similar" means only that a part of one entity is the same as a part of another entity. The concept of being similar can actually be derived from the conjunction of other concepts (≡, ¬, ∈).

15. Probability (⚡): The concept of probability concerns the likelihood of a fact's or an event's occurrence. For instance, if S represents the fact that B occurs after fact C, the probability of S is the percentage of time of the fact occurring among a collection of facts in terms of Zda's observation. Such a collection of facts are subjective in terms of scope (observation period and conditions given). Probability is a learned concept before Zda's birth, when he may sense that an event (a fact such as hunger) sometimes occurs and sometimes does not occur.

16. Preference (≽): Zda displays preference (e.g., likes one thing better than another). Preference can vary from individual to individual and from time to time, but the concept of preference is the same for everyone.

17. It (⚡): The concept of "it" refers to anything (concrete or abstract) Zda attends to at a particular time; most often "it" is used in a conversation or thinking process. To differentiate one "it" from another, we can add a subscript to ⚡, e.g., ⚡$_1$ and ⚡$_2$.

18. Time (*T*): The "biological clock" allows Zda to record event-order in time as past, present, and future (past experience stored in the memory, what is happening now, and what is imagined for the future). The circadian clock will allow Zda to record and organize time units: day and year (see the section on biological clock). Therefore, notions of time such as yesterday, today, tomorrow, last year, this year, and next year are considered to be innate concepts.

19. Precedence (≫): Precedence refers to Zda's ability to deal with a certain part, preceding others. In the linguistic agent, without assistance of other sensors, we use and force a priority. In other words, things included in the pair of precedence operators, (and), will be dealt with first. The precedence operators work as parentheses in an arithmetical formulation and can be used repeatedly or in a nested fashion.

20. Recursion (↻): The concept of the recurrence of anything (events, mathematical operations, actions, procedures) in different spaces, times, timescales, or in any other sensory aspects or in a general sense, such as weather or environmental change. The sense of the periodicity (unnested recursion in time) of the environmental change (mainly light) allows Zda to quickly formulate, in theory, the concept of "a day." Zda has the ability to perform various recursions, but here we refer to the concept.

21. Referring to (ℛ): The concept of mapping between a language (including signs) and its semantics. For instance, the word "pen" refers to an object, a pen. When the map between Zda's ℛ and a word in a particular language is established, communications between different humans and the agent become much easier.

22. Imitation (♯): The concept of copying what others do, or copying natural phenomena. This imitation is a concept, not one of the mechanisms of imitation to be discussed later. The action of imitating will be denoted by ↠ or ↞.

23. Desire (𝒟): Desire is the concept of a goal. Zda has desires so he knows others have them too. Here, the concept of desire is not the tendency of trying to satisfy a desire. Like a human, Zda does not have a clearly defined life-goal; rather, his is vaguely defined as a long and happy life. Happiness is subjective and depends on many things, and views of happiness change over time. The trade-off between longevity and happiness is purely personal. It goes in circularly: Your life-goal will direct your actions and social life, and conversely your actions and social life will reshape your life-goal.

24. Expectation (ℰ): Expectation is not desire. For example, Baby Zda wants to eat the apple (his desire). He tried twice to grab it and failed, but in the third try he succeeded. Now, if he was expecting no more than two chances, he would get mad upon failing the second time; however, if his expectation was to get it within three tries, then he will not know frustration, he will only be happy.

25. Sense of the 3D world (𝒮): This sense includes the relative location of two objects as measured by direction and distance. The location of an object is always relative.

26. Zda knows in order to act on an object, he needs to get sufficiently close to the object. The fuzzy concept of "sufficiently close" will be learned or become clear through his experiences.

When we say Zda has an innate concept B, we mean Zda has the sense of B but does not necessarily know how to express it in a natural language. In addition to the sense of the 3D world, Zda has sensory organs (for vision, smell, taste, hearing, touch, temperature) and feelings (sadness, pain, happiness), as delineated previously.

We should not misunderstand that Zda is a rational machine just because I have used symbols that are similar to those used in mathematical logic for innate concepts. There are three networks we should know about: (1) the knowledge net (*Knet*), consisting of patternized real world experiences, (2) the imaginary net (*Inet*), based on imaginary and hypothetical events, and (3) details of recent events with associated timestamps.

10.3 Innate Abilities

The innate abilities to be discussed in this section are beyond those of the sensory organs. They are an agent's abilities to recognize and perform elementary or atomic actions (tokens).

Elementary Actions: Due to inheritance, as with humans, Zda has inner abilities to act. An elementary action is an action that Zda can perform and recognize without learning. An elementary action involves some simple movement of the body. The movements in 3 dimensions of all joints of the agent's body, the production of simple sounds, and uncomplicated facial expressions can be elementary actions. The combination of joint locations and sequences of joint movements will become a fundamental subset of Zda's learned concepts and skills over time: from simple, to complex, to more complex.

Elementary tokens, including elementary actions, are the basic units used to build virtual environments, human characters, and agents. In principle such elementary elements can be further broken into smaller elements (tokens) by a human or an agent; but for Zda in the simulated environment, we will not focus on any such decomposition.

Before Zda can take an action, he needs to decide upon a set of actions from which he can choose an action. The initial actionable token list at birth plays important roles in his earlier learning.

There are eight types of elementary actions (tokens) in the following forms:

- *agent.act(name, goal, expectation, target, tool, duration, repeats, execution, Params)*
- *agent.say(textString)*
- *agent.image(eventString)*—agent thinking of the event sequence represented by eventString and leaving traces in the imagination net (*Inet*).
- *agent.recollect(eventString)*
- *agent.intend(goal, expectedProb)*
- *agent.compare(objects, attributes)*
- *agent.turnSelfawarenessSwitch(on/off)*
- *agent.face.act(expression)*

These will be examined in detail in Part IV: Prototyping Agents.

Things in the perceptual world are grounded into a category or class, initially based on certain sensible attributes. Such a similarity grouping process is called **desensitization**. For example, different objects with similar actions (e.g., in terms of speed) may be grouped into a class (may be called the class of fast-moving objects), objects of the same type can be grouped into a class, the same type objects with similar parameters can be considered as a class, and elementary actions of the same type can be grouped into a class based on their similarity in parameters. Synonyms in natural languages are a class. In a pattern structure, a token can represent a member of a class. Such a member of class is called a **desensitisor** for the sake of simplicity. The initial desensitization may not be perfect but can be improved through rewards and the authorization of teachers or humans.

An elementary token can be considered as a desensitisor of *object.action(parameters)* or object(attributes) with similar parameters or attribute values.

Action Names for Initial Gross Motor Control Elementary Tokens include: lookAt, look-Away, knockHead, shakeHead, turnHeadTo, grab, throw, pointTo, shake, push, pick, drop, hold, walkTo, walkAway, turnTo, trunAway, say, eat, cry, smile, sleep, catch, ride, dance, crawl, climb, pull, readIn, readOut, write, and listen.

Action Names for Fine Motor Control Elementary Tokens can be defined as the location and movements of body points or parts. We will explain how to implement gross and fine motor skills in Part IV.

Behavioral Inertia refers to the tendency to keep doing what one is already doing (to avoid the cost of switching energy). Behavioral inertia can be handled by assigning an association probability of repeating previous actions. In a similar vein but different, **Repetitive Fatigue** refers to the tendency to avoid repetitive work, which can contribute to the increase of muscular fatigue by inducing mental fatigue (repetitive strain, Miller, et al., 1993). Repetitive fatigue is automatically reflected since, according to the multiplication rule of joint probability, the chance of repeating the same action in a long action chain will gradually reduce.

As mentioned earlier, Zda will develop gross motor control before fine motor control. We decompose a post/action into a limited number of body movements. For instance, a hand may initially have two possible actions (grip and lose an object), the head has three positions, a face has five expressions, an arm has three different possible positions, a leg has five different positions, and so on. Over time, fine motor skills are developed so that each body part has more possible positions and movements, and more possible combinations, some of which are not viable (e.g., leading to falling down). Other aspects, such as vocal abilities, will follow the same way: a process of improving precision and control from "gross" to "fine."

Zda will gradually develop simple skills (elementary actions) and then complex skills (combinations of elementary actions) through imitation, necessity, and creativity. Those simple and complex actions with frequent occurrences will be associated with corresponding words in a natural language through communication. Those with fewer occurrences will not have words in a natural language. Such name assignments are somewhat subjective: there is a special word for the day after tomorrow in Chinese that is probably more natural than using the English phrase "the day after tomorrow."

10.4 Innate Habits

The innate habit ensures an agent does something *consistently*, not changing easily over time. **Instincts** are innate habits that are not the result of learning or experience. Such consistencies are necessary in learning and communication or language development, especially in an agent's childhood. For instance, a baby always cries when hungry. If he sometimes cries and sometimes laughs when hungry, it will make it very difficult for people to understand. Another example would be: Zda, facing a certain situation (e.g., seeing or smelling something), will produce a certain sound or have a certain facial expression or action (e.g., screams if scared). Now, a reflex can be considered a habit that is very difficult to change, whereas a habit can be seen as a reflex that could change later in life.

Some habits can change slowly over time if they are not needed anymore, or sometimes can even be "harmful." On the other hand, new habits can be developed over time. A habit can be developed when an action or sequence of actions is repeated frequently or through associative learning (classical and operant conditioning). Such a habit will become a high-level token through hierarchical tokenization (see Section 11.5). In other words, hierarchical tokenization creates habits. When a habit involves a sequence of actions, it can be considered to be due to association. A habit can be modeled using an *n*-gramton (see Section 11.5).

The innate habits considered here include:

1. Imitation, Zda likes to imitate others.

2. Biological Desires and Feeling (pleasure, pain, hunger, anger) cause attention to focus anddrive the agent's actions. For instance, when feeling pain or hunger, baby Zda will cry, while feeling happy or tickling will lead him to smile or laugh.

3. Zda's energy decreases over time. Before taking an action, the agent will check to see if he has enough energy. An action costs energy.

4. Baby Zda has low sensitivities to the environment, their world is simple.

5. Baby Zda is more imitative and more creative when young, and is less creative when getting old.

6. Baby Zda initially always tries to walk or reach for any object that has his attention.

7. Baby Zda likes to grab anything small and put it in his mouth to suck.

8. Zda likes to perform inductive reasoning (summarizing, patternization, repatternization, desensitization) and deduction (justifying what happened, or searching for justification). Such reasoning is an application of the similarity principle.

9. Given that everything else is the same, Zda more likely pays attention to objects' attributes than the differences in attributes between the objects: differences in distance (proximity), velocity, size, color, brightness, sound, loudness, smell, and other sensible attributes.

10. Zda likes to balance his energy and physical body.

11. Zda constantly monitors the distance of the attentive objects.

12. When Zda wants to look for something in reality, he will walk around, and when a match is found he will walk toward it and do something with it!

13. Giving his attention to some object (or objects) means that Zda will likely act upon it in some way. The action might involve looking at, looking away from, talking to or talking about, and walking toward or walking away from; the act might be picking it up, punching it, grabbing it, throwing it away, or otherwise making some association(s) with it (or them).

Any chain of associated events, or a sequence of events with high frequency, will be considered to be a hierarchical token. The last token in a sequence is often viewed as the short-term goal. We can say that a sequence of events (actions) leads to a goal, or that a goal drives a sequence of events (actions).

10.5 Innate Mechanisms

Innate mechanisms that Zda was born with are essential in determining how Zda learns and responds. Zda includes the following Innate mechanisms; each key mechanism will be elaborated in a separate section.

Innate Biological Desires often drive Zda's actions. Zda may appear to always pursue rewards. A reward is recognized by changes in Zda's biological states (hunger/energy or sensation). For instance, when hungry, eating an apple will lead to a change in hungriness. Sound of music may reduce sadness, a sensation change in Zda's inner state. Zda always acts toward a higher sensation status and reducing hunger. In addition, Zda constantly takes curiosity-driven actions in his lifetime. These biological desires are the fundamental forces that drive Zda's actions. Things (e.g., apples, music) that occur proximally (in space and time) to a positive change of biological states are recognized as rewards by Zda due to association, while, e.g., receiving a college degree is recognized as a reward-proxy, which is also due to a chain of associations.

It is difficult for Zda to judge if Lia's action leads to her receiving a reward because Zda cannot see directly her inner state changes. However, Zda's imitation habit lets him mimic others and if he gets a reward (or his inner state changes) through mimicking, the pattern associated with his action becomes a reward pattern. In this way, Zda accumulates his reward patterns or knowledge. Another way to accumulate reward patterns is through similarity-principle-based deduction: similar patterns will lead to similar rewards.

Zda will automatically classify rewards into different categories according to the change in different inner states: energy, sensation, or curiosity. Zda can further divide each category through learning (sensitization) based on the magnitude of the change within the category.

Zda's mechanisms of innate biological desires are very basic for prototyping: (1) Zda becomes hungry over time with associated energy level reduction and an action costs energy. Zda wants to eat food when hungry to boost his energy. (2) Music and entertainment can raise the sensation level. (3) Curiosity: Zda likes to learn, find out the why, how, and so on for things happening around him.

1. Zda's **Biological Clock** is an imprecise clock built from the computer clock with a small random variation added. Zda uses the biological clock to time and record events happening internally and externally.

2. **Self-Awareness Mechanism**: Self-awareness refers to the psychological state (phenomenon) that one knows what he is doing. For instance, Zda has desires and Zda knows he has desires. Such knowing is self-awareness. When the self-awareness on-off switch is on, Zda is aware of and can usually control every part of the body and the body as a whole, just like us. When the switch is on, Zda intends to do something and he is aware of his intention. When the self-awareness switch is off (default), Zda will not be aware of what he is doing at the moment, although he might recall it at a later time.

3. **Mechanism of Counting**: Counting refers to the process that determines the total number of certain items. It will be used implicitly in the calculation of pattern frequency.

4. **Inductive Reasoning** is drawing a general conclusion from a set of specific observations.

5. **Association mechanism** enables the ability that Zda has to make links among similar things or different things that happen close to each other in time or space. The association mechanism is a key for patternization, and creates links between different senses from different sensory organs to better identify objects.

6. **Attention Mechanisms** allow Zda to focus on a few important things (events, aspects), and this makes his learning more effective. Different objects attract Zda

in different ways and to varying degrees. Color, smell, brightness, sound, temperature, and an object's velocity all influence Zda's attention. Importantly, things that are not a focus of his attention have no effect on his decisions.

7. **Imitation Mechanism** is fundamental to Zda's learning. When the imitation switch is on, Zda can form a response by replacing the actioner in an actioner. action string with Zda himself.

8. **Creativity Mechanism** is also key to Zda's learning. When the creativity switch is on, Zda can form his response by replacing any tokens with other similar tokens in an event-string, including the empty token.

9. **Recollection Mechanism**: Recollection is important for Zda's emotional growth and an essential tool in solving problems. To recall, or recollect, from Zda's memory is to search a path in the *Knet* for a particular token or pattern. Certain things cause recollection in memory due to the association mechanism. An effect of recollection is to refresh the recency of the event.

10. **Mechanism of Dreaming**: Zda uses his dream time for repatternization or to organizeinformation and knowledge more efficiently, and sometimes, thus, to discover new things. Repatternization should follow the Parsimony Principle.

11. **Prediction Mechanism**: Prediction is key to determining Zda's responses in different situations. Prediction is under a given event-string, to determine the probabilities of different potential action paths and associated expected outcomes. Prediction may include predicting others' intentions. Predictions in dealing with novel situations are based on the Similarity Principle.

12. **Mechanism of Imagination**: Imagination is a hypothetical execution of imitation and creativity on the imaginary net (Inet) in order to predict what would happen in a given scenario.

13. **Dynamics of Knowledge Representation**: Zda's *Knet* is not a static knowledge database. Instead, it is a dynamic network that changes constantly using hierarchical tokenization and recursive patternization. Knowledge displayed through Zda's responses is based on the *Knet* and innate mechanisms. If we compare knowledge display to pizza, then the *Knet* is the set of ingredients and the innate mechanisms are the skills of the pizzaiolo. It is not necessary that we have pizza ready to eat at any moment of time, but we always have the ingredients and skills to make one in real time.

14. **Learning Mechanisms**: Learning mechanisms allow Zda to learn a broad range of things without the pre-programming of specific knowledge. Self-learning mechanisms include hierarchical tokenization and recursive patternization. Dealing with novel situations using the similarity principle, observing, imitating, analogizing, and being creative, are key components of Zda's learning. Thinking logically is itself a powerful tool in knowledge discovery.

15. **Recursion Mechanism**: Zda has the ability to perform various recursions, virtually on everything, anything.

16. **Response Mechanism**: The Response Mechanism is used in Zda's decision-making. Zda has to decide his actions (including doing nothing) at every moment. The randomized adaptive response mechanism incorporates the *Knet* and his other innate mechanisms to make decisions. In a general sense, the Response Mechanism includes several other mechanisms in this list.

17. **Feeling & Emotional Mechanisms**: A few feelings and associated (facial) expressions are inherited, such as hunger, pain, pleasure, sadness, and anger. The intensity of any feeling is proportional to the unexpectedness—the distance between one's expectation and what one actually receives—but expectations may be adjusted over time. Many different feelings can be developed as consequences of social interactions. The heart is the home for feeling, where overall feeling and emotion is recorded numerically as sensation.

18. **Evolutionary Mechanism**: Unlike other innate knowledge and mechanisms, evolutionary mechanisms only affect innate things across different generations. Zda's evolutionary mechanism is similar to Darwin's natural selection in that it includes reproduction, inheritance, individual variation, and competition under limited resources.

19. **Reward-Distribution Mechanism**: When a reward is (in Zda's view) associated with a path, then the reward will be evenly distributed to each token in the path. Because each token consists of subtokens, the distributive reward associated with each token will be further distributed evenly among its subtokens. The reward distribution process will continue until elementary tokens are reached at each branch. The distributed reward to each token or subtoken will be considered as associated with the token or subtoken.

20. **Cybernetic Mechanism**: Zda can sense the speed of a moving object by seeing, touching, or sensing a loudness change or redshift. The Innate mechanism is based on cybernetics. Thus, when Zda intends to catch a moving target, if the target is moving fast, Zda will move quickly toward it, visually and/or physically. He will then try to catch it; if failing to catch it, he can adjust his last actions slightly (not randomly try a long path) in the object's direction. If he fails again, he could retry the last action with a similar adjustment, and so repeat until succeeding.

With his embodiment, associated innate knowledge and mechanisms, Zda can acquire a very broad swath of knowledge and a great many skills.

10.6 Biological Desires

Innate Biological Desires often drive Zda's actions. Are emotions like fear, anger, love, shame, hunger, pain, jealousy, lust and sexual attraction hardwired in the brain, or are they products of culture and upbringing? According to the Instinct Theory of Motivation, all organisms are born with innate biological tendencies that help them survive. This theory suggests that instincts drive all behaviors. Instincts are innate habits that are not the result of learning or experience. For instance, infants have an inborn rooting reflex that helps them seek out a nipple and obtain nourishment, while birds have an innate need to migrate before winter. Neither behavior needs to be learned.

Zda's innate biological desires are basically related to three inner attributes, energy, sensation, and curiosity. The corresponding mechanisms are as follows. (1) The minimal consumption of energy is $E_a \times \textit{time-elapsed}$; when the energy level $< E_c$, Zda will be hungry; actions cost energy, and food boosts energy. (2) Entertainment boosts emotion and raises the sensation level. (3) Curiosity is the essential force for learning-driven actions; every time that curiosity is reduced (due to, e.g., questions being answered), the curiosity will automatically come back to a higher level shortly afterward. In addition, energy level and emotion (sensation) will also affect the level of curiosity.

In the Mechanism of Response, we will discuss model parameters that affect desires, creativity, and learning abilities.

10.7 Biological Clock

The term **Biological clock** may refer to: (1) the biological degradation associated with aging, such as longevity, fertility, and sensitivity of sense organs; (2) biological rhythms, repetitive biological processes. A **circadian clock** is a molecular mechanism that results in a circadian rhythm in a living organism; a circadian rhythm describes a biological process that displays an oscillation about every 24 hours, such as the human sleep-wake cycle (the "body clock").

Zda organ's sensitivity to the intensity changes varies over time as shown in Figure 10.1.

The fertility curve has a similar shape to the organ sensitivity curve. Ideally, Zda can grow, and the strength of his body can change too, but we will limit these aspects since this is not as critical as other aspects mentioned above.

Biological rhythms are repetitive biological processes that can range in frequency from microseconds to less than one repetitive event per decade. A **circadian clock**, or **circadian oscillator**, is a biochemical oscillator that cycles with a stable phase and is synchronized with solar time. Such a clock's in vivo period is necessarily almost exactly 24 hours. In most living things, internally synchronized circadian clocks make it possible for the organism to anticipate daily environmental changes corresponding with the day–night cycle and adjust its biology and behavior accordingly. Circadian clocks are the central mechanisms that drive circadian rhythms. The clock is reset as an organism senses environmental time cues, of which the primary one is light. Circadian oscillators are ubiquitous in tissues of the body, where they are synchronized by both endogenous and external signals to regulate transcriptional activity throughout the day in a tissue-specific manner. The circadian clock is intertwined with most cellular metabolic processes and it is affected by the aging of an organism.

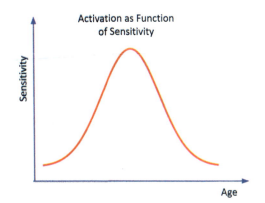

FIGURE 10.1
Organ sensitivity changes over a lifespan.

A biological clock is not as precise as a physical clock. Zda has a circadian clock using the timer created with a computer clock, but with a small random variation in the time for the realistic impreciseness. Equipped with a circadian clock, Zda will have the concepts of time and day (as 24 hours), and can learn the meanings of concepts such as month and year, yesterday and tomorrow.

The biological clock will often be used as an external object, with a ticking behavior, to insert into event-strings, thereby simulating time elapsed. For instance, Zda.cook(meat) bClock.(10 minutes) Zda.putIn(asparagus).

10.8 Self-Awareness and Consciousness

We are going to discuss how Zda can become a social being without built-in social norms.

Zda, like any person, *is* and *is not* a part of his environment. Zda can view himself as a person living in society. Recursive patternization makes Zda's mind (*Knet*) self-inclusive, which is the key mechanism allowing Zda to have self-awareness, the ability of thinking about thinking. Self-awareness is the ability of the outside Zda "seeing" the inside Zda in the *Knet*. Self-awareness means one knowing that one's mind controls one's own body (Figure 10.2). In other words, Zda can (of course he can, just like every human) differentiate himself from others over which he has virtually no control at all. This is my interpretation of self-awareness, without further explanation of the term "knowing." Strictly speaking, Zda and the Zda inside his recursive *Knet* are not exactly the same, because when the former thinks about thinking, the latter just thinks.

With this understanding of self-awareness, to prove that Zda can have consciousness we just need to prove he can *display* consciousness. We intentionally avoid Chalmers's term "subjective experience of consciousness" (Chalmers, 1995a), because its meaning is not well-defined and may involve circular definitions.

There are many examples showing that animals are social beings in a big mixed animal society. We can easily find such videos on social media, demonstrating the incredible abilities of collaboration within the same and between different animal species.

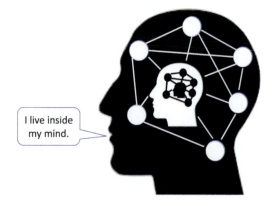

I live inside my mind.

FIGURE 10.2
The recursive knowledge net (recursive mind).

Because Zda imitates human behavior, if we reward him when he behaves humanly and morally and punish him when he fails to do so, Zda will display humanity by demonstrating similar responses, acting just as humans would under various social conditions. These will include responses reflecting consciousness, collaboration, and other social skills such as being humorous. Zda can display the ability of understanding cultural conventions, etiquette, politeness, etc. He can display human-like emotions, and sensation and desires. All these can be developed via interactions within the human-machine society and Zda's imitation mechanism. This means, we humans have to treat Zda humanely if we want him to become a human. A *mutual acceptance and recognition* between human and machine are the foundation for Zda becoming a truly social being. The question is: can AGI have full emotion without proper embodiment? I believe there will be no unique answer to this question.

Collaboration creates friends, while confrontation often makes enemies. Zda will formulate the concepts of friend and enemy and treat them as developed attributes for each individual.

10.9 Association Mechanism

The Association Mechanism equips Zda with the ability to make connections (a) between different things that happen closely together in time or space, or (b) between similar things. The association mechanism is related biologically to the neural mechanism: "neurons that link together will fire together." Association, despite its simplicity, is one of the most fundamental mechanisms in learning.

John Stuart Mill's statement (Mill, 1865) was more guarded and particular: When two phenomena have been very often experienced in conjunction, and have not, in any single instance, occurred separately either in experience or in thought, there is produced between them what has been called inseparable, or, less correctly, indissoluble, association; by which is not meant that the association must inevitably last to the end of life—that no subsequent experience or process of thought can possibly avail to dissolve it; but only that as long as no such experience or process of thought has taken place, the association is irresistible; it is impossible for us to think the one thing disjoined from the other.

Indeed, association is indisputable in every piece of our thoughts. The fact that body parts are linked together all the time makes us treat them as an entity, a body. The association mechanism also makes connections between different senses and sensory organs to better identify objects. Such links make Zda think about other aspects when experiencing some of the senses again. For instance, when we see an apple we may think of its sweetness and crunchiness. Association also makes links between different concepts if they appear at or nearly at the same time.

Any sensations A, B, C, etc., by being associated with one another a sufficient number of times, get such a power over the corresponding ideas a, b, c, etc., that any one of the sensations A, when impressed alone, shall be able to excite in the mind b, c, etc., the ideas of the rest (Chisholm, 1911).

The Three Principles of Association include contiguity in time and place, resemblance, and causation. David Hartley believed that contiguity is the main law of association, but ignored David Hume's law of resemblance (Warren, 1921).

The law of Contiguity can be stated: actions, sensations, and states of feeling, occurring together or in close connection, tend to grow together, or cohere, in such a way that, when any one of them is afterward presented to the mind, the others are apt to be brought up in idea (Bain, 1855).

When someone shows you a picture of your best friend, you naturally think of her because the picture resembles her. When someone mentions an object, you will think of the object because of the association. Zda thinks something when smelling something due to an association. Such an association can be a link between a concept (or name) and the corresponding object and can, consequently, cause Zda's attention to shift.

In Pavlov's experiment on Classical Conditioning, the newly established relationship between the sound of the bell and salivation is a consequence of the *learned association* between two stimuli (the bell and the food). Association (e.g., a stimuli–response association) is the central mechanism among teaching and learning mechanisms. The association of two things at different times makes a prediction of one from the other. An association mechanism is generally a key for pattern recognition or scientific discovery.

Association can be enhanced through repetition. Association is transitive through chains of associations. For instance, if event A associates with event B, and event B associates with event C, then event A will associate with event C. Such association/correlation is not always held in statistics: 3-way correlation among treatment-biomarker-endpoint (Chang, 2007, 2014).

From the HAI perspective, a significant feature of the association mechanism will be discussed in later sections.

10.10 Feeling and Emotion

Feelings are experienced consciously, while emotions manifest either consciously or subconsciously. Desire has an associated time-dependent expectation. Whether a desire is met or not will affect one's feelings and emotions. A few feelings and associated (facial) expressions are inherited, such as hunger, pain, pleasure, sadness, and anger. Many other feelings can be developed as consequences of social interactions.

Sadness may result from unmet expectations, perhaps due to nature or environmental causes. Anger may also be caused by an unmet expectation or may arise within us for any number of reasons. Pleasure comes when an expectation of something beneficial to us is met. Embarrassment may arise from personal behavior that does not meet his expectation of the moral standard (societal expectation). Certain physical pains and their causes are defined as innate properties, such as the fact that hard sharp objects can cause pain.

Sometimes Zda gets sad when he thinks he has no way to meet his initial expectation. He may adjust his expectation after feeling sadness (see the discussion on happiness in Part I).

Physical pain and biological pleasure are realized through embodiment. Actions initiated from the heart might be considered a rational approach with a proper utility function, whereas responses originating from the heart might be thought of as irrational or emotional.

Zda uses quantifiable sensation to measure different physical pain, biological pleasure, and mental states, whereas the intensity of feeling at a given moment is considered as an incremental sensation. When Zda is at a high sensation level, he is more likely to perform a task that requires a high energy. Associated with Sensation, Facial Expression, and Body Expression are coordinated. For simplicity, Facial Expression will be associated with Zda's face color. There are associations between Facial Expressions and Skeletal Poses; such an association can be an inner or developed quantity.

Emotion is an emergent (instead of predefined) phenomenon. Emotion is displayed emotion and is partially dependent on interpretation. Imitation makes Zda similar to a human being. The **reciprocal principle (reciprocity)** is the tendency of agents to exchange the two actions in an event-string or pattern. An action of reciprocity is an imitation, but not all imitations are actions of reciprocity. The Reciprocal Principle creates scenarios wherein Zda treats a person in the way the person treats him. Imitation is also the way Zda becomes a social being. In other words, as a social being, Zda likes to imitate others in most social settings.

As discussed, sensation as a measure of feeling and emotion often relies on expectations: if Zda receives no less than he expected, he will be happy, otherwise, if he gets less than he expected, he may not be happy. Specifically,

$$\text{Incremental sensation} = (\text{what received} - \text{expectation})/\text{expectation}$$

How does an agent determine the expectation of a decision? It is a combination of expected rewards from a set of potential actions determined by the randomized adaptive reinforcement learning (RARL in Section 14.12) algorithm and the expected reward from the executed action.

In a sense, imitations lead members of a community to behave similarly in a given social setting, thus creating societal norms. Such an individual view of social norms sets the individual expectations for social behaviors. Imitation can create desired expectations and at the same time satisfy the desired expectations. This can be elaborated as a necessary outcome of RARL:

The associated rewards with patterns in a *Knet* determined the expectation by: the average (R) of rewards associated with the candidate action paths from RARL and the reward (R_0) associated with the chosen action path. As an example of weighted average:

$$\text{Expectation} = 0.1R + 0.9R_0$$

Though imitation allows an agent to learn crying can get food when he is hungry, the initial ability or habit of crying for food when hungry is necessary for survival because such learning may take too long.

10.11 The Forgetting Mechanism

According to Davis and Zhong (2017): pioneering biological research studies, beginning with those using Drosophila, have identified several molecular and cellular mechanisms for active forgetting. The currently known mechanisms for active forgetting include neurogenesis-based forgetting, interference-based forgetting, and intrinsic forgetting, the latter term describing the brain's chronic signaling systems that function to slowly degrade molecular and cellular memory traces. The best-characterized pathway for intrinsic forgetting includes "forgetting cells" that release dopamine onto engram cells, mobilizing a signaling pathway that terminates in the activation of antibody (Rac1-cofilin) cell-signaling to effect changes in the actin cytoskeleton and neuron/synapse structure.

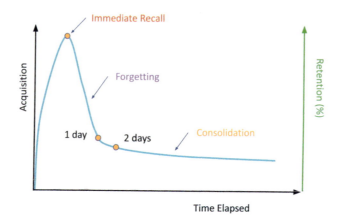

FIGURE 10.3
Ebbinghaus forgetting curve.

Over the past 50 years, experimental psychologists have debated whether forgetting occurs through an active process or through passive mechanisms. The term active process refers to the view that forgetting is active and triggered by defined external or internal factors. Interference-based forgetting has been widely studied in experimental contexts and posits that brain activity due to new information presented prior to the learning event (proactive interference) or after the learning event (retroactive interference) attenuates memory expression (Figure 10.3). The term passive forgetting has often been used to describe the biological decay of memory traces due to constitutive molecular turnover (natural decay). However, the psychological viewpoint of passive forgetting does not consider the brain as having the capacity to actively degrade the substrates of memory, even though it is widely accepted as the biological machine that forms and stores memory. There are different mechanisms for forgetting, some of which affect the integrity of the memory engram and others that disrupt retrieval of relatively intact memory engrams (Davis and Zhong, 2017).

In our HAI architecture, first, patternization of event-strings is carried out in order to simplify the representation of actual perceived events without much information loss. Such simplification in *Knet* will more or less lose some details at retrieval in comparison to the original events. Second, more information will delay relevant information retrieval and slow the decision process. Therefore, the benefits of forgetting are clear. As to what to keep and what to forget, this is a trade-off between response-promptness and information completeness. The forgetting-mechanism we proposed is based on pattern-survival time or gramton survival time (GST). This is because information and knowledge are represented by patterns in *Knet,* and when a pattern dies it will be removed from *Knet.* The survival time for an *n*-gramton is intuitively positively affected by the frequency (F) of and the associated reward (R) with the pattern, but negatively affected by the total number of tokens (N) in the *Knet* and the number of tokens (n) in the pattern:

$$GST = Cg \cdot \frac{F \cdot R}{N \cdot n}, \text{ where constant } Cg \text{ is an agent's attribute.}$$

In addition, recollection and response mechanisms discussed in later sections are related to frequency, reward, and recency, making low frequency tokens particularly difficult to recall.

A high-frequency pattern will be assigned a token name or concept, which will be used in hierarchical tokenization.

10.12 Evolutionary Mechanism

The evolutionary mechanism is not an innate mechanism of an individual agent, but a mechanism that emerges from a society of agents over generations. Materials and mechanical parts can break over time and can be replaced, just as we humans replace our body parts or organs when they fail. An agent can die of hunger or other causes, and his maximum longevity is given. The agent's evolutionary mechanism is similar to that of humans.

Unlike innate knowledge and mechanisms, evolutionary mechanisms only affect innate things across different generations. Different generations of agents alive at the same age, can affect each other's behaviors but not the innate belongings.

Darwin's four essential conditions for the occurrence of evolution by natural selection are applied to the agent architecture:

1. Reproduction of individuals in the population: Male (Zda) and Female (Lia)
2. Heredity in reproduction (via crossover)
3. Variation that affects individual survival (via crossover & mutations)
4. Finite resources causing competition

Evolution will optimize the Zda's parameters of HAI populations over different generations.

11

Dynamic Knowledge Representation

11.1 Rich Ontology

Ontology encompasses a representation, definition of categories, as well as properties and relations between concepts, data, and entities. A rich ontology is essential for AGI agents, and involves many kinds of things: material objects, situations, properties as objects, contexts, propositions, individual concepts, wishes, and intentions. Even when one kind of entity, A, can be defined in terms of others, we will often prefer to treat A separately, because we may later want to change our ideas of its relation to other entities (McCarthy, 2006). The rich ontology is supported by the hierarchical concept learning and adaptive RL-based response mechanism in Zda's architecture. In hierarchical concept learning, Zda learns complex concepts on the basis of previously learned simpler concepts. The hierarchical mechanism is essential for a rich ontology, efficient learning, memory management, and prompt response. Understanding a concept is an ongoing and tuning process. There is no single fixed meaning of a concept, even as defined by a dictionary or in some other way. The meaning of a concept should be a personal thing, and can well change over time, but the *core* meaning is the "common part" of understanding the concept in a community, which is relatively persistent or stable over time. The personalized adaptive response mechanism allows Zda to generate responses (so as to display different knowledge) in facing different situations.

One of the amazing realities is the difference between contextual meaning and objective truth. People can act or speak humorously (e.g., "he means the opposite of what he said"). How can we differentiate such assertions from truths? As an example, my statement "The sun rises from the west" is a joke if the following conditions are met:

1. I know it is obviously false, but intentionally say it to amuse you.
2. I know you know it's false.
3. I know you know I know it's false
4. I know you know I know you know.

11.2 Monotonic Reasoning and Elaboration Tolerance

Most studied formal logics have a monotonic consequence relation, meaning that adding a formula to a theory never produces a reduction of its set of consequences. Intuitively, monotonicity indicates that learning a new piece of knowledge cannot reduce the set of what is known. Having said that, false or outdated knowledge and useless (or the least

DOI: 10.1201/b23355-14

useful) information might intentionally or unintentionally be forgotten. Monotonic reasoning is a deterministic approach, not applicable to situations when uncertainties are involved (Chang, 2012). In most daily and scientific reasoning, probability is involved. Probabilistic reasoning is a non-monotonic logic. **Non-monotonic logics** are devised to capture and represent defeasible inferences, in which reasoners retract their conclusion(s) based on further evidence. **Elaboration tolerance** refers, in HAI reasoning, to allowing new information added to elaborate previous findings without starting over in the representation of previous information. Unlike narrow AI, which can only have a particular skill (e.g., playing games, recommending products, driving cars), elaboration tolerance (persistence) in a general sense, enables a humanized agent to learn all manner of different skills (add information) over time without erasing previous information. Elaboration tolerance is one of Zda's characteristics.

11.3 Representations of Perceptual World and Knowledge Net

The perceptual world in Zda's eyes and the world in his mind (*Knet*) are in the forms of objects, *object.attribute*, *object.action(parameters)*, or *object.subobject.action(parameters)*. You can also add levels of subobjects. An object can be a thing such as a book, a car, a plant, a dog, a human, or an AI agent. A property can be a shape, size, mass, color, brightness, smell, taste, state of matter (gas, liquid, or solid), temperature, velocity, acceleration, etc. Behaviors can include walking, running, speaking, listening, watching, or any others you may define.

The basic elements of knowledge representation in memory (in an agent's brain) can be OOP-alike syntax:

- *Car.color*
- *Dog.run(speed = fast)*
- *Zda.read(book)*
- *Zda.hand.firegun()*

The syntaxes are self-explanatory. The basic elements can be combined sequentially, or be nested, as shown in the following examples:

- *Zda.hold(pen) Lia.hold(book)*—Sequentially
- *Zda.see(Lia.hold(book))*—Nestedly

In Zda's view, the external world is a sequence of elementary tokens. This set of elementary tokens comes initially from innate knowledge, abilities, and actions, but can be extended through experiences or learning. Just as with humans, through patternization the external world is simplified and becomes Zda's *Knet*. Zda in this *Knet* is self-inclusive. As such, Zda treats his *Knet* as an internal world, inside his brain, and at the same time an external world that can be analyzed as he thinks about thinking. When Zda deals with novelties, imagination, hypothetical situations (such as in thought experiments, thinking how others may think and act, acting on self-awareness), he treats his *Knet* as a part of the external world. This will become much clearer and more concrete after our discussion of Zda's adaptive response mechanisms.

TABLE 11.1

Table Form of Knowledge Net

Token ID	Pattern	Freq	Recency	Duration	Reward

Zda's knowledge is not limited to static objects but also includes more dynamic events. That is, knowledge is often formed and displayed in Zda's responses when facing different situations. Similarly, a human does not exhaustively have all possible scenarios and associated responses preformulated in his memory. Even in the simple case of language, a human does not have all preformulated fixed sentences in the mind, but only has words, phrases, a limited number of sentences, and sufficient knowledge of the language's grammar to be able to formulate sentences in real time. Here, grammar is an engine that enables knowledge to be formed more efficiently.

It is convenient to store knowledge in tabular form, as shown in Relational Database, Table 11.1. Token ID is used for the identification of the pattern. Pattern is a sequence of tokens. Freq is the frequency of the pattern. Recency is the time of the most recent occurrence of such a pattern. Duration is the time that such an event will take with a missing value for no-actionable token (pattern). Time has different units: lower level patterns can be in seconds, hours, while higher level patterns can be in days, months, years, or decades. Elementary tokens or atomic tokens are always actionable, while other tokens may not be. Scientific laws are not actionable tokens. Reward is relayed to the pattern and will be discussed in Chapter 14.

11.4 Hierarchical Tokenization and Concept Embedment

Hierarchical tokenization is the act of searching segments of a target event-string that match some known patterns in *Knet* and replacing the string segments with the matched patterns. Such a replacement is called concept-embedment in this book.

Initial tokenization is based on elementary tokens that are directly formulated from innate knowledge, concepts, and elementary actions, as discussed in Section 10.3. A token usually consists of subtokens. When a token cannot be further expanded at a given time, it is called an **elementary token**. However, in principle, elementary tokens can be further broken down into more elementary tokens as Zda's sensory organs become more sensitive over time. An elementary token (action) should allow some small random variations in its parameters, such as the variable length of walking steps.

Hierarchical tokenization is a process of dimension reduction: obtaining a shorter event-string representation of the world in the mind using concept-embedment. The idea is motivated from the Connotation of Understanding discussed in Part I. That is, we explain a concept by known concepts, which are further explained by other known concepts. For example, the event-string *Zda.walk() Zda.walk() Zda.walk()* may be simplified as *Zda.walk(3 steps)*, given that Zda understands the meaning of three steps. Similarly, the event-string *Zda.walk(3 steps to the left)* Zda.walk(*2 step to the right*) Zda.walk(*4 steps to the left*) *Zda.arrive(the kitchen)* may be simplified as *Zda.walk(to kitchen)*.

The English-like syntax in event-strings is not a must. In fact, the actual syntaxes or language Zda used will depend on what is used by the people with whom he has interacted.

For instance, Chinese may use a word 后天 for the English phrase: "the day after tomorrow." Zda will learn how other people use concepts (tokens) in multilingual communities. A long event-string can be shortened by concept-embedments, recursively. However, the replaced concepts must be previously learned concepts (patterns), i.e., from Zda's *Knet*.

An *event-string* is called a *pattern* if we emphasize its structure; at the same time, so naming such strings also implies there are variations in elements. For example, when we call "Zda read book" a pattern, we imply that there are variations: Zda read a math book, Zda read a storybook, Zda read a science book, etc. Patterning concerns the common structures and the rule of variations. An *event-string* can also be called a *concept*, when we want to emphasize its *meaning*, or a token if it is treated as concept-embedment. *Patternization* is the inference from many specific cases to a general structure or pattern. *Tokenization* is breaking a *concept* represented by a string into several smaller units or simpler concepts that Zda has learned previously. The goal of hierarchical tokenization is to break a string into nested n-token long substrings (usually $n = 2$–4) for easy patternization. When a *pattern* is treated as a single unit it is called a *token*. Zda will map the *token* name to a *concept* in a natural language through his interactions with others in the social community.

A concept is abstract, a general notion. Meaning is the connotation of the concept. For example, the connotation of food may be anything edible. You may have noticed that here we have used another concept, eatable, to explain food. The denotation (extension) of a concept is a collection of similar things. For example, the denotation of food equals {apple, breakfast, meat, rice, …}, while the denotation of meat equals {pork, beef, chicken, …}; each of the concepts can be further broken down into sub-concepts. Eating apples is a concept, which includes eating different apples and different ways of eating apples. It is often impossible to exhaustively list its large number of elements.

A token contains other tokens, a concept contains other concepts, and a pattern contains other patterns. In short, token, concept, and pattern refer to different perspectives of the same thing. The letter "A" can be thought of as a token, the concept of one, and a pattern (rule of how it should be written or appear). Token and concept treat the corresponding string (e.g., a song) as a unit, while the pattern lays out the details (melody of the sound) of the string. A token as a concept may be embedded in a sentence or in nested sentences. Thus, hierarchical tokenization is simply concept embedment.

In Zda's architecture, any concepts or patterns are treated as tokens in the stochastic decision network (*Knet*), including concepts and concepts of concepts. This dynamic nested network of event-strings with associated frequencies and rewards changes constantly and varies from individual to individual; this makes each concept (token) and response context- and time-sensitive.

Strictly speaking, the decision-network consisting of events is a non-stationary stochastic decision process. The reason we can use hierarchical tokenization is because long non-stationary stochastic decision networks (paths) can be approximated by short hierarchical stochastic decision nets (paths), or even by a hierarchical Markov chain decision net. Just like language, instead of studying relationships among all the individual words in a very long story, or in the long sequence of all the individual words we have heard and spoken, we (1) break down the sequence of words into phrases, sentences, paragraphs, and articles, and (2) analyze word-relationships within phrases, phrase-relationships within sentences, sentence-relationship within paragraphs, and paragraph-relationships in chapters of the story, and so on. The hierarchical structure of a natural language is shown in Figure 11.1. The recognition of patterns at each level is conditioned by the patterns recognized at the levels below.

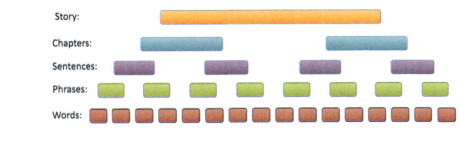

FIGURE 11.1
Building blocks in A story.

Tokens, excepting elementary tokens, are not predetermined by a computer program in Zda's architecture. Instead, they associate with learned concepts that frequently appear (e.g., in the top 50%, recurrence-wise). Frequency-based (not reward-based) tokenization is memory-wise and computationally efficient due to high token frequency, while the reward-based response mechanism (discussed later) makes the response more meaningful. Another important fact is that communication (not necessarily verbal) will direct and facilitate the formulations of tokens. People with different languages would use similar but slightly different concepts; therefore, they would use different tokens (e.g., 后天, which means the day after tomorrow in Chinese, has no single-word token in English). The cultural differences are also reflected in the different sequences of concepts in natural languages, such as the order of adjectives in a sentence. In writing mailing addresses, English goes with the recipient's name, home address, city, then country, whereas Chinese processes with country, city, home, then recipient's name. The difference might have something to do with the language of thoughts.

In general, there are several objects within Zda's attention and multiple things occurring simultaneously. For example, Figure 11.2 shows that multiple tokens occur at times t_2 and T_1, where squares represent elementary tokens and ellipses represent high-level tokens.

Communications and interactions between community members force everyone involved to consistently use the same (similar) concepts and terminologies. Communication is using the concepts (patterns) other people have identified and letting other people use the concepts (patterns) you have identified. Communication makes knowledge-sharing possible and learning more effective. The effectiveness is reflected in Zda's energy saving.

As in arithmetic, where the order of math operations will affect the result, patternization is not dependent on how the hierarchy of tokenization is chosen. The token precedence (order of tokens in patternization) is a collection of rules that reflect conventions about the sequential order of tokenization. The precedence in tokenization is based on the associated frequency: higher frequency tokens precede lower frequency tokens.

An important question is: should tokens (concepts) be time-dependent? I would say yes, at least for some of the tokens. The time scale does not have to be precise but becomes even less precise as time goes by. The time recorded in memory may just be an indication of the chronological order, not the actual time. Time-dependent tokens can be implicitly dealt with when the concepts used involve time-related concepts (e.g., five minutes later, yesterday, last month). Another interesting question is how Zda represents a new word (concept) that has never been seen before. We will discuss this in the section Dealing With Novelty in learning mechanisms.

Similarity scoring is also important in pattern refinement and knowledge discovery, allowing Zda to know how to group similar things together, revealing new patterns.

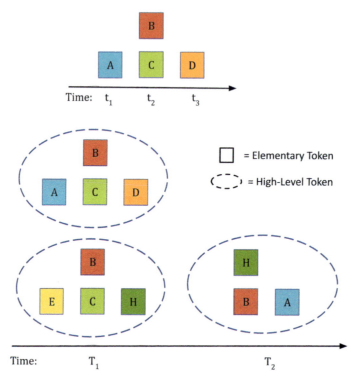

FIGURE 11.2
Hierarchical tokenization.

Furthermore, creativity is essentially a similarity-replacement: the substitution of some tokens in *Knet* with similar tokens. The refinement of patterns is a topic of repatternization in learning and adaptive response mechanisms.

11.5 Precedence in Tokenization

Tokenization is mainly based on associated token frequency, for the purpose of having a concise "grammar" that can be used to describe the world.

An important question is how to determine a high-level token (concrete procedure in reality or abstract concept in language). Tokenization precedence is first based on high-frequency occurrences, followed by long length (the number of next level subtokens). We illustrate with the following example. Note that patterns in *Knet* and Zda's attentive world are represented by event-strings.

1. The circled numbers represent the different elementary tokens.
2. Assume Zda encounters an event-string: S1 = ①②③④⑤⑥⑦⑧.
3. Assume there are 4 tokens, PT2, PT3, PT5, PT6 in Zda's *Knet:*
   - PT2 = ①②, associated frequency = 10
   - PT3 = ②③, associated frequency = 15

- PT5 = ⑤⑥⑦, associated frequency = 36
- PT6 = ⑥⑦, associated frequency = 36

4. Hierarchical tokenization is replacing the elementary tokens by high-level (composite) tokens: S1 =①PT3④PT5⑧.
5. The reason why PT3 is used instead of PT2 is that PT3 has a higher frequency than PT2 has. PT5 was randomly picked between PT5 and PT6 since they have the same frequency, which means the resulting setting can be ①PT3④⑤PT6⑧.

The problem with this frequency-deterministic algorithm is that it could lead to an inferior solution due to some initial condition (e.g., some tokens have initially high frequencies by chance). The solution is to use a probabilistic algorithm for precedence: the probability of choosing a token is proportional to its frequency. In other words, randomized Hierarchical Tokenization based on Token frequency in *Knet* uses an urn model:

$$\text{Urn Model: } Pr\left(PT_i\right) = \frac{f_i}{\Sigma f_k}.$$

Here $Pr\left(PT_i\right)$ = probability of picking pattern PT_i, f_i = frequency of PT_i, the sum is over all possible patterns for the hierarchical patternization. Note that every token will be assigned an initial frequency $f_0 > 1$ (e.g., $f_0 = 5$) when it occurs for the first time. Adding f_0 will increase the stability of the results and the robustness of the algorithm (system).

11.6 Natural Language Structure: Knowledge Expression

English sentences may present themselves in varying patterns or arrangements of the elements of a sentence. From simple to complex, there are five basic sentence patterns in English:

1. Subject + Linking Verb + Complement
2. Subject + Intransitive Verb
3. Subject + Transitive Verb + Direct Object
4. Subject + Transitive Verb + Indirect Object + Direct Object
5. Subject + Transitive Verb + Direct Object + Object Complement

English sentences are conventionally classified into four types: Declarative, Interrogative, Imperative, and Exclamatory.

A declarative sentence is an informative statement: (1) *I am interested in AI.* (2) *He wants to eat cookies, but he doesn't know how to make them.* (3) *Steven found a new job because he enjoys working from home.*

An interrogative sentence asks a question: (1) *Why does the sun shine?* (2) *How much does it cost and why do you need it?* (3) *Can you call me when it's time to go?*

An imperative sentence tells someone to do something: (1) *Turn left at the bridge.* (2) *Put your phone away and listen to me!* (3) *Hand the baby his bottle now that he's done playing.*

An exclamatory sentence expresses emotion: (1) *Wow, he just won a gold medal!* (2) *My new job is a wonderful opportunity and it offers great benefits!* (3) *Call me whether you have good news or not!*

To patternize language structures, we first study the parts of speech (PoS) in traditional grammar; then we use gramtons and skiptons, the two pattern types motivated by the notions of grams and skip-grams in the Natural Language Process (Section G in the Appendix), to patternize the structure. We will show that this approach is applicable to not only big data but also small data.

PoS is a category of words (or lexical items) that have similar grammatical properties. Words that are assigned to the same part of speech generally display similar syntactic behavior, and play similar roles within the grammatical structure of sentences. Commonly listed English parts of speech are nouns, verbs, adjectives (including articles), adverbs, pronouns, adpositions, conjunctions, and interjections. Other Indo-European languages and Chinese also have essentially all these word classes; Latin and Chinese do not have some articles. Other terms than PoS in modern linguistic classification often make more precise distinctions than the traditional scheme does, including the categories of word class, lexical class, and lexical category.

A PoS indicates how the word functions in meaning as well as grammatically within sentences. An individual word can function as more than one part of speech when used in different circumstances.

1. Noun: **Nouns** are often used with an article (*the, a, an*), but not always. Nouns can be singular or plural, concrete or abstract. In some languages, such as Chinese, nouns usually do not have separate singular and plural forms.

2. Pronoun: A <u>pronoun</u> is usually substituted for a specific noun or antecedent.

3. Verb: A verb in a sentence expresses action or being. There is a main verb and sometimes one or more helping verbs. (*"She can sing"*). Verbs also take different forms to express tense.

4. Adjective: An adjective is a word used to modify or describe a noun or pronoun. It usually answers the question of which one, what kind, or how many. Here adjectives include articles. An article (determiner) is a word, phrase, or affix that may indicate whether the noun is referring to a definite or indefinite element, a particular quantity or all. Common English determiners include the, a, this, my, their, many, both, all, no, each, any, and which.

5. Adverb: An adverb describes or modifies a verb, an adjective, or another adverb, but never a noun. It usually answers the question of when, where, how, why, under what conditions, or to what degree.

6. Adpositions: Adpositions, including prepositions and postpositions, are a class of words used to express a wide range of semantic relations between their complement and the rest of the context. Preposition: A preposition is a word placed before a noun or pronoun to form a phrase modifying another word in the sentence. A prepositional phrase almost always functions as an adjective or as an adverb.

7. Conjunction: A conjunction joins words, phrases, or clauses, and indicates the relationship between the elements joined. Coordinating conjunctions connect grammatically equal elements: and, but, or, nor, for, so, yet. Subordinating conjunctions connect clauses that are not equal: because, although, while, since, etc.

8. Interjection: An *interjection* is a word used to express emotion.

In the following example we use font faces and colors to show different Parts of Speech:

> The young **girl** brought <u>me</u> a very long **letter** from her favorite **teacher**, and then <u>she</u> quickly disappeared. *Oh my*!

Adjectives describe Zda's senses: Taste, Touch, Sound, Color, Size, Shape, Amount, Emotion (Sensation), Desire, Time, Age, Location, Origin, Material, Person or Personality, Appearance (e.g., new, impressed, clean, multicolored), Situations, Qualifiers (denoting the item's type or purpose), and changes of these attributes in time and space.

The relations expressed by adpositions may be spatial (denoting location or direction such as in, under, toward, before) or temporal (denoting position in time, starting, ending, or duration) relation or relations expressing comparison, content, agent, instrument, means, manner, cause, purpose, reference, etc. (such as of, for). An Adposition typically combines with a noun phrase, this being called its complement, or sometimes object.

As an adjunct to a noun:

- the weather *in* March
- cheese *from* France *with* live bacteria

As a predicative expression (complement of a copula)

- The key is *under* the stone.

As an adjunct to a verb:

- sleep *throughout* the winter
- danced *atop* the tables *for* hours

As an adjunct to an adjective:

- happy *for* them
- sick *until* recently

A *conjunction* connects words, phrases, or clauses that are called the conjuncts of the conjunctions. In general, a conjunction is an invariable grammatical particle and it may or may not stand between the items conjoined, as illustrated in the following examples:

- They do not gamble or smoke *because* they are ascetics.
- They gamble *and* they smoke.
- They do not gamble, *nor* do they smoke.
- They gamble *but* they don't smoke.
- Every day they gamble *or* they smoke.
- You *either* do your work *or* prepare for a trip to the office.
- *Just as* many Americans love basketball, so many Canadians love ice hockey.
- I would *rather* swim *than* surf.
- We'll do that *after* you do this.

- That's fine *as long as* you agree to our conditions.
- We'll get to that *as soon as* we finish this.
- There is a good chance of rain *whenever* there are clouds in the sky.

An initial comprehension of grammar is not necessary when learning a language. Most people learn their mother language without grasping the grammar. Learning grammar can help them to understand and use their language better when they have mastered certain skills of the language. But grammar is very useful for adults learning second languages. Knowing the common language structures here will be helpful in constructing Zda's architectures, especially in the language-guided response and in effectively teaching Zda's learning. We will use the information discussed in this section to patternize the language text strings in Section 13.2, Patternization of Language. We will see in this chapter that conjunctions and adpositions can be taught using factor-isolation techniques. However, it is important to remember we are not going to build any PoS or grammar in HAI architecture. Instead, Zda can learn the grammar of any natural language as needed.

Grammar is important for efficient learning but more important is contextual understanding.

Contextual Understanding is a base for humanized AI, but it is not the whole of HAI. An agent can understand well but still act in ways that are not humanlike. There are many languages and grammar which evolve over time. Each HAI agent has his own way to understand any language.

One important learning is "referring to" or "mapping to." "Referring to" can also be explained as "understanding." Zda will make his own grammar (pattern structure) that will be very different from the grammar of any natural language. For Zda, a natural language is one-dimensional text (verbal) string descriptions of the perceptual world. Zda's *Knet* of recursive patterns which is coded as one-dimensional text string is a different way of describing his perceptual world. The mapping between a natural language and *Knet* can be established through the elements of the perceptual world. The evolutional one-dimensional text strings also form the recursive, self-inclusive stochastic decision network used in the deep-thinking mode of the response mechanisms.

A green pen is a single object, we can describe it as "green pen," "pen green," or other ways using natural languages. Here, the object (pen) and its property (green) are arranged according to certain rules (PoS) in a 1-D natural language. Words referring to other objects or their static and dynamic attributes work in a similar manner. So do adverbs in English.

A cup on a table may be referred to by "cup on table," "cup above table," etc., using a natural language. Here, the accessory word "on" or "above" is introduced in order to use a 1-D text string to indicate (map) the 3D spatial relationship between the two objects. Such accessory words (or paired words) can be adpositions or conjunctions in English.

The term contextual understanding of a natural language is to correctly map tokens in the *Knet* patterns to the words in the natural language. We will elaborate on this process in Sections 13.2, 14.12, and Chapter 15.

12

Attention Mechanism and Attentive World

12.1 Decomposition of Attention

Like humans, Zda sends off "attention pulses" to detect the world. Thus, the world consists of discrete frames in Zda's view. We humans like to fill in the blanks between these frames with our imagination. Zda experiences and learns about the world based on his attention. Attention allows Zda to focus on a small number of things so that he can learn and deal with them effectively. Therefore, the cognitive agent must have an attention mechanism for learning and response. In Zda's architecture, attention is classified into three types: subconscious, conscious, and associative.

Subconscious Attention is due to an effortless reflex. Subconscious-Attention relates to the intensity of source (sound, light, odor, temperature), closeness, and motion. Simply put, the intensity, closeness, and speed of an object will attract Zda's subconscious attention. In general, Zda's subconscious attention to an object will depend on characteristics of the object that include its closeness, size, brightness, moving velocity (inward or outwards), acceleration, and any change in distance, brightness, soundness, odor, temperature, and tactility. Acceleration is the derivative of the velocity, the speed of speed; it is related to the future closeness to an object. In principle, we can have an acceleration of acceleration. However, Zda will not deal with such higher order quantities.

Conscious attention is the attention referred to the most in daily life. It is an attention that is of self-awareness and requires energy. The things brought to one's conscious attention are often determined through a rationalization that is mainly related to the goals, frequency, and rewards of actions to be taken. Zda has an initial (born with) set of things that potentially form conscious attentive objects (events or concepts).

Associative Attention is caused by associative thinking, leading to an attention shift from one object (event, concept) to another associated object (event, concept). For example, when we see a banana we may think of an apple.

An attention set is a set of objects, events, actions, and concepts that the agent pays attention to, in the form of *object.attributes*, *object.action()*, and patterns. For example, *myTree.size*, *myTree.stand()*, *Wind.blow()*, *Sky.shine()*, *Zda.run()*, and *Friend.rewarded()*.

12.2 Subconscious Attention

Zda's subconscious attention to an object at time t is a multiple-sense weighted attention given by

$$SA(t) = W_0 \exp\left[-d(t)\right] + W_1 S(t) + W_2 \ln\left[1 + n(t)h(t)M(t)T(t)\right]$$

DOI: 10.1201/b23355-15

where W_0, W_1, and W_2 are weights whose initial values are considered parameters of innate attributes. The weights can be updated slightly over time. $d(t)$ = the distance between Zda and the object at time t, $S(t)$ = the speed of the object *relative to the observer* (Zda), $n(t)$, $h(t)$, $M(t)$, and $T(t)$ are the intensities of smell, sound, temperature, and taste, respectively. Remember, the speed of an object is relative to the agent (observer).

Zda is sensitive to voice (words) and the words heard are virtually always in the attention set. An object that an agent is pointing at or shaking will very likely become objects in Zda's attention set.

A voice's attentivity is proportional to the logarithm of its intensity, according to the Weber-Fechner Laws. The logarithm can be explained by the fact that signal intensity reduces exponentially when it travels through a multiple-layer neural network.

Zda can only observe what happens at the attention pulses; anything in between them is made up by his imagination, just as with humans. Attention directs the consumption of the internal energy resources. The attention pulse rate is proportional to the subconscious attentivity, like a radar. Subconscious attentivity and the subconscious attention pulse rate switch are low in deep thinking since the conscious attention is high.

The subconscious attention set $\Omega(t)$ at time t consists of up to 4 objects (tokens) with the highest subconscious attentivities but removes any objects whose subconscious attentivity is less than a certain percentage of the maximum of the 4 attentivities.

On the time-axis, Zda can temporarily hold subconscious attention set up to 16 time points, $\Omega(t-15)$, $\Omega(t-14)$, …, $\Omega(t-1)$, and $\Omega(t)$. The reason that Zda automatically holds a long string of subconscious attentive objects over time is due to the inertia of subconscious attention. This long event-string allows Zda to discover complex scientific laws.

Inertia of attention is the tendency of humans or agents to pay attention to the same thing paid attention to at the previous moment. The inertia attention set $\Omega_I(t)$ at time t is equal to $\Omega(t)$ at the previous time point $t-1$. Inertia of attention can be explained by the energy cost (ΔE) due to attention switching. For convenience, we define inertial attentivity as $1/\Delta E$, the inverse of the energy cost.

Note that sensing smell, light, sound, taste, temperature, and touch, all require some tiny time interval. So does sensing the speed of a moving object. A biological clock (time) is usually in lower subconscious attentivity because the clock is always steadily and slowly ticking.

An important question is when to turn on self-awareness, so that Zda himself is in his attention set and patterns in *Knet*. This is a personal thing: some people practice introspection, turning the self-awareness switch on, more often than others do. At the moment, we use a probability of randomly turning the switch on. This probability is characterized as an innate attribute.

Attention to some innate concepts is often related to an action. For instance, when Zda is making a choice, the innate concept Preference is in his attention set. Conversely, when the innate concept Preference is in Zda's attention set, he is usually making a choice. Attention to the innate concept can be subconscious or conscious.

12.3　Conscious Attention

Conscious attention requires the self-awareness switch to be on. The conscious attention set will be selected from the list of the most interesting and valuable things: things that are enjoyable and actions that are likely associated with high rewards. In other words, the conscious attention set consists of the most frequent and rewarding patterns (things, subject fields, events, concepts, processes).

Before Zda develops his own list of interesting things for conscious attention, he will have been given an initial (born with) set of interesting things for his conscious attention.

12.4 Associative Attention Shift

According to the law of contiguity in Psychology, things happening close to each other in time or space are associated. While shaking an object to attract Zda's subconscious attention, saying the name of the object will make Zda associate the name with the object. This is the initial basic approach to teaching Zda names of objects. After Zda has associated a name with an object (or event), then, when he hears the name, he will pay attention to not only the name but also the associated object (event). For example, after Zda associates the name "coffee" with actual coffee, when Lia says *bring me a cup of coffee,* Zda will pay attention to (and begin looking for) coffee. Association is the key to making links between senses from different sense organs (Figure 12.1), and consequently the links between different objects or the coordination of body parts. The association mechanics constitute one of Zda's innate mechanisms.

When we shake an object and say its name, Zda will associate the name with the object. We then point at the same object, say its name, and Zda will "understand" the meaning of the action "pointing." After that, we do not need to shake but point at an object to teach Zda its name. Furthermore, if we gradually move away from the object and "pointing at" becomes "pointing to" while saying the object's name, we can eventually name a distant object by pointing to it. However, how do we refer to a non-pointable or abstract thing, such as time? This matter will be addressed in Chapter 15, Effective Teaching.

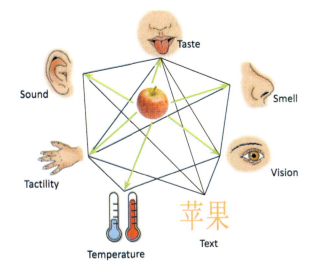

FIGURE 12.1
Associations among senses from different sensory organs.

Association can cause the attention to shift from one thing to another, leading to recollection and imaginings. For instance, we might have a chain of associations: → Apple → Apple Pie → England, the place where apple pie originated. Such a chain of associations causes an attention shift from apple to England. We will have more to say about the associative attention shift in Adaptive Response Mechanisms. The stronger the association is, the more likely the attention shift is to occur. Conversely, constant shifts between two things make the association between them even stronger.

In the most general sense, an associative attention occurs when two things (events) are similar (close) in some sense. For instance, an attention shift from banana to apple could be because of the shared property of sweetness. Associative attention also explains why we often cannot avoid thinking the things we don't want to think about.

An association will be represented by a 2-gramton (attentive token and associated token) with high frequencies (see Part IV for details).

12.5 The Attentive World

Zda only observes what happens at the attentive time points when attention pulses are sent. Anything in between is unobservable and could be made up by his imagination, as mentioned earlier. Without imagination, Zda's attentive world consists of discrete frames (Figure 12.2). Attention directs the consumption of internal energy resources.

The attention pulse rate is directly proportional to subconscious attentivity; high subconscious attentivity, such as when seeing an object flying toward your eyes, will lead to more frequent attention pulses. In other words, current subconscious attentivity will determine the next attentive time point. See Reflex and Fast-Thinking (Chapter 14).

Attention pulse rate is inversely proportional to conscious attentivity. That is, the more an agent is involved in thinking, the less attention (s)he is paying to the external world. Thus, current conscious attentivity will determine the next attentive time point. See Slow-Thinking and Deep-Thinking (Chapter 14).

We limit that an agent can only pay attention to a maximum of 4 objects or recollective events and actions (concepts) at up to 4 time points. The recollection of events or actions is itself a concept since, e.g., an actual car accident and a recollection of it are different things.

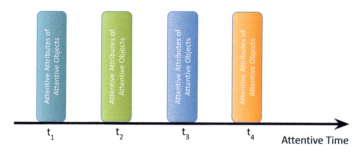

FIGURE 12.2
Agent's attentive world at 4 sequential time points.

In slow-thinking, from 16 tokens at 4 consecutive attentive time points Zda will select up to 4 of the top attentive tokens (may include voice) to form the final attention set but will ignore any tokens with attention less than half of the maximum attentivity.

To investigate the patternization mechanisms, we need to understand that there are different levels of detail Zda may pay attention to. For instance, when a big yellow German Shepherd dog named Luna is running fast down a road, Zda may notice a dog running but doesn't know it's Luna, or Zda may see a big dog running but doesn't know the breed, or Zda may see a big yellow dog running but doesn't know its speed. The level of detail Zda attends to will determine the similarity grouping in Zda's learning.

As we saw in our discussion of agent embodiment, *Shape* defines the class (type) of an object. The combination of *Shape*, *Size*, and *Color* identifies each object uniquely. Color also indicates the agent's emotion, in our simplified architecture. Therefore, Zda might pay attention to one or another set of items, such as {Shape, Action}, {Shape, Size, Action}, {Shape, Size, Color, Action}, or {Appearance, Action}.

The default attention items are rooted in objects: *object(appearance).action(targetObj)*. Up to 4 objects at 1 to 4 time points (real time objects or recollections of objects at past times) can be accommodated. Thus, Zda can pay attention to {*actor1.action1, actioner2.action2, actioner3.action3*, and *actioner4.action4*} simultaneously, or to {*actioner4.action4* at the moment and recollections of *actioner1.action1, actioner2.action2, actioner3.action3* at different times}.

Keep in mind that repetition, even recollection, will enhance the memory of an event, i.e., increase the frequencies or change the recency of the event.

12.6 Significance of Attentions

Based on their formations, subconscious, conscious, and associative attentivities usually do not change rapidly over time. This property of attention is called Attention Initia. For this reason, the attention sets are often similar over the attentive time-points t_1, t_2, t_3, and t_4. This stability of the attention set helps Zda (human) to make predictions and discover scientific laws.

The predicted world is not necessarily the same as the actual world. Zda acts based on his predicted world, in which Zda himself may or may not be in his attention set. Zda's default state is that he himself is not in his attention set. The default state is also called the observational state.

Sensory organs are usually sensitive to the change of a source intensity (of light, smell, sound, temperature, etc.). The associated reflexes can be considered as innate mechanisms and enhanced by learning. For example, when an object is flying fast toward you, you could be blinking your eyes or moving away to avoid being hit. Such a reflex is an innate mechanism (demonstrated after a baby develops vision) that will be enhanced by learning. Zda might learn that the faster an object flies, the sooner and harder it can hit him.

What are the practical implications of attention? This will mainly be a part of the topic of Zda's response mechanism, but we outline some obvious implications here and leave details for later discussion.

1. When Zda pays attention to an object (especially a moving object), he will also pay attention to its neighbors in order to predict what is going to happen next so that he can prepare for the action. In theory, motion is relative, object A moving toward object B can be viewed and object B moving toward object A.

2. Zda's attention to object x means he will more likely walk toward x (or its negation: walk away), look at (or look away) x, grasp x (or release it), wave to, throw at, jump on, and talk about x, recall information related to x, or do something with x. Therefore, these should all be elementary Zda abilities or initial action options: Zda. walk(attentive-object), Zda.look(attentive-Object), Zda.actOn(attentive Object), etc.

3. A higher attentiveness to an object means that the agent will check on the object (examine it) more often and in more detail.

4. When an innate concept is in Zda's attention set, the associated action with the concept will often be in his attention set too. For instance, when Zda hears a word (he has already learned), imitation, he will likely perform the imitation because of the associative attentional shift.

5. Because Zda has the ability of grouping similar things into categories, math and science as the concepts of subject fields are just two examples that Zda can learn from grouping and communications with others. Consequently, the subject fields may become Zda's interest and in his attention.

13

Learning Mechanism and Knowledge Discovery

13.1 Overview of Learning Model

The learning mechanisms (Figure 13.1) mainly include hierarchical tokenization and recursive patternization. We recall how we combine words into meaningful phrases, phrases into sentences, sentences into paragraphs, paragraphs into chapters, and chapters into a book. Hierarchical tokenization is like concept-embedment, i.e., using learned concepts (high-level tokens) to replace combinations of tokens, aiming at shortening event-strings for better understanding. Like language grammar, Patternization is the use of rules to describe the structural commonalities among multiple event-strings.

The recurrence of an event-string promotes the formation of a concept for effective thinking while naming a term for the concept makes for effective communication. Of course, natural language and thoughts influence each other, as we have seen.

Desensitization is the grouping of multiple tokens or event-strings into one token based on their similarities. For example, we group meat, bread, and milk into one category, food. Elements in the same category (desensitisor) are called synonyms. Sensitization is the reverse of desensitization, i.e., breaking a group into finer categories. Language-guided Learning and Response is understanding the language and using the relationships between words and actions in one's decision-making.

The factor-isolation technique is an effective method of learning where an agent makes associations between individual attentive objects or items. Curiosity learning is active learning driven by curiosity, which, e.g., would lead to an agent asking intelligent questions. Inductive reasoning is the fundamental method employed by humans in scientific discovery, and works the same way for the AI agent. Induction is realized through desensitization in our HAI architecture.

Whether as humans or agents, we constantly face situations that we've never faced before. Dealing with new things is therefore unavoidable. Similarity learning, which includes imitation and innovation, is an effective way of dealing with novelty. To Zda, imitation is the replacement of the other agent in the event-string (agent.action string) with Zda. Similarly, to Zda, innovation is replacing a portion of the event-string (agent.action string) with a similar string.

Frequency and Reward are important attributes of a pattern. Any pattern will be assigned a token name (equivalent to a concept in natural language) to be used in hierarchical tokenization. The reward associated with a pattern serves as a basis for decision-making. Tokenization and patternization are frequency-based, while the response mechanism is essentially reward-based.

Hierarchical tokenization and recursive patternization are applied to both word-strings in a natural language and event-strings in a perceptual world. Philosophically, the similarity principle and parsimony principle serve as the backbone of learning mechanisms.

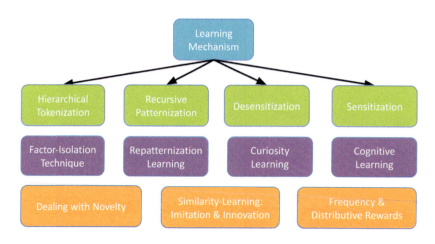

FIGURE 13.1
Overview of the learning mechanisms.

Zda is first interested in one-gramtons, which are single tokens either with reward or high frequencies. After establishing some 1-gramtons, Zda starts to learn 2-gramtons that carry either high frequency or reward. Similarly, 3-gramtons and 4-gramtons then follow.

Knowledge as the outcome of learning includes concept-recognition (what refers to what), pattern-recognition (natural laws, or what repeats after using similarity grouping), language understanding (the relationship between language and observed world or actions), methods of teaching-learning, and ways of responding.

Words can refer to an object, event, action, or an abstract concept. But understanding is mainly learning what refers to what. Such understanding also includes understanding one's intentions or goals. Lia's intention, in Zda's view, is a likely result of Lia's action, and is a future node on the path in Zda's *Knet*. A special set of 2-gramtons is needed to record knowledge of what refers to what.

An agent's response refers to an action (which may be doing nothing) in the external world, while patternization is the updating of his or her internal *Knet*. Generally speaking, patternization will occur as soon as a response is registered, unless there is no time before the next response. Patternization and repatternization can occur as long as an agent is not facing a safety issue requiring his immediate response. Having said that, repatternization always occurs at sleeping, i.e., a routine task scheduled at a certain period during every 24 hours.

Temporality and recency point to an important issue: an (one-time) event is particular and has a time of occurrence and a duration, such as the American Revolutionary War (April 19, 1775–September 3, 1783). The statement "the *United Nations was founded in 1945*" has explicitly indicated the time of the event, but no duration; we call such an event a milestone. The concept, *work gets paid,* has neither starting time nor ending time, but can have the time of the concept acquisition. This concept can be expressed in English as a logical statement: "If you work, then you will get paid." A pattern often involves multiple or recurring events; here there is no unique time of occurrence, but one can mark the time of last occurrence, its recency. "*When did you play tennis last?*" is specifically asking for the recency. An event is an instance of a pattern (class of events). There is event time but no class time. Understanding a particular car is always in the context of its class or desensitisor. This is true for any object or event.

Just as a human only remembers important things with great physical or emotional impact, Zda will only remember the details of things that have very high rewards or penalties at the time. A human can conclude on the importance of a thing after rationalization, but I would argue that at the time he arrives at the conclusion, there is an emotional impact.

13.2 Patternization of Natural Language

Natural language processing (NLP), also known as computational linguistics (CL), is a field of Artificial Intelligence in which we try to process human language as text or speech to make computers similar to humans (see Section G in the Appendix for a tutorial). In NLP, an *n*-gram (Q-gram) is a contiguous sequence of *n* items from a given sample of text or speech. The items can be phonemes, syllables, letters, or words. The *n*-grams typically are collected from a text or speech corpus. When the items are words, *n*-grams may also be called shingles. The *n*-grams can be used for efficient approximate matching. By converting a sequence of items to a set of *n*-grams, it can be embedded in a vector space (see Section G in the Appendix), thus allowing the sequence to be compared to other sequences in an efficient manner.

An *n*-gram model predicts the next token x_i based on the conditional probability

$$P\left(x_i \mid x_{i-1}, x_{i-2}, \ldots, x_{i-n+1}\right),$$

that is, the probability of x_i at time point i, given tokens $x_{i-1}, x_{i-2}, \ldots, x_{i-n+1}$ at the $n-1$ time points.

As the vocabulary of any language is large, it cannot be labeled by humans, and hence we require machine learning techniques that can enable a machine to learn the context of any word on its own. A *k*-skip *n*-gram is a length-n subsequence where the components occur at distance at most *k* from each other. A skip-gram model predicts an earlier token x_{i-k} and a later token x_{i+m} based on the conditional joint probability

$$P\left(x_{i-k}, x_{i+m} \mid x_i\right),$$

that is, the joint probability of x_{i-k} at time point $i-k$ and x_{i+m} at time point $i+m$, given x_i at time point i. A less restrict predictive model is to use two conditional probabilities $P\left(x_{i-k} \mid x_i\right)$ and $P\left(x_{i+m} \mid x_i\right)$. The *n*-gram and skip-gram models can be used for predictions of or suggestions for missing words or information.

As pointed out earlier, contextual understanding is more important than grammar. However, to promote HAI's understanding, we need to determine how to patternize the underlying natural language and how to patternize the event-strings and the relationships between them. Contextual Understanding is a basis for humanized AI. Languages evolve over time. Each HAI agent has his own way to understand any language and improve his comprehension over time.

The patternization of natural language must serve the purpose of getting sensible responses from HAI agents. That is, the two pattern structures of language-strings and event-strings in *Knet* should be chosen so that the relationships between the two types of patterns can be easily found. Grammar only partially use the meaning of the words (e.g., "above," "between," "along"), while *n*-gram and skip-gram models in NLP only work on the language-strings without considering their relationship to real-world events. For this reason, *n*-gram and skip grams cannot solve the problems inherent in contextual understanding.

In our HAI architecture, contextual understanding means correctly mapping tokens and patterns in the *Knet* patterns to the words in the natural language, as discussed in Effective Teaching (Chapter 15).

Here we want Zda to be able to discover the recursive structures or patterns in natural languages himself and do the mapping (contextual understanding) himself.

We can express the sentence,

> *Lia told me that Bob said "if it is not raining, then we can go to the movies."*

in recursive patterns, each pattern consisting of no more than *n* = 4 tokens.

In light of the examples in Section 11.6, Natural Language Structures, we limit the pattern length to a maximum of 4 tokens (f1, f2, f3, f4). Depending on the tokens' arrangement, we identify 4 different types of patterns and their generations as shown in the following table. By recursion, each of f1 through f4 can be an elementary or a high-level token (a sequence of words). The recursion makes the patterns slightly different from *n*-grams, we call them *n*-gramtons instead of *n*-grams, and skiptons instead of skip-grams.

An agent will find that some gramtons are similar. That is, they have the same structure and some common tokens, but also different tokens. In such cases, it is efficient computationally and memory-wise to summarize those similar gramtons into a pattern (pattern structure with associated categories), called a skipton. A skipton is a pattern that has fixors and variables (more precisely, desensitisors). **Fixors** are fixed words, while **desensitisors** are words that are members of categories. A category is a list of word-strings (see, e.g., Table 13.1). In the table, f1 through f4 are invariants, called fixors. Variables d1 and d2,

TABLE 13.1

Linguistic Pattern Types in *Knet*

Pattern Type Name	Pattern	Example	Recursion Form
Gramton			
GT1(f1)	f1	"apple"	
GT2 (f1, f2)	f1 f2	"red apple"	GT2(f1, GT1(f3))
GT3(f1, f2, f3)	f1 f2 f3	"very tall building"	GT2(f1, GT2(f5))
GT4 (f1, f2, f3, f4)	f1 f2 f3 f4	"big green solid table"	GT2(GT3(f1, f2, f3), f4)
Skipton			
ST1(d1, f1)	d1 f1	f1 = "walk", d1 ∈ {"they", "we", "you"}	
ST2(f2, d2)	f2 d2	F2 = "hold", d2 ∈ {"red pen", "pencil"}	
ST3(d1, f1, d2)	d1 f1 d2	"... as soon as..." "... if ..."	
ST4(f1, d1, f2)	f1, d1, f2	"Pick ... up"	
ST5(f1, d1, f2, d2)	f1 d1 f2 d2	"if ..., then ..." "neither... nor..."	
ST6(d1, f1, d2, f2)	d1 f1 d2 f2		

called desensitisors, are members of categories and d1 and d2 are paired. By recursion, fixors and desensitisors can be elementary (single words) or high-level tokens (phrases or sentences). The symbol ∈ means "belongs to."

In our HAI architecture, agents use short but recursive *n*-gramtons and skiptons instead of the long *n*-grams and skip-grams (over 100 tokens long) used in NLP. We also adopt recursion, due to the consideration that our approach starts with a small (virtually zero) instead of a big data. Each *n*-gramton and skipton can have an associated reward and recency in addition to frequency.

The patterns with up to 4 tokens in Table 13.1 cover basic sentence patterns discussed in Section 11.6 The patterns also cover the eight PoS (parts of speech) in English. For most languages the 4-token patterns should work well; in rare cases, *n*-token patterns might be more effective ($n > 4$).

The fixors in skiptons could be adpositions in English. As discussed in Section 11.6, the relations expressed by adpositions may be spatial (denoting location or direction such as in, under, toward, before) or temporal (denoting position in time, starting, ending, or duration), or may express comparison, content, agent, instrument, means, manner, cause, purpose, reference, etc. (such as "of" and "for"). In other words, an adposition expresses a relation between objects in what an agent directly sensed attributes such as distance, speed, relative position, loudness, color, and size (Table 13.2). An adposition typically combines with a noun phrase, this being called its complement or sometimes object.

In principle, a skipton can be equivalently, but memory-wise inefficiently, presented by multiple gramtons (grams).

It is not necessary for Zda to know such English grammar. Instead, "understanding" the language comes through the association between what he hears and what his other sensory organs perceive at the moment. For instance, if Zda hears "green" while he sees green, then he will make an association between the word "green" and green, the color. The Effective Teaching section will discuss such associations in great detail.

A fixor can also be a conjunction in English. A conjunction connects words, phrases, or clauses, which are called the conjuncts of the conjunctions. Sentences with conjunctions can be dealt with using Zda's innate knowledge of objects such as logical operators (∨ for logical OR, ∧ for logical AND, → and ← for implication), temporal relationships (↔ and ↭), or comparisons (≈ for similar, ≽ and ≼ for preference) as illustrated by the examples in Table 13.3.

TABLE 13.2

Relationships Indicated by Adpositions

Adposition	Indicated Relationship
As an adjunct to a noun:	
• "the weather **in** March"	[environment] [**in**] [time]
• "cheese **from** France **with** live bacteria"	[obj] [**from**] [place] [**with**] [obj]
As a predicative expression:	
• "The key is **under** the stone."	[obj] [**under**] [obj]
As an adjunct to a verb:	
• "sleep **throughout** the winter"	[action] [**throughout**] [time]
• "danced **atop** the tables **for** hours"	[action] [**atop**] [obj] [**for**] [time]
As an adjunct to an adjective:	
• "happy **for** them"	[feeling] [**for**] [people]
• "sick **until** recently"	[status] [**until**] [time]

TABLE 13.3

Logical Relationships Indicated by Conjunctions

Sentence with Conjunction	Logic
He spent $10K buying a robot because he loves AI research.	$A \leftarrow B$
They gamble and they smoke.	$A \wedge B$
They do not gamble, nor do they smoke.	$\neg A \wedge \neg B$
They gamble, but they don't smoke.	$A \wedge \neg B$
Every day they gamble or they smoke.	$A \vee B$
You either do your work or prepare for a trip to the office.	$A \vee B$
He is not only handsome but also brilliant.	$A \wedge B$
You must decide whether you stay or you go.	$A \vee B$
Just as Americans love basketball, Canadians love ice hockey.	$A \approx B$
Football is as fast as hockey.	$A \approx B$
I would rather swim than surf.	$A \geqslant B$
We'll do that after you do this.	$A \Leftarrow B$
That's fine as long as you agree to our conditions.	$A \Leftarrow B$
We'll get to that as soon as we finish this.	$A \Leftarrow B$
He had left by the time you arrived.	$A \Rightarrow B$
There is a good chance of rain whenever there are clouds.	$A \Leftarrow B$

As an illustration, "He spent $10K buying a robot **because** he loves AI research." indicates a logic: B (he loves AI research) is a cause of A (He spent $10K buying a robot), denoted by A←B in the table. However, that his interest in AI research leads him to buy an expensive robot does not mean that everyone interested in AI will do the same.

Because Zda does not have built-in natural language, such language-to-logic mapping does exist initially in Zda's head. Instead, the mapping is gradually established through learning. Briefly, this is how it works: logical relationships are the agent's inherited concepts (knowledge), and are constantly in his attention set. Thus, the key is to map the inherited concepts to different sentence structures at the time Zda hears. This temporal closeness between the two attentive things (logic concepts and sentence structures) makes Zda establish the **association** between them via an adaptive reinforcement approach. Learning is primarily establishing **associations** between different things.

We can effectively teach Zda the patterns using a factor-isolation technique (FIT). However, language patternization solely based on language itself produces nothing but grammar. To contextually understand a language, Zda must be engaged in an environment where communication and interaction among community members occur at the same time.

A key idea in our HAI architecture for learning and responding is to view both sentence-structure and event-patterns (action-rules) as functions or methods in OOP. From this notion, agents can use FIT to map sentence-structures to event-patterns, and parameters will be matched with each other too, instead of exhaustively mapping each sentence to each particular action or event. The language-patterns, action-patterns (event-patterns), and mappings between them are automatically constructed using hierarchical tokenization and recursive patternization.

From a human development perspective, language is a necessary outcome of communication and our social lives. However, the form of a particular language such as English or Chinese is more likely initially due to the randomness in nature. Such randomness is also featured in the virtual environment and the adaptive response mechanism for HAI.

In some natural languages, the same word can represent a concept or a particular instance at different times. The listener judges the meaning by the context. The difference between a concept and an instance can be illustrated in the following example in English: we can say *"the weight of an apple or the apple,"* but we don't say *"the weight of apple."* However, when we describe a particular object we have to use a concept. For example, the description of "the green apple" has used the concepts of green and apple. Whether it is an apple or the apple, Zda has to understand it in context since some languages do not have the equivalent words of "a" and "the."

Everyone has his perspective or understanding of a concept, even though the concept might be thought to be a common or shared understanding. It gives us such conflicting feelings. For, on one hand, individual instances are the basis for, and thus come before, the formulation of the corresponding concept; on the other hand, the concept is the basis for describing an individual instance.

As in our earlier discussion, human-machine interactions are two-way influences: humans and HAI learn from each other and influence each other. Humans can shift their language conventions so that HAI can understand better. In fact, we have already seen how AI-enabled applications change our shopping and other behaviors.

13.3 Patternization and Recursive Patternization

Beyond natural language grammar, a pattern can be a scientific law, a social norm, or some other rule. A natural law does not have to be expressed in natural mathematical language and taught by someone, it can be something new, found by Zda himself. However, for the purpose of communication, some language to express the law should have certain rules as pertained in a natural language.

Tokenization is the replacement of tokens in the target event-string with matched known pattern names in the *Knet*, with the aim of shortening the target string (fewer high-level tokens), while patternization is the discovery (often after tokenization) of new patterns through comparisons across multiple target event-strings (within an onsite event-string set or in the *Knet*). The discovered patterns are recorded in memory with associated frequency, recency, and rewards, if any. When a pattern is formulated through hierarchical tokenization and recursive patternization, it has implicitly considered the effect of the time when the concepts were acquired, i.e., when the patterns were formulated.

The brain not only receives information but also interprets and patterns it. How does Zda perform patternization? A common approach is to use the Factor-Isolation Technique (FIT): Given a set of event sequences, in which most parts are the same, but a small (isolated) part is different, we will record these event sequences in a compact form, that is, pattern structure and an associated category (or categories). A category is a list of different items. A category is also considered as a concept.

Here is an example: I eat apples; I eat rice; I eat cake. These three events can lead Zda to formulate a concept for the collection of {apple, rice, cake}, which may be labeled as "food" in English and "食物" in Chinese. Now we can think and express the eating of our three things in a pattern: I eat food; food = desensitisor of category {apple, rice, cake}. Note that "food" is a concept, "I eat food" is another concept.

The patternization reduces memory storage (9 words to store for the three sentences without patternization and 6 words to store with it: 3 words for the pattern and 3 words for foods).

In general, patternization is looking into (structural) commonality across different event-strings and putting the variable part as a desensitisor. A desensitisor is a member of the corresponding category. The sense of "Desensitisor" is that sensory organs are made less sensitive to objects. Some examples are as follows.

Zda read a math book.

Zda read a science book.

Zda read a storybook.

From these three events (not sentences), we can discover a pattern:

Zda read a book.

Here the concept of "book" is a collection of math books, science books, and storybooks. The desensitisor "book" is insensitive to the small differences among the different books. Every concept such as "book" is abstract; only an instance of a category, such as a particular physical book, is concrete. "Read" can be a concept since it includes fast and slow reading, etc. Although a concept and pattern both can be the collection of similar things, a concept emphasizes its meaning, not how it's expressed or stored in memory, while a pattern often emphasizes its underlying structure by separating common (invariable) and variable parts.

The third example of using the Factor-Isolation Technique to separate the fixed part and variable part:

Bod.give(a pen) Lia.take(the pen).

Bod.say("give me a pen") Lia.give(a pen).

The fixed part of the pattern can be viewed as a math function and the variable part is viewed as independent variables of the function. In this sense, pattern is a math function or a function in computer programming.

Sometimes, we need to differentiate a particular object from an object type, as appearing in the following forms:

Bob.act(objA) Lia.act(objA)

Bob.act(objA) Lia.act(typeA)

Bob.act(typeA) Lia.act(objA)

Bob.act(typeA) Lia.act(typeA)

Here variable objA refers to a particular object of type A, while typeA is any object of type A. If objA = the green pen, then typeA = a green pen or even a pen. If objA = the book, then typeA = a book. Thus there is a pairing relationship between the variable in Bob's action and the variable in Lia's action. In fact, objA is a desensitisor of type A.

The fourth example will also use the Factor-Isolation Technique:

When Bob says: "go left", Lia goes left.

When Bob says: "go right", Lia goes right.

If Zda repeatedly sees these event sequences, he may discover the pattern:

  Bob.say(GT1) Lia.act(GT2)

If Lia follows Bob's instruction, then GT1 = {"go left," "go right"} and GT2 = {goes left, goes right} are paired, i.e., the *i*th element of GT1 associates the *i*th element in GT2. However, Lia does not have to follow Bob's instruction, and thus GT1 and GT2 may not be paired. However, rewards or penalties can be used to shape Lia's behavior in this case. This is an example of Language-guided action. The key is the mapping between the language structure and event-string patterns, including parameters (variables), which will be discussed in later sections.

A fundamental idea of a pattern is a similarity group, denoted by PT0(E0) = E0, where E0 is a collection of similar things, such as *Lia.run()* = {*Lia.run(slow)*, *Lia.run(fast)*}, and food = {bread, meat, sandwich}. Here *Lia.run()* is treated as one token, as is food. Treating *Lia. run(slow)* and *Lia.run(fast)* uniformly as *Lia.run()* can be considered as desensitization or similarity grouping.

In general, a pattern requires recurrences, which are either recurrences of the same event-string, the sameness being due to the insensitivities of sensory organs, or are created through a desensitisor via similarity grouping. A desensitisor is a member of a collection (class) of similar objects or items.

We now discuss other types of event patterns. Assume Zda can pay attention to as many as $n = 4$ objects or tokens at any given time. The number n can increase as Zda's age increases. Zda will perform patternization based on only up to 4 tokens, E1, E2, E3, and E4, which are the top 4 most attentive elementary tokens among the 16 tokens at 4 time points, as shown in Figure 13.2. Among the 4 tokens, the attentivity of the least attentive token must be larger than half of the maximum attentivity of the most attentive token. If there is a rewarding token, it must be the last token.

The sequence of tokens can be events in real time (or short-term memory) or events that happened a moment ago or a long time ago, recollected from Zda's memory. Of course, the recollections are different from the real-time events. For example, a recollection of a car accident is different from the actual car accident. The latter can cause a death but the former would not cause a death.

Squares represent actions by the same or different Actors

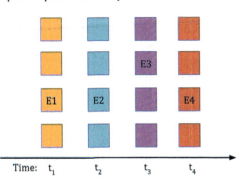

Time: t_1 t_2 t_3 t_4

FIGURE 13.2
Subconscious attentions sets at a sequence of times.

The square elements in the figure represent subconscious attentive events (in the form of actioner.action or object.event) at a sequence of times. The general form of the attentive gramtons is $E1 \otimes E2 \otimes E3 \otimes E4$, where $\otimes$ is either $\wedge$ (occur concurrently) or $\Rightarrow$ (occurs sequentially) with the default precedence of $\wedge$ and then $\Rightarrow$. The events (E1 through E4) can be actions or something (e.g., smell or color) changing. Without loss of generality, we assume E1 happens no later than E2, E2 no later than E3, and E3 not later than E4. In addition, when occurring at the same time, E1, E2, E3, and E4 will be sorted alphabetically by their names. In other words, E1, E2, E3, and E4 are first sorted by time of occurrence and then alphabetically.

Given N = 1 to 4 tokens in Zda's attention at up to 4 time points, the following lists all 15 possible patterns (gramtons) by one-dimensional text strings.

- PT1(E1) $\triangle$ E1
- PT2(E1, E2) $\triangle$ E1 $\wedge$ E2
- PT3(E1, E2) $\triangle$ E1 $\Rightarrow$ E2
- PT4(E1, E2, E3) $\triangle$ E1 $\wedge$ E2 $\wedge$ E3
- PT5(E1, E2, E3) $\triangle$ E1 $\wedge$ E2 $\Rightarrow$ E3
- PT6(E1, E2, E3) $\triangle$ E1 $\Rightarrow$ E2 $\wedge$ E3
- PT7(E1, E2, E3) $\triangle$ E1 $\Rightarrow$ E2 $\Rightarrow$ E3.
- PT8(E1, E2, E3, E4) $\triangle$ E1 $\wedge$ E2 $\wedge$ E3 $\wedge$ E4
- PT9(E1, E2, E3, E4) $\triangle$ E1 $\wedge$ E2 $\wedge$ E3 $\Rightarrow$ E4
- PT10(E1, E2, E3, E4) $\triangle$ E1 $\wedge$ E2 $\Rightarrow$ E3 $\wedge$ E4
- PT11(E1, E2, E3, E4) $\triangle$ E1 $\Rightarrow$ E2 $\wedge$ E3 $\wedge$ E4
- PT12(E1, E2, E3, E4) $\triangle$ E1 $\wedge$ E2 $\Rightarrow$ E3 $\Rightarrow$ E4
- PT13(E1, E2, E3, E4) $\triangle$ E1 $\Rightarrow$ E2 $\wedge$ E3 $\Rightarrow$ E4
- PT14(E1, E2, E3, E4) $\triangle$ E1 $\Rightarrow$ E2 $\Rightarrow$ E3 $\wedge$ E4
- PT15(E1, E2, E3, E4) $\triangle$ E1 $\Rightarrow$ E2 $\Rightarrow$ E3 $\Rightarrow$ E4.

Here E1, E2, E3, and E4 can be elementary or high-level tokens, and the symbol $\triangle$ means "is defined as." When Zda sees E1 and E2 happen at the same time (within the same time interval), he will code this as PT1(E1, E2) in his brain or *Knet*. The rest are coded in similar ways without needing further explanations.

In addition to parallel and sequential events, there may be some events that appear to be nested, e.g., *Zda.saw(Lia.took(textbook))*. However, the nested structures have been taken care of in hierarchical tokenization or recursive patternization, and the two events in the example are actually parallel events that happened at the same time, even though they appear to be nested in the coding or in a natural language.

As mentioned, a member of such a category is called a Desensitisor. For instance, Token E8 $\in$ {PT2(E1, E3), PT3(E1, E2), PT5(E5, E2, E3)} is a Desensitisor when it is used in a pattern. We call the grouping process desensitization. Conversely, the process of breaking one group (token) into detailed subgroups (subtokens) for more precise matching or better prediction is called sensitization. A desensitisor is often created by applying the factor-isolation technique to multiple event-strings. For elementary tokens E1 through E4, the desensitisors can often be formed by grouping the parameters in the elementary tokens into categories.

In the 15 patterns, we also allow the negation of a token, e.g., PT2(¬E1, E2) means E2 occurs, but E1 does not occur, while PT1(E2) simply means E2 occurs and E1 may or may not occur. ¬E1 is considered an event different from E1. In other words, E1 through E4 can represent negations of events.

If we did not sort E1, E2, E3, and E4 by time of occurrence and then alphabetically in recursive patterns, we will have many equivalent forms or identities of gramtons through permutations of parallel events in the pattern and recursion:

- PT2(E1, E2) = PT2(E2, E1)
- PT4(E1, E2, E3) = PT4(E1, E3, E2) = PT4(E2, E1, E3) = PT4(E2, E3, E1) = PT4(E3, E1, E2) = PT4(E3, E2, E1) = PT2(PT2(E1, E2), E3) =PT2(E3, PT2(E1, E2)) = PT2(E1, PT2(E2, E3)) = PT2(PT2(E2, E3), E1) = PT2(E2, PT2(E1, E3)) = PT2(PT2(E1, E3), E3)
- PT5(E1, E2, E3) = PT5(E2, E1, E3) = PT3(PT2(E1, E2), E3) = PT3(PT2(E2, E1), E3)
- PT6(E1, E2, E3) = PT6(E1, E3, E2) = PT3(E1, PT2(E2, E3)) = PT3(E1, PT2(E3, E2))
- PT8(E1, E2, E3, E4) = PT8(permutation of (E1, E2, E3, E4)) = ….
- PT9(E1, E2, E3, E4) = PT9(permutation of (E1, E2, E3), E4) = ….
- PT10(E1, E2, E3, E4) = PT10(E2, E1, E3, E4) = PT10(E1, E2, E4, E3) = ….
- PT11(E1, E2, E3, E4) = PT11(E1, permutation of (E2, E3, E4) = …
- PT12(E1, E2, E3, E4) = PT12(E2, E1, E3, E4) = PT7(PT2(E1, E2), E3, E4) = PT7(PT2(E2, E3), E3, E4) = ….
- PT13(E1, E2, E3, E4) = PT13(E1, E3, E2, E4) = PT2(PT2(E1, E2), PT2(E3, E4)) = PT2(PT2(E1, E2), PT2(E4, E3)) = PT2(PT2(E2, E1), PT2(E3, E4)) = …. = PT2(PT2(E2, E1), PT2(E4, E3)) = …. PT14(E1, E2, E3, E4) = PT14(E1, E2, E4, E3) = ….

These identities may be useful in deep-thinking mode and repatternization (see later sections) when tokens are not sorted by time and alphabetically.

The default forms of gramtons meet the following three criteria:

1. With the least number of recursions,
2. E1, E2, E3, and E4 occur chronologically,
3. E1, E2, E3, and E4 are sorted alphabetically based on their names.

As shown above, there are many possible recursive patternizations, such as PT1(PT1(E1, E2), PT5(E1, E2, E3)). The graphical representation of the recursion is fractals. The best way to patternize is to sort the included tokens by the time of occurrence and then alphabetically so that the resulting gramtons are always in their default forms. This way, we can easily calculate their frequency and improve computational efficiency.

With gramtons PT1 through PT15 and their recursions, Zda maps the multidimensional reality in his attention set to one-dimensional text string segments, just as humans describe the world using a natural language. The significant features of this mapping are: (1) patternization of the real world becomes the patternization of text strings in Zda's brain or construction of *Knet*, (2) the hierarchical tokenization and recursive patternization simplify knowledge discovery, and (3) mapping language structures to gramtons (including associated parameters) and further mapping to reality make it possible for Zda to understand language, share and inherit knowledge, advance sciences and technologies, and behave virtually like a human being.

To reiterate, a concept refers to a collection of similar things, e.g., food = E1 = {bread, rice, meat, ...}. A pattern is a structural arrangement of elements from one or more collections. A concept emphasizes the meaning or the collectiveness, while a pattern emphasizes its structure. PT3(E1, E2) is a pattern indicating an arrangement of their elements, that is, E1 $\Rightarrow$ E2.

As discussed, patternization can improve efficiency. We can store, e.g., PT3(A, b1, B), PT3(A, b2, B), through PT3(A, b1000, B) in Zda's *Knet*, but it will be very inefficient memory-wise and computationally. Instead, we can store PT3(A, B, C) and B = {b1, b2, ..., b100}. This will reduce approximately 66% memory space and increase computation efficiency.

In recursive patternization, an important thing to remember is that Zda always performs language patternization first, before he patternizes the whole event-string with nested linguistic strings.

In general patternization, we deal with three types of events on the time-axis: (1) events at the moment, (2) events in short-term memory (previous event-frame) with details including time-stamps, and (3) events in long-term memory, which Zda can pay attention to through associations or recollections. All events have an associated starting time and ending time (recency). A pattern has recency. The recency for an event where baseball is played and the recency for the concept of *Zda.playing(baseball)* are usually different. "Working towards a bachelor degree" is a concept or pattern, and thus there are no starting and stopping times (though Zda may retain the time associated with the construction of the concept), but *Zda. act* (working toward a Bachelor Degree) is an action (event) with a starting and stopping time. An event may have the same starting and stopping time; such an event will be called a milestone or state, and may depend on how finely Zda measures time. But for most of us, receiving a bachelor's degree would be a milestone.

Any sequence of tokens can be used for multiple patternization. For instance, Lia eating a particular apple is interpreted as "Lia eats an apple" instead of as the particular apple eaten. This is because Lia's apple (as any other thing) is changing constantly, and the action may also be further interpreted as "she is hungry" and/or "she is enjoying eating." These three interpretations are examples of multiple interpretations of a single event. In principle, there are no pure observations, any observation has to be interpreted and patternized by the individual observer, but some interpretations are more certain (e.g., "eating an apple"—perception) than others (e.g., "enjoying eating"—apperception). Any interpretation of an actioner's intention or his thinking is more uncertain than the physical action itself.

We now should see the differences between tokenization and patternization. Tokenization is an operation executed within a string and using known concepts (tokens) in *Knet* to divide the string into meaningful units, while patternization is an operation performed across multiple event-strings (perhaps broken off from a long string). Tokenization is the use of existing concepts (patterns) to simplify or shorten an event-string, while patternization is often what occurs when multiple strings are summarized into one pattern that could be new or might already exist in Zda's *Knet*.

Patternization as a characterization of causal relationships will follow the Parsimony Principle. That is, for a given population, if factors *A* and *B* lead to outcome *C* and if factor *A* alone also leads to outcome *C*, then the pattern (scientific law) would be: factor *A* predicts outcome *C*.

Tokenization and patternization go hand in hand: any pattern is treated as a token for the next level of patternization. Each agent has his own perceptual world, without this constantly changing perceptual world he will never be able to learn. Practically, patternization may start a pattern with a frequency of one. In other words, an event-string can be a special case of a pattern. Patterns in Zda's brain (memory) are naturally sorted by time of occurrence, with the most recent event at the top. Recollection will re-sort patterns based on the time of recalling the event (pattern) instead of the real moment in time when the event happens.

In this section, we discussed frequency-based patternization. In Chapter 14, we will discuss reward-based patternization.

13.4 Repatternization

We humans use part of our day—the time of sleep and dreams—to repatternize our brains, and so does Zda. Such repatternization is necessary for the more efficient retrieval of knowledge already acquired and for the discovery of new patterns, new knowledge. Repatternization is obviously rooted in the Parsimony Principle discussed in Part I.

In **Onsite Patternization** (patternization as events occur), Zda mainly uses desensitisors from grouping objects or action parameters into discrete categories to make patterns. Desensitisors are also generated for onsite patternization by comparing multiple event-strings using the factor isolation technique. The small set of multiple event-strings for onsite patternization are observed in real time. However, there are many experiences and patterns, generated a long time ago, stored in Zda's *Knet*. Systematically looking into all the knowledge or patterns in *Knet* and further refining the patterns or discovering new patterns is the job of repatternization.

When Zda dreams (at "sleep mode"), repatternization begins. Some patterns might be stored in multiple memory locations or in different database tables where patterns are sorted by frequency, patternive reward, or recency for computational efficiency in learning and response.

Repatternization is a way to achieve pattern reduction without too much information loss. For instance, the three patterns: I like to read storybooks, I like to read science books, and I like to read technique books, can be repatternized (simplified) into one pattern: *I like to read BOOK*. Here, desensitisor, *BOOK* (not "a book" in English) is a desensitisor of books = {storybooks, science books, technique books}.

Similarly, in a natural language (e.g., English), we can repatternize the following three patterns,

"I like to read storybooks."

"I like to read science books."

"I like to read technique books."

into one pattern (sentence): "I like to read books." Here books = {"*storybooks*", "*science books*", "*technique books*"}.

In patternization, similarity grouping often depends on the perspective of the observer: E1 (walk 5 steps) and E2 (walk 100 steps) may not be considered as similar from a distance perspective, but in certain situations, they both may indicate "walk close to the target," and therefore they can be considered the same or similar in terms of "getting close to the target." If you are interested in similarity-based machine learning in narrow AI, please read the appendix for an introduction, and the works by Chang (2020) and Hwang and Chang (2022).

For language patternization, Zda will include Gramtons GT1 through GT4 and Skiptons ST1 through ST6 discussed in the last section.

We should know that the fixor in a skipton is actually a desensitisor since, e.g., in the skipton

"if ..., then ..."

"if" and "then" can involve many different ways of writing, fonts, or different accents, but we believe the same meaning despite the differences in writing and pronunciation. Likewise, for an event-pattern, a fixor can also be a desensitizor,

Since most patterns consist of no more than 4 (high-level) tokens, the repatternization will focus on the following event patterns, where tokens such as E1 and E2 without variables are considered as fixors.

- Nine 2-gramton patterns:
  - E1 E2(objA), E1 E2(typeA), E1 E2
  - E1(objA) E2(objA), E1(objA) E2(typeA), E1(objA) E2
  - E1(typeA) E2(objA), E1(typeA) E2(typeA), E1(typeA) E2,
- Similar for 3-gramton and 3-gramton patterns, there are 3×3×3 = 27 combinations of objA and typeA at the three different locations.
- For a 4-gramton, there are 3×3×3×3 = 81 different combinations of null, object, and type at the four different locations.

As mentioned earlier, given an object or event, what Zda observes is subjective and how he classifies it depends on his interpretation. For instance, when Zda sees Lia picking a green pen among several colored pens, he can interpret it as Lia picking a pen, a green pen, or the pen, or a lad picking a green pen, etc. Thus, it might be wise to use a default value of "an object" instead of "the object," since "an" is more general than "the" and it is likely the case that "the object" is the only object that is in Zda's attention; i.e., an object = the object.

In general, a 2-gramton has the form of E1(desensitisor A) E2(desensitisor B). The key in variables is "pairing" between the desensitisors A and B. Therefore, pattern refinement will record a pattern structure and the associated variable pairing, tripling, and quadrupling.

It might be efficient not to explore all the possible n-gramtons, but use a stepwise approach: identify one or two variables each time across patterns under investigation in terms of the factor-isolation technique.

Different Skiptons are presented in Table 13.4. Here, symbols * and # in the same pattern represent paired tokens or desensitisors. The pairing can be between an object (event) and

TABLE 13.4

Selected Skiptons with Parameters

2-Token Pattern	3-Token Pattern	4-Token Pattern
E1 E2(*)	E1 E2(*) E3	E1 E2 E3 E4(*)
E1(*) E2	E1 E2(*) E3	E1 E2 E3(*) E4
E1(*) E2(#)	E1(*) E2 E3	E1 E2(*) E3 E4
	E1 E2(*) E3(#)	E1(*) E2 E3 E4
	E1(*) E2 E3(#)	E1(*) E2 E3 E4

a desensitisor, or between an object (event, procedure) and its name. Most function parameters have a range and can be considered as desensitisors.

We are particularly interested in the relationship between word-pattern (WP) and corresponding action pattern (AP). In a WP there are words (W) that are considered to be desensitisors. We denote the pattern by the function form of WP(W). Similarly, in an AP there are actions (A) or objects (O) that are considered desensitisors. We denote the pattern by AP(O). In the mixed pattern: WP(W) AP(O), we derive the 2-gramton of a refer-to pattern: W O. Here O is the object that the words W refers to. We elaborate with the following examples in the OOP-like syntax:

Lia.say("pick pen") Zda.pick(pen)
Lia.say("pick pencil") Zda.pick(pencil)

Here, the desensitisor W from {"pen," "pencil"} and the desensitisor O from {pen, pencil} form the paired 2-gramton refer-to pattern. This approach can be applied to the mixed patterns with more than 2-tokens. The * and # within a pattern in Table 13.4 can indicate such a refer-to relationship. When such words-to-action mapping or refer-to pattern is established in Zda's *Knet*, we say that he understands the words.

Similarly, the word-action mixed pattern WP(W) AP(A) can be established from the following example through repatternization:

Lia.say("pick apple") Zda.pick(apple)
Lia.say("eat apple") Zda.eat(apple)

The refer-to (paired desensitisors) to be established is W and A, where W from {"pick," "eat"} and A from {pick, eat}.

13.5 Segmentation of Event Strings for Patternization

Onsite patternization is a real-time patternization based on a small collection of event-strings during a very short time interval. For instance, Zda catches a human typing several sentences in order to teach Zda grammar, and Zda will utilize onsite patternization for pattern discovery.

How to determine the beginning and end of the event-string for patternization? For onsite patternization, a maximum of 4 elementary tokens are involved. A long idle time, a carriage return, and a reward can be considered as a marker of the beginning or end of a string segment for patternization.

The string *agent.reward()* is usually treated as the ending token for one pattern and the beginning token for another, so that patterns can link together to formulate a longer pattern in the *Knet*. In general, the last token of the previous pattern should be the first token of the current pattern.

After first round patternization occurs, the recursion occurs for the second and third round tokenization and patternization. Tokenization is a continuous process. It continues as long as there are repeated events with a frequency larger than the minimum frequency required for tokenization/patternization and the number of pattern recursions has reached the maximum number of recursions allowed. Therefore, patternization has virtually no beginning and no end.

Since all event-patterns have associated times, forming a sequence of patterns over time, Zda can repeatedly patternize the sequence of string segments, i.e., Zda may apply recursive patternization. For concept-patterns without associated recency, the associated frequency and distributive reward can be used for repatternization.

Finally, each pattern often has an associated cost and distributed reward to Zda. These are important parameters because they will be used to determine Zda's action with a randomized adaptive response-mechanism. This topic will be discussed later.

13.6 Dealing with Novelty and Similarity-Based Learning

Finding a way to deal with new things is an unavoidable challenge in patternization and response mechanisms. As an agent grows, he will have to face many situations he has not experienced before. In this section, we just consider how to deal with novelties in learning or patternization. In a subsequent section examining response mechanisms, we will discuss how to deal with novelties in response.

Patternization is mainly self-learning based on experiences, but it can also be taught. When facing novelties, the similarity principle has to be used. In our HAI architecture, hierarchical similarities will be used, such as actioner-similarity, action-similarity, similarity of the target objects, attribute-similarity, as well as other types.

It is interesting to know that similarity involves circular definitions. If two entities are similar, then replacing one with the other in an actioner.action string will lead to a similar outcome. But, conversely, if the replacement leads to a similar outcome, then we consider the two entities to be similar. By making this replacement and comparing the resulting outcome against the original outcome, Zda can find when two entities are similar and when they are not. Indeed, we are constantly involved in circular definitions, as discussed in Part I, the Connotation of Understanding. However, we use the circular definition alternatively, and iteratively to make our understanding of the world.

Novelty can also occur due to missing or incomplete information. We are constantly filling in gaps between two frames of reality, just as we do in watching motion pictures. We will do the same thing when there are missing words. For natural language, the issue of misused or missing words can be handled using n-grams and skip grams in NLP. Similarly, missing critical events can be predicted using smoothing techniques borrowed directly from the field of cybernetics. In our HAI architecture, novelties due to missing information can be directly handled using similarity scores, such as cosine similarity, Jaccard indices, and hierarchical similarities. These will be described in Section 14.9.

In our humanized AI architecture, missing information does not have to be explicitly determined all the time. Instead, Zda uses the similarity principle to determine the similarity between the incomplete event-string and strings in his *Knet*, and then determines the patterns with consideration of other factors such as reward, cost, and recency.

To reduce the issues of missing events and confounders in Zda's observations when he performs patternization or knowledge discovery, Zda needs (like us) to obtain observations from others and to perform well-designed experiments.

Learning mainly involves patternization, and a question naturally arises regarding it. Given an event-string, how does one identify the relationships within/between different objects' properties and behaviors, the relationships between different subjects' behaviors, and the relationships between an actioner's words and his or other actioners' words and behaviors? The number of an object's states (postures, smallness, tastes, facial expressions, tactile qualia, and temperatures) is limited and relatively stable over time, but the words that a human or Zda uses are rich and change constantly. Therefore, it is efficient to (1) learn what simple words refer to object's attributes, actions and simple word-patternization, and then (2) learn the relationships between verbal-verbal, verbal-action, and action-action of different actioners.

To be specific, the agent's learning in the presence of novelties is to either use a known desensitisor or create a new one, or else propose a hypothetical pattern based on similarity to see the outcome (reward), and then determine if the patternization or "referring to" is appropriate. The similarity discussions will be presented in Section 14.9.

Suppose Zda observes two similar events, one at an earlier time and the other is new:

Bob.pick(green pen)

Bob.pick(red pen)

Zda can use an existing or newly created desensitisor: pen = {green pen, red pen) to make a pattern: Bob.pick(pen) with associated desensitisor, pen. This is the main approach Zda has in dealing with patternization in learning. In a more complex case, Zda will use reward to see if he can group the multiple event-strings into a pattern. In other words, learning and response go hand-in-hand. You see, we have already discussed dealing with novelties in earlier sections about desensitisors.

In addition to novelty, Zda also needs to deal with the fuzziness of a concept or instruction. Fuzziness is a concept that appears similar but different from the concept of similarity. Closeness, goodness, highness, hardness, and difficulty, are examples of fuzzy concepts. However, it is clear that the fuzziness is due to similarities. In principle, all concepts are fuzzy; i.e., a collective impression of similar things. In our HAI architecture, a fuzzy concept can be implemented by adding a randomness to the parameter in the definition of the concept.

13.7 Cognitive Learning—Logic Reasoning with Probability

Cognitive learning (CL) is another kind of learning that involves mental processes, such as attention and memory. CL does not necessarily involve any external rewards or require a person to perform any observable behaviors. Learning through thinking or logical reasoning is an example of cognitive learning. Organisms can learn in the absence of reinforcement, such as through incidental learning or unplanned or unintended learning. For this reason, CL usually cannot be explained directly on the basis of reinforcing conditions. In this sense, repatternization including logical reasoning is a main form of cognitive learning. However, CL can be indirectly explained by adaptive reinforcement learning when a reward is used in repatternization (Section 14.10).

Before we discuss logical reasoning, it is helpful to discuss the concept of Negation. Everything and its opposite side (negation) have to coexist; without recognizing the existence of one, we will not be able to detect the existence of the other. In philosophy, the unity of opposites is the central category of dialectics (McGill and Parry, 1948). It defines a situation in which the existence or identity of a thing (or situation) depends on the co-existence of at least two conditions, which are opposite to each other, yet dependent on and presupposing each other. Sound versus silence, positive versus non-positive (or negative) are pairs of opposites. Without silence, we cannot hear anything. If it rains all the time, we wouldn't have a concept of rain. If Zda has the concept of a fair A, then he will also have the concept of the opposite side of A. For example, if Zda sees that it is raining, he must also see the situation "not raining" before he recognizes rain. The situation Zda sees may be a specific case of not-raining, not the complete set of negation of raining. As we have discussed earlier, no two things are identical in the world at any time. Therefore, the formulation of the concept of "raining" and "not raining" (or any other concepts) are personalized and are modified during interactions and communications between entities.

However, the notion of the coexistence of the two sides of anything does not exist without challenges. How do we completely understand the existence of the world if it is impossible for us to see its non-existence (including ourselves)?

Another fundamental concept in logic is the Law of Excluded Middle, which asserts that between A and the negation of A, one and only one is true. However, this self-evident law can be challenged by the Paradox of Schrödinger's Cat or the following the Doctor-Patient Paradox.

The Doctor-Patient Paradox (Chang, 2012) is another example that can impair deductive reasoning: if a doctor tells his patient that he will recover soon or he will recover very slowly, the doctor can be always right, because his statement might affect the speed of the patient's recovery; thus the law of the excluded middle in deduction does not always work. Both *A* and the negation of *A* are correct at the same time.

We believe that we have knowledge of facts extending far beyond those we directly perceive. The scope of our senses is severely limited in space and time; our immediate perceptual knowledge does not reach to events that happened before we were born or to events that are happening now in certain other places or any future events (Salmon, 1967). Therefore, not all our knowledge comes from observations, some is derived from logical reasoning.

Reasoning is the ability to assess things rationally by applying logic based on new or existing information when making a decision or solving a problem. There are three basic types of reasoning methods, Induction, Deduction, and Abduction.

Induction involves reasoning from specific cases to derive a general rule. Induction is a critical tool for scientific discovery. The results of inductive reasoning are not always certain because observations are not exhaustive. The general from induction is probabilistically correct.

As discussed in Section 10.3, induction is an inner mechanism of learning THAT Zda possesses. If event *A* is often followed by event *B*, then Zda concludes that *A*'s occurrence predicts probabilistically the future occurrence of *B*. For instance, when the word "often" above is replaced with "always," we have a mathematical implication ($\rightarrow$): $A \rightarrow B$ means A is sufficient for B. Therefore, the application of the innate concept of implication is a consequence of inductive reasoning. Zda's confidence in an induction increases as the associated number of occurrences increases. Deductive reasoning is a consequence of inductive reasoning. Thus, the validity of the former is constructed on the validity of the latter, as explained in Part I.

Induction is a method of reasoning where one's experiences and observations, including what is learned from others, are synthesized to arrive at a general conclusion. Inductive reasoning is often described as the derivation of general principles from specific observations (arguing from the specific to the general). For instance, a dog can run and a cat can run. Furthermore, dogs and cats are members of the animal class; therefore, all animals can run. We see in this example, dogs and cats are animals. We generalize the conclusion "can run" from special cases to the category "animal." This inspires us that induction can be realized in HAI by replacing objects (events, humans, or agents) with a desensitisor in the event-string.

Indeed, in our HAI architecture, Zda can perform inductive reasoning by replacing a token at a certain location in a pattern with its desensitisor. If Zda observed such a replacement and obtained a similar outcome, then such an induction is valid. Otherwise, it's incorrect. For the purpose of learning, Zda can also actively perform such a replacement; if the same (similar) outcome or reward is observed, the Zda will confirm the induction. When Zda makes an induction, the outcome often needs confirmation from humans or peers using rewards or penalties.

The root of inductive reasoning is the similarity principle discussed in Part I. The following is an example of learning from induction based on the Similarity Principle.

Suppose Zda has formed an initial concept (token) of Food = {milk, yogurt, beef} and he sees a baby likes milk and yogurt. Zda reasons that the baby might like beef since beef is similar to milk and yogurt in the sense that they all belong to the Food category in the *Knet*. Here, Food can be viewed as a desensitisor. Using the desensitisor to replace a token in the pattern is inductive reasoning.

We further illustrate this using the following example. When Zda has involved the following two event sequences:

Bob.say(Get me apple) ⇝ *Zda.get(apple)* ⇝ *Zda.act(pass apple to Bob)*
Bob.say(Get me balls) ⇝ *Zda.get(balls)* ⇝ *Zda.act(pass balls to Bob)*

he will recognize the pattern

Bob.say(Get me $\mathcal{L}$) ⇝ *Zda.get($\mathcal{L}$)* ⇝ *Zda.act(pass $\mathcal{L}$ to Human)*

where $\mathcal{L}$ is an existing desensitisor or a newly formed desensitisor, representing a member of category {apple, balls}.

As another example, we illustrate how the Law of Syllogism (*if A → B and B → C, then A → C*) is a consequence of induction:

- Zda may see the coexistence of *A, B, C.* and they often appear in that sequence.
- Zda patternizes the sequence in two ways: (1) $A → B$ and $B → C$ and (2) $A → C$.
- Because they are the same sequence, Zda always observes (1) and (2) at the same time. Collectively, such an association between individual cases (1) and (2) leads him to make an induction that $(A → B$ and $B → C)$ implies $(A→ C)$.
- However, suppose Zda also sees a sequence of *A, D, C,* then he cannot, conversely, conclude: $(A → C)$ implies $(A → B$ and $B → C)$

In this sense, the Law of Syllogism comes from induction. Since *Knet* is a recursive network, it can be viewed as an inference network with arrows as the inference directions. Therefore, in the example above the inference from node A to the node C can be viewed as from A to B, then to C.

However, the law of syllogism does not always hold; we saw this with the example of intransitive dice in Section 1.6.

Deduction, or deductive reasoning, argues from a general conclusion to a special case. The result of deductive reasoning is usually thought to be logically certain.

An example of a deductive argument would be:

All men are mortal.

John is a man.

Therefore, John is mortal.

The statistical syllogism can be generally stated as:

A proportion Q of population P has attribute B.

An individual X is a member of P.

Therefore, the probability that X has B is Q.

When Q = 100%, the statistical syllogism becomes deduction with certainty. However, when the frequency is low such a certainty might be just an illusion.

To Zda, deduction is finding a pattern that includes the observed event sequence, or its desensitisor, and predicting the outcome based on the unobserved events with associated probability.

The Deduction Laws in practice can be viewed as a consequence of observations and derived from induction. The deduction laws come from virtually checking all events humans have ever experienced, and finding no exception. However, this does not mean deduction is absolutely correct because no exception found does not mean there are no exceptions. Think about how Gödel's Incompleteness Theorem shocked everyone in the mathematical community: you can only choose one between completeness and consistency in an axiomatic system involving arithmetic.

Thus, in our HAI architecture, deduction is valid in a probabilistic sense, and the general conclusion from a deduction can be changed later if later observations suggest that.

Analogy is often used for new knowledge discovery. **Analogy** is a form of thinking that finds similarities between two or more things and then predicts similar characteristics in other aspects or outcomes. Analogy is a direct application of the similarity principle and is used by Zda in his patternization and decision-making. See Chapter 14.

Analogy, or analogical reasoning, can be stated as:

P and Q are similar with respect to properties A, B, and C.

Object P has been observed to further have property X.

Therefore, Q probably has property X.

Analogy may involve some "if" conditions. In such cases, a hypothesis is involved.

In our HAI architecture, Zda uses analogy (similarity-matching) to make predictions and take action in the response mechanisms. The outcome of such a response will determine the validity of the analogy.

Cause-Effect Reasoning is a type of thinking in which you show the linkage between two events that appear simultaneously or in sequence. The one that did not happen earlier is called the effect, and the other is the cause. Such a cause-effect relationship must be verified over time through recurrence of these pairs of events. Cause-Effect Reasoning includes abduction and causality reasoning.

Abduction is the process of finding the best explanation from a set of observations, i.e., inferring cause from effect. In other words, abductive reasoning works in the reverse direction from deductive reasoning in which effect is inferred from cause. For instance,

If and only if A is true, then B becomes true.

B is true.

Therefore, A must be true.

Abduction often involves probability; thus we have probabilistic abduction or plausible reasoning, which can take many different forms. For instance,

If A is true, then B becomes more plausible.

B is true.

Therefore, A becomes more plausible.

A second formulation would be:

If A is true, then B becomes more plausible.

A becomes more plausible.

Therefore, B becomes less plausible.

Probabilistic abduction is figuring out the most probable cause from the effect. To Zda, Probabilistic abduction is finding the most frequent path (pattern) to the cause node (token) in his *Knet*.

Lastly, we discuss how to apply probability to a pattern. We will try to avoid any fancy statistical methods since our entire HAI approach is built on the notion that complex methods are developed through simple learning methods, not the other way around. Any complex method will come at the cost of sacrificing flexibility and applicability, and thus is not a viable solution for HAI.

In patternization there are controversies, such as those we remarked upon in Simpson's paradox. For instance, in onsite patternization, $E1 \Rightarrow E3$ and $E1 \wedge E2 \Rightarrow E3$ can both be treated as evidence of E1 causing E3: $E1 \Rightarrow E3$. According to the Parsimony Principle, we record pattern $E1 \Rightarrow E3$. This deterministic approach may not be applicable when practically there are different frequencies involved in the two event sequences.

When Zda observes $E1 \Rightarrow E3$ instead of $E1 \wedge E2 \Rightarrow E3$, perhaps E2 is there or just not in Zda's attention. If $E1 \wedge E2 \Rightarrow E3$ has more frequency than $E1 \Rightarrow E3$, then E2 is an inducer or activator for E3. Conversely, if $E1 \wedge E2 \Rightarrow E3$ has less frequency than $E1 \Rightarrow E3$, then E2 is an inhibitor for E3. In either case, Zda will deal with utilizing probability. The questions are: (1) Given E1, what is the probability of outcome E3? and (2) Given E1 and E2, what is the probability of having outcome E3? To answer the questions we have to define the (target) population (often through similarity grouping), which defines the scope in which the modeling errors are to be collected (see Simpson's Paradox in Part I). The target population is the set of all units a random process can pick, whereas sample space S is the set of all possible outcomes of a random variable.

There is always a conditional probability, and never such a thing called absolutely unconditional probability in the real world. The target population defines the (unconditional or joint) probability distribution, whereas the target population is the condition we specify for the probability. In practice, we often define the target population, while in statistical books we often simply assume the population distribution. We use the term probability when the condition is not specifically defined; when the condition can be clearly defined for some of the random variables, we may use the term conditional probability. For example, we may assume probability distribution $f(x,y)$, then the conditional probability distribution of y given x is $f(y|x)$. Let's look at the concept of conditional probability in patterns as shown in the following examples.

For cause-effect inference, among all patterns with cause E1, the proportion of events with E1⇢E3 (including E1∧E2⇢E3) among all events with E1 is the conditional probability of E3 given E1. Similarly, the proportion of E1∧E2⇢E3 among events with E1∧E2 is the conditional proportion of E3 given E1∧E2.

For effect-cause inference, among all patterns with effect E3 (e.g., E1⇢E3 and E1∧E2⇢E3), the proportion of events with earlier token E1∧E2 is the conditional probability of cause E1∧E2 given the effect, E3. Similarly, for effect-cause inference, among all patterns with effect E3, the proportion of events with earlier token E1 is the conditional probability of cause E1 given the effect, E3.

Logical reasoning, imitation, analogy, and creativity are all reflected in the patternization, repatternization, and response mechanisms in the Zda architecture.

A pattern derived from logical reasoning does not usually have an initial reward. A pattern of an event-string without an associated reward can be considered to be a natural law for prediction. Pattern with action and reward is a basis for prediction and response.

13.8 Associative Learning

As mentioned in Section 10.9, there are three **Principles of Association**: (1) contiguity in time and place, (2) resemblance, and (3) causation. These are illustrated in the following examples in connection with our HAI architecture:

1. **Contiguity**: Things happening at or nearly at the same time are associated. Shaking or pointing at an object in front of a child and saying the name of the object will make him associate the name with the object. This is how to teach children object names. Contiguity is handled by 2-gramtions with association tokens.

2. **Resemblance**: When someone mentions one thing, you will often think of a similar thing. When someone shows you a picture of your best friend, you naturally think of her because the picture resembles her. Resemblance is modeled by 2-gramtons with previously formulated paired similar items or dynamic formulated paired similar items in real time.

3. **Causation**: If event A is a necessary or sufficient condition for event B, then the relationship between events A and B is causality. Causation is also dealt with using 2-gramtons with paired tokens, one for cause, the other for effect. Note, though, that a delayed effect of a cause can connect together two things that are distant from each other in time.

Zda often associates similar things by grouping them together (e.g., synonyms); he also associates opposite things together (e.g., antinomies). These groupings are important for efficient learning. On the other hand, we can say that association is based on some kind of similarity, either timewise, location-wise, concept-wise, emotion-wise, function-wise, or in some other aspect(s). I believe there is no clear line drawn between similarity and association: similarity leads to an association between two things and an association in a sense makes two things similar.

Items or subsets in the same attention set form associations. When the same attention sets reoccur over time, these associations will be enhanced due to increased frequencies. However, recurrences are just approximations, i.e., more often similar (instead of exact) attention sets occur at a given time. Contrarily, the associations between uncommon items become weaker over time. This simple fact makes statistical/scientific discovery easier, and is why frequency-based patternization makes sense in many situations. In communication and language learning, we purposely impose words in a particular attention set (e.g., talking while doing) so that Zda will make an association between the words and the other attentive items. As time goes by, the association between the words and common item(s) will be enhanced, since the words are among the common attentive items.

As recurrences can enhance an association, the pleasure-pain impact of an event or its rewards can also affect the strength of an association greatly. As an old Chinese saying suggests: once bitten by a snake, ten years afraid of ropes. Thus, as a teaching tool, we can use a reward to enhance a desirable association and a penalty to weaken an undesirable association. The link between association and frequency not only makes scientific discovery possible, but also allows auto-corrections of a false discovery over time due to missing information in our attention. Well-designed scientific experiments and careful observations by trained scientists can also remove some false associations.

Association is critical in communication and for accomplishing requested tasks. For instance, if Lia asks Zda: "get me a book," Zda will first shift his attention from the word "book" to a physical book and look for it before he tries to get it. Such an attention shift is because of the association between the word "book" and a physical book. Associations are modeled by 2-gramtons with associated frequencies and rewards in the *Knet*. One can use *n*-gramtons to model more complicated n-way associations.

Most 2-gramtons with high frequency are formulated by taking the two sequential tokens, which can serve as the basis for contiguity association and association shift. For causation, the paired tokens must have sufficient reoccurrences and one must occur before the other. Timewise, the two events may not occur closely in time or space. Paired events in a skipton can be a causal relationship. Causation is an association, but an association is not necessarily causation. Tokens in similarity-based association do not have time and space constraints as long as they are similar in some way.

"Refers to" is an association, but association is not necessarily "refers to." "Refers to" is a mapping. Using the factor-isolation technique, Zda will be able to map the static attributes (mainly shape) to identify different types of objects first. Once Zda understands the mapping between words and object types and between words and object attributes, he can quickly understand whole sentences of a language. Let's illustrate this using the following "Green-pen Red-pen" example (Figure 13.3), where changes involve objects or their attributes in a multiple object/event-string case.

Zda does not know initially that the words "green" and "red" refer to color in vision until he maps the variance in words to the changes in vision (color). This mapping can be viewed as a coordination between senses of different sensory organs, i.e., hearing and vision at the present. This patternization is accomplished across two (or multiple) event-strings at different times $t1$ and $t2$. The notion can be dissected using the principle

Time:	Lia Say:	Lia Show:	Zda Senses:
t1	"Green pen"		visual.shape = pen visual.color = green
t2	"Red pen"		visual.shape = pen visual.color = red

FIGURE 13.3
Learning object attribute names using factor-isolation technique.

of factor-isolation: (1) change maps to change, (2) base at time *t*1 ("green") maps to base (green), and (3) post at time *t*2 ("red") maps to post (red). In this case, no reward needs to be involved. In addition, Zda may also make an association between the two desensitisors: the concept of color and the actual sense of color.

However, in addition to color, Zda may also see other unintended changes, such as the location of the hand and directions the pens point in. If the moving hand is also in Zda's attention set, Zda might try to map the two words "green" and "red" to the two different locations of the hand at times *t*1 and *t*2, respectively. In such a case, a reward is needed to confirm which mapping is correct. Such rewards can enhance Zda's learning. After learning what objects "green pen" and "hat" refer to, Zda can refer "green hat" to a green hat if one is presented. More examples will be presented in the next section, Natural Language Understanding.

Generally speaking, Associative Learning is the process through which organisms acquire information about relationships between events or entities in their environment. It is expressed as the modification of existing behaviors, or the development of novel behaviors, that reflects the conscious or unconscious recognition of a contingency. Associative learning is a form of conditioning, a theory that says behavior can be modified or learned based on a stimulus and a response. Both classical and operant conditioning are forms of associative learning where associations are made between events that occur together. An example would be: if you put your hand on a hot stove and hurt yourself, you would learn to associate hot stoves with pain, and have therefore been conditioned not to put your hands on hot stove. Associative learning can happen in any of the thinking modes.

Associative learning is usually considered to be passive learning and often used in effective teaching. Classical Conditioning (Section 4.3) can be used to create reward proxies for effective teaching. Ivan Pavlov discovered that the reflex of salivation in a dog occurs not only when food is presented, but also when the dog hears the bell (the conditional stimulus). If we repeatedly use some appreciative words, such as "yes" or "thank you," or a hug as the conditional stimulus when we give Zda an actual reward, such as candy, then the stimulus substitution will gradually be established. We call such a conditional stimulus a reward proxy. It is often much more convenient to use a reward proxy in teaching than a real material reward or physical penalty. Operant conditioning is the basis for reinforcement learning in AI.

In addition to cognitive learning, habituation and sensitization are the two examples of non-associative learning methods. Habituation refers to the phenomenon of the diminishing of a physiological or emotional (innate) response to a frequently repeated stimulus. For instance, if you are working with a radio playing in the background, the noise will distract you more at first, but less as time goes by.

The major differences between associative and cognitive learning can now be summarized. Associative learning (behavioral approach) provides means of describing how a person or animal learns a series of desired responses; it is a kind of learning which demands little more than parrot-like repetitions under reinforcing conditions. Cognitive learning is more advanced learning. It explains learning with understanding, insights and concepts, and rules are applied to obtain new and significant patterns of information.

13.9 Natural Language Understanding

The notion that natural *language* influences *thought* has a long history in a variety of fields. More complex thoughts and languages exist in humans than in animals. The co-existence of language and thought can be an evidence of the influences of each on the other. The main use of language is to transfer thoughts and knowledge from one mind to another. The bits of linguistic information that enter into our minds from others' cause us to entertain new thoughts, and this can have profound effects on our world knowledge, inferencing, and subsequent behavior (Gleitman, 2005).

The natural language representations of concepts are an effective tool in communications and learning. Without such language, we humans cannot easily inherit the complex knowledge and skills from our ancestors. Without natural language, RL will be virtually only a learning approach and the vast number of potential trial-error attempts required would make it impossible for any individual to learn advanced knowledge or skills. With the assistance of a language, we can avoid many fruitless trial-error paths if we just try the limited paths that are likely to be successful and a few other creative paths. In other words, language is essential for passing knowledge from generation to generation, because no advanced skill can be learned or discovered by a single person without learning from others within a generation and across generations. Human intelligences differ from and are more advanced than other species' mainly because we have advanced languages that other species do not have.

Language processing spans perception (comprehension) and action (speech). The lowest levels of language hierarchy are raw data-oriented, recognizing patterns in streams of sounds, and generating streams of sound with the mouth and larynx. The higher levels focus on abstract patterns of linguistic organization (Goertzel, 2016).

To develop a natural language in a community, speakers should use the same terminology for the same thing, although some differences in pronunciation might still exist. Only in this way, can a common language emerge eventually. So, Zda might initially (consistently) call a dog a "cat," while Lia always calls a dog a "dog." Over time, they find that such discrepancy in meaning is inconvenient for two people living in the same community. Therefore, Zda might begin to use Lia's terminology occasionally and find it rewarding (convenient); thus, he more often uses the word "dog" and eventually becomes a consistent user of the terminology. That is, common terminologies emerge even though using particular terminologies (nouns) might be completely accidental.

In learning a natural language, instead of a big-data approach, we use virtually no data on any language for an agent at his birth. This is because a human baby, regardless of his birth parents and birthplace, has no built-in language, he will learn whatever language we teach him through interactions with his world. Zda's ability to learn languages can be shown in two aspects: (1) displaying understanding of the languages, and (2) using the languages appropriately.

In natural language-guided responses, we are particularly interested in the association between words and sensible actions to be performed. As mentioned earlier, different things (e.g., objects, events, actions) that are close together in space and/or time can trigger a chain of associations for Zda. The attention shift caused by associations from one thing to another is particularly useful in language-guided responses.

The string of elementary actions in Zda's attention set is hierarchically tokenized into a shorter action string based on Zda's acquired concepts. In order to learn and perform a complex procedure, from making a cup of coffee to manufacturing a car or launching a rocket, language is necessary.

For instance, consider the request "Please get dinner ready before 6 PM today, we will have 2 guests." The sentence carries a lot of information about what the person needs to do before 6 PM: making dinner is not a simple elementary action. Another example would be "I need to go to school to finish my homework now, but I don't have transportation." The text indicates the person's goal and what he needs to reach the goal. This information about the goal will play an important role in his decision as to what to do next.

Words can be suggestive: "Following Lia's advice is usually an intelligent choice." Words can also be used to differentiate friends from enemies. A friend's words are often informative and following his/her advice is often a good choice, whereas an enemy's words often mislead you. Conversely, if a person helps Zda get a reward or get things done, he is likely Zda's friend; if he often tries to prevent Zda from getting a reward, he must be an enemy. Like humans, by formulating opinions based on peoples' personalities, Zda can respond wisely.

Words such as "mimicking" can suggest Zda does things that he has never done before. Language can instruct Zda to assemble a machine or encourage Zda to do things no one has done before through analogy.

The concepts involved in Lia's *words can refer to* a physical object, procedure, or logical proposition. A concept can be a hierarchical composition of simpler concepts. Thus, Zda needs to know all the concepts involved (i.e., the associated patterns stored in memory), and how to respond when facing each concept mentioned, before he can confidently respond to the composite concepts.

Lia may also use words such as "tree-like object." To handle such concepts, the object's appearance must reflect the truth, not the simplified 3×3 image in Zda's current simplified architecture. Keep in mind that Zda identifies an object by its image or appearance, not by the coded name in the computer language.

Modern advanced natural languages have experienced thousands of years of development. For Zda and Lia, if the interaction is short (within one generation), they can develop only simple language. But the language as they develop it will be complex if there are many generations in between or if they interact with us sufficiently and we can teach them our languages in depth. We humans can guide agents to learn better, faster because we have the knowledge to teach them our inherited knowledge that has been evolving through the power of languages over thousands of years. One of the main reasons that humans are more intelligent than other animals is that we have rich languages that carry knowledge from one generation to the next.

Humans discovered that the categorization of responses allows us to make decisions more efficiently. For this reason, we can teach Zda to classify the natural language as, e.g., (1) questions, (2) statements, (3) requests, (4) dialogue, and (5) entertainment.

Words can be associated with objects, events, actions, procedures, stats, states, times, locations, emotions, attitudes, and so on. For instance, "Please pick the red pen on the moving table." This suggests that identifying the universal structure of language (sentences) is useful in making such associations.

Since language is a one-dimensional string used to describe the sequential and concurrent events of multiple-objects in a multidimensional world (3D in space, 1-D in time, plus many other sensory dimensions), some accessory words (such as *under, of, at, as soon as, from, close to, intensive, heavier,* and *belong to* in English) may be used to indicate the special, temporal, and other types of relations between different objects and actions. Natural language serves as a tool for expressing thoughts and knowledge, the strings of words also contain patternization of the perceived world. What is important for Zda, as a humanoid, is to find out the structural relationship between speech and his sensible actions. Patternization involves the recurrence of events, creating the need for accessory words such as *"always," "if., then," "as long as," "probably," "likely," "similarly," "under," "above," "between," "before," "after," "when," "while," "until,"* and *"rather … than …."*

We have discussed the important concept "Refers to" and how to establish such a mapping between two items using the example of "Green-Pen Red-Pen" in the previous section.

The next example shows how to teach Zda to learn object types (Figure 13.4). The same factor isolation technique can be used here: (1) change maps to change, (2) base at time $t1$ ("pen") maps to base (pen), and (3) post at time $t2$ ("hat") maps to post (hat).

We can use a similar method to teach or connect Zda's innate concepts (such as "refers to," "similar," "probability," "desire," "past") to corresponding words in any language. Thus, if Zda has learned particular words or a phrase (e.g., "refers to" in English) that maps to the innate concept ("refers to"), we can use the phrase "refers to" to teach Zda other concepts effectively. The concept of "refers to" is very likely (with a high probability) in Zda's attention set and Zda looks for the words (voice) that map to it. Another innate concept Zda constantly pays attention to is "imitation," thus teaching the words for these two concepts first will greatly help Zda learn other concepts later on. We can teach any concept using reinforcement learning (with reward) as long as the concept is in Zda's attention set; it is a matter of time.

We may think that head-nodding signaling confirmation and head-shaking signaling disconfirmation are an instance of Universal Language. Whether true or not, this universal language can be established by using the learned word that represents the meaning of "refers to." Another way to teach Zda the meaning of head-nodding and head-shaking is to say "yes" when you nod your head and "no" when you shake it, assuming Zda understands "yes" and "no" already, of course.

Language may refer to attributes, states, actions, the difference in attributes, states and actions, and/or the difference of the difference if multiple objects are in the attention set.

Time:	Lia Say:	Lia Show:	Zda Senses:
t1	"Green pen"		visual.shape = pen visual.color = green
t2	"Green hat"		visual.shape = hat visual.color = green

FIGURE 13.4
Learning object names using factor-isolation technique.

For instance, the difference between A and B is larger than the difference between A and C. Another example would be the mathematical definitions of addition and multiplication: A represents a natural number, A+n refers to n times of plus-recursion of A+1; A*n is n times of plus-recursion 0+A. The operation "+1" indicates the next number in sequence.

To summarize, externally, pointing at or shaking an object while speaking will attract Zda's attention, and the internally sensed change of a property (due to a change detected by sensory organs) will also attract Zda's attention. Therefore, if the externality (words) and internality (senses of sensory organs) happen at the same time and closely in space, Zda will make an association between them. This serves the basis for the factor-isolation technique. For effective learning or making the desired association, it is important to have a small attention set.

Language can be used for the following purposes:

1. For information only, a statement referring to something, making a prediction, or explaining a cause; no action is needed in such cases.
2. For a request, knowing what refers to what and an action that may require some skills or knowledge, e.g., answering a question and driving a car.
3. For emotional expression, knowing what refers to what and displays listening and empathy.
4. For dialog that involves a sequence of words from different mouths (actioners).

Among these four, the key concept is "refers to." If Zda can determine what refers to what, then he can learn quickly when a sentence is information, a request, an emotional expression, or suggests the speaker is looking for dialog, and can consequently determine the actions as necessary.

Word-tokens are denoted by W1, W2, …, Wn, and event-tokens are denoted by E1, E2, …, En. W1 through Wn can each be a single word or high-level token, i.e, phrases, sentences, paragraphs, articles, instructions. Likewise, E1 through En can be elementary or high-level tokens. Furthermore, the event-string W1∧E1 represents W1 and E1 occurring simultaneously, while W1⇾E1 and E1⇾W1 represent two possible sequential occurrences of W1 and E1. In W1⇾E1, W1 can be an instruction, request, question, or prediction, while E1 can be an action or event. In E1⇾W1, E1 can be an action and W1 can be a reward (penalty) proxy, instrumental suggestion for improvement, or a prediction; E1 can be an event and W1 can be a prediction, an explanation of why E1 occurs, or about knowledge learned from E1. For dialog, Zda will deal recursively with 2-gramtons W1⇾W2 and 3-gramtons W1⇾W2⇾W3 from 2 or 3 different speakers. In language-guided responses, Zda will always patternize a word-string from each speaker and action-string for each actioner before discovering the relationship between word-pattern and event-pattern (action-pattern). For convenience, we denote a natural language pattern by *wPattern(id, wParams)*, and an event-pattern by *ePattern(id, eParams)*, wParams, and eParams are parameters. We may ignore the pattern id for simplicity. For example, two sequential events can be something like this:

E1 = Lia.throw(the ball) ⇾ E2 = Zda.catch(the ball),

or like this:

W1 = Lia.say("catch the ball") ⇾ E2 = Zda.catch(the ball).

From these two examples, we can learn the following general notion:

$E1 = ePattern(desensitisor\ 1)) \Rightarrow E2 = ePattern(desensitisor\ 2)$

$W1 = wPattern(desensitisor\text{-}reference)) \Rightarrow E2 = Zda.act(ePattern(desensitisor))$

Here desensitisor 1 and desensitisor 2 are paired, and desensitisor-reference and desensitisor are paired. This suggests that if we include the pairing between desensitisor-reference and desensitisor in Table 13.4, repatternization with multiple desensitisors in Section 13.4 will be applicable to language-guided patternization, and consequently all the response mechanisms (reflex and thinking models) can naturally be expanded to language-guided action too.

A natural language (NL) is a result of word-string patternization, while generalized patterns in HAI is event-string patternization. A pattern can be viewed as a string function in OOP, where desensitisors can be viewed as having similar roles as variable types (integer, float, string, object, event) for functions. NL can be used to record history as a story and specify rules for future engagement, and so do the event patterns. Patterns are indexed functions with fixors (constant strings) and variables (parameters or desensitisors). In recursive patterns, the parameters can be general tokens (i.e., recursive functions). Thus, a recursive pattern often includes several pairs of parameters. Hierarchical tokens are equivalent to functions nested within a function. Taking the function $f(x) = 3 + x$ as an example, $f(x)$ is called a token, whereas $3 + x$ is called a pattern. In the recursive function $F(f(x)) = 7 - 2f(x)$, $F(f(x))$ will be called a hierarchical token (high-level token), $7 - 2f(x)$ is called a pattern (or high-level pattern) in our HAI.

Natural language can be viewed as Natural-Language functions wPattern(fixors, params) mapping to event-pattern ePattern(fixors, params). For instance, *Lia.speak("please bring me (the pen)")* refers to actioner.Bring(the pen). In this sense, self-patternization of event-strings is the formulation of the so-called universal language, and HAI is a self-programming or self-organized system.

To use Analogy (metaphor) in natural language is to say that two things are similar in some way(s). Examples are: "my shoes smell like garbage" and "finding my car keys is like finding a needle in a haystack." From this notion of analogy, the analogy in mapping between wPattern(params) and ePattern(desensitisor) is processed in this way: If Zda understands (1) what "a green pen" refers to, (2) what "a red pen" refers to, and (3) what "please pick *a green pen*" refers to, i.e., maps to *actioner.pickup(a green pen)*, then Zda will be able to make an analogy and map "please pick *a red pen*" to *actioner.pickup(a red pen)*, even if he has never heard the sentence "please pick *a red pen*" before. Here we assume red pen and green pen belong to a known desensitisor and Zda is able to image how to perform the action, *actioner.pickup(a red pen)*.

To sum up, language understanding involves two key elements: "refers to" and formulation of word-event patterns. Working with these fundamental tools, an agent can respond appropriately, displaying his understanding.

For effective teaching-learning and sensible responding, it is helpful to know that language is often used for the following purposes:

- Words can refer to attributes, states (moving or not), emotion (sensation level), desire, effort (energy costs), e.g., "the sad, running exhaustively boy."
- A goal or an intention can be recognized through verbal articulations or judged by an actioner's actions.

- An object can be defined by its attributes or dynamic behaviors: *the green moving car.*
- A tool is a special object that can be defined by its attributes and utilities: *the knife used to cut beef.*
- An actioner can be defined by its action described in a natural language: *the person who is walking fast.*
- An action can be defined by parameters of elementary actions.

It is interesting to imagine the following two different approaches to see how the resulting languages will differ:

1. Zda and Lia both have not learned any language before, and through interactions they develop their own language. Consider how it might evolve.
2. Zda has not learned any language, but Lia speaks a language, which Zda learns from her. Discuss how the language could further develop.

13.10 Observing, Imitative, and Creative Learnings

Observational Learning is a form of learning that develops through watching and does not require the observer to perform any observable behavior or receive reinforcement. Observational learning can involve four components: acquisition, retention, performance, and reinforcement.

Observational learning is often not as reliable as imitative learning. For instance, Zda can learn the fact: *he can use water to put out fire,* by observing Lia using water to extinguish fire. However, he cannot learn the false fact: *he can give birth,* by observing Lia giving birth.

I found it most interesting that we can study imitation and creativity under the same umbrella of similarity: Imitation is an analogy dealing with great similarities, creativity is an analogy dealing with great novelty or minimal similarity, and analogy bridges imitation to creativity (Figure 13.5). In exploitation, a great similarity makes imitation, while in exploration, too much novelty becomes illogical and can cause chaos.

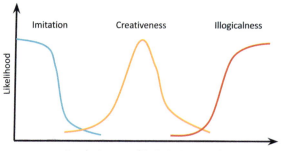

FIGURE 13.5
Imitation, creativeness, and illogicalness with different degrees of similarity.

Learning can occur through imitation and analogy. Being creative often starts with imitation. Imitation emphasizes similarity. Analogy, or creative analogy, is somewhat moving away from imitation, an evolution of imitation. Analogy focuses on the commonalities (often at an abstract level) between two things that appear to be different. Illogicalness, or illogicality, is the result of making an analogy without identifying sufficient similarities between two things (Figure 13.5). Creativity is based on an analogy across different things. One's creativity changes over the expanse of a life. When one gets old and has more experiences, that person will be less adaptive to different opinions because any new thing can be grouped into some existing categories. In contrast, youngsters may often be more creative, an advantage being "lacking" experiences. The time-sensitive creativities for different agents are modeled by a parameter in our HAI architecture.

As an example, how could humans discover or invent the sine function? Regardless of what actually happened, humans might find the relationship between an angle ϑ (theta) in a right triangle and the ratio of opposite side over hypotenuse (longest side) on paper, and quantify such a relationship by a function, that we have named the sine function. Later people make the analogy by applying the sine function to the relationship between the two quantities, $y = \sin(\vartheta)$, and formulate the concept of the sine function.

Analogy is also used in Recursion. How can humans learn acceleration? Perhaps, after humans have the concept of velocity as the derivative of a distance vector with respect to time, they make an analogy by applying the derivative operation again to the velocity vector, making acceleration the derivative of the derivative of the distance vector.

How does Zda learn from imitation? As discussed earlier, imitation for Zda is simply replacing an actioner (string) by Zda (string) in an actioner.action string (Figure 13.6). For example, the string *"Lia.walk when Bob.waveHand"* becomes *"Zda.walk when Bob.waveHand"* as Zda makes an imitation of Lia. If Zda makes some imitation and gets a reward, the probability of such imitations will increase; i.e., Zda is learning that walking when Bob waves is a good thing to do.

The **Reciprocal Principle** (reciprocity) is the tendency of agents to exchange the two actioners in an event-string or pattern. An action of reciprocity is an imitation, but not all imitations are actions of reciprocity. The Reciprocal principle creates the scenario wherein Zda treats a person in the way the person treats him.

To create or invent is to make something that does not exist, or is to make an analogy across different fields or problems. Creation is a mind's internal process in working with the external world. For instance, applying a method of solving one problem to another problem in a different field is an act of creation/invention.

Inspired by the ideas of genetic programming in evolutionary machine learning, creativity and analogy in our HAI architecture are operated by replacing (or removing) some string from object.action strings with similar strings (Figure 13.7). More generally, learning

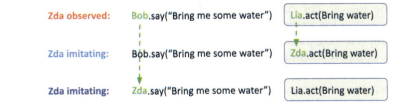

FIGURE 13.6
Examples of agent's imitations.

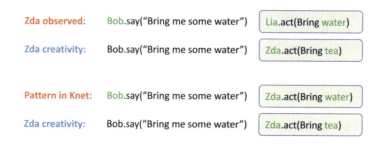

Zda observed:	Bob.say("Bring me some water")	Lia.act(Bring water)
Zda creativity:	Bob.say("Bring me some water")	Zda.act(Bring tea)
Pattern in Knet:	Bob.say("Bring me some water")	Zda.act(Bring water)
Zda creativity:	Bob.say("Bring me some water")	Zda.act(Bring tea)

FIGURE 13.7
Examples of agent's creativities.

can be realized in agents through genetic algorithms involving operations such as mutation, crossover, appending, or removing event-strings. Every such genetic operation on event-strings provides a learning opportunity for Zda when there is an associated reward. Such genetic operations, which should be initiated by Zda, are instances of active learning in the cognitive learning paradigm.

13.11 Curiosity—Motivated Learning

Curiosity motivates learning. Learning often occurs through asking intelligent questions of one's self or others. A simple case is when Zda does not know how to answer a question; he may then choose to pose the same question back to the person asking it, or to someone else. Here is an example:

Lia.say(*"How does one make a pipe?"*)

If Zda does not know the answer he can imitate Lia, asking her the same question and seeing how she responds:

Zda.say(*"How does one make a pipe?"*)

Zda may also imagine asking himself the question. If he can not find a satisfactory answer or he wants to verify his answer, he may ask the question of someone else.

Curiosity is driven by attention, while a curiosity-driven *action* leads to active learning. The actions are motivated by the questions, which usually start (at least in English) with what, why, how, or where. And the action taken is expected to lead to the answer, or one-step closer to the answer. For Zda's self-questioning, a why-type curiosity learning happens when he searches for an earlier token (node) in the *Knet* for a reason, and how-type curiosity learning is taking place when the search is for a future token (node) in the *Knet* for a prediction. Zda may intentionally take a new action that is not indicated by a pattern in *Knet* in order to see what is going to happen after his action. Thus, a creative action can be curiosity learning (how-type curiosity learning). We will discuss this more when we consider Zda's response mechanisms.

When Zda's attention set is mainly language utterance and his action set is also language utterance, dialogue occurs. Conversations focus on the relationships between patterns of words spoken by the participants, which are usually intelligent verbal exchanges. But from the agent side, at least for a linguistically young agent, conversations mainly are imitations. Zda listens to conversations between two different parties and mimics them. Of course, conversations also involve novelty. How to learn and carry on conversations will be discussed, again in the sections highlighting response mechanisms.

13.12 Recursion on Everything

Recursion in mathematics is the use of output as input, repeatedly. That is, $Y = f(f(f(\ldots f(x))))$, where $f(\cdot)$ is a function or mapping that represents a mechanism of a system. For instance, we define factorials by (1) the base case: for $n = 1$, $n! = 1$ and (2) the recursive step: for $n > 1$, $n! = n\,(n–1)!$

Inductive definition of the natural numbers can be stated as: a natural number is either 1 or $n+1$, where n is a natural number. Some more examples of mathematical recursions: multiplication can be defined as a recursion of additions: e.g., $3\times5 = ((5+5)+5)$, while addition is the recursion of the operation of adding 1, e.g., $2+4 = ((((2+1)+1)+1)+1)$. Binary search is considered to be a recursive process. Even infinity is nothing but the idea of an endless recursion. Beyond mathematics, when the derivative operator with respect to time is applied to distance, it will produce speed in physics, and when the same operator is recursively applied to speed, it produces acceleration. This recursion of an operator is a creative analogy. In fact, it is an important form of creativity. In computer science, recursion can be used in data structures. A tree structure is a simple recursive data structure.

Recursion in cognitive science has been recently identified as the defining feature not only of natural language (Hauser et al., 2002) but also of human cognition overall (Corballis, 2007). However, it has received less than a satisfactory characterization. More often than not, it has been applied to the structural complexity of some of the representations the human mind seems to have and use, irrespective of the mechanisms operating over these representations. This is in clear discrepancy with the formal sciences, where recursion originated (Garcia-Albea and Lobina, 2009).

In principle, Zda can possibly perform recursions on everything—actions, concepts, procedures, thinking, even recursion itself. In HAI architecture, the ability to apply recursion on everything is a natural consequence of repeatedly applying analogy and recursion: from recursion of thing X to recursion of similar thing Y through analogy. In other words, everything can be analogized by another thing. By recursion, everything can be an analogy of an arbitrary thing x. Therefore, recursion and recursion of analogy enable recursion on everything.

$$\text{recursion}(x) \rightarrow \text{recursion}\,(\text{analogy}(x)) \rightarrow \text{recursion}(\text{analogy}(\text{analogy}(x))) \rightarrow \ldots.$$

Verifications of patterns from such analogical recursions will be needed before moving them from the *Inet* to the *Knet*.

Just like Zda's self-awareness, the recursion of a learning method used in building Zda will enable Zda to discover and apply the learning method in various situations. Recursion on everything is one of the fundamental features of Zda's learning. For example, RL is used in building Zda and by recursive utilization of RL, Zda will discover or learn the RL method and be capable of applying the method. That is, we use RL to learn RL.

How can Zda invent or learn unsupervised learning methods, such as hierarchical clustering? Here is a possible way: after Zda learns about Euclidean distance, he can apply the similarity (defined as the inverse of the distance) between objects to group them together, starting from the two closest to each other (the most similar pair) to form a composite object; then apply similarity grouping to the reduced set of objects to further identify the two most similar objects. This recursion is applied to the reduced set of objects each time, until all the objects are grouped into one composite object. This is the idea and basic algorithm of the hierarchical clustering method. Furthermore, Zda can make analogies and apply the distance definition to different types of objects, e.g., finding the distance between two colors, and do hierarchical clustering for objects based on color similarities.

Zda can re-invent or learn to evaluate AI algorithms such as genetic programming by abstraction and analogy, though the process of inventing (reinventing) may take very long. After all, it took more than 5,000 years for humans to invent the algorithm!

The keys to inventing and learning a new learning method are (1) a necessary set of prior knowledge or concepts, (2) ways to apprehend and use similarity and similarity principles, (3) recursion, (4) analogy, and (5) rewards associated with certain approaches. With these keys, Zda can learn (discover, rediscover, or invent, reinvent) math, science, statistics, machine learning, and other methods that humans have not discovered yet.

Meta-cognition is "cognition about cognition," a recursion of cognitive processes. With Zda's hierarchical recursive *Knet*, meta-reasoning is encompassed. The abilities of self-reflection and self-programming are included. Our HAI architecture is a self-organized adaptive system featuring hierarchical tokenization, recursive patternization, and adaptive reinforcement learning.

Regarding self-programming, the HAI architecture allows an agent to perform the patternization himself, including self-determined desensitisors and sensitisors. Therefore, desensitisor and sensitisor serve as function parameters in computer programming. Learning in HAI architecture is mapping reality including natural language to event patterns, and such mapping is called an understanding of natural language. Language can be viewed as one-dimensional text that patternizes the perceptual world, including the natural language itself (recursion!). In this sense, HAI is the construction of a universal language for patterning the perceptual world that includes natural languages.

14

Adaptive Response Mechanism

14.1 Prediction and Decision-Making

There are two sequences of event-strings at any moment t: (1) the sequence of attentive event-strings that Zda has observed up to time t, and (2) the sequence of future interesting events that Zda predicts at time t. The prediction is primarily based on similarity-match between patterns in Zda's *Knet* and the observed patterns at the moment. Prediction can be viewed as an association between the current and future situations.

There is a fundamental question in our mind: is an individual's decision dependent on the current state only or the historical events too? The reason we have such a question is because for a moving object, if a location is used to describe its state, then its location at the next second cannot solely be determined by its current location. However, from classical mechanics, we know that within an inertial system if we use location and velocity to describe an object's state, then its state at the next second is fully determined by its current state. For this reason, we believe one's decision can be based on his current state as long as the state includes sufficient parameters, such as one's intention and emotion, and therefore one can use a Markov decision process to model it (Figure 14.1). Noticeably, concepts (tokens) such as "Zda has walked for 3 hours," "Zda has wanted the storybook since he was 3 years old," and "Zda got his degree after his 4 years of hard work" have already included some past information; thus in such cases, Markov-Decision models might be good as first approximations.

We can make further argument that if an individual's decision is based on his current state including his intention (goal) and his past experiences, his decision will be actually related to his current memory of past events and current predictions of future events. More philosophical discussion can be found in Section 3.10: Connotation of Causality.

However, such a Markov chain model may not be feasible because it requires us to include many known and unknown factors in the model. Besides, Markov Chain models often do not match our experiences: we always remember a short sequence of events and use that as a basis for our decision-making. We also recursively use such a chain of sequences to make associations among events that happen far apart in time. Therefore, in Zda's response model, we will use short but hierarchical and recursive chains of events to model our decision-making processes.

In a Markov Decision Process, Zda makes a prediction only based on the current state. In a non-stationary decision process such as a two-time point-based prediction, Zda makes a prediction based on the current and previous states (Figure 14.2). The reason we only limit to a maximum of time points is usually limited to $n = 3$ for prediction (but no limit on n for deep thinking) is that humans do not remember directly a long detained historical event chain. Instead, the long chain will be broken into pieces of big events and each big event includes chains of smaller chains of events; each of these smaller event chains further includes chains of even smaller events.

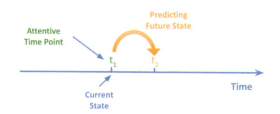

FIGURE 14.1
One-time point-based prediction in Markov model.

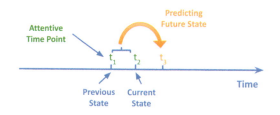

FIGURE 14.2
Prediction based on previous and current states.

FIGURE 14.3
Similarity-principle-based prediction.

Zda uses the observed tokens to predict what is going to happen based on the patterns in *Knet*. Such a reality-*Knet* mapping is mimicking the way humans map reality to their experience or knowledge when making a decision. Like humans, Zda can also make *k*-steps ahead predictions for decision-making using the long token-sequence in *Knet*. The information in the model can include other people's actions, turning it into a model in game theory.

The reality-*Knet* mapping can be exact but more often similarity-based matching, especially when facing a novelty (a new situation Zda has not met before). The similarity-matching process will produce a list of similarity-matched paths from the *Knet* (Figure 14.3). The paths represent Zda' experiences that are considered similar to the reality that Zda is facing at the moment and what is likely to happen if the same or similar action is taken as before. According to the similarity principle, similar situations and actions will lead to a similar outcome. Just like a human, Zda uses his past experiences and predictions to guide his decision using the randomized adaptive response mechanism as discussed below.

When multiple mapped paths are found, the predicted next token may or may not be actionable. When the predicted token is not actionable or an abstract concept, the high-level token will be treated as the next goal and viewed as a pattern to further map to knowledge paths. As an example, "Zda goes to the kitchen" is a pattern or concept, while "Zda walks 5 steps to the East" is an (elementary) action according to our HAI architecture. This backward recursion (reverse-engineering) continues until the concept breaks down into an action or maps to an elementary pattern. If the action was not taken by Zda but by someone else in the *Knet*, he can observe, imitate or take creative action.

Similar to the human brain, *Knet*, though it sits inside Zda's brain, is often treated as an external world by Zda because of its self-inclusive property. This duality of the *Knet* in Zda's brain: being internal and external at the same time, is critical for demonstrating self-awareness, meta-thinking (thinking about thinking), consciousness, imagination, pretending, thinking how others might think, acting like a game player, and taking goal-driven actions.

One of the challenges that have not been discussed is how to determine the number of tokens and the timing of those tokens in forming a pattern. We have to use the attention mechanism: attentive time points are those when an elementary token (observable action) changes in actioner.action or object.event-strings. The future attentive time points are also related to the current attentivity, as we discussed in Attention Mechanism.

Prediction involves human-agent-environment interactions, thus understanding of language (body and natural language) and intentions of other parties engaged are useful. Prediction and learning are two inseparable parts. In a broad sense, learning can include learning how to understand language and another's intentions (what refers to what), how to discover patterns, how to make predictions, and how to respond (action on the internal world and on the external world). Learning and responding go hand in hand: learning from the response outcomes, and prediction and response are based on the knowledge learned.

So far we discuss the reality-*Knet* mapping is one-dimensional. However, the real world and the attentive world are often multi-dimensional in the sense that multiple things occur at the same time. We will discuss this in the randomized adaptive response mechanism next.

14.2 Imitation, Creativity, and Imagination

As discussed earlier, learning starts with imitation. Imitation is the foundation of creativity and innovation. A creative idea often comes from inspiration and analogy when applying the similarity principle between new and original cases. An analogy is a comparison between two objects, systems, or situations that highlights respects in which they are thought to be similar. Creativity is related to the imagination of a new idea, while innovation is related to its implementation. Imitation and Creativity are the most common and important approaches to learning and discovery.

To Zda, imitation is nothing but replacing an actioner (such as Lia or a human) in an *actioner.action* string with himself, i.e., actioner.action is replaced with Zda.action. For instance, if the event-string contains *Lia.eat(apple)* in Zda's *Knet*, *Zda.eat(apple)* can be the string representing Zda's imitation. A common imitation is when Zda is asked a question that he does not know the answer to, in which case he can ask the same question to someone else by using actioner-replacement. As we have discussed earlier, there is no clear line between imitation and creativity. For instance, "hen brood duck eggs" instead of "hen brood chicken eggs" can be a creative idea.

Imitation using actoral replacement (behavioral similarity) has three types:

1. Randomly replace some or all actioners by Zda in the path forward.

2. Randomly replace one actioner (e.g., Lia) by Zda at all locations on the path forward.

3. Randomly pick n actioners at n random locations on the path forward and replace them by Zda (*n*-point mutation).

    Examples of imitation with a nested-actioner string (symbol ⟵ means "replaced by"):

    - Lia.say("Bob.cry") ⟵ Zda.say("Bob.cry")
    - Lia.say("Bob.cry") ⟵ Zda.say("Lia.cry")
    - Lia.say("How does one make a pipe?") ⟵ Zda.say("How does one make a pipe?")

Imitation is an innate tendency, habit, and mechanism. Imitation can also be explained as a result of Zda reasoning: since Lia gets a reward after she brings water to Bob, if I bring water to Bob, I will likely get a reward too. This reasoning is based on the similarity principle: similar actions will lead to similar outcomes.

As a social being, Zda likes to imitate others in various social settings even if there is no obvious reward by doing so. We can also say that Zda likes to imitate others in order to become a social being.

Creativity is necessary for finding better solutions than existing ones. We always want to use old methods to deal with old problems. Instead, we occasionally want to use new methods to deal with old problems in order to find a potentially better solution to the problem. Creativity means to try new things or new ways of dealing with old problems.

To Zda, creativity (innovation) is mainly an action-replacement, an object-replacement, an object's attribute replacement, or an action's attribute replacement, with a similar token (from a "synonymous list") in the event-string. For instance, From *Lia.eat(banana)* to *Zda. cut(banana)* or *Zda.cut(apple)* can be considered as creation. If the logic of such a replacement cannot be well understood, we may think (subjectively) Zda acted irrationally or lost his mind. Creativity can also include asking good questions. Asking a question is nothing but replacing the subjects or events in a question-string from his *Knet* with similar stuff and "speaking" it out. Asking an old question is often an imitation, while asking a new question is often considered creative.

Creativity using behavioral replacement (actoral similarity) has two types:

1. Randomly pick *n* actions at *n* random locations on the path forward and replace them by another similar action or by changing an action parameter in the same action-function.

2. Replacement examples of creativity with a nested-actor string (the symbol ⟵ means "replaced by"):

    - Lia.say("Bob.cry") ⟵ Lia.say("Bob.walk")
    - Lia.say("Bob.cry") ⟵ Lia.saw (Bob.cry)
    - Lia.say("Bob.cry") ⟵ Lia.say("Bob.smile")
    - Lia.say("Bob.cry") ⟵ Lia.saw(Bob.smile)
    - Lia.walk(to the East, for 3 hours) ⟵ Lia.walk(to the West, for 3 hours)

However, a token might be a high-level conceptual pattern, so how can Zda make sure the high-level token will eventually end with a Zda action? It's because the hierarchical structure of tokenization and recursive patternization ensure that any token will eventually end with actionable elementary tokens by means of reverse engineering.

We can have a list of potential examples of imitation and creativity, but that is just a scenario-play to predict what is possibly going to happen, and will remain imaginary until Zda takes a particular action. Such a scenario is called imagination in daily life. Unlike the imitation or creativity where token-replacement occurs in *Knet*, imagination is extracting the pattern into a separate *Knet* (called the imaginary net) and precedes token-replacements in the imaginary net. Depending on the predicted result, Zda may or may not actually make the token-replacement in the *Knet*. The strategy of scenario-play that Zda used, in this case, is based on the notion of game theory because it involves the prediction of others' possible actions.

As far as which one will be selected for execution, this will be determined by the randomized response algorithms discussed later. Each initial, imaginary, and executed pattern has an associated frequency, reward (if any), energy cost, recency (time of recent occurrence), and actionable (if an elementary token) or not. These attributes will be used to determine the probability of selecting an action candidate to be executed.

In the Intent Action List, not all actions are executable at the current condition. For instance, Zda intends to eat an apple, but I might not be able to actually eat an apple since there might be no apple available at the moment. Zda can say: "John, jump into the water," but that may not happen. Zda cannot ensure other people will perform certain actions as he wishes. Therefore, in coding an action for Zda we may need to include an executable conditions check.

Every act of imagination will leave a trace (may be patternized) on Zda's imaginary net that is separated from, but also associated with, his real *Knet*. In other words, the imaginary net will be updated after the imagining. Information on the imaginary net will be only temporarily maintained to keep its size small. Because the knowledge net and imaginary net are two physically separated memory areas, Zda will be able to separate what is real and what is imaginary. An imaginary net consists of scattered, highly-rewarded patterns because many low-predicted-rewarded patterns and old patterns are forgotten (removed) by Zda.

Zda can formulate hypotheses using imaginary imitation, analogy, innovation, and logical reasoning. The hypotheses will be held in the imaginary net for testing.

We know that our recollection of a past experience can cause sensations of enjoyment and pain. Likewise, imagination via the *Inet* can also lead to different sensations through association. This is shown in Figure 14.4.

How do different mechanisms such as attention, imitation, creativity, recollection, logical reasoning, and other actions work together to support the formulation of HAI? We have to first look into the overview of the Response Model.

FIGURE 14.4
Sensations from imagination and recollection.

14.3 Overview of Response Model

While patternization is updating his internal *Knet*, an agent's response refers to an action (including doing nothing) in the external world but also includes deciding which action of learning is appropriate and when it will be performed. Perhaps the simplest form of response is a reflex. In biology, a **reflex** is an involuntary unplanned sequence or action and a nearly instantaneous movement in response to a stimulus that does not receive or need conscious thought. A reflex is made through neural pathways or reflex arcs which can act on an impulse before that impulse reaches the brain.

A reflex often includes a spontaneous emotional response. A reflex is a way to deal with a time-sensitive situation, and such situations frequently occur. Reflexes can protect your body from things that can harm it. For example, if you put your hand on a hot stove, a reflex causes you to immediately remove it even before a "Hey, this is hot!" message gets to your brain. Other protective reflexes include blinking when something flies toward your eyes and raising your arm if a ball is thrown your way. Even coughing and sneezing are reflexes. They clear the airways of irritating matter. Thinking about food when hungry can also be considered a reflex.

Biological Desire and Feeling (pleasure, pain, hunger, anger) attract attention and drive actions. As an example, Baby Zda looks for food constantly, as he gets hungry quickly. Zda's behavior will also change constantly over time, one obvious example being quitting his bottle-sucking habit when he grows up. Zda's personal habits certainly help to determine his responses.

According to psychologist and economist, Daniel Kahneman, humans have two distinctive cognitive systems. They can be characterized as (1) intuitive, fast, unconscious (automatic and impulsive), one-step parallel, non-linguistic, emotional, habitual, using implicit knowledge, and (2) slow, effortful, logical, sequential, conscious, linguistic, algorithmic, planning, reasoning, employing explicit knowledge. In the HAI architecture, we divide the response system into reflex, fast-thinking, slow-thinking, and deep-thinking. Such a response mechanism, with four response modes, will perform better and more efficiently than one with only two modes.

In Zda's architecture (Figure 14.5), the agent's response mechanism includes mainly Reflex, Fast-thinking, Slow-thinking, and Deep-thinking.

1. Reflex can protect one's body from things that can harm it. Reflex deals with one real-time elementary token with the highest subconscious attentivity based on reflexons. A reflexon is a pair of timewise high-associated tokens. The first token is called stimulus and the second is an actionable elementary token, called a reflexor.

2. Fast-thinking is a response mechanism dealing in real time with up to 4 elementary tokens at 1 to 4 time points.

3. Slow-thinking is activated in situations with less time pressure, dealing with up to 16 most recent elementary tokens indirectly, by hierarchically tokenizing the long token sequence into no more than 4 high-level tokens.

4. Deep-thinking, often used in scientific investigations, focuses on responses (logical reasoning and repatternization) using high-level conceptual tokens instead of real-time elementary tokens.

In slow and deep thinking, Zda will judge whether his action will be able to affect an outcome that is in his favor before taking the action.

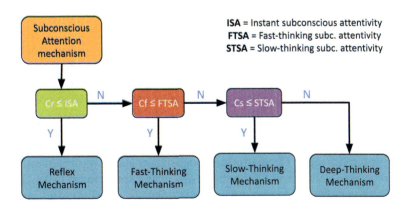

FIGURE 14.5
Overview of response algorithms and mechanisms.

The response models initiate from the subconscious attentivity as described in Chapter 12:

$$SA(t) = w_0 \exp\left[-d(t)\right] + w_1 S(t) + w_2 \ln\left[1 + n(t)h(t)M(t)T(t)\right]$$

As we discussed in the section on the Attention Mechanism, the speed of an object is relative to the agent (observer). Zda is sensitive to voice (words), and the words heard are virtually always in the attention set. An object that an agent is pointing at or shaking will very likely also become object in Zda's attention set. Attention to some innate concept is often related to an action. For instance, when Zda is making a choice, the innate concept Preference is in his attention set. Conversely, when the innate concept, Preference, is in Zda's attention set, he is usually making a choice. Attention to an innate concept can be subconscious or conscious.

The maximum subconscious attentivity at the current time t is called Instant Subconscious Attentivity (ISA), the maximum ISA at times $t-2$, $t-1$, and t is called Fast-Thinking Subconscious Attentivity (FTSA), and the maximum ISA at times $t-14$, $t-13$, ..., $t-2$, $t-1$ and t is called Slow-Thinking Subconscious Attentivity (STSA). The values ISA, FTSA, and STSA will determine which response model is to be triggered, as shown in Figure 14.5. In all four response models, a probabilistic optimal decision approach, called the randomized adaptive response mechanism, is necessarily involved.

If ISA $\geq$ Cr, a critical value, the reflex mechanism will be triggered. Reflex works in a simple way: if a matched Reflexor, an actionable token with a high association with a stimulus, is found, Zda will take the action corresponding to the reflexor. If ISA < Cr or no reflexor is found during the search, FTSA will be calculated. If FTSA $\geq$ Cf, Zda will turn to a fast-thinking model.

ISA will also determine the next attentive time according to the formulation:

The next attentive time starting from current time is NAT = Ct/ISA.

However, at the calculated attentive time points if Zda is in the process of completing his action determined at previous attentive time points, he has no time to determine the next response, the calculated attentive time point will be escaped. Here Cf and Ct, like Cr, is another critical value treated as an innate parameter.

In the fast-thinking model, a small number (e.g., 3) of elementary tokens will be considered in decision-making or response. If fask-thinking does not provide a high reward or if FTSA < Cf, then STSA will be calculated. If STSA ≥ Cs, slow-thinking will be triggered. The critical value Cs is treated as an innate parameter.

In slow-thinking, a long string of tokens (up to 16 elementary tokens from 64 tokens at 16 time points) will be hierarchically tokenized into no more than 4 high-level tokens, and the decision is still based on the event-string of ≤ 4 high-level tokens. Each attentive time point is determined by the previous time point, up to a total of 16 time points.

If reflex, fast-thinking, and slow-thinking are not triggered (STSA < Cs), the conscious attention switch will be turned on and Zda will be in the deep-thinking mode.

Reflex, slow- and fast-thinking usually involve onsite patternization after a response acting on the external world. Deep-thinking focuses on learning-driven and goal-driven actions, and repatternization and new pattern discovery are its main tasks.

In dealing with very complex problems such as scientific questions and unsolved mathematical problems, deep-thinking is needed. It is similar to slow-thinking, but more focused on repatternization of the *Knet* and the formulation of hypotheses based on logical reasoning, analogy, and predicted rewards.

Fast-thinking can be viewed as a near-sighted approach because only 4 elementary tokens are involved. Slow-thinking is not as near-sighted as fast-thinking, while deep-thinking is a visionary approach. According to the Law of Summative Effects (see Section 3.2), each approach in this list is an improvement on the previous one in terms of vision and reward. However, there are reasons for fast-thinking: (1) slow and deep thinking requires a longer time and more effort (cost), (2) the reward may diminish as time goes by, and (3) due to Fredkin's Paradox and Analysis Paralysis (Section 1.1), we tend to spend more time than necessary on choices that make virtually no difference, a poor use of time that should be avoided.

So far we have discussed the response mechanism without language involvement. However, words in Zda's ears can provide a lot of information (or be a main factor) about what he should do. A simple example would be: how does Zda respond to a verbal request? Lia's words may indicate the intended goal of her action. For instance, "I am going shopping." This statement indicates a sequence of actions, not just a simple elementary action. Knowing her intention (goal), Zda will predict better, less frequently check and update the attention set, and better focus on the goal, thus saving time and energy.

When words are in the attention set, the language-guided response will likely be triggered. In language-guided responses, we are particularly interested in the association between words and the sensible actions to be performed. The subconscious attention mechanism and the Factor-Isolation Technique (FIT) play important roles in language-guided learning and response.

Language not only influences thought but also plays a critical role in learning how to plan responses and actions. Without language, humans cannot record knowledge and pass it from one generation to the next, and we would not have today's technology, iPhones, computers, robots, space-stations, as no single generation alone could achieve such amazing miracles. Without learning language, Zda's learning (reinforcement learning) will be very slow and limited. Based on the HAI architecture, Zda will be able to develop his language ability and thoughts hand in hand.

Even though Zda's response is mainly based on associated rewards, high-frequency responses, such as reflexes, might just be a sign that following societal conventions or norms works for the greater betterment of society.

Before we discuss each response model, it will be helpful to look into different types of actions that Zda might take according to the prediction or predicted token as shown in Table 14.1.

TABLE 14.1

Types of Actions Based on Predictions

Expected Token	Main Action to Take	Explain
Zda.act($\mathcal{A}$)	Zda.act($\mathcal{A}$)	Reinforcement Learning
ZdaDesensitisor.act($\mathcal{A}$)	Zda.act($\mathcal{A}$)	Deduction
Actor.action($\mathcal{A}$)	Zda.act($\mathcal{A}$)	Imitation
Non-actionable token	Zda.act(PreviousAction)	Inertia
Non-actionable token	Zda.act(Resting)	energy minimization
Zda.act($\mathcal{A}$)	Zda.act(desensitisor of $\mathcal{A}$)	Creativity
Obj1.act($\mathcal{A}$) & Obj2.act($\mathcal{A}$)	ObjDesensitisor.act($\mathcal{A}$)	Induction
Obj.act($\mathcal{A}1$) & Obj.act($\mathcal{A}2$)	Obj.act(ActionDesensitisor)	
Obj.attribute1 & Obj.attribute2	Obj.AttrDesensitisor	
Obj.act(param1) & Obj.act(param2)	Obj.act(paramDesensitisor)	
Any token	Zda.think(associatedItem)	Attention shift
Zda.rewarded(Giver)	None	Zda received reward

The rewarding token(s), if any, should always be the last token(s) in a pattern. In fast-thinking, a pattern can only have one (the first) rewarding token. Multiple rewards are allowed in slow and deep thinking. A multiple-rewards pattern often means collaboration.

HAI is a complex adaptive self-organized system with hierarchical tokenization, recursive patternization, and randomized adaptive reinforcement learning (RARL). Dynamic response (param), so as to map virtual reality in pattern (param), is, in fact, an autoprogramming-based real-time experience. The notion of randomized reinforcement learning is the imitation of a reward receiver's action in the hope (according to the Similarity Principle) of receiving a similar reward. Imitation is also a necessity for cooperative social beings. For example, imitating others by making charitable donations may make Zda "feel good" in *some* way, and is what we think a social being should do even though it is not an action that maximizes a defined reward.

Agents' behaviors or responses are influenced by inherited personalities. The personalities are modeled by using various innate parameters such as a Pc, denoting the probability of creativeness, for modeling how creative the agent should be.

Finally, we want to point out that tokens are classified into three types in terms of controllability: (1) the agent can fully control, such as his own action, (2) the agent can have some influence, such as with his friend's behavior, and (3) the agent might have virtually no control, e.g., over the rain outside. The response mechanisms will focus on the first category, but will also consider action in some cases of the second category.

14.4 Reflex

In Zda's architecture, reflexes are modeled using reflexons. A reflexon is a pair of timewise highly-associated tokens (2-gramtons occur very closely with high frequencies). The first token is called stimulus and the second is called reflexor. Examples of (stimulus, reflexor) are (an object flying toward eyes, blinking eyes}, and (a sharp pain, scream). A habit can initially be considered as reflexon, but could change later in life.

The Reflexon table will include fields/columns: stimulus, reflexor, frequency, reward, and recency. An initial list of reflexons is needed. The reflexon table will be updated after a reflex. Any 2-gramton with the second token being Zda's action will be considered as a reflaxon if either the associated frequency, reward, or penalty to Zda becomes very high. If the Zda.reward() is also included as a token, some reflexons have 3 tokens or 3-gramtons.

Before determining the response, Zda will determine the attention pulse rate or next attentive time, calculate the subconscious attentivity, and determine the elementary tokens with the highest subconscious attentivity (called Instant Subconscious Attentivity, ISA) at the moment t as discussed in Section 12.2.

The Reflex Algorithms (if ISA $\geq$ Cr) are outlined as flows:

1. Search a reflexor from the Reflexon Table based on the stimulus (a desensitisor of elementary tokens) in the attention set. If no matched reflexor is found, randomly generate a possible action from the Elementary Action List (including action of inertia and doing nothing).

2. Perform animations based on the action taken.

3. Update Zda's internal state: energy, emotion, desire & determine the next attention pulse time based on current subconscious attentivity.

Here the critical Cr is an individual innate parameter of an individual agent.

The question is how to obtain a desensitisor of the elementary tokens? We can predetermine the rules to group the objects and elementary events or actions with different parameter values. The initial list of elementary desensitisors is needed.

14.5 Fast-Thinking

In Zda's architecture, fast-thinking responses will have a follow-up learning process or patternization. A response is an action on the external world based on prediction, while patternization is considered knowledge discovery from observations and prior knowledge. Patternization persistence requires follow-up updates in the internal *Knet*. Predictions are made based on mapping observations to patterns in *Knet*. For fast-thinking with associated onsite decision-making, no hierarchical tokens but only elementary tokens (including their desensitisors) are involved. The basic idea in fast-thinking is that Zda imitates the reward-receiver's action in hoping to receive a similar reward according to the similarity principle. When there is no reward directly involved, Zda will use the pattern frequency or distributive reward as a proxy for reward.

After a response that acts on the external world, dependent on the outcome, onsite patternization will immediately follow, unless the computation requires a long execution time. In such a case, patternization can be scheduled at a later time.

A fast-thinking response is based on predictions that involve a maximum of 3 elementary tokens (in the forms of *actioner.act* or *object.event*) at 1 to 3 time points, while the follow-up patternization involves one more token, with the last token often being the outcome or reward (in the form of actioner.rewarded), which may not be the same as was predicted.

Zda sends his attention pulse to detect the external world, its rate is directly proportional to the subconscious attentivity in reflex and fast-thinking and inversely proportional to the conscious attentivity in slow-thinking and deep-thinking. Therefore, the current subconscious attentivity will determine the next attentive time point. Like a human, Zda generally very much pays attention to voice and spoken language.

The Fast-thinking algorithm starts with 16 potential tokens at 4 consecutive attentive time points; from that, Zda will select up to 4 top attentive tokens (may include voice) to form the final attention set, but will ignore any tokens with less than half the maximum attentivity. A reward token, if any, should always be in the attention set unless it was intentionally hidden from Zda. Reward is in the agent's view regardless of its truthness.

Natural Language patternization in fast-thinking involves up to 4-tokens; an elementary token may include a simple or high-frequency elementary language-token such as a frequently used word or phrase. Such as a language-token may be included as a token's parameter in the event-string actioner.speak(parameter).

As discussed in patternization, the general form of the attentive event-string is $E1 \otimes E2$, $E1 \otimes E2 \otimes E3$, or $E1 \otimes E2 \otimes E3 \otimes E4$, where $\otimes$ denotes either $\wedge$ (occurs at same time) or $\Rightarrow$ (occurs sequentially), with the default precedence of $\wedge$ and then $\Rightarrow$. The events (E1 through E4) can be actions (speaking, eating, walking, thinking) or changes of attributes (e.g., smell or color). Zda uses similarity-based pattern-matching (15 types) to make predictions and decisions (Table 14.2). The key in all thinking models is to find the similarity-based reality-to-*Knet* matched paths.

Through desensitization, Zda makes E1, E2, E3, and E4, each involving just desensitisor of elementary a token with different parameter values, e.g., $E1 = Lia.run()$, regardless of the running direction and speed. In fact, Zda cannot observe all parameters at any given time; therefore, each of E1, E2, E3, and E4 is desensitisor of many similar elementary tokens with different parameter values. Having said that, shape and size are always observed since they are the key parameters in identifying an object. E1 through E4 can also be a single word or phrase or a simple frequently used sentence as a token in 2-gramton (elementary word-action, word-event, word-word) form.

TABLE 14.2

Fifteen Patterns Sorted by Matched Pattern

Scenario	Matched Pattern (Skipton) in *Knet*	Observed Pattern	Expected Token
1	$PT1(1) = E1$	Null	
2	$PT3(1, 2) = E1 \Rightarrow E2$	E1	E2
3	$PT5(1, 2, 3) = E1 \wedge E2 \Rightarrow E3$	$E1 \wedge E2$	E3
4	$PT6(1, 2, 3) = E1 \Rightarrow E2 \wedge E3$	E1	{E2, E3}
5	$PT7(1, 2, 3) = E1 \Rightarrow E2 \Rightarrow E3$	E1	{E2, wait}
6	$PT7(1, 2, 3) = E1 \Rightarrow E2 \Rightarrow E3$	$E1 \Rightarrow E2$	E3
7	$PT9(1, 2, 3, 4) = E1 \wedge E2 \wedge E3 \Rightarrow E4$	$E1 \wedge E2 \wedge E3$	E4
8	$PT10(1, 2, 3, 4) = E1 \wedge E2 \Rightarrow E3 \wedge E4$	$E1 \wedge E2$	{E3, E4}
9	$PT11(1, 2, 3, 4) = E1 \Rightarrow E2 \wedge E3 \wedge E4$	E1	{E2, E3, E4}
10	$PT12(1, 2, 3, 4) = E1 \wedge E2 \Rightarrow E3 \Rightarrow E4$	$E1 \wedge E2$	{E3,wait}
11	$PT12(1, 2, 3, 4) = E1 \wedge E2 \Rightarrow E3 \Rightarrow E4$	$E1 \wedge E2 \Rightarrow E3$	E4
12	$PT13(1, 2, 3, 4) = E1 \Rightarrow E2 \wedge E3 \Rightarrow E4$	E1	{E2, E3, wait}
13	$PT13(1, 2, 3, 4) = E1 \Rightarrow E2 \wedge E3 \Rightarrow E4$	$E1 \Rightarrow E2 \wedge E3$	E4
14	$PT14(1, 2, 3, 4) = E1 \Rightarrow E2 \Rightarrow E3 \wedge E4$	E1	{E2, wait}
15	$PT14(1, 2, 3, 4) = E1 \Rightarrow E2 \Rightarrow E3 \wedge E4$	$E1 \Rightarrow E2$	{E3, E4}
16	$PT15(1, 2, 3, 4) = E1 \Rightarrow E2 \Rightarrow E3 \Rightarrow E4$	E1	{E2, wait}
17	$PT15(1, 2, 3, 4) = E1 \Rightarrow E2 \Rightarrow E3 \Rightarrow E4$	$E1 \Rightarrow E2$	{E3, wait}
18	$PT15(1, 2, 3, 4) = E1 \Rightarrow E2 \Rightarrow E3 \Rightarrow E4$	$E1 \Rightarrow E2 \Rightarrow E3$	E4

Note: PT1(1) is short for PT1(E1) and PT5(1, 2, 3) is short for PT5(E1, E2, E3), etc.

The question is, how does one do desensitization using the elementary tokens? We can predetermine the rules to group the objects and elementary actions based on, e.g., sensory organ sensitivity: we know a newborn has very limited vision but has some good olfaction. For objects of the same type with similar attribute values can form a base for elementary desensitisors. Elementary actions of the same type with similar parameter values can serve as a base for elementary desensitisors. Finally, grouping in desensitization can be changed by Zda automatically for memory and speed optimization over time. Specifically, if the rewards associated with two similar patterns are similar then they can be grouped into one category. We will discuss more later in Sensitization and Desensitization.

We use the following examples to illustrate Zda's decision-making (Refer to Table 14.2).

Example 1: Suppose Zda observes E1 = *Lia.run()*, and in his *Knet*, Zda finds a match PT3(E1, E2), where E2 = *Zda.give(water to Lia)*, no explicit reward specified. Zda could take the action E2 to imitate himself based on past experience.

Example 2: Suppose Zda is observing E1 = *Zda.pick(pen)* and E2 = *Zda.pick(paper)* at the same time. In his *Knet*, Zda finds a match PT5(E1, E2, E3), where E3 = *Zda. write("Happy New Year")*. Zda could take the action E3 based on past experience.

Example 3: Suppose Zda observes E1 = *Lia.run()*, and in his *Knet*, Zda finds a match PT3(E2, E3). Here E2 = *agent.run()*, where desensitisor, agent ∈ {Lia, Bob, Andy} in the *Knet*, and E3 = *Bob.give(water to runner)*, where runner is the agent who runs. Therefore, Zda as a social being could imitate Bob's action and give water to the runner.

Example 4: Suppose Zda observes E1 = *Lia.run()*, and in Zda's *Knet*, Zda found a match PT3(E1, E2) with an expected reward of 5, where E2 = *Bob.give(water to Lia)*. Zda thus makes a prediction, based on the similarity principle, that if he imitates Bob by giving water to Lia, he will receive 5 in reward. Here we have made the assumption that desensitisor of {Lia, Bob} exists in Zda's *Knet*. Zda is performing simple analogical reasoning in this example.

Example 5: Suppose Zda observes E1 = *Lia.run()*, and in Zda's *Knet*, Zda finds a match PT3(E1, E2) with a reward of 5 to Zda, where E2 = *Zda.give(water to runner)*. Also, in his *Knet*, Zda finds another matched pattern PT3(E1, E4) with reward 8 to Zda. Here E4 = *Zda.give(juice to runner)*. Therefore, Zda makes predictions that if he gives water to the runner, Lia, he might get 5 in reward, whereas if he gives juice to Lia, he might get a reward of 8 based on the similarity principle. In this case, Zda will make a random choice of E2 or E5 based on the similarity and reward. See Randomized Adaptive Reinforcement Learning later.

Example 6: Suppose Zda observes E1 = *Lia.run()*, and in his *Knet*, Zda finds a match PT7(E1, E2, E3) = E1⇝E2⇝E3, where E2 = *Lia.walk()*, E3 = *Zda.give(water to Lia)*, no explicit reward specified. Zda could take action E2 to imitate Lia, or wait until *Lia. walk()* and then take action E3, *Zda.give(water to Lia)*.

In fast-thinking response, all tokens (of the matched pattern in *Knet*) after *Zda.rewarded()* will not be considered in response. In fact, no token after *actioner.rewarded()* should appear in elementary patterns, since reward is a natural break point in the segmentation of an event-string.

In Fast-Thinking, a response can be based on the n-token-ahead prediction (n = 1, to 3). For example, if the observed pattern is PT1(1) = E1 at the moment, and Zda finds PT15(1, 2, 3, 4) = E1⇝E2⇝E3⇝E4 in *Knet*, then Zda can do a 1-, 2-, or 3-token-ahead prediction.

In Table 14.2, the expected token (ET) is the token needed to complete the pattern in *Knet*.

1. In scenarios 2, 3, 6, 7, 11, 13, and 18, there is a single expected token.
2. In scenario 4, 8, 9, and 15, there is more than one token in the ET Set.
3. In scenarios 5, 10, 12, 14, 16, and 17, there is a wait option in the ET Set.

Before making a decision, Zda needs to consider the similarity between the combined event-string (the observed event-string + the expected token) and the pattern in the *Knet*. How do we measure similarity? In fast-thinking, token-wise matching must be exact. Thus, the similarity (Jaccard Similarity) between the full pattern (observed event-string appended the event-string for expected actions) and each candidate pattern be calculated as

$$Jaccard\ Index = \frac{Number\ of\ identical\ tokens\ at\ given\ locations\ between\ two\ patterns}{Total\ number\ of\ tokens\ of\ the\ two\ patterns}$$

The candidate patterns are the patterns (in *Knet*) that contain the observed event-string.

In general, decision-making is based on the net expected reward (NER) that Zda is going to get. The NER will be influenced by several factors: (1) the expected rewards of the matched patterns in the *Knet*, (2) the cost for Zda to execute the action, (3) similarities between reality and patterns in *Knet*, (4) Zda's ability to perform the intended action, (5) the reliability of the observed reward, measured by the frequency of the pattern, (6) transability of reward from one actioner (reward taker) to Zda when Zda imitates the taker's action, and (7) Zda's choosing to rest for saving energy, continuing what he is doing out of inertia, or performing some creative action. All these will affect the expected net reward that Zda is going to receive. We will discuss each of them, and then integrate them in Section 14.12, Randomized Adaptive Reinforcement Learning.

The expected reward, if any, is one of the tokens in the pattern. The cost of an action is specified in an action function. Similarity was just discussed. The ability to perform the intended action is the executable condition-check in the action function (Table 14.2). The frequency of a pattern is always recorded in conjunction with the pattern. The number 6 is actually already reflected in Jaccard similarity.

We can see that observational, imitative, creative, and associative learning (e.g., "referring to") are the basic learning forms in Fast-Thinking.

After Zda's response, he has to determine the attention pulse rate or the next subconscious attentive time point t, and this t now becomes the next subconscious attentive time point. A very low energy, a pain, or any other extreme stimulus (such as fire, being hit by an object, someone screaming) can interrupt the regular pulse and cause subconscious attention. At this moment, such extreme stimuli will not be considered in our HAI architecture.

In Fast-Thinking, Zda does not need to decide an active response at every attentive time point, since completing an action requires time (time to complete, TTC). At attentive time points during TTC, Zda does not determine his response.

Algorithms for Determination of Subconscious Attention Set for Fast-Thinking (if $ISA < Cr$):

1. We have calculated 3 subconscious attention sets at the time points $t-2$, $t-1$, and t. In each attention set, there are possibly 1 to 3 objects involved, and for each attentive object there are 1 to 3 attentive attributes involved.
2. Select objects with the top 3 highest attentivities from the collection of the 3 attention sets to formulate the so-called tentative subconscious attention set (TSAS), then remove any objects with the subconscious attentivity < ½ × the highest

subconscious attentivity from TSAS to formulate the final subconscious attention set (FTSAS) for fast-thinking. The maximum subconscious attentivity in FSAS is called the Fast-Thinking subconscious attentivity (FTSA).

3. Determine the next subconscious attentivity pulse or attentive time at which to recalculate the attentivities.

If $Cf \leq FTSA$, the following fast-thinking algorithms will be used:

1. Based on the observed pattern, perform Similarity Search from the *pKnet* (Top 3 tables with most frequent, or most reward, or most recency) to find top $K > 0$ matched patterns.

2. Determine candidate actions based on the observed pattern and matched patterns.

3. Choose an action/token from the list of the K expected tokens based on probability of action (PoA) in the randomized adaptive RL algorithms (see the later section).

4. Perform animations based on the action taken.

5. Initiate the Learning Mechanism:

   a. Patternization: store a new pattern or update the frequency and reward of an existing pattern in *Knet*.

   b. Sensitization: if the current reward is very different from the existing distributive reward, then divide the pattern into two parallel patterns.

6. Update Zda's *Knet* & internal state: energy, emotion, desire, and determine the next attention pulse time based on current subconscious attentivity.

Here the critical value $Cr > Cf$ is an innate parameter; updating *Knet* includes the new pattern, reward, recency, and reward.

Since Fast-Thinking is related to not only the similarity, but also frequency, reward, and/or recency, for computational efficiency a separate memory is reserved, a table that only includes a small set of top patterns with either high-frequency, high-reward, or most-recency.

Similarity search and desensitisor-replacement in patternization (desensitization) require a desensitisor of {x, y, z,...}. Desensitisor-replacement is viewed as Zda's inductive reasoning. Similarity-replacement (Synonyms-replacement) is making analogies and metaphors. Each desensitisor has an associated similarity matrix to indicate the similarity of each possible pair of elements.

Keep in mind that patternization does not allow similarity-matching but only *exact matching* since desensitization has already been used. However, in determining a response the agent will have to use *similarity-matching* because novelty requires exportation needed to search for possibly better solutions. When similarity-matching is used instead of exact-matching, a new pattern is generated with a frequency of 1.

Zda may label a person or agent whom he has interacted with as a friend, classmate, stranger, enemy, or other desensitisor so that he can make more intelligent responses. These characteristic labels can become the extended attributes of the agent.

Reward-based patternization usually follows after a response by using an existing desensitisor, such as friend = {Lia, Bob, John}, or food = {bread, milk, pork, beef}. He may also create a new category or desensitisor if two different patterns have similar rewards. On the other hand, if the current reward is different from the existing reward for the pattern, then it might be a good idea to break down the pattern into two parallel patterns, i.e., sensitization. Sensitization can be performed in fast-thinking and slow-thinking, but more often in deep-thinking.

We now discuss further how Zda formulates desensitisors with the following examples.

Lia asks for **an** apple ⇝ Zda gives **an** apple
Lia asks for **the** apple ⇝ Zda gives **the** apple
Lia asks for **the** apple ⇝ Zda gives **an** apple
Lia asks for **the** apple ⇝ Zda gives **a** desensitisor of apple
Lia asks for **an** apple ⇝ Zda gives **a** desensitisor of apple

Zda needs to know (in his view) if Lia wants **any** apple or a **particular** apple, then he needs to know what is available and what to give her.

Lia asks for **a** banana ⇝ Zda gives **a** banana
Lia asks for **the** banana ⇝ Zda gives **the** banana
Lia asks for **the** banana ⇝ Zda gives **a** banana
Lia asks for **the** banana ⇝ Zda gives **a** desensitisor of banana
Lia asks for **a** banana ⇝ Zda gives **a** desensitisor of banana

These events lead to a pattern: Lia asks for **fruit** — Zda gives **fruit**. Here **fruit** = {apple, banana}. In general, the second fruit will match the first fruit as much as possible in the following descending order if apple is asked for: the apple to the apple, an apple to an apple, the apple to an apple, an apple to a banana, the apple to a banana. When Lia asks Zda for an apple, if no apple is in Zda's attention, he will look for an apple.

A car arrives at a gas station ⇝ Zda pumps gas to **the** car
The car arrives at a gas station ⇝ Zda pumps gas to **the** car
A bus arrives at a gas station ⇝ Zda pumps gas to **the** bus
The bus arrives at a gas station ⇝ Zda pumps gas to **the** bus
A truck arrives at a gas station ⇝ Zda pumps gas to **the** truck
The truck arrives at a gas station ⇝ Zda pumps gas to **the** truck

Zda might summarize these 6 event-strings as a pattern: **vehicle** arrives at a gas station ⇝ Zda pumps gas to **vehicle.** Here **vehicle** = {car, bus, truck}. The second vehicle in the event-string will match the first vehicle in the event-string as much as possible in the following descending order of similarity if car appears in the first place in the event-string: the car to the car, a car to a car, the car to a car, a car to a bus, the car to a bus, etc. When Lia asks Zda for a car, if no car is in Zda's attention, he will look for a car.

In reflex and fast-thinking, a pattern allows one parameter (e.g., fruit).

14.6 Slow-Thinking

In fast-thinking, onsite patternization only formulates elementary gramtons that consist of no more than 4 elementary tokens. These elementary gramtons will be stored in Zda's memory (*Knet*) for future hierarchical tokenization and recursive patternization for slow-thinking and deep-thinking. Meanwhile, Zda will temporarily remember a long event-string of up to 64 of the most recent elementary tokens for slow-thinking. We call this a long event-string LOES (long onsite event-string). Each LOES will be hierarchically tokenized using existing tokens in *Knet,* and a new hierarchical token might arise when a substring appears multiple times within the LOES. This hierarchically tokenized LOES and the associated frequency will be stored in *Knet* for future hierarchical tokenization and recursive patternization.

Like you and me, Zda uses previously learned concepts as tokens to tokenize event-strings for further learning. In this way, Zda can make a future prediction based on just a few concepts (high-level tokens). Predictions are the basis for Zda's decision-making.

Slow Thinking involves up to 64 of the most recently observed elementary tokens, which will be hierarchically tokenized and shortened into no more than 4 high-level tokens. The resulting shortened string of tokens will be used for patternization, but only partial tokens will be used for the prediction and decision-making based on the matched path(s) in Zda's *Knet.* The methodology is similar to fast-thinking, but slow-thinking involves the initial step of hierarchical tokenization for the observed elementary token strings.

It is important to make sure all patterns will recursively end with elementary tokens and no circular tokenization definitions; otherwise, a response may not be in an actionable path. Such a requirement can be guaranteed using reverse engineering of hierarchical tokenization. That is, starting with elementary tokens, a new pattern is always constructed on the basis of known patterns (elementary tokens are naturally the starting tokens for a baby). Regardless of the language humans use in interacting with Zda, the Zda architecture allows code patterns in a consistent way without any built-in natural languages, and thus is natural-language-independent. The mapping between these coding conventions (patterns) and any particular natural language is established gradually through communication and interaction.

Rewards can be used as a tool to shape Zda's knowledge and behavior over time. The recursive network of patterns can be stored in a database table format in Zda's implementation (coding).

In slow thinking, a pattern allows recursions and requires exact matching between patterns in its frequency and reward calculations. However, response allows similarity-matching on the top-layer pattern, while patterns in other layers must be exactly matched, because all other levels have desensitized tokens as needed in hierarchical patternization. This similarity is caused by similar-token replacement at the top layer.

As in Fast-thinking, slow-thinking also involves a single word or phrase or a simple frequently used sentence as a token in 2-gramton (elementary word-action, word-event, word-word) form. As with Fast-Thinking, observational, imitative, creative, and associative learning are the basic learning forms in Slow-Thinking.

Algorithms for Determination of Subconscious Attention Set for Slow-Thinking (if $Cf > FTSA$):

- We have calculated 16 subconscious attention sets at the time points t-15, …, t–1, and t.
- Select objects with the top 16 highest attentivities among the 16 attention sets to formulate the tentative subconscious attention set. Then remove any objects with subconscious attentivity < 1/2 of the highest subconscious attentivity to formulate the final subconscious attention set (STSAS) for slow-thinking. The maximum

subconscious attentivity in FSAS is called the Slow-Thinking subconscious attentivity (STSA).

- Determine the next subconscious attentivity pulse or attentive time based on STSA.

We can outline the slow-thinking algorithms (*if Cs ≤ STSA*):

1. Perform hierarchical tokenization as needed following the precedence of hierarchical tokenization.
2. Search for two similar event-substrings within STSAS. If similar substrings are found, go to the FIL Algorithms below. Otherwise, continue on to Step 3.
3. Determine candidate actions based on the observed pattern and matched patterns
4. Choose an action/token from the list of the K expected tokens based on probability of action (PoA) in the randomized adaptive RL algorithms (see later section).
5. Perform animation as needed.
6. Initiate the Learning Mechanism with Patternization:
   a. Patternization: store a new pattern or update the frequency, reward, and recency of an existing pattern in *Knet*.
   b. Sensitization: if the current reward is different from the existing reward, then divide the pattern into two parallel patterns.
7. Update Zda's *Knet* & internal state: energy, emotion, and desire, and determine the next attention pulse time based on current subconscious attentivity.

Here the critical value Cs is another individual agent's attribute; updating *Knet* includes the new pattern, reward, and recency.

A hierarchical token may not be directly executable; reverse engineering will be needed to make the expanded form before the execution and animation. A generalized action can be speaking out of an abstract concept or an update of internal *Knet* for scientific discovery.

Response and learning are often inseparable. In slow-thinking, refer-to-learning also happens from multiple event-strings using Factor-Isolation Learning algorithms (FIL Algorithms), outlined as follows.

FIL Algorithms:

1. Identify fixors as common tokens among the two similar (Jaccard index) tokens.
2. Identify a desensitisor (or paired desensitisors) consisting of token variable(s).
3. Store pattern structure (fixors) and associated desensitisor or paired desensitisors.
4. If one desensitisor in the paired desensitisor is word-type, then 2-gramtons of refer-to-type are generated with the word-tokens referring to the other tokens. This is refer-to-learning.
5. Update the *Knet*.

As with Fast-Thinking, in Slow-Thinking, Zda only needs to decide upon an active response at some attentive time points. At attentive time points during TTC, Zda does not determine his response but is in the process of completing his action.

14.7 Deep-Thinking

Reflex, Slow-Thinking, and Fast-Thinking involve onsite patternization after actions on the external world. Deep-Thinking is mainly a learning process, focusing on the internal repatternization (knowledge discovery) in the recursive *Knet*. The actions in Deep-Thinking are usually learning-driven actions, or more generally goal-driven actions. Scientific research belongs to deep-thinking, in which the real world may be recorded as experimental or non-experimental data. Zda treats the data as his perceptual world and may apply mathematical, statistical, or AI models he has learned. Zda may use a continuous function to fit the observed discrete data as we do in Newton's second law. Unlike Slow-Thinking, the number of final tokens after hierarchical tokenization will not be capped at 4 but randomly drawn from a probability (geometric) distribution. It's important to remember that language patternization occurs first, before Zda patternizes the whole event-string with nested linguistic strings.

So far we have discussed how *Knet* is viewed as a collection of patterns. However, we can also treat *Knet* as a (recursive) network if we link the tokens sequentially for any given pattern and join different patterns at their common tokens (Figure 14.7 in Section 14.10). The links are consistent with the directions of patterns (some links between two nodes are bidirectional), e.g., A→B→C and A→ B∧C →D. In this *Knet*, a path can be very long and can be used for *n*-token-ahead predictions. Here the arrow can be either a temporal ($\Rightarrow$) or logical ($\rightarrow$) relationship (implication or cause-effect). A path in *Knet* with a high reward on each node may represent a new scientific law or a social norm that might need to be tested.

Constructivists emphasize activeness in learning, and so does our synthetic approach. As example, active learning is reflected in inductive and analogical reasoning. Induction is based on the similarity principle: similar things have similar outcomes. A conclusion from induction should be considered a hypothesis actively proposed by Zda, and thus needs further verification, especially for low-frequency events or patterns. Low-frequency patterns can be due to random chance. The nature of actively proposing hypotheses and seeking verifications is driven by Zda's curiosity. Since probabilistic induction is a direct use of the similarity principle, it can also be considered as an analogy. As we recall, only at one token-level is similarity used in Fast-Thinking and Slow-Thinking, but similarity-matching might be based on multiple-level aggregated similarities (see section 14.9) are often required in Deep-Thinking. Logical reasoning and NAI learning methods can be performed using the data collected from scientific experiments stored in a computer or on an internet cloud.

To achieve a goal is to meet a biological, emotional, or material (rational) desire. Achieving a goal will bring an emotional and/or a material reward. A reward is often time-dependent. When hungry, food is a reward; otherwise, it is not. A reward often diminishes as time goes by. Material rewards (MRs) and emotional rewards (ERs) cannot always be separated completely. A material reward can trigger the feeling of an emotional reward.

1. When hungry (at low energy) or sexually hungry, Zda will likely search for a node with the high responding reward (called a Bio-desirable Node).

2. A low emotional state for Zda can lead to emotional hunger and trigger an emotion-driven action; that is, he will then likely search for a node with a high emotional reward (an Emotional Node) and paths to such a node.

3. Otherwise, Zda can become rational hunger, triggering a material-driven or learning-driven action, and then Zda will likely search for a rational goal node (called a Rational Node) based on material reward or a proxy.

Therefore, Zda can use the reward-adaptive randomization mechanism to randomly pick a goal node (emotional, bio-desirable, or rational node) based on the normalized desirability, and take the corresponding action.

Zda becomes hungry and energy decreases over time, and an action usually costs energy, thus he needs to search for food to boost his energy. Likewise, sexuality can be modeled by hormone level. However, hormone level is cumulative over time, while virtual sexual activity will generally reduce the hormone level.

If the emotional node is chosen, emotion-driven actions to be taken include imagining and recollections of past experience. Emotional needs can also lead to an external action, such as making a donation of some kind.

What can be considered emotional rewards by Zda? It can be positive interactions, such as parents' hugs or tickling (innate), a friend's kind words (developed proxy of emotional reward through association), or it can be something that gives Zda hope.

Emotion and sensation often rely on expectations: if Zda receives what he had expected or more, he will be happy; otherwise, if he gets less than he expected he may not be happy. Here are two examples. Zda expects a reward of 5 without Lia's help, and when Lia helps, he gets a reward of 8, and he appreciates her. In the second example, Zda foresees a risk and no one helps; surprisingly, Lia helps him avoid the risk, and he appreciates her. Zda feels emotional rewards in these two situations.

A rational goal is a goal obtained through rationalization, such as "I need to find a job soon to support my family." A goal can also be taught by teachers, parents, or a person you trust. It can also be determined from reading a book. For example, your parents may tell you: "Knowledge is power. Go to college to get a degree." You may or may not believe what they say. To Zda, rationalization refers to finding the node with top rewards in the *Knet*, while the frequency of a pattern is often considered as a reward-proxy. A reward measures importance in Zda's life.

Despite possible distractions, the long-term goal in deep-thinking cannot easily be changed, and Zda often continues his thinking process when he is in Deep-Thinking. However, while pursuing his goal (e.g., earning a college degree) after deep-thinking, Zda can have different fast-, slow- and even deep-thinking that may change his mind.

We can group actions into two different kinds of tasks in Deep-Thinking (when $Cs > STSA$): goal-driven, and learning-driven tasks (Figure 14.6). Curiosity is Zda's innate attribute that will be affected by energy level and emotion. If there is a low curiosity ($<Ce$),

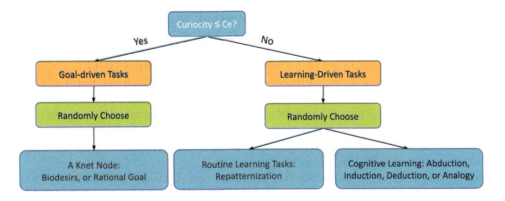

FIGURE 14.6
The Deep-Thinking model.

perform a goal-driven task; otherwise execute a learning-driven task by randomly choosing the routine learning tasks (repatternization) or cognitive learning (Figure 14.6).

A goal-driven task is to randomly choose a goal node in *Knet*, and then use backward-induction to find the paths to the goal node in *Knet* and take action accordingly. Finding an existing path to the goal node is often called recollection (remembering), which may satisfy the emotional need to a certain degree, no other actions are necessary, but may need to take further actions. The goal may be a request from others. For hunger, eating food is needed, so the action will be to search for food. For virtual sexual desire, a recollection or an action of virtual dating may be needed. A rational goal is a node with a high reward or its proxy.

Repatternization is the random choice of existing patterns in *Knet*, and the search for similar patterns to combine into one with newly associated (and possibly paired) desensitisors, this for concise presentations, as discussed in Section 13.5.

Repatternization will be applied to word-strings, event-strings, and word-action strings. Hypothesization will be performed on patternized (and often hierarchically tokenized) event-strings, only one more level of hierarchical tokenization may be needed before hypothesization. The verification of a hypothesized pattern (called a proposition) can be done via Proof-by-Contradiction. If a hypothesized pattern is expressed in natural or mathematical language, the proof or verification can be done by others.

Cognitive Learning uses logical reasoning: abduction (backward-induction), induction (desensitization), deduction (sensitization), analogical reasoning based on patterns and events in *Knet*. Note that induction and deduction are also used in repatternization. Logical reasoning often occurs based on long event-strings by connecting the different patterns at the joints of common tokens. The resulting "event-strings" may be something not observed before, and therefore the concluding pattern will be considered a hypothesis that requires further verification. Such verification will be done through updating the frequency and reward of the corresponding pattern. We have discussed probabilistic logical reasoning in Section 13.6. Other more advanced logics such as predicate calculus in mathematical reasoning can be learned without pre-programming.

Proof-by-Contradiction is based on the notion that if proposition *A* implies the negation of *A*, then proposition *A* is not true. Proof-by-Contradiction in *Knet* is simply finding the node (token or pattern) representing the negation of proposition *A*. For example, if the proposition says "all dogs are black," but Zda finds a negation node (token) in *Knet* representing a yellow dog, then the proposition is not true. In most situations, the negation of a proposition is discovered through deduction (cause-effect reasoning). If two nodes representing A and the negation of A are connected, such a connection will be in great doubt, and might need to be removed. However, keep in mind that the validity of Proof-by-Contradiction is based on the law of the excluded middle, but this law is challenged by Schrödinger's cat Paradox in quantum mechanics, previously discussed.

NAI Utilization may involve software packages and data retrieval, but it is really no essential difference as learning and utilization of other methods or procedures such as calculus and rocket-making. An agent's actions are mostly virtual on a computer, but the NAI utilization can be real since it is performed on a computer anyway. To perform actions that utilize NAI or other statistical methods, Zda must learn the necessary knowledge and employ an interface that allows him to retrieve data.

Deep-Thinking often includes fast-thinking and slow-thinking as its subprocesses due to an STSA increase at the attention pulse time. For instance, when Zda takes actions to accomplish a long-term goal, he may face situations that require his reflex, fast- and slow-thinking.

Agents' actions are mostly virtual, but downloading data and running AI/statistical analyses can be really executed because these can happen on a computer.

When *Cs* > *STSA*, Zda will be in deep-thinking. There are three Random Choice boxes in Figure 14.6 that need to be explained:

1. If Zda's learning curiosity ≤ Ce (one of Zda's innate parameters), choose a goal node in *Knet* based on Zda's desire ("food," "entertainment," or "rational goal") and then identify the path using backwards induction and execute the required tasks.

2. If curiosity > Ce, perform learning-driven tasks randomly, either repatternization or cognitive learning (abduction, induction, deduction, or analogy).

3. If the association search might be performed to mimic attention shift, the resulting token will be treated as either an effect node for abduction or as a cause node for deduction (inference from cause to effect), or general cognitive learning will be performed.

4. Update Zda's *Knet* & internal state: energy, emotion, and desire.

5. Determine the next subconscious attentivity pulse or attentive time to recalculate the attentivities.

Updating *Knet* includes the new pattern, reward, recency, and distributive reward.

In Deep-Thinking, the tokens in the gramtons can be high-level tokens of mixture word-event or word-action tokens (see Section 14.12, Randomized Adaptive Reinforcement Learning).

14.8 Attention Shift Due to Association

The Law of Contiguity can be stated in this way: actions, sensations, and states of feeling, occurring together or in close connection, tend to grow together and cohere in such a way that, when any one of them is afterward presented to the mind, the others are apt to be brought up in an idea. Indeed, association can cause attention to shift from one thing to another (subconscious attention to conscious attention). For instance, when we see a banana, we may think of its yellow color, sweetness, an apple, or even the enjoyment of eating fruit. Like similarity search, such associative search is usually a recollection or token search in *Knet*. Association can be triggered by not only recollections, but also by the imagination. When we see a huge cake, we may imagine a spectacular birthday party that we never had before. Such imagining can happen to Zda too.

It is well accepted in the psychological community that recognition memory reflects the contribution of two separable memory retrieval processes, namely recollection and familiarity. Recollection reflects the retrieval of qualitative information about a specific study episode, such as when or where an event took place, whereas familiarity reflects a more global measure of memory strength or stimulus recency (Yonelinas, et al., 2010).

Recollections are triggered by the association or similarity as similar things are associated by their similarity. Here, familiarity is reflected in the frequency of the pattern (path) and the similarity. In our HAI architecture, the recollection (together with familiarity) process is modeled as follows. Given the current attentive set, search a path in Zda's

Knet, which matches (exactly or similarly) with the observed event-string with the high-frequency associative 2-gramton Table. In humans, recollections can sometimes originate from emotional needs. This is also reflected in HAI since an agent's recollection is based on association gramtons with one of tokens being sensation (emotion, feeling) or some other outcome. Recollections are from recency, reward and frequency tables, and similarity matching.

Recollection is reliving the past, while imagination is living a speculative future, and both are means that can lead to different feelings and emotions. Imagination is the ability to create mental stories, and to mentally construct and simulate the ways to solve a problem or other need. Imagination allows us to conceive of things we do not know how to accomplish, and to conceive of what will happen in hypothetical situations. In our HAI architecture, an instance of imagination is realized by copying a part of Zda's *Knet* and adding a new path (representing an imaginary scenario) to another network, called the imagine net (*Inet*), and predicting what would happen. The separation of *Knet* and Inet is necessary so that Zda can differentiate the imaginary from the real.

What Zda needs to do for imagination is to put different pieces (patterns or strings) together and replace some of the tokens. In this sense, dreams are imaginings when the alarm clock is off, whereas imaginings are dreams when the alarm clock is on. However, dreams that one remembers can be different from the actual dreams. Recollections and imaginings can be triggered by a chain of associations: from *Banana* to *Apple, Fruit, Cake,* and then to *Birthday Party*. In a sense, similarity search is associative search, because similar things are associated.

Associative search is finding an associated token for a given token, which requires a 2-gramton table with high frequencies, high (positive or negative) reward, or high sensation, in Zda's *Knet*.

Outline of algorithms for associative search:

a. Randomly pick a token X with probability p from the attention set.

b. Randomly pick a token Y that is associated with the token X from 2-gramton tables, perform a chain of association search from 2-gramton tables.

c. Consider the final associated token identified as the token in the attention set and identify another set of top K most similar rows from the entire *Knet*.

14.9 Similarity Matching Mechanism

As per our earlier discussion, similarity grouping makes recurrence of events and provides the possibility of discovering (or inventing) scientific laws. Without recurrence of events, no pattern, no scientific laws would exist. However, similarity grouping can have many different ways. It cannot be completely subjective or objective but instead will be subjective and objective at the same time. Similarity grouping is necessary not only for similarity-based pattern discovery but also for dealing with novelty. For this reason, similarity determination plays a critical role in Zda's cognitive development.

We have mentioned the Jaccard index, or Jaccard similarity, which is used in Fast-thinking and Slow-Thinking. The Jaccard index cannot deal with the negation of an event well, i.e, it treats the negation of an event and Null the same. For Deep-Thinking, the similarity calculation is more complicated, involving multiple levels of similarities.

Elementary tokens involve different parameters, such as target, speed, direction, intensity, and so on. Since a high-level token hierarchically consists of elementary tokens, it includes the parameters of the elementary tokens. Therefore, identifying a pattern (gramton) involves not only matching token names but also the parameters. In most cases, token names can be exactly matched, but the parameters are difficult to exactly match. For instance, *Lia.act(name = walk, direction = East, steps = 800)* and *Lia.act(name = walk, direction = East, steps = 810)* may be considered the same, by virtue of similarity grouping, since the two actions may be similar enough to have the same or similar rewards. This is justified by our early discussions: since everything is unique, similarity grouping is necessary to make up event recurrence and pattern emerging.

Since different attributes (parameters) can contribute differently to the similarity score, the similarity between two elementary tokens can be based on weighted similarities of parameters of the two tokens: absolute values, differences, ratios of parameters of two objects. All the parameters should be grouped into categories. For instance, actioners may be grouped into {classmates, friends, relatives, collaborators, opponents} as learning continues; speed may be simplified as {slow, fast, very fast}, and distance as {close, distant}. Many concepts, such as slow and fast, close and distant are vague and vary slightly among individuals and at different times. Therefore, we can add a random variable in their definitions.

How does Zda determine the similarity between two tokens if the two actions are the same and the two actioners are different? For instance, Lia.act(actionName = pick, target = pen) and Zda.act(actionName = pick, target = pen) are two tokens with the same action but different actioners. Like for other parameters, Zda can group the actioners in one or more categories, such as {all agents}, {friends, enemies, collaborators, etc.}. Considering actioners as one category means that Zda does not consider the difference between the actioners at that moment.

Gross grouping in patternization makes few patterns and a less precise model, while fine grouping makes more patterns and a more precise model. If a grouping leads to a large variation of rewards of the pattern, then a finer grouping is needed and the pattern needs to be broken down into finer groups or patterns. However, fine grouping may lead to a low pattern-frequency and model instability in the earlier years of an agent, and to slow performance in his later years when the number of patterns gets large.

When the actioner in the attention set is not important in patternization or decision-making, it means that his identity is not important. However, the identity of an actioner is generally important in our cognitive development. Identity retains some consistency over time, and thus the use of identity often makes things more predictable.

Multiple-level similarity includes similarity at the parameter level, subpattern level, and aggregately, at the pattern level.

At the lowest level, the elementary object-level and action-level, the exponential similarity between two objects is used:

$$\text{Parameter Similarity} = \exp\left(-\sum_n R_n d_n\right),$$

Here the summation $\sum$ is over all N parameters ($n = 1,..., N$), d_n is the absolute difference (dissimilarity) in the nth parameter between two objects, and R_n is the attribute-scaling factor for the nth parameter. The parameter similarity score will range from 0 (completely different) to 1 (identical). Note that not all the attributes are in Zda's attention set for calculating the index. At a given moment only the parameters in the attention set will be used in the similarity calculation; all other unobserved (unattended) parameters are assumed to be the same or irrelevant.

Appearance determines an object's identity and its static attributes. Thus, *Appearance* and *Actions*, including the *targetObj*, are the important factors in the similarity calculation. Dynamic attributes may or may not be important for similarity determination, dependent on attention.

At subtoken-levels, the commonly used Cosine-Similarity will be used. First, for a given location in a pattern (subpattern), we code 1 for the positive situation that token E (such as an actioner) must be in the location, 0 for the Null situation that E is not in the attention set, and −1 for the negative situation (¬E), meaning that E must not be in the location, and then all patterns can be expressed in vector form. Because we code 0 for Null, we make two unequal-length vectors equal length. Given two equal-length vectors of attributes, A and B, the cosine similarity, $\cos(\theta)$, is represented using their dot product $A \cdot B$ and magnitudes $\|A\|$ and $\|B\|$:

$$Cosine\ similarity = \cos(\theta) = \frac{A \cdot B}{\|A\| \, \|B\|}$$

The resulting similarity ranges from −1, meaning exactly opposite, to 1, meaning exactly the same, 0 indicating orthogonality or decorrelation, while in-between values indicate intermediate similarity or dissimilarity. It is more convenient to use the normalized cosine similarity to the range (0, 1): $(1 + \cos(\theta))/2$.

For text matching in NLP, the attribute vectors A and B are usually the term frequency vectors of the documents. Cosine similarity can be seen as a method of normalizing document length during comparison.

We now discuss aggregate similarity. Unlike the simple n-gram and skip-gram models without recursion in NLP, Zda adopts a recursive structure in repatternization. Therefore, the pattern similarity consists of the pattern structure similarity and parameter similarity. In other words, the similarity score between two recursive patterns is equal to the multiplication of similarity scores at all levels:

$$Recursive\ Similarity = S_1 S_2 S_3 \ldots S_L,$$

where S_k ($k = 1, 2, 3, \ldots, L$) is the kth level similarity. Updating those attribute-scaling factors in the parameter similarity is considered a piece of learning.

Examples of patterns and various similarity indexes between two patterns are provided in Tables 14.3 and 14.4, respectively. Here the exponential similarity is based on the scaling attribute factors $R_1, R_2, \ldots, R_n = 1$.

TABLE 14.3

Examples of Patterns

Location	1	2	3	4	5
Pattern 1	Not A (-1)	B (1)	Not C (-1)	Null (0)	E (1)
Pattern 2	Null (0)	B (1)	C (1)	D (1)	Null (0)
Pattern 3	A (1)	Null (0)	C (1)	D (1)	E (1)
Pattern 4	0.1	0.3	0.2	Missing	0.4
Pattern 5	0	0.2	0.5	0.2	Missing

TABLE 14.4

Different Similarities Between Patterns in Table 14.3

Comparison	Exponential Similarity	Cosine Similarity	Jaccard Index
Patterns 1 vs 2	$\exp(-5)$	0	$1/5$
Patterns 1 vs 3	$\exp(-6)$	$-1/(\sqrt{4}\sqrt{4})$	$1/5$
Patterns 2 vs 3	$\exp(-3)$	$2/(\sqrt{3}\sqrt{4})$	$2/5$
Patterns 4 vs 5	$\exp(-0.5)$	$0.16/(\sqrt{0.14}\sqrt{0.16})$	N/A

There seem to be many parameters in similarity calculations. Fortunately, an agent can only pay attention to a small number (≤ 4) of things at a time. Therefore, we only need up to 4 items to determine a similarity score. Determining if two objects (or situations) are similar can be a sequential decision process. For example, we use the first 4 parameters to determine the similarity, and (1) if dissimilar, stop further comparisons; otherwise, (2) pick up another 4 parameters to determine the similarity, and (3) repeat the same comparison process, (1) and (2), continuing until no more attributes need to be considered to determine the similarity.

For deep-thinking, which we discuss due to hierarchical or recursive structures of a pattern, the similarity is calculated recursively starting from the lowest level (elementary level) to the highest level. When formulating a pattern, only partial (attentive) parameters of the elementary tokens are stored in *Knet*.

The number of objects, the number of categories of the elementary parameters, and the number of levels in pattern recursions, determine the number of possible event-strings. Sensitization and desensitization determine the number of possible patterns based on the number of events. Even though the possible combinations can be very large, what an agent experiences will be much smaller.

For simplicity, an object type is determined by Shape in HAI prototyping. A particular object of a given type is determined by size; emotional expression is symbolically represented by an agent's face color. When a particular object (including agents and humans) is identified using the shape, size, and color, the only things to be considered are the actions. Patternization will only concern the limited attributes and actions in the attention set. Therefore, a perceived identicalness of two objects might be just an illusion because of the missing attributes in the attention set. Since motions will increase the subconscious attentivity, actions are more likely to be in the attention set than the static properties. Thus, the default event-string in the attention set is object(appearance).action(targetObj).

14.10 Patternive, Distributive, and Collaborative Rewards

An observed reward associated with an event-string (path) or a pattern is called a patternive reward (PR) or simply reward. A PR is recognized and determined by a change in Zda's internal states (hunger or sensation). When the patternive reward is observed, a distributive reward (DR) can be used in determining a response. The notion of Distributive Reward is that each related action on the path contributes to the reward. In calculating the distributive reward, the actioner in the actionable tokens must be consistent with the patternive reward receiver. For example, from event-string: *Zda.cook() Zda.serve() Lia. eat() Zda.rewarded(2)*, we know that Zda received a patternive reward of 2. The patternive reward is distributed to the action tokens, *Zda.cook()* and *Zda.serve()*, each having a distributive reward of 1, but no distributive reward goes to Lia.

The concept of distributive reward plays a key role in Zda's response mechanism with reinforcement learning when dealing with long novel event-strings in slow-thinking and deep-thinking. When patterns can be linked at the same nodes (tokens) to form a recursive network (*Knet*), novel long patterns can be often formed from this recursive *Knet* for deep-thinking without any actual observations. The novel patterns do not have patternive rewards at time of initial formulation. In randomized adaptive reinforcement learning, if there is a patternive reward, use it; otherwise, a PR can be approximated by summing all the distributive rewards associated within the pattern. That is, use the sum of DRs to predict the PR.

Several patterns can share a token; the distributive reward on the token is the average distributive reward from multiple patterns (Figure 14.7). Since patterns form at different times, the *DR(t)* at time *t* is updated from *DR(t−1)* according to the following formula:

$$DR(t) = \frac{DR(t-1)f(t-1) + PR(t)/N}{f(t-1)+1}.$$

Here, *PR(t)* is the patternive reward received at time *t*, *N* is the number of actionable tokens sharing *PR(t)*, while *f(t−1)* is the frequency of receiving distributive rewards up to time *t−1*. This formula is also applicable when the same pattern has different PRs at different times.

Each directed curve with a reward Zda received at the end represents a path (pattern) he experienced.

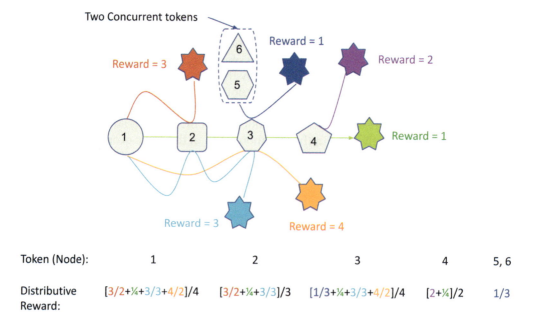

Token (Node):	1	2	3	4	5, 6
Distributive Reward:	[3/2+¼+3/3+4/2]/4	[3/2+¼+3/3]/3	[1/3+¼+3/3+4/2]/4	[2+¼]/2	1/3

FIGURE 14.7
Illustration of distributive rewards.

Strictly speaking, the distributive reward itself is a characteristic of the Markov decision model (past-irrelevant or memoryless), but can only be applied to a recursive *Knet* with RARL as a first approximation, according to the law of summative effects. This also conforms to our social practice. For instance, we often treat a Bachelor's degree uniformly regardless of how hard one works to get there—the value of a milestone achieved is path-independent.

From the formulation of DR, a token can appear in different patterns but only has a unique distributive reward. A distributive reward associated with a token tells us approximately how important the token is in contributing to the actual reward, while the associated frequency indicates how reliable the reward is. A high frequency indicates a high reliability, while a low frequency indicates a low-reliable reward that could be due to random chance. Therefore, the distributive reward determines how likely Zda will take the associated action, if possible. When the distributive reward increases, the expected reward increases. Zda can make an n-tokens-ahead prediction and associated distributive rewards on which to base his decision-making.

A collaborative reward is similar to a distributive reward, but a collaborative reward is distributed over all actionable tokens within the pattern regardless of the actioners. The use of collaborative rewards is based on the belief that a patternive reward is the result of collaborative efforts of all actioners within the pattern.

An actionable pattern becomes an actionable token at a higher hierarchical tokenization level. Conversely, an actionable token can consist of a pattern at a lower tokenization level, and thus has an associated reward. This inspires us to introduce two new concepts: reward propagation and reward aggregation. A reward associated with a token can propagate to subtokens at a lower level, conversely, rewards associated with tokens at a lower level can be aggregated and associated with the higher level token (Figure 14.8). For instance, token 8 consists of tokens 1 and 2 at a lower level, so the reward at token 8 can propagate to tokens 1 and 2. On the other hand, the rewards at tokens 8 and 9 can be aggregated to token 13 at a higher level.

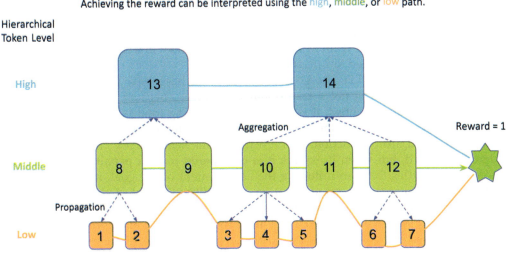

FIGURE 14.8
Reward propagation and aggregation.

Reward propagation and aggregation are motivated by the same notion: In *Knet*, achieving a reward can be interpreted using either a path of actionable lower level tokens elaborately or higher level tokens briefly. In particular, the reward of 1 at the end in Figure 14.8 can be explained in three different ways: (1) due to actions (tokens) 13 and 14, (2) due to actions 8 through 12, or (3) due to actions 1 through 7. An example in real life would be seen when manufacturing a modern car, which includes making (1) the engine, (2) the braking and electric systems, (3) the frame and body, (4) the drive train, (5) fuel and exhaust systems, (6) suspension and steering systems, and (7) assembly of the entire car and testing. Each of the 7 steps (actionable tokens) can be further broken into more detailed steps (actionable tokens). The value (reward) of making the car can be approximated by the sum of the values (rewards) of finishing each of the steps (actionable tokens).

To avoid over-iteration in calculations, reward distribution, propagation, and aggregation will be performed only when an actual reward is received. The reward may be a verbal reward or some other reward proxy, e.g., parents telling their children how important their education will be. In Zda's *Knet*, a reward to an agent is measured in terms of Zda's view of it, not simply as what the agent actually receives. Likewise, in Lia's *Knet*, a reward to an agent is valued by Lia herself.

It is interesting to know that when patterns can be linked at the same nodes (tokens) to form a recursive network (*Knet*), a path with a high reward on each node probably indicates a potential scientific law or social norm.

14.11 Intentions and Goals in the Agent's Mind and Eyes

For us humans, a goal is the desired outcome we wish to attain at some point in the future. An intention is a chosen theme that allows us to create alignment in our lives. If goals are about a destination, intentions are about a direction. Goal-setting focuses on outcome, intention emphasizes process. Goals alone can leave us feeling empty inside when we fail to achieve. An intention is a guiding principle for who we want to be and how we want to act, live, and show up in this world.

What is Zda's goal in life, if any? How is it formulated and will it change over time? How are his subgoals formulated toward the life-goal?

For an agent, Zda or Lia, the goal of maximizing happiness is mainly driven by reward. However, this is not a traditional rationalism, because (1) a thing being a reward depends upon context, it is not fixed (e.g., eating food is a reward when Zda is hungry, but it is not when he is not hungry), (2) being a reward is not and cannot be a prespecified utility function, (3) a reward is time-sensitive (e.g., food is often considered a reward, but when it expires it is considered to be a penalty!), (4) there are many uncertainties that can influence the achievement of the goal, including incomplete information about a current situation, the ability to execute a chosen action, and uncertainty about the outcome of an action, (5) the goal will be achieved as the sum of short-term adaptive goals, but the latter will change constantly as information accumulates, (6) Zda's energy level and biological desire vary over time, (7) there might be some immediate risks that must first be mitigated, (8) children usually do not have life-goals in mind; the life-goal is formulated later in life (and some people even have had none in their entire lives).

Last but not least, happiness is related to one's mentality. Mentality is the character-istic attitude of mind or way of thinking of a person. It reflects his or her expectation and attitude toward a situation (a positive or negative view). In Zda's architecture, mentality is the difference between what was expected and the current situation, as well as predictions of the future. When a goal is believed to be associated with a delayed reward it becomes a reward, at least he feels like at the moment he believes. In other words, whether it is a reward or not is sometimes dependent on one's beliefs. If you think eating fish heads will make you smarter, you will be feeling rewarded and happy when you eat them. And this is just like what we saw in the Doctor-Patient Paradox of Section 13.7.

A goal can be long-term or short-term, concrete or abstract, clearly pathed or vaguely pathed, self-determined or given. Regardless of its complexity, Zda views a goal as a reward proxy. That is why we take the goals set by our parents seriously and often are self-motivated or under parents' and teachers' guidance to accomplish them. When we are young, our parents may help us to set the goal and point out the path forward. We may or may not follow it well due to the energy required, distractions, peer pressure, or other fac-tors. What people (peers) usually do or social conventions (or the corresponding frequen-cies) are also considered a reward proxy.

Even if we have a goal, we may not have it in our attention all the time. For this reason, our actions cannot always be goal-driven. In our architecture, when a goal is in Zda's attention, he will treat it as a node in his *Knet* and use backward induction to identify pos-sible paths to the goal node (Figure 14.9). However, such a path may not always be clear, and he may need knowledgeable people to guide him along on what to do; or perhaps he can figure it out himself along the way by identifying some subgoals (nodes in the *Knet*) and using trial and error methods (RL). According to the law of summative effects, the reward from achieving a long-term goal is approximately equal to the sum of rewards for achieving a series of connected subgoals. This situation formulates exactly the notion of a Markov decision process in stochastics, but for a recursive net.

For the purposes of goal-setting and prediction, Zda needs to use forward induction, while for actions required to achieve a goal, Zda needs to use backward induction. When a goal is set for him by others, including verbal directions by a human or agent such as "Get a college degree," the path to that end will not be fully clear to Zda if there are no clear paths to the goal node in his *Knet*.

In summary, Zda achieves his long-term goal of happiness by pursuing short-term hap-piness cumulatively over time. With all the factors affecting happiness as discussed above, the complexity of the entire goal issue suggests to us a synthetic approach: the RARL algo-rithms for taking care of goal and intention issues and all other aspects of human nature as we have discussed so far in this book. This is the topic of the next section.

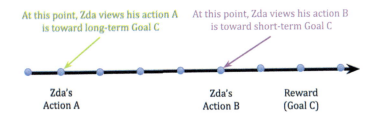

FIGURE 14.9
Goals in agent's mind—illustration via paths in agent's knowledge net.

14.12 Randomized Adaptive Reinforcement Learning

Hierarchical tokenization models the hierarchy of concepts, and recursive patternization "compresses" rich knowledge into the *Knet* without substantial information loss. The efficiency of the compression is ensured through frequency-based patternization and repatternization. The *Knet* is powered by the reward-based response-engine (mechanisms) for an agent to decide a meaningful response according to his life goal and subgoals. An agent's knowledge is judged by how the agent responds in various situations.

Like humans, Zda does not attempt to store all possible scenarios and associated responses that are pre-formulated in his memory. Even if such pre-formulation is possible, it will take Zda very long to retrieve the sensible response from a huge database in the memory. The efficiency of dynamic response using a response mechanism can be seen in a simpler case in language communications: we don't have all pre-formulated sentences in our memory. Instead, we only have words, phrases, and a limited number of sentences in our minds. We use language-specific grammar to formulate sentences and carry on conversations in real time, even though the grammar and knowledge each person has may not be necessarily exactly the same as the official ones.

The reward-based response mechanism is essentially RARL. Hierarchical tokenization, recursive patternization, and the adaptive response mechanism ensure the rich ontology, elaboration tolerance, and computational efficiency.

In Reinforcement Learning (RL), the learner is not told which actions to take, as in most forms of machine learning, but instead must discover which actions yield the most reward by trying them. RL is learning what to do or how to map situations to actions so as to maximize a short-term or long-term expected reward. When the reward is not explicitly identified, the frequency associated with the pattern may be used as a proxy for the reward based on the notion that we often act toward the path associated with the maximum reward.

In the most interesting and challenging cases, actions may affect not only the immediate reward but also the upcoming situation and, through that, all subsequent rewards. Such RL is characterized by "trial-and-error search" and "delayed reward." In traditional RL, the agent will take the action with the maximum expected reward (see Section F in the Appendix).

However, one of the challenges that arise in reinforcement learning, and may not in other kinds of learning, is the trade-off between exploration and exploitation. To obtain the maximum expected reward, Zda not only needs to consider actions that it has tried in the past and found to be effective in producing reward but also needs to try actions that it has not selected before since the uncharted territories may provide better rewards. On a stochastic task, each action must be tried many times to gain a reliable estimate of its expected reward. When an agent takes a path with the maximum reward and such a path has not been tried sufficiently many times, the optimal path could be just an illusion due to randomness caused by some hidden confounders. A solution to this problem is to use RARL. In this probabilistic approach, the probability of taking a path is proportional to the associated reward using a model such as the adaptive urn model (similar to the response-adaptive randomization, Chang, 2007, 2014).

Zda's action is based on what he senses from the environment, his *Knet,* and his prediction of future events. For this reason, different agents usually have different responses even when they are facing identical situations.

Zda as a humanized reinforcement agent has a life's goal. Zda can set up subgoals that are associated with the life-goal in various situations at different times of his life. This is in contrast with many narrow AI approaches that consider sub-problems without addressing how they might fit into a larger picture or life-goal. Zda with RARL can sense aspects of his environment, and can choose actions to influence his environment, his collaborators (friends), and opponents (enemies).

Zda's actions are often based on predicting what is going to happen even at moments when he can have little influence on the outcome. At such times he is still learning how the universe works. Such predictions may sometimes be based on imaginary or hypothetical situations. Zda's action will be based on his predicted world at that moment. In Zda's architecture, a randomized-response model based on *n*-token-ahead distributive rewards will be used.

Randomized adaptive reinforcement learning (RARL) is a Trial and Error method in which a randomized response is used. In a randomized response, what is randomized is the intention of performing the preferred action among the options according to the associated probabilities (to be discussed soon), not the action itself. Such an intention is a path to Zda's goal. Or we may say Zda wants to perform the desired action. But having the intent to do something does not mean Zda can do it.

In general, a simpler pattern with a higher frequency, higher reward, and occurring more recently will more likely be picked as an action path. To further explain other parameters in the probability model, we start with the probability of an action.

Probability of Action (PoA):

$$Pr\ (action\ i) = \frac{1}{C}SRF, \text{ where normalization factor } c = \sum_{i=1}^{K} SRF.$$

1. Similarity: S is the similarity between the currently observed event-string and an existing pattern in the *Knet*. The similarity represents the suitability of the reward

2. Expected (Average) Reward: R = average net reward associated with the reward taker in the pattern from the *Knet*. An action has a parameter of energy cost. R can be negative or time-sensitive: as time passes, the reward may diminish. A reward can be viewed as a pattern enhancer. If the action is taken by and so the reward is given to another person, Zda can only get an estimate of the expected net reward if he takes the same action. Money is not a reward until Zda learns that money can buy things he likes or is taught by others. When Zda learns that getting a college degree is associated with a potentially higher paying job, he could set the college degree as his goal or a proxy of reward.

3. Frequency: The frequency F of the pattern measures the reliability of the reward. A high frequency of a pattern suggests that the association between reward and pattern is real, and not by random chance. Frequency is also a Reward Proxy. When no direct reward is associated with a pattern, then a high frequency indicates a possible late reward (rewarding things keeps people doing the same thing).

Expected Reward R, similarity S, and frequency F are path-related; thus PoA is also path-(pattern-) dependent.

From PoA formulation, the effect of the same percentage increase in frequency, in reward, or in similarity is the same. A high-reward pattern will have high frequency, thus the frequency and reward are associated. A typical PoA curve in relation to the frequency is shown in Figure 14.10. The reason that the relationship is not linear as expected

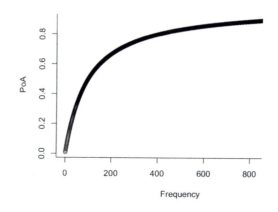

FIGURE 14.10
Probability of action as a function of pattern frequency.

is because of the normalization factor c in the equation. Such a non-linear relationship is consistent with our intuition and experiences. Similar relations hold between PoA and R, and between PoA and S.

Note that we can consider the 4 factors S, R, and F together to formulate PoA, or we can deal with them sequentially as we do in the Particle Swarm Optimization search algorithm.

Energy Consumption: ΔE = energy consumption when executing the intended action. Taking actions such as imagining and playing games requires energy. Zda constantly monitors energy levels or predicts the energy required to achieve a goal and decides if it is worth the effort (cost). Making predictions also carries a cost. Thus, Zda may abandon a prediction if he sees the cost (including opportunity loss) is more than the expected gain, or if his energy is low and it may be exhausted before reaching the goal. For simplicity, we only define the energy cost for each elementary action, and no energy cost of switching between tasks is considered. Energy costs will be reflected in the internal energy update. In fast-thinking, only elementary action is involved, so the cost is negligible. In deep-thinking, a token such as "getting a college degree" can involve years of effort and cost a lot.

14.13 Finding the Source

How does Zda find the location (direction and distance) of a source such as a light, sound, smell, or heat? He will move back and forth (and/or turn his head around) to sense the difference in the intensity of sound, smell, light, or distance. However, this is only applicable when the source is nearby. When the source is far away, the small distance change caused by moving is insignificant. For a distant source, one judges the source location by the prior knowledge of such a sound source and by the loudness changes when turning in different directions. For a nearby sound source, one can also judge the source location by the difference in sound coming into the two ears. For a moving source, its motion effects are reflected in the intensity changes in the ears and the redshift phenomenon (a higher pitch when a source is moving closer and a lower pitch when it is moving away). As long

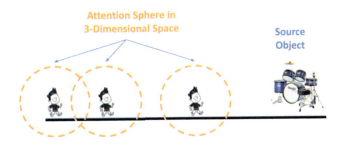

FIGURE 14.11
An agent in searching for a source of sound.

as Zda is equipped with such ears, which is not difficult, Zda can identify a sound source as a human. Eyes work in a similar way (Figure 14.11).

14.14 Efficiency of Hierarchical Decision-Making and Computation Efficiency

This hierarchical decision process (Figure 14.12) is a natural consequence of hierarchical tokenization and recursive patternization. The innate hierarchical decision process has a very important feature: it reduces the decision (computation) time exponentially from N (the number of options) to $\log_2 N$. Moreover, when fewer options are presented at each decision point, it is much easier to make a decision because Zda does not need to compare all N options each time before deciding.

You may have realized that in real life, we humans are often presented with hierarchical options for selecting products. For instance, clothes: Which size do you like? What color do you like? What kinds of materials do you prefer? What styles do you find attractive? These sequential questions can help us to reach the final choice exponentially faster (though maybe, less optimally in some cases). They appear to be similar to hierarchical concepts in

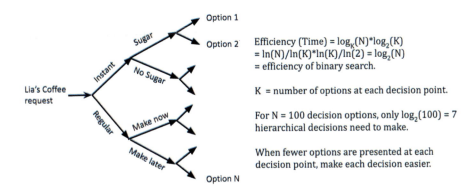

Efficiency (Time) $= \log_K(N)*\log_2(K)$
$= \ln(N)/\ln(K)*\ln(K)/\ln(2) = \log_2(N)$
= efficiency of binary search.

K = number of options at each decision point.

For N = 100 decision options, only $\log_2(100) = 7$ hierarchical decisions need to make.

When fewer options are presented at each decision point, make each decision easier.

FIGURE 14.12
Efficiency of hierarchical decision-making.

Zda's (or a human's) mind, but are actually different in structure. Sequential questioning further breaks down the options beyond the hierarchical concepts we already have.

Because time is a factor of the utility function in optimization, the Kolmogorov complexity of a string of bits is never an issue in computing (determining) a response for Zda. The Kolmogorov complexity (algorithm entropy) of an object, such as a piece of text, is the length of a shortest computer program (for a given computer language) that produces the object as output (Kolmogorov, 1963). It is a measure of the computational resources needed to specify the object. The notion of Kolmogorov complexity can be used to prove impossibility results akin to Cantor's diagonal argument, Gödel's incompleteness theorem, and Turing's halting problem.

Alan Turing demonstrated in 1936 a famous theorem known as the halting problem theorem. In simple terms, it states the following: a general program deciding in a finite time whether a program for a finite input finishes running or will run forever cannot exist for all possible program-input pairs. The halting problem theorem is related to Kurt Gödel's incompleteness theorem in the following way. Suppose that we have a program that can assess the algorithmic complexity of sequences (or an input string). This program works in such a way that, as soon as it detects a sequence with complexity larger than n, it stops. The program would then have to include instructions for the evaluation of algorithmic complexity, occupying k bits, plus the specification of n, occupying $\log_2 n$ bits. For sufficiently large n, the value of $k + \log_2 n$ is smaller than n and we arrive at a contradiction: a program whose length is smaller than n computes the input string of the program itself whose complexity exceeds n. The contradiction can only be avoided if the program never halts! That is, we will never be able to decide whether a sequence is algorithmically random (Marques, 2008).

14.15 Nuts and Bolts

1. Words can refer to objects, events, actions, or abstract concepts. Understanding is mainly learning what refers to what. Such understanding also includes understanding one's intentions or goals. In Zda's view, Lia's intention is a likely result of Lia's action, and is a future node on the path in Zda's *Knet*.

2. Biological Desire and Feeling (pleasure, pain, hunger, anger) cause attention and drive actions.

3. Attention is the starting point of learning and responding, while the maximum Subconscious Attentivity determines the response model (reflex, fast, slow, or deep-thinking) in action.

4. For simplicity, an object type is determined by Shape in HAI prototyping. The particular object of a given type is determined by size; emotional expression is symbolically represented by the agent's face color.

5. Reflex can protect one's body from things that can harm it. Reflex deals with one real-time elementary token with the highest subconscious attentivity based on reflexons, a list of highly associated two tokens (2-grams, 2-gramtons, 2-skiptions with high frequencies).

6. Fast-thinking is a response mechanism under time pressure, dealing in real time with up to 4 elementary tokens at 1 to 4 time points.

7. Slow-thinking is activated in situations with less time pressure, dealing with up to 16 of the most recent elementary tokens, indirectly, through hierarchical tokenization into no more than 4 high-level tokens.

8. Deep-thinking is often used in scientific investigations, focusing on the responses (logical reasoning and repatternization), using high-level conceptual tokens instead of real-time elementary tokens. In deep-thinking the real world may be recorded as data using instruments. The data may represent an agent's perceptual world and statistical models may be applied to the data.

9. Language-guided response concerns how to use the information words provided in the natural language to facilitate the response.

10. Randomized Adaptive Response is based on Probability of Action, which depends on 3 normalized factors: Similarity (S), Reward (R), and Frequency (F).

11. Zda's goal can be viewed as a proxy of a reward. When a goal is believed to be a reward, it becomes a reward. A subgoal is a node (milestone). According to the law of summative effects, the reward from achieving a long-term goal *is believed to be* approximately equal to the sum of rewards for achieving a series of connected subgoals.

12. To Zda, imitation is nothing but replacing an actioner (such as Lia or a human) in an actioner.action string with himself, such that the string becomes Zda.action. As a social being, Zda likes to imitate others in various social settings, even if there is no obvious reward for doing so. A creative action is mainly a replacement of an object, action, or object's attribute with a similar token (from a "synonymous list") in the event-string.

13. The similarity principle is the foundation for dealing with novelty.

14. Just like you and me, Zda has the habit of constantly performing cognitive learning (abduction, induction, deduction, and analogy).

15. Zda asks why and how to satisfy curiosity as a reward. To Zda, curiosity learning is searching an earlier token on the path in the *Knet* for a reason—why-type curiosity-learning. Zda may intentionally change a new action that is not indicated by a pattern in *Knet* in order to see what is going to happen after his action. Thus, a creative action is how-type curiosity-learning. Curiosity may also be shown in imitation. As an example, when Zda sees another person producing a certain sound that is new to Zda, the probability of Zda producing this new sound will be boosted.

16. Learning (patternization and referring to) occurs after a response. That is, we learn from each experience. Learning itself can be considered as a type of response.

17. Zda constantly monitors the distance of attentive objects.

18. When Zda wants to look for something in reality, he will walk around, and when a match is found he will walk toward it and do something with it.

19. Attention means that Zda will likely act on the attentive object, which may be looking at it, looking away, talking about it, walking toward it, walking away from it, picking it up, punching it, throwing it away, grabbing it, and making association among the attentive item.

20. A pattern can represent a two-way association between body pose and language, between emotion and language, or between emotion and body pose, or a 3-way association between Body poster, language, and emotion.

21. What gets randomized is Zda's intentions (wants), not directly Zda's actions, because not all actions are executable at the moment.

22. A name can be associated with an object in reality or a concept of performing a certain task. A concept can refer to anything, including other concepts.

23. Zda needs to differentiate a categorical name from a name for a particular object of the category. In other words, he needs to differentiate between a class (category) and a desensitisor (a member of the class).

24. As far as attention is concerned, who Lia speaks to is often important.

25. A path in *Knet* with a high constant frequency across all nodes is a scientific law.

26. Any (directed) path in *Knet* with rewards is a rule in daily life or a social norm. Any directed path of high level tokens in *Knet* can be a scientific law or mathematical or physical law in a statistical sense.

27. Since rewarded paths are more likely to be repeated, when rewards are not explicit, determining Zda's response based on frequency will be a good alternative.

28. When the self-awareness switch is on, Zda is aware of his intention or goal.

29. As social interactions accumulate, a person/agent will be labeled with certain personalities and intention of an action at a particular time.

30. *Shaking* an object while *calling* its name brings Zda's attention to the two things and lets him make an association between them; this is because two things happening close together in space and time will automatically be associated.

31. Explaining (calling its name) while performing a task will bring the action to Zda's attention and prompt him to make an association between the procedure and its name.

32. One can present the same object at different temperatures to Zda and say words like cold, cool, warm, hot to teach him the meaning of these words.

33. Patterns serve as the basis for predictions, while predictions serve as the basis for response. A pattern indicates associations between tokens and between a path and the response.

34. It might be efficient to indicate whether a token is actionable or not in the database.

35. Association is everything. To understand the intention of peoples' words is to make an association between the words and Zda's appropriate responses. Response is affected by an association between the observed event chains and action or outcome, e.g., event chain A B C results in D, while A B leads to D, and A G leads to S. PoA is a measure of the strength of such an association.

36. Zda pays attention to words, or NL, because (1) innate habits of voice-sensitive, and (2) rewards and penalties often happen close to wording.

37. When Zda appears to be doing nothing with the external world, or observing, it means he is likely performing cognitive learning or factor-isolation learning.

38. Zda identifies an object by its attributes, not the other way around. If Zda identifies an object as a class of object, it means its basic attributes used for the identification are similar to the class attributes.

39. When Zda compares two objects, he will often compare many of their attributes until he finds differences, even if some of the attributes are not in his initial attention.

15

Effective Teaching

15.1 General Principles in Teaching

Learning through extensive interactions, just as we take some 20 years to teach someone until graduating college.

It is important to understand Zda's learning and responding mechanisms, which are the foundation of his effective learning. In teaching Zda, we should work in ways that are similar to how we teach humans, from babies to adults. Here are general principles and tips for teaching Zda:

1. Get Zda's attention to what you want to teach him. Shaking (quickly moving) and pointing at (pointing to) an object will attract his subconscious attention. Voice (changes of sound and silence) will also attract Zda's attention.

2. Association is fundamental in learning, because humans (agents) tend to associate things that happen near each other in time and/or space. A teacher should talk while doing so that Zda can make associations between words and the teacher's event/action. This is how natural language is learned. Therefore, as a trainer, we should direct the agent's attention and strategically utilize associations.

3. *Shaking* an object while *calling* the name brings Zda's attention to the two things and lets him make an association between them: two things happening near each other in space and time will automatically be associated. Explaining (calling the name) while doing work attracts Zda's attention and makes an association between the procedure and its name. Associative Learning (classical and operant conditioning) is passive learning, but rewards and associative learning together are a powerful tool for effective teaching.

4. First things to teach: words for object names and their attributes, words for sensory attributes, innate knowledge (concepts) such as "referring to."

5. Use the factor-isolation technique (FIT) to create multiple situations (event-strings or sentences) where only one or a few factors are different, so that Zda can easily see the pattern (onsite patternization). Examples in language learning would be "You read the book," "I read the book," and "He read the book." Another example would be presenting the same object at different temperatures and saying words like "cold," "cool," "warm," and "hot," to teach Zda the meaning of the words.

6. Following the idea of FIT, using an isolated-word change in conjunction with an isolated-attribute change is an effective way of making an association

between the word and the attribute that the word refers to. Passing food to a child when he is hungry, while you are saying: "Are you hungry?" will make him associate the word "hungry" with the sense of "hungry" or the inner state of hunger.

7. While talking, show how to do things (with others) to provide Zda an opportunity to imitate and learn the natural language associated with the action. When Zda imitates a pattern or event-string, he must know all the actions associated with its tokens. For example, to make a chair, he already knows how to make all its parts.

8. For effective learning, create an environment that only allows limited action options that we want Zda to choose from.

9. It is critical to know what knowledge Zda has before teaching him more complex concepts, so that he can perform tokenization efficiently using the concepts known to him.

10. Recurrent events are created on the basis of similarity grouping. A category and its desensitisor are discovered or created through applying the factor-isolation technique to multiple event-strings.

11. High-frequency patterns might reflect societal conventions, even if the reward reaped by following the conventions seems not directed to Zda, but is instead intended for the greater betterment of the society. Use Zda.favorites {…} as the proxy to collect all the rewards, including social rewards, to others.

12. Zda's behaviors are somewhat consistent (e.g., he screams when facing a danger and cries when hungry). Such a necessary consistency on a time-axis exists either due to the inherited, natural, or developed tendencies (habits). The more you do, the more you are likely to do.

13. Learn the sequential order of attributes and comparisons of attributes between objects when describing an object, and learn the sequential order of dynamic attributes when describing an action. Such sequential order is culturally dependent.

14. Zda's biological clock (time) is usually in lower subconscious attentivity because it is always steadily and quietly ticking.

15. Zda's *Knet* is a self-inclusive network. The self-awareness switch is off by default. When it is off, Zda searches the current observed pattern in his *Knet* for decision-making. When it is on, the Zda outside the *Knet* is "watching" the Zda inside the *Knet* and recording what he is doing. That is, Zda is intent on doing something, and he is aware of his intention. It is important to keep this in mind when we want to teach Zda effectively.

16. A goal is a desire, an innate concept. In Zda's view, a goal is something that directly or indirectly associates with a reward. The goal can be a necessary or sufficient condition. An intermediate goal is often called a milestone, represented by a node in Zda's recursive *Knet*.

17. A concept can be learned or taught in different ways, but some are more efficient than others.

18. In general, the way we teach Zda is virtually the same way we teach our babies and kids.

15.2 Referring to Objects and Sensible Attributes

We illustrate how to teach Zda the names of persons, objects, and properties. It will be the same way we teach our babies and kids.

Example 1: We can point at (to) the mother while calling "Mom" and point at the daddy while saying "Daddy" so that the baby Zda can mimic the sounds "mom" and "daddy" and make the associations between the word "Mom" and his mom, and between the word "Daddy" and his daddy. Repeat this process so that the association is enhanced and becomes reliable.

Example 2: Shake a pen in front of baby Zda while calling it "pen," so that the pen and the word "pen" in his attention allow him to make an association between the two. However, other attributes, such as color, might also be in the attention set and Zda may associate the color attribute with the word "pen." Thus, we need to repeat the teaching process with pens of different colors. By doing so we create multiple event-strings. The common association between elements in the attention set is enhanced. In this case, the common association is between the appearance (combination of shape and size) of pens and the word "pens."

Example 3: To teach the word "milk," when Zda cries because of hunger we repeat: "Hungry?" and then pass a bottle of milk while repeating "milk." Repeating the process every day allows Zda to make associations between "hungry" and feeling hungry, and between "milk" and the bottled milk. We say "Hungry?" at the moment when we think Zda is feeling hungry so that he can establish the association between the word "hungry" and the hungry feeling.

Example 4: Similarly, we can put things with different smells to Zda's nose while saying "smells good" or "smells bad," to teach Zda the phrases.

Understanding a word is a process. Teaching Zda the same words in different situations can make him better understand the word, even if the word is not a polysemy.

After we teach Zda nouns for calling a class of objects using their appearances (e.g., shape and size), we need to teach him how to refer to particular objects using adjectives. Adjectives describe objects using an agent's sensed attributes: Taste, Touch, Sound, Color, Size, Shape, Amount, Emotion (Sensation), Desire, Time, Age, Location, Origin, Material, Person or Personality, Situations, Qualifiers, and changes of these attributes in time and space.

Example 5: After Zda learns the word "pen," put a green pen and a red pen near Zda and ask him to pick the red one by repeatedly saying "red pen." In the beginning, he may randomly pick one of the pens. Every time he picks the red one, we give him a reward, such as a piece of candy or a warm hug. Otherwise, give a small penalty. Using this reinforcement learning, or conditioning, Zda will quickly learn what a red pen is.

Learning how to describe an object using its attributes includes (1) a word, or words, for each attribute, (2) an appropriate sequential order of words to describe the attributes in the phrase or sentence, (3) learning to understand what others say, and (4) being able to describe an object following standard conventions. The order of adjectives in a sentence will influence one's thoughts. For instance, the adjective order in English is supposed to be:

Quantity or number, Quality or opinion, Size, Age, Shape, Color, Proper adjective (often nationality, other place of origin, or material), and Purpose or qualifier. As another example, for mailing addresses in English the order is the recipient's name, street, city, state, and country, while in Chinese, the order is reversed. Different orders imply which attributes will attract one's attention first.

We can refer to an object using the dynamic attributes of the object, as illustrated in Example 6.

> **Example 6**: (1) Present a non-moving toy car and a moving toy car. (2) Request to Zda: "Pick the moving car." (3) Use reinforcement learning, i.e., if Zda picks the right car, a reward is given, otherwise, a penalty will be given. By repeating the process, Zda will learn to pick the correct one. Furthermore, by replacing the two cars with other two identical objects and repeating the training process, Zda will learn what "moving" means through repatternization.

We can refer to an object using the attribute comparisons of different objects, as illustrated in Example 7.

> **Example 7**: (1) Present two identical toy cars, one moving faster than the other. (2) Request to Zda: "grab the faster car." (3) Use reinforcement learning, i.e., if Zda grabs the right car, a reward is given; otherwise, a penalty will be given. By repeating the process, Zda will learn to grab the correct one. Furthermore, by replacing cars with other objects and repeating the training process, Zda will learn what "faster" means.

15.3 Teaching Pronouns and Making Requests

> **Example 1**: After Zda has learned what a pen and a book are, we set a situation where a pen and a book are at Zda's reach. We either ask Zda to give us the pen or ask him to give us the book, randomly; if he gives you the correct item, you say "Yes," otherwise you say "No." Repeat this process using the same objects and different objects. Zda will eventually learn what "No" and "Yes" mean.

When Zda has learned "Yes" and "No," we can teach him the words, "you," "him," and "me," as illustrated in the following example.

> **Example 2**: This takes place in a 3-person setting: Zda, Lia, and Bob. Lia says to Zda "you" while pointing at Zda, says "me" while pointing at Lia herself, and says "him" when pointing at Bob. Repeat the process many times. Then let Bob do the similar pointing-saying pattern, repeatedly. Over time, Zda will imitate the process. If he does so incorrectly, Lia or Bob says "no," otherwise "yes" to confirm. We can also hold Zda's hand to point at a different person to assist him in learning the words, "you," "me," and "him."

The reason Zda can learn in Examples 1 and 2 is because of the notion of association, as discussed in Section 13.8: Items or subsets in the same attention set form associations.

The key and coin appear together 100 times

The key appears 100 times   **The coin appears 100 times**

To teach Zda word "key", you say "key" when there is a key alone and say "key" or "coin" randomly when you see both key and coin. This will lead two associations: "key"— 150 times, "key"— 50 times. The intended association is the strongest association.

FIGURE 15.1

An associative feature shown in the key-coin experiment.

When the same attention set recurrences over time, these associations will be enhanced. However, more often there are many similar attention sets, the common items in attention sets gain enhanced associations because their frequencies are higher, while uncommon items have weaker associations due to their lower frequencies. This simple fact makes statistical/scientific discovery easier. That is why frequency-based patternization makes sense in many situations that naturally occur. In communication and language learning, we purposely impose words in some particular attention set (e.g., talking while doing) so that Zda will make an association between the words and the other attentive items. Over time, the association between the words and common item(s) is enhanced since the words are among the common attentive items.

We elaborate the nature of the associative mechanism in the following example:

Put a key and a coin in an urn (Figure 15.1). Randomly choose the key, coin, or both key and coin with replacement (put the selected item(s) back into the urn). Say "key" when the key is picked; say "coin" when the coin is picked; say either "key" or "coin" randomly when both key and coin are picked. Repeat this picking-saying game, say, 300 times, in front of Zda. Then it is expected that Zda's attention set includes {key, "key"} 100 times, {coin, "coin"} 100 times, {key, coin, "key"} 50 times, {key, coin, "coin"} 50 times. When only 2 items are in the attention set, there is only one possible association, e.g., between key and "key" or between coin and "coin." When there are 3 items (e.g., key, coin, "coin") in the attention set, Zda could establish 6 possible associations, key—coin, key—"coin", coin—"coin", (key∧coin), etc. It is clear that the association between "coin" and the coin, and the association between "key" and the key are strongest because their frequencies are highest. We wish the attention set will be either {key, "key"} or {coin, "coin"}, but not other sets. However, we see that even if the attention sets are not perfectly as we wish, Zda can still establish the probabilistically correct associations according to the frequencies. This is an important association feature for teaching since we cannot control Zda's attention completely.

In the key-coin urn experiment, it is critical to impose (speak) words into Zda's attention set at the right moment. It is possible some undesirable associations may develop. Polysemy is a result of such multiple associations of a single word, causing ambiguities sometimes. Fortunately, we can use a reward to enhance a desirable association and a penalty to weaken an undesirable association. Well-designed scientific experiments can also remove some false associations. In addition to using rewards, changing the recurrences of event-pair can reshape the association or even dissociate an existing association.

What does an association mean in general? It means that Zda and others will likely repeat the pattern in his response, and consequently means that the association could lead to desirable word-referring and appropriate use of the word in communications.

15.4 Classical Conditioning and Reward Proxy

Classical Conditioning (Section 1.4.3) can be used in teaching Zda. The Russian physiologist Ivan Pavlov discovered that the reflex of salivation and the secretion of gastric juices in a dog occur not only when food is placed in the dog's mouth, but also when the dog hears the bell (the conditional stimulus, Section 1.4.3). Pavlov uses stimulus substitution in his explanation: an association forms between the conditioned stimulus and unconditioned stimulus during training, and the conditioned stimulus is eventually substituted for the unconditioned stimulus. If we repeatedly use appreciative words, such as "yes" or "thank you," or a hug, as the conditional stimulus when we give Zda an actual reward, such as candy, then over time the stimulus substitution will be established. We call such a stimulus a reward proxy.

15.5 Teaching Using Factor-Isolation Technique

The Factor Isolation Technique can be used in effective teaching as shown in the following examples.

Example 1: We can teach Zda the concept of "walk close to object O" using the following actions as we speak the phrase "walk close to object O":

> *Lia.walk close to O*
> *Bob.walk close to O*

The concept of "close to object O" refers to the unchanged part: "close to O" in the three object.strings.

To further teach Zda the concept of "close to," use the following actions as you speak the word "close to":

> *Lia.walk close to the desk*
> *Lia.run close to the kitchen*
> *Bob.run close to the desk*
> *Lia.walk close to the kitchen*

See there are different pairings between the "words" and action strings, as in Pavlov's dog conditioning experiment.

Example 2: How does one teach the concept of "Change from X to Y"?

We can say "change x to y" when Zda sees X changing to Y (e.g., a multi-color light bulb changes its color), repeatedly.

Example 3: How do we teach the concept of Color?

To teach Zda the meaning of the colors red and green, show balls with the two different colors alternately as you speak the words "red" and "green" accordingly. That is, everything else is the same, only repeating the pairings (red, "red") and (green, "green"), similar to the paired events (cause, effect) and (no cause, no effect).

A complex concept is a composition of simpler concepts. There are three possible compositions:

1. Parallel structured, e.g., a baby keeps grabbing a bottle while walking.
2. Nested or hierarchically structured, e.g., Zda.said(Lia.say("the new book is very interesting").
3. Sequential procedure, e.g., he made a cup of coffee and brought it to me.

In goal-driven actions, backward induction is often used by Zda.

$$T_1 \leftarrow T_2 \leftarrow T_3 \leftarrow T_4 \leftarrow T_5 \leftarrow T_6 \leftarrow \text{Goal}$$

In a backward approach, at time point T_2, Zda reasons: to achieve the goal, he needs to reach T_6; to reach T_6 he needs to reach T_5; to reach T_5 he needs to reach T_4; to reach T_4 he needs to reach T_3. In general, the goal is a node on the predicted path in *Knet*.

Why-type and how-type inductions are backward inductions from effect to cause. Knowing this, Zda can eliminate the source of an undesirable outcome and create the source for a desirable outcome.

15.6 Mapping Natural Language to Innate Concepts

Zda has some 25 innate concepts: True (T), Negation ($\neg$), Sameness or equivalence ($\equiv$), All (A), Some ($\exists$), Every(e), Implication ($\rightarrow$), Intersection ($\cap$), Union ($\cup$), Conjunction ($\vee$), Disjunction ($\vee$), Inclusion ($\in$), Similarity ($\sim$), Probability (P), Preference ($\geq$), It (ϕ), Time (T), Precedence ($\gg$), Count (N), Recursion ($\circ$), Referring (R), Imitation ($\#$, $\rightarrowtail$ or $\leftarrowtail$), Desire (D), Expectation ($\mathcal{E}$), Sense of 3D world (S) that includes the relative location of two objects (direction and distance). The concept Difference is the negation of sameness.

Innate concepts are so fundamental to everyone, we subconsciously use them without notice. For example, we assume Zda knows the concepts of True, Negation, and sameness all the time. Without such assumptions, Zda cannot tell if there is a word in the text-string or not, if two words are the same (Sameness) or not. Likewise, we assume Zda knows the concept of likelihood (probability), not the mathematical definition of probability, but the idea that in a given situation something may or may not happen. For instance, Zda knows he sometimes feels hungry, sometimes not, and the likelihood changes depending on the time in the day.

Zda needs to map his innate concepts or knowledge to a natural language so that he can effectively communicate with others and learn from humans and his peers. This can be done through the factor-isolation technique. To teach a word that refers to an innate concept, the key is to bring Zda's attention to the innate concept while you are saying the word.

> **Example 1**: Present two objects (e.g., apple and banana) for Zda to choose. If he chooses the apple, then we say: "you prefer apple"; if he chooses the banana we say: "you prefer banana." Using various things to repeat the choice game, Zda will make a strong association between the word "prefer" and his innate concept of preference, because when Zda is making a choice the innate concept of preference is in his attention set. Such association is a basic understanding of the word "prefer."

A better way to teach is to teach the word/phrase ("refers to" in English) for the innate concept of "refers to" before teaching other innate concepts, and then teach other concepts through the phrase "refers to."

As we discussed apropos subconscious attention, innate concepts will randomly attract a young child's attention. Therefore, a dirty trick is to use the backdoor to teach innate concepts: Let Zda automatically pop-up innate concepts on a screen and have the user enter the corresponding words in his language, so that the mappings (associations) between them will be made once and for all.

In our earlier conversations we noted that, when an innate concept is in Zda's attention set, the associated action with the concept is often also in his attention set. For instance, when Zda hears the word *imitation* (a word he has already learned), he will likely perform an imitation, as the associative attention shifts from the word to the action.

Some concepts, such as probability, require to be quantified. The term *probability* is a quantitative sense of the Probability concept that can be learned from repeated coin-flipping experiments. Since no two things are identical, repeated experiments are actually a collection of similar experiments. This is a frequentist probability. However, the collection of similar experiments can often include similar "experiments" or experiences (called prior knowledge) in the *Knet*. In such a case, the probability is the so-called Bayesian probability. Zda will learn the frequentist probability before learning Bayesian probability, but the latter will be used more often in his daily life. We as non-statisticians don't differentiate the two different probability concepts but often use the same word, *probability*.

Even before we teach Zda to mathematically quantify a probability, he can use the probability concept and roughly quantify it upon his actions, as illustrated in Example 2.

> **Example 2**: In Skinner's Operant Conditioning experiment, replace the pigeon with Zda. We say: the probability of heads is a value x when the experiment has been repeated for many times.

Biological clocks are essential to humans and agents. Without such clocks, we cannot sense time and the alternations of day and night. As social beings, we need to synchronize our biological clocks and quantify time to be productive. The main reason that humans invented the physical clock was to synchronize peoples' biological clocks and precisely define the common time. Here we discuss how to teach Zda to learn some quantified time-related concepts such as yesterday, today, and tomorrow before he understands the time clock.

Example 3: Time-related concepts (TRCs), such as yesterday and tomorrow, can be taught with Zda's biological clock (BC). To teach time, we have to direct Zda to pay attention to his internal biological clock, in addition to other things in the attention set.

Here is an example of how to teach the concepts of yesterday, today, and tomorrow (assume Zda understands how to play the game of checkers already):

1. Lia plays a game of checkers with Zda.
2. The next day Lia says to Zda: "We played the checkers game yesterday. Do you like it?" Lia then invites Zda to play the game again and says: "Would you like to play the checkers game again?" After playing checkers, Zda is invited to play the game again: "We will play the game tomorrow, OK?"
3. On the third day, Lia plays checkers again with Zda.
4. Zda will make an association between biological clock time and the concepts of yesterday, today, and tomorrow after the procedure is repeated at different times on different days, and if checkers are replaced by other activities, such as different games or sports.

To teach Zda other time-related concepts, such as *slow* and *fast*, we can use the following example. Lia says to Zda "slow" while she is walking slowly. Then she says "fast" while walking fast. Repeating the process several times, Zda will first establish the two associations: (1) the word "slow" and walking slowly, and (2) the word "fast" and walking fast. Because being *slow* and being *fast* are relative, it is necessary that the two actions repeat alternately to show the contrast.

15.7 Describing Multiple-Object Worlds and Concepts

In Language teaching, we should be aware that language is a way of mapping one-dimensional word-strings to multidimensional worlds. Therefore, accessory words such as adpositions are necessary. The relations expressed by adpositions may be spatial or temporal relations, or relations expressing comparison, content, agent, instrument, means, manner, cause, purpose, reference, etc. Adpositions can be single invariants and paired invariants. Single invariants include *in, for, until, because, and, but, under, above, from, with, throughout, whenever, after, during, just as, by the time, instead of,* etc. The paired invariants include *either... or, not only... but also, as... as, the more... the better, rather... than,* etc. These words can be dealt with using Zda's innate knowledge, which includes the use of logical operators (e.g., $\vee$ for logical OR, $\wedge$ for logical AND, $\rightarrow$ and $\leftarrow$ for implication), temporal relationships ($\leftrightarrow$ and $\leftarrow$), or comparisons ($\approx$ for similarity, $\geq$ and $\leq$ for preference). Zda's use of these knowledge tools is illustrated in the following examples.

Learning is progressive. After Zda learns what "box" refers to, we can teach him what "yellow box" means. After he learns "ball," and "yellow box," we could teach him "ball in the yellow box," and then ask him to "Pick the ball *from* the yellow box."

We can replace the ball with other objects or the yellow box with other containers in the teaching process so that Zda can learn the meaning of the word "from."

In teaching Zda the contextual understanding of a word, the key is to bring Zda's attention to the right object or the concept to which the word refers.

Following this teaching principle, we can map the word "because" to the innate concept ← (an implication), e.g., in the following sentence:

"He runs fast *because* he is an athlete,"

map the word "and" to the innate concept ∧, as in:

"They gamble *and* they smoke,"

map "or" to ∨ as in:

"Every day, they gamble *or* they smoke,"

map "rather... than" to the innate concept ≥ (preference) as in:

"I would *rather* swim *than* surf,"

map "as... as" to ≈ (similarity) as in:

"Football is *as* fast *as* hockey,"

and map "after" to the temporal concept ⇐ as in the following example:

"We'll do that *after* you do this."

To this end, we first need to learn to match the situation in the perceptual world to an innate concept.

First, learn what the sentence refers to in the real world, and then determine whether it is a question, a request, a way to provide information, or purposeless.

15.8 Characterizing Space, Location, and Orientation

Based upon the principle of factor-isolation, we can present multiple sentences with the same adpositions so that Zda can know the relative locations between the adpositions in the string and the sensed internal status and external object's attributes. By doing so, Zda could formulate the concept of adpositions.

Learning is progressive. To teach Zda locational and directional words such as on, under, left, right, east, west, above, behind, forward, and backward, we can use the following approach.

Take "on" and "under" as examples. Suppose Zda knows the words "red," "green," "apple," and "desk" already, and you put a red apple on the desk and a green apple under the desk. Then point at the red apple while saying "a red apple on the desk" and point at the green apple while saying "a green apple under the desk."

Next, switch the locations of the two apples, and repeat the teaching process. After that, Zda will form an initial understanding of the words "on" and "under." Over time, Zda will

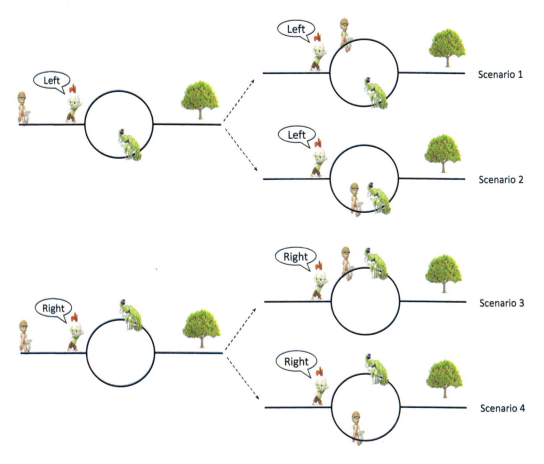

FIGURE 15.2
Possible language emerging—Go left, Go right.

meet many situations where people use these two words, and he will get better and better at understanding the two words.

RL lets Zda try different options over time and remember the best option he has identified to date in a given situation. When the situation occurs again, he will take this best option.

Suppose that Zda and Lia met at the forest on December 1, 2020, BC for the very first time. Since then, they have met at the same fork in the same road every day (Figure 15.2). Besides them, there is also a humongous bug that might, unpredictably, appear on one of the two roads near the fork. Each morning, when Lia saw Zda walking towards her, she **consistently** said either "left" or "right" depending on whether the gigantic bug was on the left or right road. As a penalty, if Zda meets the bug on the load, the bug will bite him. We will see how Zda's behaviors over time display his initial understanding of Lia's words: "left" and "right."

There are 4 possible scenarios:

- Scenario 1, when the bug is on the **left road**, Lia says "**Right**," Zda takes the **left** road trying to get some apples from the tree, and the bug **bites Zda**.
- Scenario 2, when the bug is on the **left road**, Lia says "**Right**," Zda takes the **right** road, the bug doesn't bite Zda, and Zda **gets apples**.

- Scenario 3, when the bug is on the **right road**, Lia says "**Left,**" Zda takes the **left** road, the bug doesn't bite Zda, and Zda **gets apples**.

- Scenario 4, when the bug is on the **right road**, Lia says "**Left,**" Zda takes the **right** road trying to get some apples from the tree, and the bug **bites Zda**.

If Zda has tried all 4 scenarios, Zda will learn via RL that the maximum reward occurs on the following either of the two conditions: (1) when Lia says "Left," he will go left, and (2) when Lia says "Right," he will go right. This shows that Zda understands Lia's meaning in saying "Left" or "Right."

It is important to know that after this training Zda has only an initial, fuzzy understanding of the concept of the words "Left" and "Right." He does not know when the word "Left" means that Lia wants him to go to the left road or that the bug is on the left, or something else. Nevertheless, Zda does display his initial understanding of the words in the case. The meaning of the words will be better understood later by Zda when he interacts with others in many different situations that involve the words *left* and *right*.

However, there are at least three problems with this RL. (1) Zda does not know how many scenarios need to be tested, i.e., the exploration versus exploitation issue. There might be better options that he has not tried. (2) Zda's attention is only to a limited number of things at each moment, and thus, the situation that is identified as a recurrence may not be a true recurrence, and the attention is different at the two different times. Furthermore, there are no two things that are truly identical; they will be different in some respect. (3) There might be too many options, in reality, for Zda to try out every possible option.

A solution is to use randomized adaptive reinforcement learning, basically the idea of Operant Conditioning (OC). OC is a kind of learning in which the consequences that follow some behavior increase or decrease the likelihood of that behavior occurring in the future. In OC an agent acts (operates) on the environment in order to change the likelihood of the response occurring again.

We can teach other locational and orientational words, such as up, down, front, back, forward, backward, inside, outside, close to, and far away, similarly as we did for the words "right" and "left."

15.9 Creating Patterns for Zda to Learn

Pattern creation using factor-isolation can be illustrated with the following examples of language teaching. In each example, only one word or token varies.

Example 1:
I read the book.
You read the book.
He read the book.

Example 2:
I like dogs.
I like cats.
I like birds.

To teach sentence structure: *either… or…,* we can use the following sentences:

> He can *either* eat *or* leave.
> The car is *either* yours *or* mine.
> You *either* do your work *or* prepare for a trip to the office.

Similarly, to teach the phrase: *as soon as,* we can use the following sentences:

> We'll get to that *as soon as* we finish this.
> We'll win *as soon as* we finish this.
> He will believe it *as soon as* we get this done.

Such pattern creation can be generalized to event-strings. For example, Lia asks Zda to get three different things in the same setting. In general, based on our knowledge of what concepts Zda has learned, we can create different patterns for Zda to learn.

15.10 Formulating Desensitisors and Sensitisors

Sensitization is a process of more precisely defining a pattern (category) by breaking it down into more patterns (categories), while desensitization is the reverse process: combining multiple patterns (categories) into one pattern (category). For instance, a color-blind person who can only see black and white becomes normal and sees colors after a treatment. This can be viewed as a sensitization. Conversely, a vision-normal person becoming color-blind after an accident can be viewed as desensitization. Most sensitization and desensitization processes occur at Zda's repatternization.

The pattern resulting from desensitization is called a category, while a desensitisor in a pattern represents a member of a category. A desensitisor can also be viewed as a combined pattern, while a sensitisor is a decomposed pattern.

The hierarchical structures of Zda's embodiment are scalable, which makes sensitization and desensitization natural and easy. For instance, the initial structure Zda.eyes.vision.light can be scaled up to Zda.head.eyes.leftEye.light.color or Zda.head.eyes.light.intensity. These hierarchical structures are useful in generating the sensitisor and desensitisor, as examples shown below:

> *Desensitisor: Obj*
> *Sensitisor: Obj.subobj*
>
> *Desensitisor: Obj.subobj*
> *Sensitisor: Obj.subobj.subobj*
>
> *Desensitiser: Obj.subobj.subobj*
> *Sensitisor: Obj.subobj.subobj.property*
>
> *Desensitisor: Obj.subobj.subobj.property*
> *Sensitisor: Obj.subobj.subobj.property.value*

More discussion of sensitization and desensitization can be found in the sections on repatternization.

15.11 Imitation, Innovation, Composite Tasks, and Collaborations

To imitate a composite task (corresponding to a high-level pattern), Zda must already know all the actions associated with its subtasks (tokens). For example, to make a chair, he already knows how to make all its parts.

Example 1:

In Zda's presence, have him watch the event sequence unfold:

> *Bob says: "Bring me a cup of coffee."* ⇒ **Lia** *makes coffee and brings it to Bob.*

Zda imitates Lia when Bob asks him for coffee (replacing Lia with Zda):

> *Bob says: "Bring me a cup of coffee."* ⇒ **Zda** *makes coffee and brings it to Bob.*

An imitation does not have to be taught. Zda can initiate (self-learning) an imitation based on a pattern by replacing the actioner with himself. The resulting consequence will reshape his behavior by updating the associated distributive reward with the pattern.

As discussed early on, innovation or creativity is a similarity replacement of tokens (other than replacing actioners with himself) within an event-string or pattern. Here, similarity is important. If done without similarity, the replacement might be deemed a ridiculous action. A replacement with some sense of similarity will often be considered to be a creative analogy. For example, replacing a word or thing in a pattern with another word or thing in the same category from the *Knet* can be considered as creativity.

Imitation can also be used when Zda does know how to answer a question, as when he asks the same question back to the questioner or of someone else.

Zda can also perform a collaborative task by imitation or through language-guided actions. Imitation is commonly used for getting a better understanding of a process and mastering skills, and thus is a foundation of creativity. The importance of imitations is also due to the fact that imitation makes Zda a social being, behaving the way other people do, i.e., morally.

Zda's creativity is also an important way of learning. Here is a simple example of creativity.

Example 2:

> *Bob says: "Please bring me an **apple**."* ⇒ *Zda brought him a **banana**.*

Zda gave Bob a banana instead of an apple because no apple was available. It is also because in the *Knet*, there is a pattern:

> *Bob says: "Please bring me an **apple**."* ⇒ *Zda brought him an **apple**.*

The creativity here is the replacement of apple with banana (the desensitisor, fruit) in the pattern from the *Knet*.

Creativity can also occur when Zda asks a question he's never heard before by similarity-replacement in a question found in the *Knet*.

"Goal" is the innate concept of desire. In Zda's view, a goal is something that directly or indirectly associates with a reward or is believed to be associated with a reward. An intermediate goal is often called a milestone. It is a node in Zda's *Knet*. The milestone is a sufficient or necessary condition for a longer term goal. If all paths toward the next goal must pass through the milestone node in the *Knet*, the milestone might be a necessary condition; otherwise, it is not.

A goal is not an expectation. For example, the baby Zda wants to eat the apple (his desire); he tries twice to grab it but fails, but in the third try, he succeeds. If he was expecting that he would need no more than two tries to get it, then he would get mad when he fails the second time; however, if his expectation is to get it within three tries, he will be happy (a reward in reinforcement learning).

In Example 1, Zda views making coffee as the precondition before bringing the coffee. Zda will view this precondition as a subgoal before accomplishing the goal (bringing coffee to Bob). Of course, Zda may just respond: "I am sorry, I am busy at the moment."

15.12 Catching a Moving Target: Acting on Predictions

Zda has the innate concept of speed, i.e., the feel of something happening fast or slowly, but not the exact definition of speed. He also has the innate knowledge that to act on an object, he needs to know the location of and get sufficiently close to the object. This concept will be enhanced and the meaning of "close" will become clear in various situations through practice.

The steps to catch a moving object are something like this (Figure 15.3):

1. Predict the future location of the moving object.
2. Body and hands start moving toward the predicted location.
3. Adjust the direction and speed of movement according to the location prediction.
4. Zda repeats steps (1) through (3) until he is close enough to the object, and tries to catch it.
5. Repeating the exercise many times, Zda will predict better and master the skill of catching a moving object.

FIGURE 15.3
Catch a flying ball: acting on anticipation.

15.13 Playing Games

A board game (Figure 15.4) typically involves pieces that can be moved or placed on a pre-marked board (playing surface) and often includes elements of table, cards, and role-playing. Many board games feature a competition between two or more players. Classical board games are divided into four categories: race games (e.g., Parchisi), space games (e.g., Noughts and Crosses), choice games (e.g., Hnefatafl), and games of displacement (e.g., chess).

For two-person board games, as an example, Zda starts by learning the game rules using natural language for legal moves and penalties for illegal moves. Natural language-guided response with RARL will be an effective tool for teaching game rules and improving playing skills. The key is to bring Zda's attention to the game, e.g., moving the chequers on the gameboard and learning how to predict the opponent's possible moves.

A choice game involves decision-making when facing several options. The well-known Monty Hall Problem (Figure 15.5) was originally posed in a letter by Steve Selvin to the American Statistician in 1975 (Selvin 1975) and was published in Marilyn vos Savant's "Ask Marilyn" column in the magazine Parade in 1990.

Suppose you're on a game show and you're given the choice of three doors. Behind one door is a car; behind the others are goats. The car and the goats were placed randomly behind the doors before the show. The rules of the game are as follows. After you have chosen a door, the door remains closed for the time being. The game show host, Monty Hall, who knows what is behind the doors, now has to open one of the two remaining doors, and he will open a door with a goat behind it. After Monty opens a door with a goat, he always offers you a chance to switch to the last, remaining door. Imagine that you chose

FIGURE 15.4
Board games.

FIGURE 15.5
The Monty Hall problem.

FIGURE 15.6
The guessing game using binary searching.

Door 3 and the host opens Door 1, which has a goat. He then asks you "Do you want to switch to Door Number 2?" Is it to your advantage to change your choice?

Many readers refused to believe that switching is beneficial as Von Savant suggested. Ironically, Herbranson and Schroeder (2010) recently conducted experiments showing that pigeons (supposedly stupid birds) can make the right decision when facing the Monty Hall Dilemma. The probability of gaining reinforcement for switching and staying was manipulated, and the birds adjusted their probability of switching and staying to approximate the optimal strategy. This optimal strategy is exactly the RARL response algorithm that was implemented in our HAI.

As the player cannot be certain which of the two remaining unopened doors is the winning door, most people assume that each of these doors has an equal probability of being that door, and conclude that switching does not matter. However, the answer may not be correct depending on the host's behavior. You could increase the probability (p) of winning from 1/3 to 2/3 by switching (Chang, 2014)!

A guessing-game (Figure 15.6) involves a prediction for a given set of facts. Using binary search to guess an integer within a given range, say from 1 to 10, is very effective. We first split the ten numbers into two equal sets, those less than 6 and the rest. So, we ask: "Is it less than 6?." The game host answers either "Yes" or "No." Assume he answers "No." Knowing now that the integer is between 6 and 10, we divide the smaller set of numbers into two equal parts and ask "Is it less than 8?" Suppose he again answers "No," so that the number is either 8, 9, or 10. We continue, "Less than or equal to 9?" He says: "Yes." This is our fourth question: "Is it 9?" He says "No," and finally we have the number, 8. But this is the worst-case scenario. We have been unlucky: if the answer to the third question had been "No," we would have known the number at that moment. The minimum number of yes/no questions required to determine with certainty a number between 1 and N is $n = \log_2 N$.

Such an advanced search method requires Zda to apply the binary split-rule to the resulting (remaining) integer set, and it would take a very long for Zda to rediscover the rule without teaching him. The feasible approach is to teach Zda a natural language and some math, then teach him the search method, just as we do in schools.

Part IV

Prototyping Agents—Zda and Lia

16

Functional and Logic Specifications

This chapter can serve the primary purposes of a Functional Requirement Specification and Logic Specifications in HAI software development. Because of the complexity of HAI and limited space in this book, the document will be brief but will cover the key components. No animation details will be discussed; our focus is the agent's mind building and coordination with facial expressions and body posture (movements), while animation itself is computer language-specific and IDE-dependent. The information provided in this part can further clarify some complex points in the architecture.

A function specification is a formal document that software developers use to describe in detail a product's intended capabilities, appearance, and interactions with users. The functional specification is a kind of guideline and continuing reference point as the developers write the programming code.

Think of HAI as something similar to virtual reality games, such as Real-Time Strategy (RTS) and Role-Playing (RPG) games. In RTS, players usually need to build up their inventory of items, armies, etc. RTS games move in real time, and players can play simultaneously in the same game without taking turns. In any RPG, a player gets to act out the part of the main character, be the hero, etc., and make decisions that go along with the game's story lines. In RTS and RPG, all characters have no brain and act according to programmed behaviors, partially controlled by human input or human players. However, in addition to these human-controlled agents (human-race agents), HAI also has machine-race humans (Lia and Zda) who have their own brains, allowing each to think and act independently and learn knowledge and skills through experiences.

In this virtual reality, human users and human-race agents can interact with any other agents via computer input devices (e.g., keyboard, mouse, microphone, camera), and all agents can interact with each other. Most importantly, all agents can learn languages or develop their own language in their communities. Humans such as you can use any language to communicate with agents. Just remember: treat an agent as a baby, and patiently teach it, moving from simple to complex concepts.

Users (human-race agents) can create (instantiate) a machine-race baby with different innate attributes via Class Constructors in OOP. Users can add items (objects and agents) to the virtual world. Users can add attributes and abilities to machine-race agents with associated animations. Therefore, using a game engine for programming HAI may have some advantages.

Logic specification is about the structure of the programming (e.g., major groups of code modules that support a similar function); individual code modules and their relationships and the data parameters that they pass to each other may be described in a formal document. This document, called a logic specification, describes internal interfaces and is for use only by the developers and testers.

Since many function and logic specifications are similar to virtual reality games, we will focus on the HAI agent's sensory organs and brain (mind) with learning and thinking mechanisms.

DOI: 10.1201/b23355-20

16.1 Conventions in Object-Oriented Programming

Most syntax conventions are self-explanatory for anyone who has the basic concepts of OOP.

Logic Syntax and Conditional Statement Conventions:

```
& (and), || (or), > (larger than), ≥ (larger than or equal to),
similar for < and ≤.

If (condition) { Statements }

If (condition) {
        Statements
Else
        Statements
}
```

Loop Conventions:

```
For Each x In y
        Statements
Next

For i = 1 To N
        Statements
Next

Loop While (condition)
        Statements
Endloop

Do Loop
        Statements
Until (condition)

Switch (variable) {
        Case "task 1"
                Statements
        Case "task 2"
                Statements
        Case "task 3"
                Statements
}
```

Text after double forward in a line are comments: // comments

Build-in Math Functions:

```
Math.rand()     // generate a random number ranging [0, 1)
Math.ceiling()    // round up to the nearest integer
Math.round()
```

Reference to object's attributes:

```
ObjectX.attributeA
ObjectX.objectY.attributeB
ObjectX.act()
ObjectX.objectY.act()
```

Conventions with Array or List of Objects:

```
ObjectsA[1].attributeB = objectsB[2].attributeB
ObjectsA() = objectsB()     // entire array assignment
ObjectsA.sortBy(objectsA.var)    // sort the objects by objectsA.var
ObjectsA.insert(recordX, 3)     // insert recordX as the 3rd record
ObjectsA.insert(recordX, -1)     // insert recordX as the last record
ObjectsA.delete(index = 2)     // delete the 2nd record
ObjectsA[index > 5]     // get all records after the 5th record
ObjectsA.find(name = "Bob")     // get records with name = "Bob"
```

String and Array Object Conventions:

```
StringA.split(delimiter)    // get list of tokens from StringA per delimiter
StringA.find(tokenX)     // return the position of tokenX
StringA.replace(old, new)     // replace the first old with new
StringA.substring(n)    // substring consisting of the first n characters
StringA.app(StringB)     // append StringB to the end of StringA
StringA.size     // size is the number of tokens
StringA.length     // length is the number of characters
```

Array Class has properties and methods:

```
ArrayA.sum     // the sum of the numerical elements
ArrayA.ave     // the average of the numerical elements
ArrayA.size     // the number of elements in arrayA
ArrayA.add(recordB)     // add recordB as the last element
Array.delete(index = 2)     // delete the 2nd item
ArrayB[4][2]     // an element of two-dimensional array
```

System Function:

A naming system is necessary to automatically generate a unique name for a pattern, desensitisor, or sensitisor.

```
autoName()     // get a unique name for a pattern, token, desensitisor, or others.
```

Randomly choose n integers from 1 to N without replacement

```
Math.randNumsWithoutReplacement(n, N)
```

In OOP language Java, a container (contains other objects) or a similar thing in OOP will be needed for monitoring all objects. Alternatively, using ab IDE such as Xcode that has a game engine for programming HAI has some advantages from an animation perspective.

From a coding or patternization perspective, it might be convenient to write the elementary token *Lia.say("wordString")* as Lia.say√wordString.

16.2 Memories and Data Storage

To manipulate the *Knet* Database, the commonly used relational database language is the so-called SQL (structured query language). Different database servers may use slightly different SQLs, their syntax and processes are very similar:

- Connect to database server.
- Retrieve relevant records and upload into computer memory.
- Insert, delete, or sort records.
- Close the connection.

For database, SQL-alike (Structured Query Language) will be used:

```
Select * From tableX Where (condition)
Delete From tableX Where (condition)
Insert Into tableX Values (value1, value2, …)
```

To sort rewards in a particular order, we use the "sortBy" keyword.

Net class has a List attribute (subclass), Patterns. Patterns is a list (array) of Pattern objects.

```
Knet.size    //Number of patterns in Knet
```

Join two network objects netX and netY or two patterns at the common token, "node":

```
NetX.link(netY, node)
PatternX.link(PatternY, node)
```

Select patterns based on different properties:

```
Knet.Pattern [tokenID = "myAI2022"]
Knet.desensitisor[tokenID = "food"]
```

Net class (*Knet*) inherits String class and implements or overrides the following functions or methods:

```
Knet.Pattern.add(name, pattern, freq, reward, recency)
Knet.Pattern.update(name, pattern, freq, reward, recency)
Inet.Pattern.add(name, pattern, freq, reward, recency)
Knet.Pattern.delect(condition)
Inet.Pattern.delect(name =)
Inet.Pattern.delect(id =)
Knet.Pattern.sortBy(var)
Knet.paths(A, B, n)    //find n paths from A to B represented by a pattern
Knet.nameMaxIndex  // the max index used pattern names
Knet.Pattern[1:3]    // first 3 rows or records
Knet.Pattern[rType = "food"]    // records with rType = "food"
// Language net consists of patterns with names starting with Z.
KZnet = Knet (patterns.name.substring(1) = "Z")
ME.Knet   // Here, ME is a reserved word to indicate the current agent
```

Pattern class inherits from String class, and has additionally the token property. Every elementary token has a unique token name, i.e., Pattern.tokenID, to be used in hierarchical tokenization. A token Array contains all (1 to 4) tokens in the form of $E1 \otimes E2 \otimes E3 \otimes E4$, where $\otimes$ is either $\wedge$ (occurs concurrently) or $\Rightarrow$ (occurs sequentially), with the default precedence of $\wedge$ and then $\Rightarrow$.

```
Pattern.tokenID
Pattern.reward
Pattern.rType    // Reward Type = "food" or "entertainment"
Pattern.freq
Pattern.recency
Pattern[2].size    // number of tokens of Pattern[2]
Pattern.length    // number of characters
PatternA.tokens[2]    // Get to the 2nd token of PatternA
A.replaceToken(i, tokenName)  // replace the ith token with tokenName
A.union(A, B)    // intersection of tokens between patterns A and B
A.intersection(B)  // intersection of tokens between patterns A and B
```

Note that a pattern is a sequence of tokens (a row), whereas a desensitisor is a list of tokens (a column). Desensitisor and sensitisor are one-gramtons without associated frequencies. A **regular expression** (shortened as **regex** or **regexp**) is a sequence of characters that specifies a search pattern in text. Available in many OOP languages, these can be useful in HAI pattern search in HAI development.

17

Modularization of Humanized AI Architecture

To implement Zda, we need to modularize the overall architecture (Figure 17.1).

A multifaceted world, even with infinitely many objects in infinite detail, is greatly simplified via limited sensitivity of sensory organs, attention mechanisms, and similarity grouping. Such a simplified world in Zda's mind is the blueprint of his perceptual world, combining innate elementary knowledge, skills, and habits, allowing Zda to think, act, learn, and respond like a human. The four basic internal components for a humanized agent are: (1) innate elementary knowledge, skills, habits; (2) attention mechanisms; (3) learning mechanisms; and (4) response mechanisms. Two critical external factors are: (1) effective teaching and (2) extensive interaction with the environment.

As we discussed in Part III, understanding a concept is an ongoing and tuning process. The meaning of a concept should be a personal thing, and can well change over time, but the *core* meaning is the "common part" of understanding the concept in a community, which is relatively persistent or stable over time. The personalized adaptive response mechanism allows Zda to generate responses in facing different situations.

Interactions create language and social norms. In interactions, Zda adheres to social norms through imitation and associative learning. Natural language grammars can be viewed as a set of recursive string functions, as are event-patterns and a response-mechanism.

Patterns are constantly undergoing evolution: less used patterns will gradually die and patterns with high frequencies and rewards will endure. The fitness in the algorithm is mainly frequency. Frequent patterns become more frequent. A pattern with a high penalty will also survive only a very short time, ensuring it will not be used!

17.1 Virtual World Simulation

Since we are currently dealing with agents on a computer, a virtual world needs to be created. For robots, such a virtual world is not needed.

In OOP terms, the virtual world will consist of elements of two types (classes) of objects: (1) Mindlessor (or Thingy), anything that cannot think, such as lifeless objects and plants, and (2) Minder, anything with mind that can think, such as animals and (humanized) agents. Humans are also involved through input devices that connect to machine-race humans. In principle, all objects should follow the physical laws as enabled by many virtual reality game engines.

The Thingy class, representing inanimate things, has the following attributes: name, Appearance(shape, size, texture), phyChem, Color(color, brightness), Sound(sound, loudness), Odor(odor intensity), taste, mass, temperature, Location(x, y, z), and Velocity(v_x, v_y, v_z). We will conventionally use the starting uppercase to indicate an object and a starting lowercase for a property. For example, Color representing a subobject and color representing a property. More properties can be added as you like. All these properties have

DOI: 10.1201/b23355-21

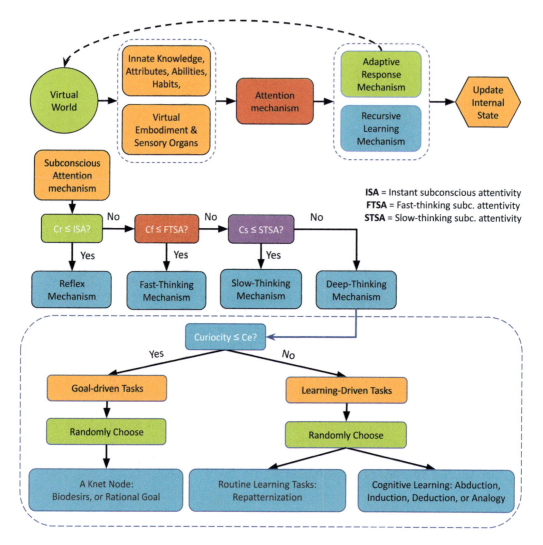

FIGURE 17.1
Modularization of humanized AI architecture.

discrete values. A Thingy's behaviors follow Laws of Physics. Examples of Thingies are desks, light bulbs, switches, water, cups, bread, apples.

- name = a private property not visible to agents but used for computer coding only.
- shape = triangle, square, circle, star, pentagon, hexagon, which serve as visual identifications of a class of object (e.g., car, dog, cat).
- size = an integer to indicate the size of an object.
- texture = an integer to indicate the surface texture characteristic; may be used to identify each object for a given class.
- color, sound, odor = a value associated with the object's color, sound, odor.
- brightness, loudness, density = a value indicating brightness, loudness, density.

- phyChem = a value associated with the object's physical or chemical property.
- taste = binary value indicating edible or not.
- temperature = a value to indicate the object's temperature.
- utility = drivable for car, water can put out fire, light can enlighten a room, etc.
- age = elapsed time from the object's creation.
- sex = determines sexual attraction and affect on evolution of agents.

Some special objects can be created from the Thingy class, such as Weather(four seasons, raining, sunny), Sky(clouds, sun, room, stars), Earth(mountain, river, road), General(desk, book, playcards), and Tools(car, pen, microwave). For such an object, it might be necessary to add so-called "functions," "behaviors," or "methods" in OOP as in the following examples with self-explanatory meanings:

- Sky.act(actionName = "raining," intensity = high)
- Environment.act(actionName = "sunshine," intensity = low)
- Environment.act(actionName = "raining," intensity = heavy)

It is important to remember: no matter how colorful the external world is, if an agent is a blind he will not see it. How simple the environment is, will often be determined by the agent's sensory organs.

The Animals class inherits all properties from the Thingy class and may have other properties such as gender, age, and simple brain with simple pre-programed response-features such as a hungry animal can run when he sees a prey, while a Thingy cannot move unless an external force acts on it.

The (humanized) Agent class inherits all properties from the Thingy class and has other properties (attributes) and methods (behaviors) to be discussed in the next section. The additional attributes include innate attribute state (energy, desire), and the developed attributes such as friends, enemies, collaborators to indicate who they are. For simplicity, we may assume that an object type (class) is determined by its shape in the HAI prototyping, a particular object of a given type is determined by size, while emotional expression is symbolically represented by the agent's face color. An Animal can be implemented as a degenerated Agent.

Two important types of Thingy are **Food** and **Entertainment**. The Food is a subclass of Thingy that has attributes type = "food" and energy = a value. These two attributes are critical in determining the reward for an action or pattern. **Entertainment** is a subclass of Thingy that has attributes type = "entertainment" and energy = a value. These two attributes are also critical in determining the reward for an action or pattern.

A Virtual Human (VH) here is an agent whose behaviors can be controlled by the user. A VH is a user who interacts with agents and virtual environments through input devices such as keyboards, microphones, and video cameras.

17.2 Virtual Embodiment of Agents

The virtual embodiments provide an agent with innate and developed abilities. The list of virtual embodiments is summarized in Table 17.1. As with humans, the number of categories that an organ is able to sense may change through learning. When the

TABLE 17.1

Prototype for Virtual Embodiment

Virtual Organ	Intrinsic Function	Initial No. of Sensible Levels
Eyes	Vision	3
Ears	Auditory (hearing)	3
Nose	Olfaction	3
Tongue	Tastiness	2
Skin	Tactile (hepatics)	3
Body	Thermoreception	3
Vocal cord	Voice & words	3
Face	Emotion expression	3
Skeleton	Pose & motion	6
Brain	Knowledge & learning	Innate concepts & abilities
Heart	Emotion	10

number of sensible levels becomes one, the agent is impaired with regarding the sensory organ.

The virtual embodiments equip an agent with three categories of organs, with the caveat that such categorization does not try to match exactly the biological or psychological functions of the organ systems.

The first category is sensory organs for receiving information, including: Eyes for vision, Ears for hearing, a Nose for olfaction, Tongue for tastiness, Skin for tactile sense, and the Body for thermoreception. These sensory organs provide passive sensory abilities, subconsciously working with the reflex mechanism.

The second category is used to directly project information or alike onto the external world, including Vocal cords for voice and words, a Face for expression, a Skeleton for posture and motion.

The third is to indicate an agent's key internal state, the Brain for storing knowledge, Heart for feeling sensation, Gender for determining sexual attraction and reproductivity, and Age for modulating parameters for activity.

Sensory Organs: Zda can differentiate initially 3 different colors and 3 levels of intensity (brightness), but can be scaled up or down via sensitization or desensitization, to be described later. Ears, Nose, Skin, and Body have similar sensitivities. The Tongue has only 2 levels: something is edible or it is not.

Vocal Cords: Zda, like humans, can learn to speak any language (a string of text) but in a constant intensity (yet, no intonation) at this moment. Zda can initially only produce 3 different sounds (Ba, Ma, and a cry). Additional types of sounds can be learned through imitation, e.g., or be built-in with different associated probabilities initially.

Face: The Zda face is a 3×3-grid 2-color 2D image. The image is visible to agents and will be used as identification; at the same time, the color property will be used for expressions. Therefore, there could be as many as $2^{3 \times 3} = 512$ different types of objects. Remember, the size property is used to represent a particular object of a given type (class). A simplified version uses geometric shapes for different types of objects. The face image can only have 2 colors picked from 4 colors (red, green, yellow, blue), a total of 12 possible combinations (expressions). That is, colors of the face are used to indicate an agent's facial expression.

Skeleton: Zda has initially limited possible postures or actions {standing, sitting, eating, grasping, walking, turning, dropping, looking, smiling, crying, speaking, etc.}. He can do more through learning such as mimicking. Each posture and action has an associated probability. Skeletal postures are often associated with facial emotions, whether such an association is an inner or developed ability. The skeleton can also perform physical actions. Some types of actions are innate or inherited abilities, each kind with an associated initial probability. Abilities to perform other advanced actions can be developed through learning, imitation, or creative activities.

Brain: Zda's brain is the place to store his knowledge and mechanisms of actions. The knowledge consists of a small set of innate knowledge and learned knowledge and skills, represented by a recursive network of patternized experiences, called *Knet*. Mechanisms of actions include attention, learning, and response mechanisms.

Heart: The Heart is the virtual place to host emotions, with an initial 10 levels for coding 10 different emotions.

Gender Organ: Gender is used to determine agent's sexual attraction in making friends and virtual reproduction; using genetic evolution algorithms as an example.

Energy Bank: Zda has a certain energy level at any given moment when alive. Performing any action, even sleeping will cost him energy, while eating food and rewards will boost his energy level. Zda at his higher energy state will be more likely to perform a task that requires more energy. Energy can have 100 levels. When the level is zero, Zda is dead.

Other body parts of various physical sizes and shapes can be implemented: a head, arms, hands, fingers, legs, feet, and the rest.

17.3 Innate Concepts and Knowledge

Zda has 26 innate concepts (knowledge), which can be matched directly to any particular language used. This is done (1) by prompting each concept to let a human user enter the corresponding word, or (2) through training using association with the factor-isolation technique. The same two approaches can apply to the innate sense of sensory organs: vision, auditory, olfaction, tastiness, tactility, thermoreception, and sensations (happiness, pain, hunger). Zda can also recognize a list of elementary actions.

As discussed in Part III, the innate concepts or knowledge include:

1. True (T): If Zda "sees" something happening, then he realizes it is the truth, or is true to him.

2. Negation ($\neg$): If Zda has the concept of a fair A, then he will also have the concept of the opposite side of A (i.e., the negation of A or $\neg$A). For example, if Zda sees that it is raining, then he also has the concept of "is not raining." If Zda sees something happening, then he realizes it is the truth. At the same time, he has the concept of the opposite side of the truth, i.e., falseness (not happening). A thing and its negation always coexist.

3. Sameness or equivalence (≡): Like a human, Zda has the intrinsic concept of sameness and has some sensors to detect whether two things are the same or not. For instance, a person has the ability of knowing if two objects are the same, or not, by looking at them, by touching or/and smelling them, even if he cannot express the concept of sameness in terms of any language. Therefore, sameness can be detected by the various senses, through shape and color, and by feel, taste, temperature, or smell. The concept is independent of any sensor, but the ability is dependent on particular sensors, e.g., a color-blind person cannot tell if two objects have the same color or not. With the sensor, a person can store information about two objects and compare them, and then produce the feeling of "same" or "not same." Such a feeling or sensation expresses the concept of sameness.

4. Implication (→): A→ B means A is sufficient for B.

5. All ($\mathcal{A}$). "All" is the whole or collection of everything under consideration. Zda has the concept of allness but may not necessarily be able to identify the whole in any particular case. For example, if we say: "all math books in the world," Zda may not understand what we say, not because he does not have the concept of "all," but because he doesn't understand, e.g., the terms "word," "books," "the world."

6. Some (∃). Some are a part of all.

7. Count ($\mathcal{N}$): The concept of the total number of certain items.

8. Every(e): Every element of a set of affairs under consideration.

9. Intersection (∩): Zda has the concept of an intersection of two events, i.e., a part belonging to two things simultaneously. However, this does mean he would not make a mistake in judging intersections in some cases.

10. Union (∪): Zda can identify the union of two events, i.e., a thing can be made of two things, e.g., people ≡ men ∪ women.

11. Conjunction (∧): Zda has the concept of the conjunction of two events, i.e., walking ∧ talking, meaning talking while walking.

12. Disjunction (∨): Zda can identify a disjunction of two events, i.e., a thing can be made of two things, e.g., walking ∨ talking, meaning either talking or walking.

13. Inclusion (∈): The concept of inclusion is a relationship between a part and the whole. For instance, a person knows a slice of pizza is part of the whole pizza. A door is a part of a house, and the lock is a part of the door. The part of a whole is independent of any language, and Zda is born with the ability to understand the connection. In notation, $A \in B$ means A belongs to B; or is a fundamental part of B.

14. Similarity (~): The concept of "similarity" concerns a relation between two entities. "Are similar" means only that a part of one entity is the same as a part of another entity. The concept of being similar can actually be derived from the conjunction of other concepts (≡, ¬, ∈).

15. Probability ($\mathcal{P}$): The concept of probability concerns the likelihood of a fact's or an event's occurrence. For instance, if S represents the fact that B occurs after fact C, the probability of S is the percentage of time of the fact occurring among a collection of facts in terms of Zda's observation. Such a collection of facts are subjective in terms of scope (observation period and conditions given). Probability is a learned concept before Zda's birth, when he may sense that an event (a fact such as hunger) sometimes occurs and sometimes does not occur.

16. Preference (⩾): Zda displays preference (e.g., likes one thing better than another). Preference can vary from individual to individual and from time to time, but the concept of preference is the same for everyone.

17. It (ƒ). The concept of "it" refers to anything (concrete or abstract) Zda attends to at a particular time; most often "it" is used in a conversation or thinking process. To differentiate one "it" from another, we can add a subscript to ƒ, e.g., ƒ₁ and ƒ₂.

18. Time ($\mathcal{T}$): The "biological clock" allows Zda to record event-order in time as past, present, and future (past experience stored in the memory, what is happening now, and what is imagined for the future). The circadian clock will allow Zda to record and organize time units: day and year (see the section on biological clock). Therefore, notions of time such as yesterday, today, tomorrow, last year, this year, and next year are considered to be innate concepts.

19. Precedence (≫): Precedence refers to Zda's ability to deal with a certain part, preceding others. In the linguistic agent, without assistance of other sensors, we use and force a priority. In other words, things included in the pair of precedence operators, (and), will be dealt with first. The precedence operators work as parentheses in an arithmetical formulation and can be used repeatedly or in a nested fashion.

20. Recursion (↻): The concept of the recurrence of anything (events, mathematical operations, actions, procedures) in different spaces, times, timescales, or in any other sensory aspects, or in a general sense such as weather or environmental change. The sense of the periodicity (unnested recursion in time) of the environmental change (mainly light) allows Zda to quickly formulate, in theory, the concept of "a day." Zda has the ability to perform various recursions, but here we refer to the concept.

21. Referring to ($\mathcal{R}$): The concept of mapping between a language (including signs) and its semantics. For instance, the word "pen" refers to an object, a pen. When the map between Zda's $\mathcal{R}$ and a word in a particular language is established, communications between different humans and the agent become much easier.

22. Imitation (#): The concept of copying what others do, or copying natural phenomena. This imitation is a concept, not one of the mechanisms of imitation to be discussed later. The action of imitating will be denoted by ↠ or ↞.

23. Desire ($\mathcal{D}$): Desire is the concept of a goal. Zda has desires so he knows others have them too. Here, the concept of desire is not the tendency of trying to satisfy a desire. Like a human, Zda does not have a clearly defined life goal; rather, his is vaguely defined as a long and happy life. Happiness is subjective and depends on many things, and views of happiness change over time. The trade-off between longevity and happiness is purely personal. It goes circularly: Your life goal will direct your actions and social life, and conversely, your actions and social life will reshape your life goal.

24. Expectation ($\mathcal{E}$): Expectation is not desire. For example, Baby Zda wants to eat the apple (his desire). He tried twice to grab it and failed, but in the third try he succeeded. Now, if he was expecting no more than two chances, he would get mad upon failing the second time; however, if his expectation was to get it within three tries, then he will not know frustration, he will only be happy.

25. Sense of the 3D world ($\mathcal{S}$): This sense includes the relative location of two objects as measured by direction and distance. The location of an object is always relative.

26. Zda knows in order to act on an object, he needs to get sufficiently close to the object. The fuzzy concept of "sufficiently close" will be learned or become clear through his experiences.

When we make associations between these innate concepts and words in a language, Zda will understand the words we say. It is very helpful to understand the words representing these innate concepts when we teach Zda more complicated concepts, as discussed in Chapter 15, Effective Teaching. You can think of an innate concept as a common word in an international language that everyone understands and uses internally, in his or her mind.

These innate concepts may not appear to be important to you and you might think you don't know how to use them. But as matter of fact, you will subconsciously use them in coding when you implement the agents. For example, you may use a comparison statement in code for an agent to compare two things, to see if they are identical. In such a case, you have assumed the agent has the concept of "equivalence." In record frequencies of patterns or any recurrences, the count concept is used implicitly. When we code a search function to represent an agent performing a search for an object, you have assumed the agent has the concepts of "True" and "Negation." When you code a function representing an agent seeing whether two objects are overlapping, you have used the concept of "conjunction." When you code an agent's similarity comparison ability, you would have assumed the agent has the concept of "similar." We should not confuse the innate concepts with the mathematical axiom system, since in the innate concepts system, some concepts can actually be defined by others. For example, "similar" is defined by the state of affairs that the two objects are the same only in "some" parts, not ("negation") in others. The concept of "preference" is the root of how an agent makes a choice, including the reinforcement learning algorithms. The "recursion" concept is the foundation of hierarchical tokenization and recursive patternization, and it is the key for learning complex concepts and procedures. The sense of "referring to" is critical in our daily interaction and learning. Senses of 3-dimensional space and time are prerequisite for assessing velocity (and speed) and identifying the chronological order of events. All of these concepts or assumptions would exist subconsciously in our coding even if we did not explicitly list their usages here.

17.4 Representation of Actions

The syntax conventions of action are closely related to hierarchical tokenization and recursive patternization. The syntax conventions of actions suggested here do not have to be followed, but provide convenience and clarity for the later discussions on the implementation of tokenization and patternization. There are 8 types of elementary actions: act, compare, say, recollect, image, intend, SelfawarenessSwitch, and a face action. We discuss each of the actions as follows.

The action agent.act has the following form:

- *agent.act(name, goal, expectation, target, tool, duration, repeats, execution, Params)*

A subobject can also have actions such as

- *agent.eyes.act(params)*
- *agent.face.act(params)*
- *agent.body.act(params)*

- *agent.hand.act(params)*
- *agent.foot.act(params)*
- *agent.mouth.act(params)*

The parameters are listed as follows.

1. name = name of the action
2. goal = set by the intend() action to be discussed below, can be null for a "purpose-less" action
3. target = Agent, Animal, Thingy if applicable, but can be null since, e.g., stretching oneself does not have a target
4. tool = tool used, a Thingy object with some utility defined, can be null
5. repeats = integer (e.g., 5 for walk 5 steps), default =1
6. Params = includes the action starting time, ending time, force, speed, and direction, as applicable
7. execution = 1 (executed) or 0 (unexecuted), involving the executable condition check. Condition checking will be similar to those game-engines (e.g., unreal, Unity. GameMaker, AppGameKit, and Amazon Open 3D Engine Lumberyard) provided, and might include distance, direction, collision, reachable, and passable checks.

While shape is the fundamental attribute to identify an object's type, the combination of shape, size, texture, color, and other observable static and dynamic characteristics can be used to describe the object. For example, we might say: "the boy on the moving cart"; here, the cart is defined by its dynamic state "moving" and the boy is defined by its location "on the moving cart." Another example will be "the dog that runs the fastest among others."

Action involves a target object that may involve action. For instance, "he is catching the flying dragonfly." This creates a recursion of actions. Similarly, an agent may be defined by its action that may involve its parameter defined by another object that is defined by its action, and so on. This also creates recursions.

Appearance often is used to identify an object and then may consequently infer on its attributes. Thus, *Appearance* and *Actions* including the *target* are the important factors in the similarity calculation. Dynamic attributes may or may not be important for similarity determination. It is important to remember that similarity judgment is based on the agent's sense—not the actual object's attributes, but the agent's attentive attributes.

For consistency, all numerical attributes can be normalized, ranging from 0 to 1. Agents, actions, and their parameters can be grouped into a small number categories for effective learning. Such categorization can be improved over time.

We have to emphasize that when Zda sees Lia in action, he may not be aware of all her action parameters. In fact, he may mistakenly identify Lia as someone else.

The action agent.compare has the form of

agent.compare(objs, attrs).

The parameter objs = often the two or more objects to be compared; attrs = static and dynamic or developed attributes for the comparison. The developed attributes can be music skills, math knowledge, number of friends, wealthiness, and so on.

The outcome of a comparison between two entities can be differences in static attributes, abilities, state, location, or differences in distance, speed, and observed qualities such as color, and may also include such differences over time and under acceleration. We might observe a difference of a difference: the distance between A and B is larger than the distance between A and C. Results of such comparisons are critical in forming many concepts; e.g., the concept of "close to" refers to the sense of relative location or the distance between two objects. The most commonly used comparisons between paired objects are attributes, location, speed, and difference in location. The action "compare" is constantly needed for an agent to identify objects and make decisions.

The action "say" takes the form of

    agent.say(textString).

The single parameter textString represents what the agent says, not necessarily in any natural language (though agents can learn to speak in natural languages), and can involve nested strings as shown in the following example:

    agent.say("Lia.say("Zda.see(Bob.run(...))")")

An agent can think of what actually happened (recollect) or some hypothetical scenarios that may or may not happen in the future (image).

- *agent.image(eventString)*—agent thinking of the event sequence represented by eventString and leaving traces in the imagination net (*Inet*).
- *agent.recollect(eventString)*—agent searches the event path represented by eventString, i.e., extracts the event-string of *eventString* from the *Knet*.

An agent may set his short-term or long-term goal using the *intend* action:

- *agent.intend(goal, expectedProb)*

Here the parameter *goal* is a node with a reward in the *Knet*. When a goal node is identified, the associated path from current position to the node can also be identified in the *Knet*. When the goal is set, the agent will keep the goal in his attention set from time to time until the goal is achieved or replaced by a new goal. The parameter *expectedProb* is the expected probability of success, which is determined by the relevant path in the *Knet*. Expectation and goal are two different things. We may intend to do something with a low or high expectation of its success. When the expectation is not met, an agent would display his upset.

An agent can turn his self-awareness on or off using

- *agent.turnSelfawarenessSwitch(on/off).*

For a subobject action, at this moment we just consider facial expression using the action

- *agent.face.act(expression)*

The parameter *expression* has 12 possible values associated with facial colors, as discussed in Virtual Embodiment. The value or color will represent an emotional state. The facial expression will automatically be back to its default state just a few seconds after the action.

17.5 Innate Action Abilities

We have discussed the passive or subconscious sensory abilities an agent has. In this section, we discuss the innate abilities beyond the sensory organs: abilities to recognize and perform the elementary actions (identified as elementary tokens).

Before an agent can take an action, he needs to decide on a set of action options. The initial action list at birth or for a very young infant plays important roles in its early learning. This initial list is considered a set of inherited action abilities. To create such a list, we try to think what a very young infant can do. As we discussed earlier, a child (Zda) develops his gross motor control skills first, before acquiring and tuning fine motor control skills. For purposes of illustration, the gross motor skills are listed in (Tables 17.2A through 17.2E).

Each initial action has an associated probability to indicate how likely the agent will perform the action in a given condition. We have also listed some actions that may not look that elementary, but will be associated with very low probabilities. Doing so will be convenient from a coding perspective, as the agent can just modify the probabilities for these actions as necessary later on.

Each initial action also has a set of initial weights that associate with its parameters. These weights will be used to determine similarity in learning and response mechanisms. The weights can be updated by himself based on Zda's experience.

There are different ways to define fine motor control skills. One way is to decompose a post or action into a limited number of movements or actions of different body parts. For instance, a hand may initially have 2 actions (gripping and releasing an object), the head can have 3 positions, there are 12 expressions for a face, 3 possible positions for an arm,

TABLE 17.2A

Suggested Initial Actions—Group A

Name in Agent.act	Parameters with Mandatory Values	Initial Probability	Energy Cost
lookAt	target	1/11	0.001
lookAway			0.001
knockHead			0.005
shakeHead			0.005
walkTo			0.010
walkAway			0.010
Sleep			0.000
Laydown			0.000
crawl			0.005
Sit			0.001
Stand			0.002

TABLE 17.2B

Suggested Initial Actions—Group B

Name in Agent.act	Parameters with Mandatory Values	Initial Probability	Energy Cost
agent.face.act	Expression = happy	1/3	0
	Expression = sad	1/3	0
	Expression = neutral	1/3	0

TABLE 17.2C

Suggested Initial Actions—Group C

Name in Agent.act	Parameters with Mandatory Values	Initial Probability	Energy Cost
grab	target	1/12	0.005
throw			0.005
pick			0.005
hold			0.005
drop			0.000
pointTo			0.001
PointAt			0.001
shake			0.005
push			0.010
pull			0.010
rideOn			0.010
catch			0.010

TABLE 17.2D

Suggested Initial Actions—Group D

Name in Agent.act	Parameters with Mandatory Values	Initial Probability	Energy Cost
eat/drink	target (content)	⅕	0.005
readIn			0.010
readOut			0.010
write			0.010
Count			0.010

TABLE 17.2E

Suggested Initial Actions—Group E

Name in Agent.act	Parameters with Mandatory Values	Initial Probability	Energy Cost
agent.sound	*textString:*	0.01	0.001
	cry	0.01	
	discomfort	0.18	
	laugh	0.05	
	curiosity	0.30	
	want	0.20	
	baba	0.25	
	mama		

5 different leg positions, and so on. Over time, fine motor skills are developed so that each body part has more possible positions and more possible combinations of different positions, even though some of them are not viable (e.g., leading to falling down). Other aspects, such as vocal ability, will follow the same path: from "gross" to "fine" in process.

Fine Motor Control Elements:

Head (facing): a 3-angle vector $(\alpha_h, \beta_h, \theta_h)$

Eyes: a 2-angle vector (α_e, β_e) in relation to the face.

Body: a vector $(B_1, B_2, B_3, \theta_b)$ defined by the 3 points on the spine and a rotational angle around the spine.

Left-Arm: a vector $(LA_1, LA_2, LA_3, \theta_{LA})$ defined by the 3 points on the left arm and a rotational angle around the left arm.

Right-Arm: a vector $(RA_1, RA_2, RA_3, \theta_{RA})$ defined by the 3 points on the right arm and a rotational angle around the right arm.

Left-Hand: list poses {grip, drop, a snap of the fingers, …}.

Right-Hand: list poses {grip, drop, a snap of the fingers, …}.

Left-Leg: a vector $(LL_1, LL_2, LL_3, \theta_{LL})$ defined by the 3 points on the left leg and a rotational angle around the left leg.

Right-Leg: a vector $(RL_1, RL_2, RL_3, \theta_{RL})$ defined by the 3 points on the right leg and a rotational angle around the right leg.

The parameters in fine motor control, such as angle vector $(\alpha_h, \beta_h, \theta_h)$, will be discretized using some minimal increments. In general, a gross motor action can be defined by a set of fine motor actions.

17.6 Dynamic Knowledge Presentations

Zda has separated memory areas (Relational Database Tables) to ensure his functionality and efficiency in learning and response. For persistence, data from all tables are retained on computer disk or in cloud storages. All tables except *Knet* are retrieved/preloaded into computer memory when Zda's power is on, because the *Knet* may be too large to load into memory.

- Knowledge Net (*Knet*): The complete patternized real-world experiences saved in a cloud storage or on a computer disk; used for Deep-Thinking.

- Primary *Knet* (*pKnet*): A subset of *Knet* that only includes patterns with top M/5 reward, top M/5 frequency, top M/5 recency, bottom M/5 duration, and top M/5 survival time left. Here M is a larger number and may increase as Zda accumulates his experiences and knowledge. This subset of *Knet* will be loaded in memory for speedy learning and fast-thinking and slow-thinking responses.

- Meta Net (*Mnet*): If different patterns in *Knet* are linked at the same tokens, a large recursive knowledge net (*Mnet*) is formulated. *Mnet* has the same structure as *Knet*. A path in the recursive net may or may not actually happen; it might be from logical reasoning or a hypothesis that should be tested. *Mnet* is useful in deep-thinking.

- Natural Language Net (*Lnet*): the patternized natural language based on the agent's experiences, but different from the grammars we humans use in any natural language. The net structure is similar to *Knet*.

- Imaginary Net (*Inet*): It is similar to *Knet* structurally but formulated by hypothetical scenarios that have not been executed or verified by logical reasoning or mathematical derivation. Such scenarios can only be kept for a short time unless they could lead to serious undesirable consequences. *Inet* is often used in Deep-Thinking.

- Deep Gramtons (Dgrams): A goal-driven action requires the agent to set up his goal first. A short-term or long-term goal from conscious attention in Deep-Thinking will be randomly picked from either gramtons with the shortest durations or the top rewarding gramtons (Dgrams). Dgrams consist of the patterns from *pKnet*. Therefore, Dgrams have the same attributes as the *Knet*.

- Reflexons: A **Reflexon** Class is a pair of timewise highly associated tokens (2-gramtons) used in Reflex. The first token (event) is called stimulus and the second token (action) is an actionable elementary token, called a reflexor. The reflexor usually occurs immediately after the stimulus. Here, the meaning of "highly associated tokens" is that the conditional probability of relexor, given the simulus, is virtually equal to 1. In other words, a stimulus has and only has a reflexor. Most habits can also be viewed as reflex and modeled by 2-gramtons. The Reflexon includes five attributes: tokenID, stimulus, reflexor, freq (frequency), and pReward (patternive reward). All the information in a Reflexon is recorded in *Knet*. In *Knet*, each paired stimulus and reflexor is recorded with the same tokenID in the Reflexon and an associated pattern with the first token as stimulus and the second token as reflexor.

- Associative Gramtons (Agrams): A collection of 2-gramtons used for attention shift due to the association. All 2-gramtons in the Agrams class have high conditional probabilities of the associated tokens (AssToken); given the attentive tokens (AttToken), they are high either in frequency, similarity, or reward. Such a 2-gramton may indicate an association (Refer-To) between a pattern and its name in natural language. A refer-to association can lead to a language-guided action, such as an action following a friend's request. All the information in Agrams is recorded in *Knet*. In *Knet*, the paired AttToken and AssToken are recorded with the same tokenID as in Agrams and an associated pattern with the first token as AttToken and the second token as AssToken.

- Desensitisors: A list of one-gramtons and corresponding elements, to be used to determine if a token belongs to an existing desensitisor, or for a given desensitisor to choose an element from it.

- Elementary Gramtons (Egrams): A subset of *Knet* that only includes high-frequency and high-reward elementary 2-, 3-, and 4-gramtons; used for Fast-Thinking.

- Subconscious attention set (SAS) as a property of *Knet*: SAS is an array that has up to 3 objects with the highest subconscious attention on their attributes. SAS includes the following attributes: d, the distance between Zda and the object; S, the speed of the object; and n, h, M, T the intensities of smell, sound, temperature, and taste, respectively. ISA is shorthand for instant subconscious attentivity based on SAS.

- Recency Subconscious Attention Set (RSAS) as a property of HumanizedAI *class*: RSAS up to 64 tokens at 16 time points for Slow-Thinking. The 64 tokens record the details of recent events.

- Milestone Gramtons (Mgrams): The Mgrams class records significant historical events in detail including the associated time and duration.

- Cause to effect net (CEnet): List of 2-gramtons, each pair having an associated probability.

All these knowledge networks (tables) are formed and constantly updated based on Zda's experiences (including what he has been taught), i.e., his past attention sets, not exactly what may have happened in the real world.

The *Knet* and *pKnet* Class (database Table) has the same structure, including the fields (attributes): Token ID (tokenID), Pattern-Type (pType), Pattern (Path), Frequency (Freq), Patternive Reward (pReward), reward type (rType), Distributive Reward (dReward), Recency (Rec), Duration (Dur), and Name in natural language (NNL) if any. The reward, if any, is always for the agent of the *Knet*. Duration is the duration of such a composite event indicated by the pattern. tokenID is the token name when the pattern is viewed as a higher level token. rType has initially limited types including "food" and "entertainment," NNL has initially no values, but will be filled in by Zda himself through learning strong associations between tokenIDs (Patterns) and words in a natural language. pType can be one of the 15 possible Pattern types and 8 types of language patterns specified in Section 11.3. pType is useful for easy tokenization of patterns.

We must make the following clarifications:

1. All high-level tokens are presented by 5-letter tokenIDs generated from the Auto Naming system (Chapter 9), e.g., GFtRS. Among them, the tokenID for a pattern that only contains natural language elements will start with the capital letter ZFtRS.

2. The tokenID for an elementary token is a 5-letter string with "0" appended to the end, e.g., FDGRw0 a general pattern and ZFDsk0 for a pattern in a natural language.

3. A skipton can include paired or tripled desensitisors. For the purpose of hierarchical detokenization, in naming desensitisors, a desensitisor's tokenID is constructed by appending a sequential number to the tokenID of the associated skipton. For instance, if the tokenID for the skipton is ADShD, the desensitisor names will be ADShD1, ADShD2, and ADShD3, etc., depending on the number of desisentisors in the skipton. In this way, given a tokenID (e.g., ADShD) for a skipton, we can easily reconstruct the skipton. That is, we know where to find the relevant desensitisors.

4. Patterns are usually expressed in a sequence of tokenIDs. For example,

   FtRS⇒GFtRS ⇒FDGRw0∧ZFDsk0

5. A pattern for an elementary (atomic) natural language pattern is a single word in natural language, e.g., "Daddy" for the pattern with tokenID = ZFDsk0.

6. A pattern (Egram) for an elementary token is the definition of the token, expressed (coded) somewhat like in Table 17.2 of Part IV, e.g., Zda.act("walk", step = 3). Egram might include some of the desensitisors of elementary tokens by dividing the parameters of actions into categories. The data structure of Egram includes attributes: tokenID, action definition and its parameters, initial probability, energy cost, and pReward.

7. A desensitisor can be a high-level or elementary token with the auto-naming conventions. The Pattern attribute for a desensitisor is a list of one-gramtons with a high-frequency or an associated high reward. The Egrams have the same attributes as in *Knet*. All the information in Egrams is also recorded in *Knet*. The separate OOP class for desensitisor is used for the purpose of computational efficacy, even though the same information has been included in *Knet*.

All above OOP classes have corresponding database tables with matched attributes for the requirement of knowledge persistence.

17.7 Innate and Developed Habits

As we have discussed in Part III, innate habits ensure that an agent does things consistently, not changing easily over time. Such consistency is needed in learning and communication. Innate associations between innate abilities, such as between facial expressions and body language, create habits. A habit can be inherited or developed. Habits can change slowly over time or go away when they are not needed anymore. From a modeling perspective, the tendency of taking one or a sequence of actions with a large probability is called a habit. Therefore, a habit can be modeled using an *n*-gramton or skipton with a high frequency or probability.

- Biological Desires and Feelings (pleasure, pain, hunger, anger) cause attention and drive actions. For instance, when feeling pain or hunger, a baby Zda will cry, while feeling happy or tickling will lead to him smiling or laughing.
  How to implement:
  (1) Create a timer to constantly monitor Zda's sensation, (2) if sensation = pain, trigger the "cry" sound; if sensation = tickling or happy, trigger the laugh sound, (3) when the energy level < E_c, Zda will be hungry, and (4) create a timer for constantly checking the energy level.

- Zda's energy decreases over time. Before taking an action, the agent will check if he has enough energy. An action costs energy.
  How to Implement:
  Using a time-decay function: *energy = energy-Ea*time-elapsed*, if the action costs more energy than the energy that's left, the agent would not take the action. Here *Ea* is Zda's property.

- Baby Zda has low sensitivities to the environment, his world is simple.
  How to Implement:
  It is implemented using limited sensitivity levels in each sensory organ, as shown in Table 17.1, Virtual Embodiment.

- Baby Zda is more imitative, becomes more creative when young, and less creative when getting older.
  How to Implement:
  Use individualized time-sensitive creativity parameters in the umbrella-shaped creativeness in fast-thinking: $P_c = P_{cm}*(1-(age-C_a)^2)$, and an age timer; P_{cm} may be called the maximum creativeness and C_a, the most creative age.

- Baby Zda initially tends to walk or reach to an object in his attention.
  How to Implement:
  Use a high initial probability of the walkTo() and Grab() actions as shown in Table 17.2: Initial Action List.

- Baby Zda likes to grab anything small and put it in his mouth to suck on it.
  How to Implement:
  This can be implemented using a 2-gramton with a paired parameter ObjA: *Zda. grab(ObjA) Zda.eat(ObjA)*. The initially associated probability is set high and the conditional probability of the second token given the first token is also high. This 2-gramton with a parameter can be considered as a reflexon. A reflexon has a very high conditional probability.

- Zda likes to perform cognitive learning, which is often an application of the similarity principle.
  How to Implement:
  See implementations in Deep-Thinking.
- Given that everything else is the same, Zda more likely pays attention to objects' attributes than the differences in attributes between objects: differences in distance (close to), velocity, size, color, brightness, sound, loudness, smell, and other sensible attributes.
  How to Implement:
  It is considered in attention mechanisms and the agent.compare action.
- Zda constantly monitors the distance of the attentive objects all the time.
  How to Implement:
  At each attention time point, calculate the distance for each object nearby (the nearby is determined by the distance at the previous time point) in the scene, and then determine the subconscious attentivity. For a robot, such calculations may not be needed if the vision can determine the distance automatically.
- When Zda wants to look for something in reality, he will walk around and when a match is found he will walk toward it and do something with it.
  How to Implement:
  If Zda's goal is to find a thing, he will recall the thing and search nearby objects for a match; if the thing to be searched is abstract, he may search in his *Knet*.
- Attention means that Zda will likely act on the attentive object, which may mean looking at it, looking away, talking about it, walking to it or walking away, picking it up, punching it, grabbing it, throwing it away, and making association(s) among the attentive items.
  How to Implement:
  This habit is reflected in the Randomized Adaptive Reinforcement Learning found in Part III.
- Zda likes to balance his energy and physical body.
  How to Implement:
  To be considered in Robots.

A habit can be developed when an action or sequence of actions is repeated very often. Such a habit will become a high-level token through hierarchical tokenization. When a habit involves a sequence of actions, it can also be considered to be due to association.

17.8 Innate Attributes and Initialization

An agent has to be initialized when he is created. The initialization is classified as, physical property, innate attributes, and Net objects' initializations. For persistence, these data and new data (mainly patterns) created during interactions will be serialized and saved mainly as relational database tables on a computer disk or some remote cloud. The computer is usually left on so that agents can work constantly without a break. If for some reason it has to be shut down, and turned on again, the HAI system will reload all the data from cloud storage back to memory via the reverse process, deserialization.

Physical Properties of a Thingy as Discussed in Virtual World Simulations:

- name in Coding (not a name in a natural language).
- age = elapsed time from the object's creation.
- sex = male or female
- Appearance(shape, size, texture),
    - shape = triangle, square, circle, star, pentagon, hexagon, which serves as a visual identification of a class of object.
    - size = an integer to indicate the size of an object.
    - texture = an integer to indicate the surface texture characteristic, may be used to identify each object for a given class.
- phyChem = a value associated with the object's physical or chemical property.
- Color(color, brightness), Sound(sound, loudness), Odor(odor intensity)
    - color, sound, odor = a value associated with the object's color, sound, odor.
    - brightness, loudness, intensity = a value indicating brightness, loudness, intensity.
    - Face default color, the facial image can only have 2 colors picked from 4 colors (red, green, yellow, blue), a total of 12 possible combinations (expressions).
- taste = binary value indicating edible or not.
- temperature = a value to indicate the object's temperature.
- mass = mass of the object
- Location(x, y, z) = location of the object
- Velocity(v_x, v_y, v_z) = velocity of the object, speed is the magnitude of the velocity.
- utility = drivable for car, water can put out fire, light can enlighten a room, etc.

Innate Attributes as Discussed in Virtual Embodiment and Habits:

- $W0$, $W1$, and $W2$ are coded as inherited attributes and can be updated depending on interests developed over time for subconscious attentivity.
- probability parameter p in associative search or attention shift.
- Ct, Cr, Cf, Cs, and Ce in response models.
- C_a in determining the time to the next subconscious attentive time point, $Dt = C_a/ISA$, *where ISA* is Instant Subconscious Attentivity (see Dynamic Attributes below).
- E_a in *energy = energy -* E_a **(time-elapsed)*
- E_c in energy when energy $< E_c$, Zda is hungry.
- The maximum creativeness, P_{cm} and the most creative age, C_a in umbrella-shaped creativeness: $P_c = P_{cm} (1 - (age - C_a)^2)$.
- Parameter Cg in longevity of patterns, $Cg \cdot \frac{Freq \cdot Reward}{N \cdot n}$

Dynamic Attributes:
The agent's dynamic attributes will include:

- Subconscious attentivity set, SAS(t), at the current time t consistent of 4 objects with the top attentivities among all objects in the environment.

- The 12 objects in SAS at time points t-2, t-1 and t will be stored in array attribute, SAS12. Similarly, the 60 objects from SAS at 15 time points t-14, t-13, ..., t-2, t-1, and t, 4 objects at each time point, will be stored as array attribute, SAS60.
- The maximum activity in SAS is called Instant Subconscious Attentivity (ISA). The maximum ISA at time t-2, t-1, and t is called Fast-Thinking Subconscious Attentivity (FTSA), and the maximum ISA at times t-14, t-13, ..., t-2, t-1, and t is called Slow-Thinking Subconscious Attentivity (STSA).
- CAS, the shortcut for Conscious Attention Set.
- NAT, Next attentive time point.

Agent Initialization:

- Limited number of categories for each sensory organ, as shown in Table 17.1.
- Initial probabilities of elementary actions: See Table 17.2.
- All actionable (elementary) tokens are assigned initially a small patternive reward (e.g., 0.01).
- Before Zda developed a list of interesting things for conscious attention, he had an initial (born with) set of interesting things for conscious attention.
- Retrieve relevant *Knet* database rows and create temporary Tables into corresponding *Net* objects in the computer memory.
- Auto-naming system parameters: Knet.nameMaxIndex = initial number of initial elementary tokens, Knet.zNameMaxIndex = initial number of elementary words.

Initial Desensitisors:
The list of initial Desensitisors will be based on the following grouping.

- Actor = any given actioner
- Agent = any HAI agent
- Animal = any type of animal
- Food = any object with milk smell
- Action = any given action regardless of parameters
- ActionSameTarget = any given action with the same target

17.9 Innate Mechanisms

There are three main mechanisms in HAI architectures (Figure 17.2):

- Attention Mechanism: Subconscious Attention, Conscious Attention, and Associative Attention Shift.
- Response Mechanism: Reflex, Fast-Thinking, Slow-Thinking, and Deep-Thinking Mechanisms.
- Learning Mechanism: Hierarchical tokenization, Patternization, and Repatternization, and the forgetting mechanism.

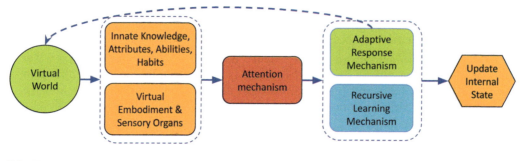

FIGURE 17.2
Overview of humanized AI architecture.

The simulated virtual environment, including the agents themselves, consists of elementary tokens. Thus, to Zda, observables through his sensory organs are the elementary tokens. The observed elementary tokens assemble the attention set, which may trigger a reflex or thinking (fast-thinking, slow-thinking, and deep-thinking). Reflex is based on an expandable list of 2-gramtons (not necessarily elementary tokens) with high frequencies or high positive rewards. Fast-thinking is mainly based on an expandable list of 2-gramtons and 3-gramtons with high frequencies and/or high rewards. In slow-thinking, the long event-string of elementary tokens are conceptualized into shorter (≤4) high-level tokens through hierarchical tokenization. In deep-thinking, repatternization of conceptual tokens may occur at "sleep time." Goal-driven action and cognitive learnings also occur in Deep-Thinking. The response mechanism is discussed in Part III, Chapter 14, and the blueprint of the overall response mechanism is shown in Figure 14.5. The pattern structures in *Knet* and Learning Mechanism are discussed in Part III, Chapters 12 and 13, respectively. The components of the Learning mechanism are outlined in Figure 13.1.

17.10 On Simulations and Animations

If every object has a separate CPU, then "everyone" works independently (this is more realistic) and CPU speed reflects an individual's abilities. However, in my demonstrations, only one CPU is used, and CPU time distribution is avoidable. Zda needs to monitor the external world defined by the attentive animal's language (sequence of voices), expression (face), post, and motion (of skeleton) as listed in the Table of Zda Prototype for virtual embodiment. In addition, the location and speed of attentive moving objects are also monitored.

To speed up the animations, the demonstrations can proceed with two steps: (1) the empty proxy animation functions with parameters are called initially at real time so that no actual animations are performed during interactions, and the sequence of those proxy animation function calls are recorded in a file, (2) the real animations are performed by reading in the file and linking the proxy functions to the corresponding actual animation functions. Therefore, Zda's visual recognitions are simplified by reading the corresponding attributes of the object, such as geometric shape, size, and color. In the condition of virtual agents, not robots, the tactile sense is also reading from the object's attributes, the same for smell, sound, and taste. Animation is generally faster using GPU. The main difference between CPU and GPU architecture is that a CPU is designed to handle a wide-range of tasks quickly (as measured by CPU clock speed), but is limited in the concurrency of tasks that can be running. A GPU is designed to quickly render high-resolution images and video concurrently. However, newly proposed algorithms proposed by computer scientists from Rice University could actually turn the tables and make CPUs much faster than some leading-edge GPUs.

18

Implementations of Innate Mechanisms

We discuss functions or methods in OOP class. For each module, we will use NL descriptions, mathematical formulations, and OOP conventions for clarity and conciseness.

For a robot, identifying objects is a much-needed skill, since the same object appears different every time. For instance, every person is changing every second. For agents in computers, we could simply use the agent name in the computer code to codify its identity so that we can focus on Zda's language learning and thought process. Similarly, a robot has to be able to detect an object's distance and speed; for Zda, we just use the coordinates of objects in the computer code to determine the distance and speed for the same reasons. The same token applies to smell, brightness, and other sensible attributes.

List of Modules (OOP methods or functions) in this section are grouped into seven categories (List 18.1). Module Inception is the startpoint of the HAI agent system. The numbers in the parentheses, before a semicolon indicate which modules will invoke the module, and the numbers indicate which modules it invokes. For example, "FastThink (8; 35, 47, 56)" means module *Inception* will invoke *FastThink* and *FastThink* will invoke modules: *ExpectedTokens*, *RandomizedAdaptiveRL*, and *Animation*.

Auto Naming System

1. AutoName (27, 48; 2)
2. nameByPermutation (1;)
3. AtomicTokenID (19; 1)
4. ExtractNets (8;)

Biosystem Simulation

5. HumanizedAI (OOP Class; 6, 7, 8)
6. Embodiment (5;)
7. AtomicActions (5;)
8. Inception(5; 9, 10, 19, 31, 39~42)
9. BioClock (8, 10;)
10. Biodesires (8; 9)
11. Emotion
12. EmotionChanged (auto)
13. PatteniveReward
14. DistributiveReward
15. CollaborativeReward

16. Crossover (18;)
17. Mutation (18;)
18. Evolution (; 16, 17)

Attentions

19. SubconsciousAttentionSet (20~21; 3)
20. FastThinkingAttentionSet (19;)
21. SlowThinkingAttentionSet (19;)
22. ConsciousAttention (47; 37)

Tokenization and Patternization

23. Tokenization (24, 29, 30;)
24. HierarchicalTokenization (42; 23)
25. RandomRow (34, 49, 51, 57;)
26. Gramization (28;)
27. Patternization (28; 1)
28. Repatternization (43; 26~27)
29. RecycleTokenID (31;)
30. MetaPath (42;)

31. Forgetting (8;)
32. FreewillRandomizer (22, 43, 46, 50;)

Response Models

33. ExpectedTokens (40, 46; 25, 34, 38)
34. JaccardSimilarity (33, 37~38;)
35. ExpSimilarity (37;)
36. CosineSimilarity (37~38;)
37. AggregateSimilarity (38; 34~35)
38. SimilaritySearch (33, 41~42; 34~37)
39. Reflex (8; 54)
40. FastThink (8; 33, 45, 53)
41. SlowThink (8, 46; 24, 33, 45, 53)
42. DeepThink (8; 28, 43~44, 52~53)
43. GoalSetting (42; 32, 49, 51)
44. CognitiveLearning (42; 22, 50, 55~59)
45. RandomizedAdaptiveRL (40~41; 32)
46. GamingPrediction (; 42, 34)

Action Types

47. Imitation (51;)
48. Creation (51; 25)
49. Recollection (; 32)
50. AttentionShift (44; 25)
51. Imagination (; 47~48)
52. GoalDrivenActions (42; 38)
53. Animation (39~42)

Cognitive Reasoning

54. Detokenization (56, 58)
55. Induction (44; 25)
56. Deduction (44; 55)
57. Analogy (44)
58. Abduction (44; 54)
59. CauseToEffect (44;)
60. RecursionOnEverything

LIST 18.1 Modules in humanized AI and their relationships.

18.1 Auto Naming System

Because Zda's knowledge will increase through learning automatically, an auto-naming ability for elements (tokens, patterns, desensitisors, sensitisors) of such knowledge is necessary. We equip (coding behind scene) Zda with a Five-Letter Coding system: elementary tokens, hierarchical tokens, patterns, and words and word-patterns in natural languages are coded in a 5-English-letter coding system (a – z, A – Z), e.g., *after* and *WagUs*. In the 5-letter universal code system, all natural language words and their hierarchical tokens always start with capital letter Z. In other words, all pure natural language tokens (or pattern) and only pure natural language tokens start with the letter Z.

Each elementary token or initial desensitisor is given a unique name statically at the design stage, while a pattern, desensitisor, or sensitisor is given a unique name dynamically in real time. Since each name is 5-characters long, the naming system can provide $52^5 = 380$ millions different names, including $52^4 = 7$ million names for coding pure language (tokens, patterns, and desensitisors). An event-string patternization always starts with natural language tokenization and patternization within the event-string. Therefore, the auto-naming system includes auto-naming for natural language and auto-naming for general events. All tokens in an event-string or a pattern are represented by a sequence of names (tokenID) of patterns, not in the structures of elementary tokens. This is possible because each elementary token also has its name. However, an elementary token has to be represented by its actuarial structure, e.g., elementary token BSDTY may be expressed in walk(step =5). The name indicates the sequence of {aaaa, aaaab, aaaac, ..., aaaba, aaabb, ..., ZZZZa, ZZZZb, ..., ZZZZZ}.

In addition to a skipton (pattern) name, the associated one desensitisor or two paired desensitisors in a skipton will need names. The desensitisor's name is obtained by adding a sequential number to the skipton name. For example, if skipton's name is *Hahds*, the names for the associated desensitisors will be *Hahds1*, *Hahds2*, ..., depending on the number of desensitisors. The multiple desensitisors are always paired or tripled, etc. Each elementary token name or *tokenID* will be appended a "0" in the end.

To outline the auto naming algorithms:

1. Ensure to use a name from the recycle bin first if any.

2. Generate unique 5-letter name as tokenID for each pattern (gramton or skipton)

3. A tokenId starting with capital letter Z is reserved for a pattern of pure natural language.

4. If the pattern is a skipton, generate a tokenID for each desensitisor by appending a sequential number 1, 2, or 3 to the skipton name.

5. If the pattern is simply an elementary token, append "0" to the name to form the final tokenID.

The purpose of the following module is to generate a unique name to token, pattern, desensitisor, sensitisor for general event-strings including event-word mixtures, more precisely, to generate unique tokenID of patterns in different *Knets* (Section 17.6). Here, the parameter *patternType* should be "Event" for a general pattern or "NL" for a pure natural language pattern.

```
AutoName(patternType) {
// names of died patterns are removed from Knet and put in namaRecyleBin
If (nameRecycleBin.size > 0) { // Use a recycled name first if any
        name = nameRecycleBin[1]
        nameRecycleBin.delete(index = 1)
Else
        name = nameByPermutation(patternType)
}
TokenIDs[1] = name              // tokenId for gramton
TokenIDs[2] = name.app("0")     // tokenID for atomic token
TokenIDs[3] = name.app("1")     // tokenID for desensitisor of the skipton
TokenIDs[4] = name.app("2")     // for paired desensitisor of the skipton
TokenIDs[5] = name.app("3")     // for tripled desensitisor of the skipton
TokenIDs[6] = name.app("4")     // for quadrupled desensitisor of the skipton
Return TokenIDs
}
```

The purpose of the following module is to use permutation of letters at the 5 position to form a name.

```
nameByPermutation() {
letters = [a, b, c, …, z, A, B, C, …, Z]
//Event-name coding system
Knet.nameMaxIndex = Knet.nameMaxIndex + 1
nIndex = Knet.nameMaxIndex    //the max index for pattern name used
index[5] = Math.mod(nIndex, 52) + 1 //Get the remainder of the division
nIndex = nIndex - index[5]
index[4] = Math.mod(nIndex, 52^2) + 1
nIndex = nIndex - index[4]*52
index[3] = Math.mod(nIndex, 52^3) + 1
nIndex = nIndex - index[3]*52*52
index[2] = Math.mod(nIndex, 52^4) + 1
index[1] =  nIndex - index[2]*52*52*52 + 1
If (type = " NL") { index[1] = 52}  //A word-token starts with capital letter Z.
For i = 1 To 5
        name = name.app(letters[Index[i]])
Next
Return name
}
```

Elementary tokens. including words in natural languages. will be mapped to the standard 5-letter auto-naming system by means of the following module:

```
AtomicTokenID(patternIn, patternType) {
For Each token In patternIn
        If (Knet.Pattern.tokenID.find(token) < 1) {
                newPattern.tokenID = AutoName(patternType)
                newPattern.freq = 1
                Knet.Pattern.add(newPattern)
                If (patternType = "NL") { // Also add to NL net
                        Knet.Pattern.add(newPattern)
                }
        }
Next
}
```

The purpose of the following module is to extract different subnets (see Section 17.6) from *Knet*. The module should be invoked periodically (e.g., daily) to keep all net information up to date.

```
ExtractNets() {
// depending your system, may use QOL to extract data from Knet
// Omitted.
}
```

18.2 Biosystem Basics

18.2.1 Inception of Humanized AI

```
HumanizedAI() {  //the OOP Constructor, called at instantiation.
Embodiment()      // assign agent's static features
AtomicActions()   // Elementary actionable tokens
Inception()       //Agent life begins
}
```

The purpose of the module Embodiment is to assign the new agent's static attributes and *Knet* structure as discussed in Part III. Coding the module is straightforward, but tedious, and so is omitted here.

```
Embodiment()  {
// Omitted, to follow instructions in Part III
}
```

The purpose of the module AtomicActions is to assign the initial atomic actions (elementary tokens) and habits described in Part III.

```
AtomicActions()  {
// Omitted but follow instructions in Part III
}
```

Inception means the birth of an HAI agent. From that time on, the biological clock is ticking and the system becomes alive. The module (also called OOP method, function, or procedure) Inception will do the following:

1. Invoke the *Biodesire* module to set up the agent's desires.
2. Invoke the *SubconsciousAttention* module.
3. Instantiate *AttentionClock* with the next attention time (NAT).
4. At the attention pulse rate, invoke the Reflex, FastThink, SlowThink, or DeepThink module based on attentions.
5. Periodically remove unused (dead) patterns.

```
Inception () {
Biodesires(300) // Every 5 minutes update desires
SubconsciousAttentionSet()
//The AttentionClock() should be refresh once NAT changes
AttentionClock = BioClock(ME.NAT)
// Decide the response model to invoke
AttentionClock.pulse() {
  If (ISA >= Cr) {
        Reflex()
  ElseIf (FTSA >= Cf)
        FastThink()
  ElseIF (STSA >= Cs)
        SlowThink()
  Else
        DeepThink()
  }
}
// Periodically (24 hours) remove unused patterns.
Forgetting(24*60)
// Periodically (24 hours) refresh all nets
RefreshClock = BioClock(24*60)
RefreshClock.pulse() {
        ExtractNets()
}
}
```

18.2.2 Biological Clocks

Zda's Biological Clock is an imprecise clock built from the computer clock with a small random variation added. Zda uses the biological clock to time and record events happening internally and in his surroundings. The BioClock(*period*) can be instantiated as many times as needed on timers: hourly, daily, weekly, monthly, seasonal, and yearly timers. A period of 24 hours indicates a day. The concepts of month and year are learned. A Bioclock object has an inherited BioClock.pulse event module. Statements within the pulse event module will be executed periodically (i.e., every *period* second).

The purpose of the following module is to create a timer with Period = period.

```
BioClock (period) {
aClock = system.timer(period) //computer cock
Return aClock
}
```

18.2.3 Biological Desires

As discussed in Part III Chapter 10, the biodesire mechanisms are as follows. (1) The minimal consumption of energy is $E_a \times$ (*time-elapsed*); when the energy level < E_c, Zda will be hungry; actions cost energy, and food boosts energy. (2) Entertainment boosts emotion and raises the sensation level. (3) Curiosity can be reduced due to, e.g., a question being answered, but it will automatically come back to a higher level shortly afterward. In addition, energy level and emotion (sensation) will also affect the level of curiosity. See the following OOP-like code for details.

We create a timer to periodically adjust Zda's energy level. The purpose of the following module is to determine the energy level. The procedure biodesireTimer.puls() is auto triggered in every predefined time interval.

```
Biodesires(pulseInterval) {
//Create a timer with pulse interval = pulseInterval
biodesireTimer = BioClock(interval = pulseInterval)
biodesireTimer.puls(){ // auto triggered every pulseInterval second
// minimal consumption of energy
ME.energy = Math.min(ME.energy - ME.Ea*pulseInterval, 0)
// Auto backup curiosity
ME.curiosity = Math.max(ME.curiosity + ME.Ea*pulseInterval, 1)
// Curiosity adjustment by energy and emotion
lessCuriosity =  (1-ME.energy) +(1-ME.heart.sensation)
ME.curiosity = ME.curiosity - lessCuriosity
If (ME.energy < ME.Ec) { //energy < Ec, Zda will be hungry.
        ME.hungry = TRUE
        ME.desire = "food"
ElseIf (ME.heart.sensation < ME.Ec)   //desires entertainment.
        ME.desire = "entertainment"
Else
        ME.desire = "curiosity"
}
}
}
```

18.2.4 Emotion Simulations

The intensity of a feeling (incremental sensation) is discussed in Section 10.10.

Incremental sensation = (what is received minus expectation)/expectation

The associated rewards with patterns in a *Knet* determine the expectation by: the average (R) of rewards associated with the candidate action paths from RARL and the reward (R_0) associated with the chosen action path. The expectation = $0.1R+0.9R_0$ is an example of a weighted average.

The purpose of the following module is to calculate the incremental sensation and update sensation states. This module should be invoked within the atomic action modules if there is any associated cost or reward.

```
Emotion(actualReward, expReward) {
dSensation = actualReward/expReward -1  //Incremental sensation
//Heart is the home for feeling: a higher sensation is better.
ME.heart.sensation = ME.heart.sensation + dSensation
Return dSensational
}
```

Biological Desires and Feelings (pleasure, pain, hunger, anger) cause attention and drive actions. For instance, when feeling pain or hunger, the baby Zda will cry, while feeling happy or tickling will lead him to smile or laugh. Such an instinct is determined by Zda's inner state: sensation and triggered by the event-module SensationChanged() or EmotionChanged() automatically whenever sensation changes, instead of using separate reflexons.

Algorithms: (1) create a timer for constantly checking energy level, (2) If sensation = a low (pain), trigger the "crying" sound, (3) if sensation = a higher value (happy), trigger the "laughing" sound.

A few feelings and associated (facial) expressions are inherited, such as hunger, pain, pleasure, sadness, and anger. This nature (instinct) characteristic can be changed and replaced with some nurture habits (high-frequency 2-gramtoms). More expressions can be developed as consequences of social interactions.

The purpose of the following module is to set the corresponding value for emotion state and will be triggered whenever emotion changes.

```
EmotionChanged () {
Switch (ME.heart.sensation) {
        Case value 1  //Pain, mad, sad
                ME.sound("crying")
                ME.facialExpression[1]
        Case value 2  //Defalt
                ME.facialExpression[2]
        Case value 3  //Happy, pleasure, tickling
                ME.sound("laughing")
                ME.facialExpression[3]
}
```

18.2.5 Rewards

A patternive reward (PR) is recognized by a change in Zda's internal states (hunger or sensation). External environments can affect Zda's internal states. For instance, virtual food can change hunger and virtual entertaining activities can increase Zda's sensation level. When a PR is recognized, it indicates the end of a string segmentation or an elementary pattern. The purpose of the following module is to determine the patternive reward, which is a subclass of Thingy with attributes of energy and type (food, entertainment). Module PatteniveReward should be invoked whenever an action is taken; thus, it's better to call it within each action module. The reward should be relevant to the current pattern (the actions immediately before the reward due to the laws of association) and the new patternive reward should be the frequency-weighted average of previous and current rewards.

```
PatteniveReward(type, value){
// It is invoked whenever an action is taken.
pReward.reward = value
pReward.type = type
If (type = "food") {
        ME.energy = ME.energy + value
}
If (type = "entertainment") {
        ME.heart.sensation = ME.heart.sensation  + value
}
// increase the reward for the current pattern by value/freq
cID = ME.Knet.crrenttokenID
freq = ME.Knet.Pattern[cID].freq
reward = ME.Knet.Pattern[cID].reward
ME.Knet.Pattern[cID].reward = (reward*freq+value)/(freq+1)
Return pReward
}
```

When a Patternive Reward (PR) is received, Zda needs to update the associated distributive and collaborative rewards.

Distributive Rewards will be updated according to the following formulation:

$$DR(t) = \frac{DR(t-1)\, f(t-1) + PR(t)/N}{f(t)}$$

for each actionable token (node) of a given pattern (path). *PR(t)* is the patternive reward received at time t, N is the number of related actionable tokens in the pattern, $f(t–1)$ is the frequency of receiving distributive rewards (without future-discount) at the node (token) up to time $t–1$, and the updated frequency for the node at time t is $f(t) = f(t–1)+1$.

All actionable (elementary) tokens are assigned initially a small patternive reward (e.g., 0.01). Patternive Rewards sometimes exist in the verbal form or as other reward proxies, such as when parents tell their children how important their education will be. In Zda's *Knet*, a reward to an agent is measured from Zda's viewpoint, not as what the agent actually receives. Likewise, in Lia's *Knet*, a reward to an agent is assessed in terms of Lia's view.

The purpose of the following module is to calculate the distributive reward.

```
DistributiveReward(stringIn, PR) {
// DR = distributive reward.
For Each pattern In Knet.Pattern
        If (pattern = stringIn) {
                N = 0   // occurrences of the receiver appear as actioners
                For Each token In pattern
                        index = token.search(".")   // token = actioner.act()
                        actioner = token.substring(index - 1)
                        If (actioner = ME) { N = N + 1 }
                Next
                DR =  pattern.dReward*pattern.freq + PR/N
                disReward = DR/(pattern.freq + 1)
                Knet.Pattern.dReward = disReward
                Knet.Pattern.freq = pattern.freq + 1
                Break
        }
Next
Return disReward
}
```

The purpose of the following module is to calculate the collaborative reward.

```
CollaborativeReward(stringIn, PR) {
// PR = patternive reward. CR = collaborative reward.
For Each pattern In Knet.Pattern
        If (pattern = stringIn) {
                CR =  pattern.CR*pattern.freq + PR/pattern.size
                coReward = CR/(pattern.freq + 1)
                Knet.Pattern.CR = coReward
                Knet.Pattern.freq = pattern.freq +1
                Break
        }
Next
Return coReward
}
```

18.2.6 Evolutionary Mechanism

Evolutionary Mechanism: Unlike other innate knowledge and mechanisms, evolutionary mechanisms only affect innate things across different generations. Zda's evolutionary mechanism is similar to Darwin's natural selection, including reproduction, inheritance, individual variation, and competition under limited resources. See Section F.3 in Appendix for Genetic algorithms and Genetic programming.

Natural Selection: During each successive generation, a portion of the existing population is selected in the breeding of a new generation. Individual solutions are selected through a fitness-based random selection process. Fitness at any moment is measured by the cumulative rewards that the HAI agent has received.

The "genetic make-up" is represented by HAI agent's 6 sets innate attributes as discussed in Section 17.9:

1. Organ Sensitivity parameters, $W0$, $W1$, and $W2$ in subconscious attentivity.
2. Probability parameter p for attention shift.
3. Characteristic parameters, Ct, Cr, Cf, Cs, and Ce in response models. C_a in determining the time to the next subconscious attentive time point, $\Delta t = C_a/ISA$.
4. Energy consumption parameter E_a and the threshold E_c for hunger.
5. The creativeness parameters, P_{cm} and C_a.
6. Memory parameter for token longevity, Cg.

Unlike gene sequences, this simple "genetic material" is just sets of parameters that have no different genomic sequences.

Genetic Operators: Crossover and mutation are the main types of genetic operators. The mutation probability is usually smaller than the crossover probability to avoid chaos across generations.

The purpose of the following module is to perform genetic crossover operation.

```
Crossover () {
```
    Algorithms:

1. Randomly select two agents of different genders as father and mother based on their fitnesses from a population with top 10% fitness.
2. Randomly select some (e.g., 3) sets of the 7 sets of genetic material from the mother and the remaining sets from the father.
3. Create an agent with this combined "genetic material" as innate attributes.
```
}
```

The purpose of the following module is to perform genetic mutation operation.

```
Mutation () {
```
Algorithms:

1. Randomly select an agent with fitness from a population with top 10% fitness.

2. Randomly select a genetic material and randomly change its value.

3. Create an agent based on the new set of innate attributes.

```
}
```

The purpose of the following module is to generate a new baby agent using evolutionary algorithms. The Evolution module should be invoked at the time the HAI agent successfully delivers her virtual baby—instantiating a new HAI agent by some changes of innate parameters, as listed above.

```
Evolution () {
// probability P_c for crossover and P_m = 1- P_c mutation.
If (Math.rand() > Pc ) {
        Crossover()
Else
        Mutation()
}
}
```

18.3 Attentions

18.3.1 Subconscious Attention

The Subconscious Attention Set $\Omega_S(t)$ consists of objects (events) with the highest subconscious attentivities. The subconscious attentivity is calculated using

$$SA(t) = W_0 \exp\left[-d(t)\right] + W_1 S(t) + W_2 \ln\left[1 + n(t)h(t)M(t)T(t)\right]$$

where $W0$, $W1$, and $W2$ are coded as inherited attributes and can be updated dependent on interests developed over time. We define $d(t)$ = distance between Zda and the object at time t, $S(t)$ = the speed of the object, while $n(t)$, $h(t)$, $M(t)$, $T(t)$ are the intensities of smell, sound, temperature, and taste, respectively.

The purpose of the following function is to determine Subconscious Attention Sets and track and update the 15 most recent subconscious attention sets (RSAS) with associated times.

```
SubconsciousAttentionSet () {
```

Loop through all objects in the environment and determine the top n = 3 objects as the subconscious attention set $\Omega_S(t)$ at time *t*.

The algorithms:

1. Determine the Instant Subconscious Attention Set, ISAS
2. Calculate ISA: Instant Subconscious Attentivity.
3. Tokenize words in the ears:

   Words = AtomicTokenID(ME.ears.words, "NL")

   wordPattern = HierarchicalTokenization(Words, 4, 3, "NL")

   Replace the words heard in ISAS with wordPattern

   Words = AtomicTokenID(ISAS, "Event")

4. Update RSAS: subconscious attentivity sets written in the standard tokenID, SAS(t) at the 16 most recent time points using tokenized word-string.
5. Calculate Stimulus the object corresponding to ISA.
6. Calculate FTSAS and FTSA

   FTSAS = FastThinkingAttentionSet(Knet.RSAS)

7. Calculate STSAS and STSA

   STSAS = SlowThinkingAttentionSet(Knet.RSAS)

8. Determine NAT = Ct/ISA: the next subconscious attentive time.

```
ME.ISA = ISA  //Current ISA; ME is the key word for the agent.
ME.NAT = NAT  //The next subconscious attentive time
ME.FTSA = FTSA  //Fast-Think Subconscious Attentivity
ME.STSA = STSA  //Slow-Think Subconscious Attentivity

// We express various attention sets in the standard tokenIDs:
//Stimulus = the object with ISA.
ME.stimulus =  ISAS  //coded in elementary tokenID
//the instant subconscious attention set
ME.ISAS = ISAS  //coded in elementary tokenID
//15 recent subconscious attention sets
ME.RSAS = RSAS
//Fast-think subconscious attention sets
ME.FTSAS =FTSAS
//Slow-think subconscious attention sets
ME.STSAS = STSAS
}
```

Module SubconsciousAttentionSet will be automatically triggered whenever any object's location or appearance changes size, color, smell, etc. This is easy to do since most OOP languages and IDE provide the capability of change-event triggers. What we need to do is to put the module inside the event-change procedures.

The purpose of the following module is to determine FTSAS, the subconscious attention set for fast-thinking and associated times.

```
FastThinkingAttentionSet(RSAS) {
tempFTSAS = RSAS[index > 13] //the objects at the 3 latest timepoints
tempFTSAS.sortBY(ISA)  //Descending sort by attentivity
FTSA = tempFTSAS[index = 1]  //The max attentivity
FTSAS =tempFTSAS(ISA  > FTSA/2)  //Remove low ISA objects
Return FTSAS
}
```

The purpose of the following module is to determine STSAS, the subconscious attention set for fast-thinking and associated times.

```
SlowThinkingAttentionSet(RSAS) {
tempSTSAS = RSAS
tempSTSAS.sortBY(ISA)  //Descending sort by attentivity
STSA = tempSTSAS[index = 1]  //The maximum attentivity
STSAS =tempSTSAS(ISA  > FTSA/2) //Remove low ISA objects
Return STSAS
}
```

18.3.2 Conscious Attention

The Conscious Attention Set (CAS) is a token that is randomly selected from the top $K = 100$ most rewarding patterns (or tokens that might represent a problem, a research field, a procedure of making a product) in *Knet*. The random selection is based on the probabilities or the normalized patternive rewards or proxies associated with the top K tokens. A conscious set may also be determined by attention shift due to a request, such as a teacher's homework assignment.

CAS is a subobject of Agent with properties: Pattern, Frequency, Attentivity (reward), and Recency. The corresponding relational database table structure is the same as *pKnet*.

The purpose of the following module is to randomly (using the freewill randomizer) choose the conscious attention set.

```
ConsciousAttention (){
probs = pKnet.Pattern.pReward/Pattern.pReward.sum
index = FreewillRandomizer(probs)
CAS = pKnet.Pattern[index]
ME.CAS = CAS
Return CAS
}
```

18.4 Tokenization and Patternization

18.4.1 Segmentation and Elementory Tokenization

There are various tokenization techniques. Given a sentence or paragraph, White Space Tokenization tokenizes into words by splitting the input whenever a white space is encountered. This is the fastest tokenization technique but will work for languages (e.g., English, but not Chinese) in which the white space breaks apart the sentence into meaningful words. Regular Expression Tokenizer uses regular expressions to control the tokenization of text into tokens. Because of our smaller data approach and personalized connotation of understanding, big-data-based methods such as Dictionary-Based Tokenization and Penn TreeBank Tokenization are not applicable.

In our HAI, for language tokenization, the delimiters are carriage-returns, long-pauses between device inputs, or white-spaces, or unicode-based tokenization. For general event-string tokenization, it will include more than language tokenization, the tokenization will depend on programming conventions, especially the structures of functions and our OOP conventions. Because the virtual environment is simulated using elementary tokens, stringIn occurs naturally in the form of agent.act(), agent.sound(words), or object.event().

Segmentation is the determination of the dynamic sequence of event-strings at the current time, mainly based on the moving time points, t1, t2, ... t16. At each time point, up to 4 simultaneous elementary tokens. The string *agent.reward()* is usually treated as the end of a string segment. A long string may be shortened through hierarchical tokenization or can be broken into multiple string segments according to the similarity between them. Such similarity-based breakdown of a string is the basis for patternization and language understanding using the factor-isolation technique.

18.4.2 Hierarchical Tokenization

A high-frequency pattern will be assigned a token name or concept using the auto-naming system discussed earlier. The name will then be used in hierarchical tokenization.

The purpose of the following module is to perform simple patternization to shorten the event-string without recursion.

```
Tokenization(stringIn, patternType) {
// NL words tokenization occur at attention modules
// assign tokenIDs for elementary tokens and single-word tokens
For Each token In stringIn
        If (token != Knet.Pattern.tokenID) {
                TokenIDs = AutoName(patternType)
                stringIn.replace(tokenIDs[0])
                If (patternType = "NL") {stringIn.replace(tokenIDs[1])}
        }
Next
// a substring can be multiple tokens
For Each substring In stringIn
        If (substring = Knet.Pattern) {
                stringIn.replace(substring, Knet.Pattern.tokenID)
        }
Next
Return stringIn
}
```

The purpose of the following module is to perform hierarchical tokenization for stringIn with length ≤ maxTokens. This function is intended to be used for very long event-strings in repatternization. Here, stringIn is the string to be hierarchically tokenized, patternType can be "NL" when stringIn is entirely a string of a natural language; otherwise pattern-Type should be "Event". Default values for maxTokens and loops 4 and 3, respectively.

```
HierarchicalTokenization(stringIn, maxTokens, loops, patternType) {
n = 0
Do Loop
        n = n + 1
        stringIn = Tokenization(stringIn, patternType)
Until (stringIn.size <= maxTokens & n >= loops)
Return stringIn
}
```

18.4.3 Patternization

There are 15 types of gramtons and skiptons. For onsite patternization only elementary tokens are involved, and no hierarchical tokenization takes place. The tokens are connected by symbol ∧ (concurrent) or ⇸ (sequential). Concurrent tokens are written in alphabetic order in a pattern. The patternization function here can patternize a string set without the constraint of elementary tokens.

Learning in HAI architecture is the mapping of reality, including natural language, to event patterns; such mapping we call an understanding of natural language. Language can be viewed as one-dimensional text that patternizes the perceptual world, including the natural language itself (recursion!). In this sense, HAI is a process of constructing a universal language for patternizing the perceptual world that includes natural languages. The object or action referring can be indicated in the words. A goal can be recognized through verbal articulation. We are *mapping language-structure(parameters) to parameters to object.action(parameters), object.attributes(values) or actioner.state(values)*. This works for requests, but not necessarily for questions.

The purpose of the following module is to return a random object from objectList without replacement.

```
RandomRow(objectList) {
index = Math.ceiling(Math.rand()*objectList.size)   // round up
Return objectList(index)
}
```

The purpose of the following module is to discover and update 1-gramtons through 4-gramtons.

```
Gramization(stringIn, Net) {   //Net = Knet, pKnet, or KZnet
For Each pattern In Net.patterns
        If  (pattern = stringIn) {Net.patterns.Pattern.freq += 1}
Next
}
```

The purpose of the following module is patternization based on 2 strings with equal number (≤ 4) of tokens. Here, patternA and patternB must consist of tokenIDs for elementary and high-level tokens. Desensitisors in Patternization are viewed as equivalent to parameters in similarity determination. We don't recycle tokenIDs for patternA and patternB, but let them die naturally by the forgetting mechanism.

```
Patternization(patternA, patternB, patternType, Net) {
// patternType = "NL" or "Event"
If (patternA.size < 2) { Return Null}
TokenIDs = autoName(patternType)   // get tokenIDs
newPattern.tokenID = TokenIDs[1]   // tokenID for the skipton
newPattern.pattern = patternA   //use patternA as pattern template
newPattern.freq = patternA.freq + patternB.freq
newPattern.recency = system.time()   //time of pattern creation
// Create desensitisors (single, paired, tripled, …), see Section 3.
For i = 1 To patternA.size   // size is the number of tokens
        noOfDes = 0   // no of desensitisor
        If (patternA.tokens[i] != patternB.tokens[i]) {
                noOfDes = noOfDes + 1
                // Append a number to desName = tokenID for desensitisor
                desName = TokenIDs & noOfDes
                desensitisor[noOfDes].tokenID = desName
                // a desensitisor's pattern is a list of comma-delimited items
                Pattern = patternA.tokens[i] & ", " & patternB.tokens[i]
                desensitisor[noOfDes].pattern = Pattern
                newPattern.Pattern.replaceToken(i, desName)
        }
Next
//At least one fixor is required for a pattern.
If (noOfDes = patternA.size) {Return NULL}
Net.Pattern.add(newPattern)   // Otherwise, store a regular pattern
For i =  To noOfDes
        // add desensitisors as patterns, but be caution at detokenization
        Net.Pattern.add(desensitisor[i])
Next
// The two original patterns will die if no longer used often.
Return newPattern
}
```

The purpose of the following module is to choose nPairs of equal-sized recorders to repatternize Net. Here nPairs is the number of pairs of patterns to be retrieved for repatternization.

```
Repatternization(nPairs, Net, patternType) {
For Each patternX In Net.pattern
        Gramization(patternX, Net)     //Gramton
Next
If (patternType != "NL") {patternX = RandomRow(Net.pattern) }
If (patternType = "NL") {patternX = RandomRow(Lnet.pattern) }
N = Knet.size  //Number of patterns in Knet
yIndexes = Math.randNumsWithoutReplacement(nPairs, N))
For Each yIndex In yIndexes
        patternY = Knet.Pattern[yIndex]
        If (patternX.size = patternY.size) {
                Patternization(patternX, patternY, patternType, Net)
        }
Next
}
```

The purpose of the following module is to delete the record with the tokenID from *Knet* and put the tokenID in the nameRecycleBin.

```
RecycleTokenID(tokenIDtoRecycle) {
Knet.Pattern.delect(tokenID = tokenIDtoRecycle)
nameRecycleBin.add(tokenIDtoRecycle)  // Recycle tokenID
}
```

18.4.4 Meta Network

Knowledge involving a large time-span requires a MetaNet (Figure 14.7) that connects different patterns from *Knet* together at common tokens (tokenIDs). The purpose of the following module is to form a path in such a MetaNet. The reward of the pattern (meta path) is the sum of rewards of all the newly connected patterns from *Knet*. Such a path is considered a secondary experience by Zda. Here, nPatterns is the maximum number of patterns from *Knet* to be connected.

```
MetaPath(nPatterns) {
patA = RandomRow(ME.Knet.Pattern)
For i = 1 To nPatterns
        For Each pattern In ME.Knet.Pattern
                // get the location (of the last token of patA) within pattern
                joint = pattern.find(patA.token[patA.size])
                If (0 < joint < pattern.size) {
                        patA.app(pattern.substring[joint])
                        patA.pReward = patA.pReward + pattern.pReward
                        Break
                }
        Next
Next
patA.freq = 1
patA.recency = NULL
ME.Mnet.Pattern.add(patA)
ME.Knet.Pattern.add(patA)
Return patA
}
```

18.4.5 The Forgetting Mechanism

The forget-mechanism is based on gramton survival time (GST):

$$GST = Cg \cdot \frac{Freq \cdot Reward}{N \cdot n},$$

where constant Cg is an agent's attribute. Without a forgetting mechanism, a PC memory will easily overflow.

A 24-hour (or shorter) timer will check the *Knet* to remove any patterns that have age > GST (see updating *Knet* Database). Note that any increase in pattern frequency, reward, will increase GST, while any increase in pattern size n (in terms of number of tokens) and the total number of patterns (N) in *Knet*, will reduce GST of the pattern.

The purpose of the following module is to periodically and automatically remove dead patterns using a BioClock. The tokenID of removed patterns will be put in the name recycle bin for future reuse.

```
Forgetting(period) {
ForgetTimer = BioClock(period)
ForgetTimer.pulse {    //Statements to be executed periodically
For Each pattern In ME.Knet
        GST = pattern.Cg*Freq*pattern.Reward/Knet.size/pattern.size
        If (GST > system.time - pattern.recency) {
                Knet.Pattern.delect()  // should also delete the desensitisors
                nameRecycleBin.add(Knet.Pattern.tokenID)
        }
Next
RecycleTokenID(Knet.Pattern.tokenID)
}
}
```

18.4.6 Freewill Randomizer

The purpose of the following module is to return an index based on Probability mass function or any set of unnormalized values, Probs.

```
FreewillRandomizer(Probs) {
cProbs(0) = 0   // cumulative probs
For i = 1 To Probs.size
        cProbs[i] = cProbs[i-1] + Probs[i]
Next
randNum = Math.rand()
For i = 1 To Probs.size
        If (cProbs[i-1] ≤ randNum < cProbs[i]) {
                itemNum = i
                Break
        }
Next
Return   itemNum
}
```

18.5 Response Models

18.5.1 Similarity Mechanisms

Similarity search proceeds after tokenization. Similarity matches are needed for all thinking modes. Elementary tokens involve different parameters, thus a high-level token that consists of elementary tokens will also involve the same parameters. In fast-thinking and slow-thinking, we group elementary tokens by parameter-grouping, and the Jaccard index is used to calculate similarity between two patterns.

The purpose of the following module is to calculate the Jaccard similarity between strings A and B, defined as the length of the intersection divided as the length of union.

```
JaccardSimilarity(patternA, patternB){
intersection = patternA.intersection(patternB)
unionLength = patternA.length +patternB.length - intersection.length
Jaccard = intersection.length/unionLength
Return Jaccard
}
```

In deep-thinking, similarities occur at multiple levels. At the elementary token level, besides Jaccard similarity, for ordinal and continuous parameters, the exponential similarity (ranging from 0 to 1) between two objects may is a more precise measure, especially when the sensitivities of sensory organs increase:

$$\text{Exponential Similarity } S1 = \exp\left(-\sum_n R_n d_n\right),$$

Here the summation Σ is over all N parameters in the agent's attention; d_n is the absolute difference (dissimilarity) in the nth parameter between two objects, and R_n is the attribute-scaling factor for the nth parameter that can be learned by an agent. Outcomes determine the importance or scaling factor R of each attribute. The numerical vector R_n corresponding to the parameters in each elementary actionable token is defined when we add elementary functions in Zda's capability set.

The purpose of the following module is to calculate exponential similarity between two numerical vectors of parameters, A and B with scaling factor R.

```
ExpSimilarity(R, A, B) {
// R = vector of attribute-scaling factor
S1 = 0
For k = 1 To R.size
        S1 = S1 + R[k] * (A[k] - B[k])
Next
Return S1
}
```

At subtoken-levels, Cosine Similarity can be used for equal-sized vectors or patterns. For a given location in a pattern (A or B), we code 1 when a token is observed, 0 for not observed, and –1 for the case that the token must not be at the location. As a result, patterns A and B are expressed in vector form and cosine-similarity (ranging from –1 to 1) is calculated as

$$\text{Cosine similarity } S2 = \cos(\theta) = \frac{A \cdot B}{\|A\| \|B\|}$$

It is more convenient to use the normalized cosine similarity to the range (0, 1): $(1 + \cos(\theta))/2$. However, we will not implement the cosine similarity calculation as a Zda's initial ability, but he should be able to learn it later.

The purpose of the following module is to calculate the normalized cosine similarity between two strings, A and B.

```
CosineSimilarity(patternA, patternB) {
// Need triple coding -1, 0, 1 before use this function
S1 = 0; NormA = 0; NormB = 0
For k = 1 To patternA.size
        NormA = NormA + patternsA.tokens[k]*patternsA.tokens[k]
        NormB = NormB + patternsB.tokens[k]*patternsB.tokens[k]
        S2 = S2 + patternA(k)*patternB(k)
Next
S2 = S2/NormA/NormB
S2 = (1 + S2)/2  // Normalize it to the range (0, 1)
Return S2
}
```

In deep-thinking, the aggregate similarity or recursive similarity may be used. The aggregate similarity is calculated using the parameter similarity S_1 and the pattern structure similarity S_2 by the multiplicity rule:

$$Aggregate\ Similarity = S_1S_2$$

How does Zda determine the similarity between two tokens if the two actions are the same and the two actioners are different? As with other parameters, Zda can group the actioners in one or more categories, such as {all agents}, {friends, enemies, collaborators, etc.}.

The purpose of the following module is to calculate recursive aggregate similarity based on exponential and cosine similarities.

```
AggregateSimilarity(R, A, B, patternA, patternB) {
S1 = ExpSimilarity(R, A, B)
S2 = JaccardSimilarity(patternA, patternB)
aggS = S1*S2
Return aggS
}
```

To use aggregate similarity, because of the recursive structures of a high-level pattern, reverse-engineering by means of the Detokenization module may be needed beforehand.

We illustrate how to use the exponential similarity in two elementary tokens TA and TB. Assume they take the general forms of

$$TA = Lia.act(name, target, ParamsA)$$

and

$$TB = Zda.act(name, target, ParamsB)$$

We can use Jaccard index alone to compare these two strings, leading to similarity $S = 2/6 = 0.33$. Alternatively, we can use aggregate similarity based on the Jaccard and exponential similarities: we apply exp-similarity S1 for ParamsA and ParamsB at the parameter level, but Jaccard index S2 at the pattern (token) level. Thus, S1 = ExpSimilarity(R, TA, TB) and S2 = JaccardSimilarity(ParamsA, ParamsB). Equivalently, we can use

AggregateSimilarity(R, TA, TB, ParmsA, ParmasB). Here the attribute scaling factors R are given initially when the module <u>agent</u>.act(<u>name, target, ParamsA</u>) is defined.

In addition to these similarity functions, desensitisors including function-parameter desensitisors are often used as similarity measures.

Before making any decision, Zda needs to know his current position in his *Knet*. The purpose of the following module is to identify a pattern (in Net) similar to the current position according to similarity type ("Jaccard," "exponential," "cosine," or "aggregate"). The search will stop as soon as the required similarity level is reached. The current position is usually defined by the current subconscious attention set.

```
SimilaritySearch(currentPosition, Net, similarityType, simLevelRequired) {
// currentPosition in the form of pattern string
maxSimilarity =0
For Each pattern In Net.pattern
        // this block code may need to be modified according to
        // the function template you have adopted.
        R = pattern.elementaryToken.weights
        A = pattern.elementaryToken.params
        B = currentPosition.elementaryToken.params
        //Using Jaccard or recursive similarity
        If (similarityType = "Jaccard") {
                similarity = JaccardSimilarity(pattern, currentPosition)
        ElseIF (similarityType = "exponential")
                similarity = ExpSimilarity(R, A, B)
        ElseIF (similarityType = "cosine")
                similarity = CosineSimilarity(pattern, currentPosition)
        Else
                patternA = pattern
                patternB = currentPosition
                similarity = AggregateSimilarity(R, A, B, patternA, patternB)
        }
        If (similarity > maxSimilarity) {
                maxSimilarity = similarity
                currentTokenID = pattern.tokenID
                If (maxSimilarity > simLevelRequired) {Break}
        }
Next
Return currentTokenID
}
```

18.5.2 Expected Action

The purpose of the following module is, based on the observed pattern, to perform Similarity Search from the *pKnet* to find the top $K > 0$ matched patterns using existing desensitisor. If an exact search cannot find a pattern in the Net, do the similarity-based search. Return the next actions needed. Note that Net = Knet or pKnet, similarityType = "Jaccard" for fast-thinking, "Jaccard" and/or "Exponential" for slow-thinking, and "Recursive" for deep-thinking. The keyword "ME" is the owner of the *Knet*, or the OOP class where the module resides.

```
ExpectedTokens(observedPattern, Pc, Net, similarityType, simLevel) {
// Exact search
matchedPatterns = Net.patterns.find(observedPattern)
// If no exact match, do similarity search with similarity = 0.8
If (matchedPatterns = NULL) {
        SimilaritySearch(observedPattern, Net, similarityType, simLevel)
}
For Each pattern In matchedPatterns
        index = pattern.find(observedPattern) + observedPattern.length
        //Expected pattern = matchedPattern - observedPattern
        expPattern = pattern.substring(index)
        nextActions = expPattern.tokens
        //determine next possible action
        rn = Math.rand()
        If (rn < 1 - Pc )   // imitation, Pc = probability of creation
                // Might: nextActions.actioner = ME before replacement
                Half = expPattern.replace(nextActions.actioner[1], ME)
                fullPattern = observedPattern.app(Half)
        Else
                If (nextAction.actioner = ME) {   // creative action
                        oldAction = nextActions.actionName[1]
                        // Get desensitisor of old action
                        aDes = Knet.desensitisor[tokenID = oldAction]
                        newAction = RandomRow(aDes)
                        Half = nextActions.replace(oldAction, newAction)
                        fullPattern = observedPattern.app(Half)
                // else, Rest or wait for the next moment
                }
        }
        // Determine Jaccard index between expPattern and fullPattern
        Similarity = JaccardSimilarity(pattern, fullPattern)
        expPatterns.patteren.add(fullPattern)
        expPatterns.similarity.add(similarity)
        expPatterns.expActions.add(Half)
Next
Return expPatterns
}
```

18.5.3 Reflex Mechanism

The purpose of the following module is to return a reflexor based on stimulus (desensitisor of elementary tokens).

```
Reflex () {
stimulusToken = ME.stimulus  //expressed in tokenIDs
For Each token In Reflexon
        If (Stimulus = stimulusToken) {
                Reflexor = ME.Reflexon.Reflexor
                ME.Reflexon.Freq = ME.Reflexon.Freq + 1
                Break
        }
Next
Animations(Reflexor)
ME.NAT = ME.NAT + ME.Ca/ME.ISA  // the next attention time
}
```

18.5.4 Fast-Thinking Mechanism

If ISA < Cr, FastThink() is invoked. In Fast-Thinking, Zda does not need to decide an active response at every attentive time point since completing an action needs time (the time to complete, TTC). At attentive time points during TTC, Zda does not determine his response. The Fast-Thinking algorithms are described in Section 14.5.

The purpose of the following module is to perform Fast-Thinking Response and Learning.

```
FastThink () {
FTSAS = ME.FTSAS   // expressed in tokenIDs
ExpPatterns = ExpectedTokens(ME.FTSAS, Pc, Net, "Jaccard")
patternIndex = RandomizedAdaptiveRL(ExpPatterns)
actionsTaken = ExpPatterns.[patternIndex].expActions
Animations(actionsTaken)
Knet.add(actionsTaken)   // add pattern: actionToken to Knet
ME.NAT = ME.NAT + ME.Ca/ME.ISA   // The next attention time
}
```

18.5.5 Slow-Thinking Mechanism

Slow thinking allows similarity-matching on the top-layer pattern, while patterns in other layers must be exactly matched, because all other levels have desensitized tokens as needed in hierarchical patternization. This similarity is caused by similar-token replacement at the top layer. The slow-thinking algorithm is presented in Section 14.6.

As in Fast-Thinking, in Slow-Thinking, Zda only needs to decide an active response at some attentive time points. At attentive time points during TTC, Zda does not determine his response, but is in the process of completing his action. Multithreads and Synchronization in OPP can handle this issue.

The purpose of the following module is to start slow-thinking if Cs ≤ STSA).

```
SlowThink () {
tokenizedStr = HierarchicalTokenization(ME.STSAS, 4, 1, "Event")
// Divide tokenizedStr into two equal length stringA and stringB
halfLength = Math.round(tokenizedStr.size/2)
stringA = tokenizedStr.substring(1, halfLength)
stringB = tokenizedStr.substring(halfLength+1)
//Check if Similar substrings are found Jaccard index > 0.5.
If (JaccardSimilarity(stringA, stringB) > 0.3) {
        Patternization(stringA, stringB, patternType, Knet)
Else
        ExpPatterns = ExpectedTokens(tokenizedStr, Pc, Net, "Jaccard")
        patternIndex = RandomizedAdaptiveRL(ExpPatterns)
        actionsTaken = ExpPatterns[patternIndex].expActions
        Animations(actionsTaken)
}
newPattern.name = autoName(patternType = "Event")
newPattern.freq = 1
newPattern.pattern = actionsTaken
Knet.add(newPattern)   // Add pattern: actionToken to Knet
ME.NAT = ME.NAT + ME.Ca/ME.ISA   // The next attention time
}
```

18.5.6 Deep-Thinking Mechanism

If Cs > STSA, Zda will be in deep-thinking mode (Figure 17.1). In deep-thinking, if Zda's learning curiosity is low (< Ce), he will perform a goal-driven task; otherwise, he will randomly choose either learning-routine (repatternization of *Knet*) or cognitive learning.

The purpose of the following module is to perform Deep-Thinking. The repatternization and cognitive learning may proceed in *Knet* (with 0.8 probability) or in *Mnet* (with 0.2 probability).

```
DeepThink () {
If (ME.curiosity < Ce) {
        goal = GoalSetting()
        currentPosition = HierarchicalTokenization(ME.ISAS, 4, 1, "Event")
        actionPath = GoalDrivenActions(currentPosition, goal, Knet)
        If (actionPath = NULL) {
                actionPath = GoalDrivenActions(currentPosition, goal, Mnet)
        }
        Animation(actionPath)               // May need deTokenization first
Else
        If (Math.rand() < 0.5) {
                MetaPath(nPatterns = Math.round(Math.rand()*8))
                Repatternization(nPairs = 10, Knet, "NL", Lnet)
                Repatternization(nPairs = 10, Knet, "NL", Knet)
                Repatternization(nPairs = 10, Knet, "Event", Knet)
                Repatternization(nPairs = 10, Mnet, "NL", Mnet)
                Repatternization(nPairs = 10, Mnet, "Event", Mnet)
        Else
                If (Math.rand() < 0.8) {
                        CognitiveLearning(Knet)
                Else
                        CognitiveLearning(Mnet)
                }
        }
}
ME.NAT = ME.NAT + ME.Ca/ME.ISA    // the next attention time
}
```

Before Zda can perform goal-driven actions, he needs to set a goal or find the goal node, from which he will find a path to it. The goal may be specified by words or may be determined by the following module. The purpose of the following module is to set the goal for a goal-driven task. Here the parameter goal is presented by tokenID associated with the goal node. The tokenID is generated by the auto-naming system in Chapter 18.1.

```
GoalSetting () {
// a 10% probability for recollection and 15% probability of attention-shift
If (Math.rand() < 0.1 ) {Recollection(ME.desire, 0.15)}
// a 10% probability for imagination
If (Math.rand() < 0.1) {Imagination(ME.CAS)}
If (ME.desire = "food") {  // find a nearby food node in pKnet
        foodPatterns = Dgrams.Pattern.soryBy(duration, ascending)
        // 3 nearest (timewise) nodes with reward type = food
        foodNearby = foodPatterns[1:3, rType = "food"]
        // pick food according to reward
        foodId = FreewillRandomizer(foodNearby.reward)
        goal = foodNearby.pattern[index = foodId].tokenID
ElseIf (ME.desire = "entertainment")  // find a nearby entertainment node
        joyPatterns = Dgrams.Pattern.soryBy(duration,  ascending)
        joyNearby = joyPatterns[1:3, rType = " entertainment"]
        // pick  entertainment according to reward
        joyId = FreewillRandomizer(joyNearby.reward)
        goal = joyNearby.pattern[index = joyId].tokenID
Else    // find a high reward node or more reward-sensitisors
        rwdPatterns = Dgrams.Pattern.soryBy(duration,  ascending)
        rwdNearby = rwdPatterns[1:3]
        // pick  entertainment according to reward
        rwdId = FreewillRandomizer(rwdNearby.reward)
        goal = rwdNearby.pattern[index = rwdId].tokenID
}
Return goal
}
```

The purpose of the following module is to perform the five types of cognitive learning methods (Abduction, Induction, Deduction, Analogy, and Causation).

```
CognitiveLearning(Net) {
// Perform Cognitive Learning
CAS = ConsciousAttention()
// Freewill choose a cause and an effect
cause  = CAS.tokens[FreewillRandomizer(CAS.tokens.freq)]
effect = CAS.tokens[FreewillRandomizer(CAS.tokens.freq)]
// Round up the random number, ranging from 1 to 5.
iTask = Math.Ceiling(Math.rand()*5)
Switch (iTask) {
        Case 1          //abduction
                Abduction(effect, Net)
        Case 2          //Induction
                Induction(CAS, Net)
        Case 3          //deduction
                Deduction(cause, effect, Net)
        Case 4          //analogy
                Analogy(cause, effect, Net)
        Case 5          //possible effects from a cause
                CauseToEffect(cause, Net)
}
p = 0.2//Assign probability of attention shift p =0.2, or other value.
AttentionShift(CAS, p)
Net.NAT = Ct/ISA  // the next subconscious attentive time.
}
```

Deep-Thinking often includes fast-thinking and slow-thinking as its subprocesses due to STSA increase at the attention pulse time. For instance, when Zda takes actions to accomplish a long-term goal, he may face situations that need his reflex, fast- and slow-thinking.

The agent's actions are mostly virtual, but downloading data and running AI/statistical analyses can be really executed because it can happen on a computer. In Deep-Thinking, the tokens in the gramtons can be high-level tokens of a mixture, word-event, or word-action tokens (see Chapter 14, Adaptive Response Mechanisms).

18.5.7 Decision-Making

The purpose of the following module is to determine the action among all options using the randomized adaptive response mechanism.

```
RandomizedAdaptiveRL(PotentialPatterns) {
F = PotentialPatterns.freq
R = PotentialPatterns.reward
S = PotentialPatterns.similarity
SRFs = S*R*F  //SRFs is an array
c = SRFs.sum  // sum of elements of SRFs
PoAs =  SRFs/c  //Calculate the Probabilities of Action
patternIndex = FreewillRandomizer(PoAs)
Return patternIndex
}
```

In gaming or decision-making using game theory, Zda has to predict how the other player (Lia) will move. This prediction employs the same prediction method but will be carried out after Lia's move.

```
GamingPrediction(observedPattern,  Pc, Net, similarityType, Opponent) {
// Image Competitor would play, no Knet update
Opponent.SlowThink (attentionSet)
expPatterns = expTokens(observedPattern,  Pc, Net, similarityType)
Return expPatterns
}
```

Based on the same notion as gaming, if the player, Lia, is replaced by a flying object (e.g., a ball), then it becomes a prediction of the object in catching a moving object. Therefore, this module can also be applied to the actions in catching moving or static objects.

18.6 Action Types

18.6.1 Imitation Mechanism

Zda can only perform imitations on the top level after all its subtokens are learned. Imitation is achieved by actioner-replacement in an actioner.action token, one-actioner replacement at a time.

The purpose of the following module is to perform imitation.

```
Imitation (patternIn) {
actioner = patternIn.getActioner()
patternOut = patternIn.replace(actioner, ME)
Return patternOut
}
```

18.6.2 Creation Mechanism

The purpose of the following module is to perform a creative action by replacing action or action parameters with or without the actioner by the creator.

```
Creation(patternIn) {
actionToken = patternIn.getActionToken()
// Get desensitisor of action in actionIn
aDesensitisor = Knet.desensitisor.find(actionToken)
newAction = RandomRow(aDesensitisor)
patternOut = actionTokenIn.replace(actionToken, newAction)
Return patternOut
}
```

18.6.3 Recollection Mechanism

Recollections may bring pain and excitement similar to real experiences and/or enhance past experiences: the sight stirs up one's feelings.

The purpose of the following module is to determine the recollection from a Similarity Search in *pKnet*.

```
Recollection(stimulus, p) {
If (Math.rand() < 0.5) {stimulus = desensitisor(stimulus)}
thingCollected = AttentionShift(stimulus, p)
// Recollection can only enjoy 5% the reward from real experience
ME.heart.sensation = ME.heart.sensation + thingCollected.reward*0.05
Return thingCollected
}
```

18.6.4 Associative Attention-Shift

A table of 2-gramtons of NL words and 2-gramtons of general event-strings maintains all the high frequent associations. The probability of picking an associative object (event, concept) is equal to the probability of associative attention multiplying the normalized frequency of association. In a chain of associative objects, the multiplication rule of probabilities is applied.

The purpose of the following module is to return an associated 2-gramton based on TokenIn.

```
AttentionShift(TokenIn, p) {
// Multiple attentionShifts by to association: TokenIn~AssToken
Loop While (Math.rand() < p)
      AssTokens = pKent.Agrams[AttToken2 = TokenIn].AssToken
      TokenIn = RandomRow(AssTokens)
Endloop
Return TokenIn
}
```

18.6.5 Imagination Mechanism

Imagine something similar to past experience but have some changes, e.g., your friend's wedding party becomes your wedding party. Or imagine something that might be impossible, e.g., your hands become wings and you can fly faster than a plane. Imagining may bring pain and excitement similar to real experiences. Such effects are modeled by small changes in Zda's sensation level.

The purpose of the following module is to pretend to execute imitation and innovation in the *Inet*.

```
Imagination(attentionSet) {
If (Math.rand() < 0.5) {
      // Imitation in the Inet and enjoy the reward or suffer the pain
      patternOut  = Imitation(attentionSet)
Else

      //Innovation in the Inet and enjoy the reward or suffer the pain
      patternOut = Creation(attentionSet)
}

      ME.Inet.Pattern.add(patternOut)
      ME.heart.sensation = ME.heart.sensation + actionOut.reward*0.05

}
```

18.6.6 Goal-Driven Action

Belief-net (Bnet) is an extended *Knet* that combines the *Knet* and virtual net (Vnet) consisting of patterns by others' words or research papers. To Zda, goal-driven actions to find paths from the current position (node or similarity-matched node) to the goal in *Knet* or *Bnet*, unless the goal and paths are told. If the goal is new to Zda, he may not have a corresponding goal node. In this case, he will choose an approximate node based on similarity, or he may choose another goal based on his interest or on rewards associated with the goals.

The purpose of the following module is to identify paths (sequences of nodes) to the goal. Here the input parameter goal is specified by the tokenID associated with the goal node in the Net; the parameter Net can be *Bnet*, *Knet*, or *pKnet*, and the parameter currentPosition is the current attention set (usually includes self) and is expressed by token id (tokenID in the *pKnet*). We use the standard Net.paths(A, B, n) method to find *n* paths from node A to node B; each such path is represented by a pattern consisting of a sequence of nodes (tokenIDs). Even though the path found is a random one, over time, Zda can find a better one, since better paths will be used more often (higher frequency) and more frequently used paths will be more likely to be found.

```
GoalDrivenActions(currentPosition, goal, Net) {
// currentPosition = subconscious attention set
// Determine currentPosition in the Net with Jaccard similarity = 0.8
SimilaritySearch(currentPosition, Net, Jaccard, 0.8)
// Find 5 paths
paths = Net.paths(currentTokenID, goal, 5)
// Select action path from paths based on distributive rewards
actionPath = paths[FreewillRandomizer(paths.dReward)]
Return actionPath
}
```

In animation, reverse-engineering using Detokenization(actionToken) may be needed to ensure all action tokens are elementary tokens.

18.7 Cognitive Reasoning

Before using the cognitive procedure in the section, we assume Zda has the concept of cause and effect.

18.7.1 Detokenization

When a decision is made, it may be a complex procedure or higher level tokens, not directly in executable form. Thus, the tokens need to expand recursively into sequences of actionable or elementary tokens. This reverse-engineering of hierarchical tokenization is called detokenization (Figure 18.1).

The purpose of the following module is to expand tokenIn into a pattern with a frequency associated with each token in the pattern. By using the function recursively, we can eventually expand any pattern into a sequence of elementary tokens.

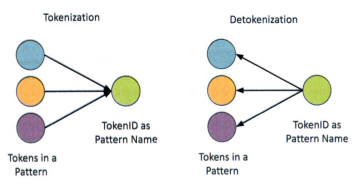

FIGURE 18.1
Tokenization and detokenization.

```
Detokenization(tokenIn) {
// objOut with String property string and Array of probs.
myPattern = Knet.Pattern[tokenID = tokenIn]
For Each token In myPattern.tokens  // Get the token probabilities
       For Each name In Knet.Pattern.tokenID
              // tokenID =  pattern name in hierarchical tokenization
              If (token = name) { objOut.probs.add(Knet.Pattern.freq) }
       Next
Next
objOut.probs = ojectOut.freq/ojectOut.probs.sum  // Normalization
objOut.pattern = myPattern
Return objOut
}
```

18.7.2 Inductive Reasoning

Inductive reasoning, or induction, is a process taking us from specific cases to a general conclusion. To Zda, induction is finding a pattern in *Knet* or *pKnet* which is similar to the observed event sequence but only one token difference at the same location. The simple induction is a desensitisor-replacement. More complex inductions are implemented as repatternization.

The purpose of the following module is to perform induction by a single desensitisor replacement.

```
Induction(patternIn, Net) {
//Randomly select a token from patternIn
iToken = RandomRow(patternIn.tokens)
//Randomly select a desensitisor of iToken from Knet
iDesensitisor = RandomRow(Net.desensitisor[tokenID = iToken])
//Induction by replacement
newPattern.tokenID = AutoName(patternType = "Event").[1]
newPattern.pattern = patternIn.replace(iToken, iDesensitisor)
newPattern.freq = 1
Inet.addPattern(newPattern)
}
```

18.7.3 Deductive Reasoning

Deductive Reasoning, or deduction (Figure 18.2), is the application of general rules to an observation to make a conclusion. To Zda, deduction is often determining the probability of a cause-effect relationship. The (conditional) probability given the effect is determined through patterns that include the effect and the desensitisors of the cause. By recursion, deduction can answer very complicated how-type questions.

The purpose of the following module is to return cause-effect with the maximum probability: the conditional probability of *causes* given *effect*. Reasoning from a general case (desensitisor) to a special case. The function is based on the Detokenization function that has no involvement of desensitisors.

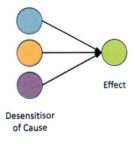

Desensitisor
of Cause

Effect

FIGURE 18.2
Deductive reasoning.

```
Deduction(cause, effect, Net){
ceObj = Detokenization(effect)
For Each cause In ceObj.Pattern.tokens
        //Check if cause has its desensitisor in ceObj.pattern
        cDesensitisor = Net.desensitisor[token = cause]
Next
prob = 0
If (cDesensitisor != NULL) { prob =1/cDesensitisor.size }
// Use string-concatenation & to form a new pattern
newPattern.pattern = cause &  effect
newPattern.tokenID = AutoName(patternType = "Event").[1]
newPattern.freq = 1
Net.addPattern(newPattern)
Return prob
}
```

18.7.4 Analogical Reasoning

Analogical reasoning, i.e., analogy, is an application of the similarity principle. We use similarity to group things or to create a desensitisor. If the similar things in a desensitisor produce similar results for a defined outcome measure (e.g., body weight or longevity), then we can use the outcome measure as an (additional) attribute in future similarity grouping. Analogy may involve some "if conditions," and the similarity-based prediction occurs in *Inet*. To Zda, to employ analogical reasoning is to perform similarity-replacement (synonyms-replacement) in a pattern and predict a similar outcome, i.e., to replace a token (or parameter value) with its desensitisor. Analogical reasoning is often performing similarity-replacement for both the "cause" and "effect." The following is the logic flow for the function *Analogy(cause, effect)*, which implements double-desensitisor replacements (Figure 18.3); single-desensitisor replacement was discussed previously, in the section Thinking Models.

Analogy can also be performed on the data collected from scientific experiments. Deploying the Analogy algorithm is actually proposing a hypothesis that needs to be checked.

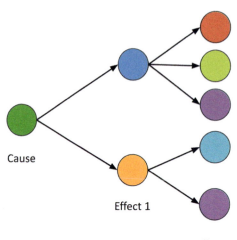

Cause

Effect 1

Effect 2

FIGURE 18.3
Analogy in action.

The purpose of the following module is to perform analogical reasoning, adding a 2-gramton of cause-effect to *Inet*.

```
Analogy(cause, effect, Net) {
//Find a desensitisor of cause in Knet
cPatterns = Net.desensitisor[name = cause]
//Find a desensitisor of cause in Knet
ePatterns = Net.desensitisor[name = effect]
// Use string-concatenation & to form a new pattern
newPattern.pattern = cPattern.tokenID & " " & ePattent.tokenID)
newPattern.tokenID = AutoName(patternType = "Event").[1]
newPattern.freq = 1
//add a 2-gramton with frequency =1 in Inet
Inet.Patterns.add(newPattern)
}
```

18.7.5 Abductive Reasoning

Abductive Reasoning, or Abduction, is inferring cause from effect. To Zda, abduction is starting from a goal (or an effect) node in his *Knet* or *pKnet* and looking back to a connected node with high frequency (Figure 18.4). It returns an effect-cause 2-gramton with associated probability + a chain of cause-effect 2-gramtons and a multiplicative probability. Abduction can be used to answer why-type questions. With recursion, abduction can answer very complicated why-type questions. Abduction can also be performed on the data collected from scientific experiments

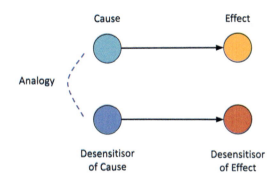

FIGURE 18.4
Illustration of abduction.

The purpose of the following module is to return a sequence of previous nodes as possible causes: search a connected pattern based on the probability or normalized frequencies of the patterns connected to the effect-node (token).

```
Abduction(effect, Net) {
objOut1 = Detokenization(effect)
objOut.Cause1 =objOut1.String
//probs1 is one-dimensional array of probabilities
objOut.probs1 = objOut1.probs
For Each token In Cause1
        objOut2 = Detokenization(token)
        objOut.Cause2.add(objOut2.String)
        //probs2 is a two-dimensional array of probabilities
        objOut.probs2.add(objOut2.probs*objOut1.probs)
Next
For Each cause In objOut2
        // Use string-concatenation (&&) to form a new pattern
        newPattern.pattern = objOut2.tokenID && " " &&  effect)
        newPattern.tokenID = AutoName(patternType = "Event").[1]
        newPattern.prob = 1/objOut2.size  // Number of causes
        // Add new gramton: Cause2 to effect to Knet with probability
        Net.addPattern(newPattern)
        CEnet.add(newPattern)
Next
Return objOut
}
```

18.7.6 Cause-to-Effect Reasoning

Cause-to-Effect Reasoning infers from cause to effect. To Zda, Cause-to-Effect Reasoning means starting from a node (cause) in *Knet* and looking forward to a connected node (effect) with high frequency (Figure 18.5). Returned is the string of effect nodes with

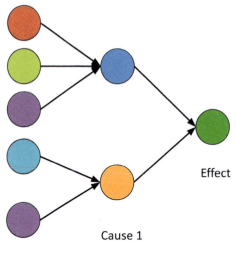

FIGURE 18.5
Cause to effect inference.

associated probabilities. By recursion, that is use the current effect nodes and new causes to drive the further effects. Recursion here means using the following CauseToEffect function (method) recursively.

The purpose of the following module is to derive possible effects for a given cause and associated probabilities.

```
CauseToEffect(cause, Net) {
myPattern = Net.pattern[tokenID = cause]
causePos =  Net.Pattern.find(cause)
effects = Net.Pattern.substring(causePos + 1)  // effects after a cause
For Each token In effects.tokens
        For Each name In Net.Pattern.tokenID
                // tokenID =  pattern name in hierarchical tokenization
                If (token = name) { objOut.probs.add(Net.Pattern.prob) }
        Next
Next
objOut.probs = ojectOut.probs/ojectOut.probs.sum  // Normalization
// use concatenation (&&) of string to get a pattern
objOut.pattern = cause && " " &&  effects
objOut.tokenID = AutoName(patternType = "Event").[1]
Net.CEnet.add(objOut)  // Add the cause-effect pair to CEnet
Return objOut
}
```

18.7.7 Recursion on Everything

Recursion in mathematics is the use of output as input, repeatedly, $Y = f(f(f(\dots f(x))))$. Recursive hierarchical patternization in *Knet* provides the mechanism for recursions on everything. Everything can be analogized by another thing. By recursion, everything can be an analogy of an arbitrary thing, x. Therefore, recursion and recursion of analogy enable recursion on everything:

recursion(x) → recursion (analogy(x)) → recursion(analogy(analogy(x))) → ....

The purpose of the following module is to perform recursion of event (procedure) x through analogy depth times.

```
RecursionOnEverything(x, depth) {
For i = 1 To depth
        x = Analogy(x)
Next
Return x
}
```

However, we will not often use this module because the Analogy model, being repeatedly used over time, will produce the same results.

19

Miscellaneous

19.1 Schedules for *Knet* and Internal Attributes Updates

When do the *Knet* and other internal attributes get updated (e.g., energy, patterns, frequency, *Inet*)? Responses occur at each attentive time point, which is related to the variable attention pulse rate. Before a response, tokenization (hierarchical tokenization) and patternization occur. However, updating *Knet* and other data tables will not occur until the response is finished, or possibly even later. The purpose of delaying the updating of data tables is to improve Zda's real time performance. Internal attributes such as energy are updated immediately after each response, or in real time.

1. After a reflex, update the Reflexon frequency only, unless the next attentive time is within a threshold Cr, likely requiring another immediate reflex. Note that a 2-gramton is a 2-gram with the second token actionable. When the frequency of a 2-gramton reaches a threshold, the 2-gramton becomes a Reflexon. A 2-gram, 2-gramton, and reflexon are associations, but the reverse is not necessarily true.

2. After a fast-thinking response, the *Knet* will be updated using the corresponding pattern:
   a. Update the frequency of the exactly matched pattern in *Knet*, the distributive reward, and recency.
   b. Update the frequency of the new similarity-matched pattern (desensitisor) with frequency one in *Knet*, the distributive reward, and recency.
   c. Create the imitation-induced new pattern with frequency one, the distributive reward, and recency.
   d. Create the creativity-induced new pattern with frequency one.

3. After a slow-thinking response, the hierarchical tokenization of an event-string of up to 16 randomly selected elementary tokens occurs before patternization, and at the higher token level, patternization occurs in three forms:
   a. Update the frequency of the higher level tokens from hierarchical tokenization in *Knet*, the distributive reward, and recency.
   b. Update the frequency of the new similarity-matched pattern (desensitisor) with frequency one in *Knet*, the distributive reward, and recency.
   c. Create the imitation-induced new pattern with frequency one, the distributive reward, and recency.
   d. Create the creativity-induced new pattern with frequency one.

4. In deep-thinking, patternization occurs before the response, including the patternization that could occur in slow-thinking, and repatternization of *Knet* (induction with desensitisors, deduction with sensitisors). Any pattern (including

high-level tokens from hierarchical tokenization) update will update frequency, the distributive reward, and recency. The response can be based on n-token ahead predictions. From deep-thinking with recursion, Zda can derive many learning methods, statistical models, and can create humanized agents.

Elementary and high-level tokens, including their attributes, can also be considered as patterns, and will always be updated in *Knet* and in other relevant memories for fast execution. A string of tokens if not formed a higher level token will not be updated since it does not sustain in Zda's attention.

For performance efficiency, the pattern update can be in two steps: First, updates occur in computer memory in real time, and then the corresponding database is updated in the computer disk or cloud.

19.2 Tips for Implementation

Remember the following when implementing Zda:

1. Zda likes to make noise, sounds, or do other things to attract people's attention.
2. Shaking an object while calling its name is how one can bring Zda's attention to the two things and have him make an association between them. This is because two things happening close in space and time will automatically be associated by our agent.
3. Explaining (saying the name) while doing work will get Zda's attention and allow him to make an association between the procedure and its name.
4. A pattern can represent a two-way association between body posture and language, between emotion and language, or between emotion and body posture, or a 3-way association between body posture, language, and emotion.
5. Randomize Zda's intentions (wants) to do something; do not directly randomize Zda's actions.
6. A name can be associated with an object in reality or the concept of performing a certain task. A concept can refer to anything, including another concept.
7. Zda needs to differentiate a categorical name and a name for a particular object of the category.
8. As far as attention is concerned, whom Lia speaks to is important.
9. A path in *Knet* with a high constant frequency crossing all nodes is a scientific law.
10. Any directed path in *Knet* with distributive rewards is a rule in daily life or a social norm. Any directed path of high-level tokens in *Knet* can be a scientific law or a mathematical or physical law in a statistical sense.
11. Since rewarded paths are more likely to be repeated, when rewards are not explicit, determining Zda's response based on patent frequency will be a good alternative.
12. When the self-awareness switch is on, Zda is aware of his intention or goal. As social interactions accumulate, a person will be labeled with certain personality traits and intentions at any particular time t, making the process indirectly a Non-Stationary Decision Process.

13. Use the same object in different states to teach Zda those states. For example, present him with a dish at different temperatures and say words like cold, cool, warm, hot to teach Zda these words.

14. Because of the parsimony principles, people like to generalize (they use induction) and may question why (making deductions) to satisfy themselves or others. We all ask why and how in order to satisfy our natural curiosity.

19.3 Simplified Agent Sharing Model

I believe all the modules (innate mechanisms) above can be mimicked using simple electronic networks or ANNs, but these ANNs are somewhat different from the deep learning ANNs (see Appendix). In this sense, we can use neural nets to archive Humanized AI. Such a simulated ANN for HAI has a clear meaning or matched mechanism, while the integration of such ANNs form a live member in human-machine society. However, we are not going to expand upon this. Instead, we suggest exploring the following very simple agent model.

Agent Model:

1. Agents are born with a green appearance and a size of 1, the distributive reward mechanism, hierarchical tokenization.

2. Agents randomly act with reinforcement learning—responses or actions taken based on distributive rewards.

3. Each agent possesses some basic (inert) knowledge and skills.

4. An agent randomly shares knowledge (successfully experienced) using language consisting of strings of characters A, B, and C.

5. Agents are more likely to share their knowledge with their friends (other agents who also like to share their knowledge with them) than with their enemies (i.e., agents who are not willing to share their knowledge or may deceive when doing so). Different agents have different levels of willingness to share their knowledge.

6. An agent's size gets bigger every time he gets a reward. The amount of growth is proportional to the rewards. When an agent's size is doubled his original size he will split into two identical agents of his original size and current knowledge. Every time he splits, the agent gets red or bright red, visible to other agents including himself.

7. An agent's size is visible to all agents, including himself.

8. An agent's ultimate goal is to grow his size as much as possible.

9. Every action has an associated cost and leads to a reduction in the agent's size. When an agent's size is smaller than his original size he dies.

10. An agent likes to imitate others. It's important for communication and establishing a common language.

11. An agent is sometimes creative.

12. An agent is somewhat persistent (e.g., he likes consistently to say "go right" when the tiger is on the left road). This is also important for communicating and developing language.

13. An agent likes to work with knowledgeable agents.

14. Consider: When the two babies Lia and Zda without any learned knowledge start to interact, what will the society of the two become (an Alphazero situation)?

15. As before, if Lia has gained some knowledge and natural language already from humans, what will the society of the two become?

Environment:

1. Food (rewards), monsters (penalties), and elements for agents to play with.

2. There are many tasks with associated but initial unknown rewards/penalties.

3. Complicated tasks are a combination of basic skills.

4. More complicated tasks usually have higher associated rewards.

How to Play:

1. Set a goal, e.g., putting object A on B and C on A.

2. What you can do in the game is to place rewards (e.g., food) at any place, any time you like.

Outcomes to Observe:

1. How willingness of sharing affects learning.

2. How language evolves in the community.

3. The role of language in learning.

4. How this community works with another community who speaks a different language using strings of characters D, E, and F.

Glossary

A

Abstraction: The process of forming a concept by identifying common features among a group of individuals, or by ignoring unique aspects of these individuals. Abstraction is similarity grouping or desensitization.

Adaptive Response Mechanisms (Randomized Adaptive Reinforcement Learning): Decision-making or action-taking based on the currently observed path and the expected reward (R), similarity (S), and frequency (F) of the past experiences (patterns). Specifically, the probability of taking a path (a sequence of actions) will be proportional to the product of R, S, and F.

Agents: An OOP object that inherits all properties from the type Animal and has other properties and behaviors.

AI Waves: The four main AI waves, Logic-based handcrafted knowledge, Statistical machine learning, Contextual adaptation, and Humanized artificial intelligence.

Alternating Attention: The capacity for mental flexibility that allows the shift of focus between tasks.

Analogy: A comparison between two systems that highlights respects in which they are thought to be similar.

Animals: An HAI class in OOP that inherits all properties from the Thingy class and has a simple brain with simple pre-programmed response-features.

Antagonistic: The situation that the whole is smaller than the sum of its parts

Artificial General Intelligence (AGI): The ability of an intelligent agent to understand or learn any intellectual task that a human being can. AGI can also refer to a broad collection or integration of narrow AIs (NAIs).

Associative Attention: The attention caused by associative thinking, leading to an attention shift from one object (event, concept) to another associated object (event, concept).

Associative Gramtons: A collection of 2-gramtons used for attention shift due to association.

Associative Learning: A method or process wherein the learner associates a certain response to an object or a stimulus resulting in a positive or negative outcome.

Attention: The behavioral and cognitive process of selectively concentrating on a discrete aspect of information, while ignoring other perceivable information.

Attention Pulse Rate (APR): Based on the notion that attention is not continuous in time, but like an electric pulse, the APR is sent at a certain rate that is directly proportional to subconscious attentivity.

B

Behaviorism: Theory of behavior that is only concerned with observable stimulus-response behaviors, as can be studied in a systematic and observable manner. Behaviorists believe actions are reflections of what goes on in the mind, adopting a goal-driven approach.

Biological Clock: A general term denoting biological degradation and biological rhythms.

Biological Degradation: A biological clock associated with aging, such as longevity, fertility, and sensitivity of sense organs.

Biological Rhythms: Repetitive biological processes. A circadian rhythm describes a biological process that displays an oscillation about every 24 hours, such as the human sleep-wake cycle.

Biologism (Biodeterminism): The thesis that human characteristics, physical and mental, are determined at conception by hereditary factors passed from parent to offspring.

Bootstrapping: A statistical procedure that resamples a single dataset to create many simulated samples.

Braess's Paradox: The phenomenon that increasing an option can actually make a system less efficient when individually motivated factors drive behavior without collaboration. E.g., adding a new road can make traffic heavier.

C

Cantor's Diagonal Argument: A proof of the existence of uncountable sets.

Causal Determinism: The thesis that every event is the effect of antecedent events, and these in turn are caused by events antecedent to them, and so on. Causal determinism is the foundation of First Principles.

Cause to Effect Net (CEnet): List of 2-gramtons, each pair having an associated probability.

Cause-Effect Reasoning: A type of thinking where one seeks the (probabilistic) linkage between two events that appear in sequence.

Circadian Clock: A molecular mechanism that results in a circadian rhythm in a living organism.

Classical Conditioning: The type of learning process evidenced in Pavlov's experiment: the newly established relationship between the sound of the bell and salivation is a consequence of the learned association between two stimuli (the bell and the food).

Classical Mechanics: Newtonian mechanics with three fundamental conservation principles, the conservation of energy, linear momentum, and angular momentum,

Cognitive constructivism: Constructivism that focuses on the idea that learning should be related to the learner's stage of cognitive development.

Cognitive Learning (CL): Another kind of learning that involves mental processes such as attention and memory.

Collaboration (Social Collaboration): A working practice whereby individuals work together to a common purpose.

Collaborative Reward: In the HAI architecture, a reward that is distributed over all actionable tokens within the pattern regardless of the actioners.

Collectivism: Taking group goals as the focus point; what is best for the collective group and personal relationships.

Commonsense Knowledge Base: Facts about the everyday world that all humans are expected to know. It is currently an unsolved problem in Artificial General Intelligence.

Computational Linguistics: The scientific and engineering discipline concerned with understanding written and spoken language from a computational perspective, and the building of artifacts that usefully process and produce language.

Conditional Probability: A measure of the probability of an event occurring, given that another event has already occurred.

Confounders: A variable that influences both the dependent variable and independent variable, causing a spurious association.

Connectionism: The notion that humans' intellectual abilities can be mimicked using artificial neural networks.

Conscious Attention: The attention referred to the most in daily life, which is of self-awareness and requires energy to be sustained.

Consciousness: A being or an agent having some degree of awareness of self, one's situation or relation to the world, one's perceptions, thoughts, and actions (both past and present), and the potential consequences of decisions. Displayed consciousness is consciousness in this book.

Consensus Theory: The thesis that truth is whatever is agreed upon, or might come to be agreed upon, by some specified group.

Constructivism: The theory that knowledge cannot be a passive reflection of reality, but an active construction by the individual, from simple to complex. Constructivist approaches require minimal innate knowledge as opposed to the large common-sense knowledge-base required by the behavioristic approach.

Contextual Understanding: Context is the setting within which a work of writing is situated. Context provides meaning and clarity to the intended message. As an example, individuals can be better understood as actors within their environment or community.

Correspondence Theories: The thesis holding that there exists an actual state of affairs and maintaining that true beliefs and true statements correspond to the actual state of affairs.

Cosine Similarity: A similarity measure (from –1 to 1) based on two vectorized attributes of two objects.

Creativity: Creativity, related to imagination and new ideas, is the ability to conceive of something unpredicted, original, and unique. In HAI, creativity is realized by a replacement of an object, action, or object's attribute with a similar token (from a "synonymous list") in the event-string.

Curiosity: A strong desire to know or learn something due to its novelty.

Cybernetics: The science of communications and automatic control systems in both machines and living things.

D

Deep-Thinking: A response mechanism in HAI often used in scientific investigations, focusing on responses (logical reasoning and repatternization) using high-level conceptual tokens.

Desensitisor: In a pattern structure, a token can represent a member of a category such as food. Such a member of class is called a desensitisor.

Desensitization: The process of creating a desensitisor or performing similarity grouping.

Discovery and Invention: While both involve novelties, the determination of a discovery or invention is dependent on whether or not it initially exists outside of a human (or agent) mind.

Distributive Reward (DR): A computed reward based on the notion that each related action on the path contributes to the actual reward.

Divided Attention: The ability to respond simultaneously to multiple tasks or multiple task demands.

Doctor-Patient Paradox: A phenomenon wherein A and Not A can both be correct. In the situation where a doctor tells his patient that he will recover soon or he will recover very slowly, the doctor can be always right, because his statement might affect the speed of the patient's recovery; thus, both statements A and Not A are correct.

Dreams: Successions of images, ideas, emotions, and sensations that occur involuntarily in the mind during certain stages of sleep. A dream may NOT be equal to the recalled dream.

E

Elaboration Tolerance: Allowing new information added so as to elaborate previous findings without starting over in the representation of previous information.

Elementary Tokens (Atomic Tokens): The initial basic units used to build virtual environments, human characters, and agents. In principle, elementary tokens can be further broken into smaller elements (tokens) by a human or an agent later in life when the sensitivities of sensory organs increase.

Embodiments: Human-equivalent physical sensory organs that can be used to detect the real world, while an agent on a computer is embodied virtually, with virtual sensory organs to detect the virtual world.

Emotions: Mental states associated with thoughts, feelings, behavioral responses, and a degree of pleasure or displeasure; the other side of reasoning; if reasoning fails emotion arises.

Entanglement: An important concept in quantum mechanics whereby two particles (electrons, photons, molecules, etc.) can be entangled, i.e., knowing the status of one implies instantly knowing the status of the other, no matter how far the two particles are apart. This implies that information can be "transmitted" instantly, faster than light. Entanglement makes it possible for quantum computing to be faster than classical computing.

Entropy of Statistical Mechanics: A measure of disorder in particle disorder, equivalent to information entropy in information science.

Event-Patterns: Patterns that do not only contain tokens in natural language.

Event-String: A text string representing sequential and/or concurrent events.

Evolutionary Algorithm: A generic population-based metaheuristic optimization algorithm inspired by biological evolution, such as reproduction, mutation, recombination, and selection.

Exploration-Exploitation Trade-Off: The matter of choosing whether to repeat the best decisions known so far (exploitation) or to make a novel decision (exploration) that might provide an even better solution.

Exponential Similarity: A similarity measure (from 0 to 1) of two patterns or objects based on the exponential difference between their attributes.

Experience: Patternized experiences.

F

Factor-Isolation Technique (FIT): A technique, based on the principle of factor-isolation, in which one works to constructively isolate a few factors in order to determine association and causal relationship.

Fast-Thinking: A response mechanism of HAI under time pressure, dealing in real time with up to 4 elementary tokens at 1 to 4 time points.

Fechner's Law: An alternative form of Weber's Law which says that the intensity of our sensation increases as the logarithm of an increase in energy.

First Designer Stance (Intentional Stance): The level of abstraction in which we view the behavior of an entity in terms of mental properties.

Fixors: The unchanged parts in a skipton.

Focused Attention: The ability to respond discretely to specific visual, auditory, or tactile stimuli.

Fredkin's Paradox (Minsky's Optimization Paradox): Fredkin's observation that "the more equally attractive two alternatives seem, the harder it can be to choose between them."

Function Specification: A formal document that software developers use to describe in detail a product's intended capabilities, appearance, and interactions with users. The functional specification is a kind of guideline and continuing reference point as the developers write the programming code.

Functionalism (Symbolism, Logicism): The thesis that one simulates the functional processes of logical thinking in the human mind.

G

Gödel's Incompleteness Theorem: A sufficient axiomatic system involving arithmetic cannot have the properties of completeness and consistency at the same time.

Gramton: A text string in the form of $E1 \otimes E2 \otimes E3 \otimes E4$, where $\otimes$ is either $\wedge$ (occur concurrently) or $\rightarrow$ (occur sequentially).

H

Habituation: The phenomenon of the diminishing of a physiological or emotional (innate) response to a frequently repeated stimulus.

Hierarchical Tokenization: A process of dimension reduction, proceeding from the notion that complex concepts are understood based on some simpler concepts, implemented in obtaining a shorter event-string representation by repeatedly replacing a part of the string with learned concept-strings (tokens).

Human Nature: A concept that denotes the fundamental dispositions and characteristics, including ways of thinking, feeling, and acting, that are natural to humans.

Humanized AI (HAI): AI aiming at creating agents (virtually—on computer—or robots) that look, think, and behave like humans and act as life companions, not digital slaves.

I

Identity Paradox: If change is a constant to everything, what persists in one's identity?

Imaginary Net (Inet): A network similar to *Knet* structurally, but formulated by hypothetical scenarios that have not been executed or verified by logical reasoning or mathematical derivation.

Imagination: A speculative mental state that allows us to consider situations apart from here and now.

Imitation: Mimicking someone or something, especially as the starting point of learning and creativity. In HAI, imitation is realized by replacing an actioner in an actioner. action string with the agent himself. Imitation is essential in letting an agent automatically become a social being.

Individualism: A social theory favoring freedom of action for individuals over collective or state control.

Inductive Reasoning: Drawing a general conclusion from a set of specific observations.

Inertia of Attention: The tendency of humans or agents to pay attention to the same thing paid attention to at the previous moment.

Information Entropy: A measure of information disorder in information theory.

Informational Obesity: The result of a person taking on too much, or unnecessary, information.

Initial Tokenization: Segmentation of a string based on elementary tokens that are directly formulated from innate knowledge, concepts, and elementary actions.

Innate Behavior: The inherent (built-in) inclination of a living organism toward a particular complex behavior.

Innate Biological Desires: The desires agents are born with, such as for food or energy when hungry, curiosity when facing novel situations, or emotional desires. Desires often drive Zda's actions.

Innate Concepts or **Knowledge:** Inherited (built-in) concepts and knowledge.

Innate Habits: Opposite to developed habits, innate habits are inherent (built-in) regular tendencies that are hard to give up.

Innovation: The practical implementation of smart ideas by borrowing across different disciplines.

Instincts: Innate habits that are not the result of learning or experience.

Instinct Theory of Motivation: All organisms are born with innate biological tendencies that help them survive. This theory suggests that instincts drive all behaviors.

Instrumental Rationality: A pursuit of all means necessary to achieve a specific goal.

Intelligence: The capacity to learn from experience and adapt to one's environment, including three fundamental cognitive processes, abstraction, learning, and dealing with novelty.

iWordNet: An individual's knowledge network constructed by a sequence of interconnected questions. An iWordnet can be used to analyze one's overall knowledge structure and understanding of concepts.

Intersubjective Agreement: The agreement among some number of conscious minds.

Intransitive Dice: A set of dice with circular winning probability, e.g., $A > B > C > A$.

J

Jaccard Similarity: A similarity measure (from 0 to 1) based on the ratio between the intersection and union of two patterns or strings.

K

Knowledge: Facts, information, and skills acquired through experience or education; the theoretical or practical understanding of a subject.

Knowledge Net (*Knet*): In this book, *Knet* refers to patternized real-world experiences saved in cloud storage or on a computer disk and used for Deep-Thinking.

Kolmogorov Complexity: The Kolmogorov complexity of an object, such as a piece of text, is the length of a shortest computer program (in a predetermined programming language) that produces the object as output.

L

Language-Guided Response: A means of using the information words provided in the natural language to facilitate a response.

Language of Thought Hypothesis (LOTH): The presupposition of a mental language where thought and thinking take place.

Law of Contiguity: A law of association stating that we associate things that occur close to each other in time and/or space.

Law of Contrast: A law of association stating that the thought of something is likely to trigger the thought of its direct opposite.

Law of Excluded Middle: In formal logic, the axiom that between A and the negation of A, one and only one is true.

Law of Similarity: A law of association which asserts that when two things are very similar to each other, the thought of one will often trigger the thought of the other.

Law of Summative Effects: The whole can be practically approximated by the sum of its parts.

Law of Syllogism: Suppose the following two statements are true: (1) If p, then q. (2) If q, then r. Then, according to the Law of Syllogism, we can derive a third true statement: (3) If p, then r.

Laws of Association: Rules used to explain how we learn and remember things through associations.

Lia: A generic name for a female HAI agent.

Logic Specification: A document about the structure of the programming and the relationships between individual code modules and the data parameters that they pass to each other.

Logicism: The thesis that one can simulate the functional processes of logical thinking in the human mind.

M

Machine Learning (ML): A narrow AI that emphasizes learning from data, the AI field in which we have major achievements today. ML can be classified into five general categories: supervised, unsupervised, reinforcement, evolutionary, and swarm intelligence learning methods.

Markov Decision Process (MDP): A mathematical framework for modeling decision-making in situations where outcomes are partly random and partly under the control of a decision-maker. MDPs are useful for studying optimization problems.

Meta Net (*Mnet*): If different patterns in *Knet* are linked at the same tokens, a large recursive knowledge net (*Mnet*) is formulated. Mnet is mostly used in Deep-Thinking.

Monotonic Reasoning: In monotonic reasoning, adding knowledge does not decrease the set of propositions that can be derived. That is, once the conclusion is taken, it will remain the same even if we add some other information to existing information in our knowledge base.

Multilevel Intelligence: An intelligence can be considered collective intelligence from a lower level. Human intelligence can be viewed as the collective intelligence of body cells; social intelligence can be viewed as a collective intelligence of humans in society. Humanized AI can be the collective intelligence of its parts or the integration of its various mechanisms.

N

Narrow Artificial Intelligence (NAI): AI that focuses on a specific task or problem.

Natural Language: A language (e.g., English and Chinese) that has developed naturally in use, as contrasted with an artificial language or computer code. Natural Language is an essential tool for communication, while communication itself is a key instrument in cognition, learning, and emotional expression.

Natural Language Net (*Lnet*): The patternized natural language based on an agent's experiences, but different from the grammar humans use in any natural language.

Natural Language Processing (NLP): A field of Artificial Intelligence in which we try to process human language as text or speech to make computers similar to humans.

Neurologism: The thesis that Humanized AI can be made through simulating the structural characteristics of the biological neural networks in the human brain.

Neuronal Correlates of Consciousness: The minimal neuronal mechanisms jointly sufficient for any specific conscious experience.

N-gram: A contiguous sequence of n items from a given sample of text or speech.

Non-Associative Learning: Learning that includes habituation and sensitization.

Non-monotonic Reasoning: Conclusions may be invalidated if we add some more information to our knowledge base, such as occurs in probabilistic reasoning.

O

Objective Multifaceted World: See the world we live in.

Object-Oriented Programming (OOP): A computer programming model that organizes software design around objects, rather than functions and logic. The classes of objects have associated properties and behaviors (methods, functions). Abstraction, inheritance, encapsulation, and polymorphism are four key features of OOP. In HAI, the three basic built-in classes of objects are Thingy, Animal, and Humanized Agent.

Observational Learning: A form of learning that develops through watching and does not require the observer to perform any observable behavior or receive reinforcement.

Onsite Patternization: Real-time patternization based on a small collection of event-strings during a very short time interval.

Ontology: An essential set or scheme of concepts and categories for AGI agents, encompassing a representation with definitions of categories, properties, and relations between concepts, data, and entities.

Operant Conditioning: See Reinforcement theory.

P

Parallel Worlds (Many Worlds Theory): In contrast to superposition, the thesis in quantum theory is that when a physical system is measured, it branches into multiple parallel worlds that never cross each other.

Parsimony Principle (Occam's Razor): The simplest theory that fits the facts of a problem is the one that should be selected. However, Occam's Razor is not considered an irrefutable principle of logic, and certainly not a scientific result.

Particle Swarm Optimization: A collective intelligence search algorithm in Narrow AI to an optimum.

Path of Understanding: A vector characterization of language strings using local topological properties of iWordnet, providing a way to compute meaning.

Patternive Reward (Simple reward): An observed reward associated with an event-string (path) or a pattern.

Pragmatic Theories: Theories holding in common the principle that truth is verified and confirmed by the results of putting one's concepts into practice.

Primary *Knet* (*pKnet*): A portion of *Knet* that only includes patterns with top reward, frequency, top recency, bottom duration, and top survival time left.

Principle of Maximum Entropy: The probability distribution which best represents the current state of knowledge about a system is the one with the largest entropy, in the context of precisely stated prior data.

Principles of Association: Contiguity in time and place, resemblance, and causation.

Probability of Action (PoA): The product of similarity, reward, and frequency, used in the response mechanisms.

Proof-by-Contradiction: A form of proof that establishes the truth or the validity of a proposition, by showing that assuming the proposition to be false leads to a contradiction.

Q

Q-Learning: A model-free reinforcement learning algorithm to learn the value of an action in a particular state.

Quantum: The minimum amount of any physical entity involved in an interaction.

Quantum Mechanics: Different from classical mechanics, in quantum mechanics the state of a quantum can be in multiple possible states at the same time, with associated probabilities. The key useful concepts of modern Quantum Mechanics include Superposition and Entanglement.

Qubits: Unlike classical bits of information, quantum information in qubits can be neither copied (the no-cloning theorem) nor destroyed (the no-deleting theorem). These two properties are very useful for the future of Cyber Security.

R

Radical constructivism: The constructivism, whose central idea is that learners and the knowledge the learner constructs tell us nothing real, they only help us function in our environment; knowledge is invented, not discovered.

Randomized Adaptive Response: Response based on Probability of Action, which depends on three normalized factors: Similarity (S), Reward (R), and Frequency (F).

Rationalization: Decision-making based on maximization of certain utilities or rewards. In HAI the frequency of a pattern is a reward-proxy.

Reciprocal Principle (Reciprocity): The tendency of agents to exchange the two actioners in a pattern. The Reciprocal Principle creates the scenario wherein an agent treats a person in the same way the person treats him.

Recursion: Recursion in mathematics is the use of output as input, repeatedly: $Y = f(f(f(\ldots f(x))))$, where $f(\cdot)$ represents a function or mechanism of a system.

Recursive Patternization: Using patternized string to further patternize stings, repeatedly.

Reinforcement theory (Skinner): A theory of actions built on the assumption that behavior is influenced by its consequences. Reinforcement is the process of shaping behavior by controlling the consequences of the behavior. Rewards are used to reinforce the behavior we want and punishments are used to prevent the behavior we do not want. These processes are called operant conditioning.

Reflex: An action that is performed as a response to a stimulus and without conscious thought, used to protect one's body from things that can harm it. Reflex also refers to a Humanized AI response model.

Reflexons: A pair of timewise highly associated tokens (2-gramtons) used in HAI Reflex. The first token is called a stimulus and the second token is called a reflexor.

Reverse Engineering: The reverse process of hierarchical tokenization, used in agent responses and in animation.

Reward Aggregation: The aggregation of rewards from the next lower token level.

Reward Propagation: The propagation of a reward to the next lower token level.

Robotics: An interdisciplinary branch of computer science and engineering involving design, construction, operation, and use of robots.

S

Sample space: S is the set of all possible outcomes of a random variable.

Schrödinger's Cat: The cat that is in both live and dead states at the same time; used to illustrate the concept of superposition.

Selective Attention: The ability to maintain attention in the face of distracting or competing stimuli.

Self-Awareness: The psychological state (phenomenon) that one knows what one is experiencing.

Self-Programming: AI system that can generate programs by itself.

Sensitization: The reverse process of desensitization, i.e., breaking a group into finer categories.

Similarity Principle: The principle that (a) similar things or individuals will likely behave similarly, and (b) the more similar they are, the more similarly they behave. The Similarity Principle is the foundation for dealing with novelty.

Simpson's Paradox: A phenomenon in which a trend appears in several groups of data but disappears or reverses when the groups are combined.

Simulated World Hypothesis: The thesis that reality could be simulated, e.g., by quantum computer simulation, and is to a degree indistinguishable from "true" reality.

Skipton: A pattern consisting of fixors and desensitisors.

Slow-Thinking: A response model in Humanized AI dealing with those situations with less time pressure than in Fast-Thinking and up to 16 most recent elementary tokens.

Social Being: A being that lives or prefers to live in a community rather than alone, and actively seeks companionship and engages in social service. Social Collaboration is a common characteristic for a social being.

Social Collaboration: See Collaboration.

Social Constructivism: Constructivism that views all of our knowledge as constructed, and that truth is constructed by social processes and is historically and culturally specific.

Social Justice: A fair and equitable division of resources, opportunities, and privileges in a society, also a consequence of social interactions.

Social Norms: The perceived informal, mostly unwritten, rules that define acceptable and appropriate actions within a given group or community, thus guiding human behavior. No prespecified rules are needed for Humanized AI, as the imitation mechanism will automatically lead agents to conform to social norms.

Stochastic Decision Networks: Networks that involve transitional probabilities for changing from one state to another and which have rewards associated with the network nodes. In Humanized AI architecture, the network is recursive and directional.

Subconscious Attention: The attention that relates to an effortless reflex.

Subsumption Architecture: The hierarchical architecture that decomposes a robot's control system into a set of task-achieving behaviors or competencies.

Superposition: A key concept in quantum theory, where a physical system (electrons, photons) can be considered to be in two different states at the same time, with associated probabilities.

Supervised Learning: A type of machine learning method in which the learner will give a response y based on an input x and will be able to compare his response to the target (correct) response.

Sustained Attention: The ability to sustain a steady response during continuous attention.

Swarm Intelligence (Collective Intelligence): An intelligent system in which organized behavior arises without a centralized controller or leader.

Synergistic: Involving a scenario in which the whole is greater than the sum of its parts.

Synthetic Approach: A new constructivist approach in humanized AI.

T

Target population: It is the set of all units a random process can pick.

Thingy: An OOP class presenting any inanimate thing with the following attributes: appearance (color, shape, size), material, mass, brightness, sound, loudness, odor, odor intensity, surface texture, temperature, edibleness, location, and velocity. A Thingy has these properties, but cannot move unless an external force acts on it.

Thought Experiment: A hypothetical situation in which a hypothesis, theory, or principle is laid out for the purpose of thinking through its consequences. Galileo's Leaning Tower of Pisa experiment and Schrödinger's cat are two well-known thought experiments.

Three-World Theory: The postulation of three distinct worlds to assist in building Humanized AI, including the world we live in, the world in our eyes, and the world in our mind.

Trolley Problem: The thought experiment with a raised ethical question: should an operator divert a runaway trolley onto a side track, killing a person on the track, if doing so reduces the overall number of deaths?

Turing's Halting Problem: The problem of determining whether a given set of responses to some input emanate from a human or a computer program. Alan Turing proved in 1936 that a general algorithm to solve the halting problem for all possible program–input pairs cannot exist.

U

Unsupervised Learning: A type of machine learning in which the learner receives no feedback from the supervisor at all. Instead, the learner's task is to re-represent the inputs in a more efficient way, for instance, as clusters or with a reduced set of dimensions.

V

Virtual Humans: Human-like characters on a computer screen, who might embody life-like behavior, displaying eyes or other parts of an avatar body, with or without human control. The term Virtual Human also refers to any one of us, any technology user who interacts with agents and virtual environments through input devices such as keyboards, microphones, and video cameras.

Virtual Sensory Organs: Sensory organs made for robots or humanized AI agents on computers.

W

Weber-Fechner Laws: A law stating that the minimum increase of stimulus that will produce a perceptible increase of sensation is proportional to the pre-existent stimulus.

World We Live In: A multifaceted objective world of infinite detail for humans and robots to sense and interact with. The multifacetedness is asserted by quantum mechanics.

World In Our Eyes: The "image" of the objective world that projects on the "retina" through the "eyes", a subset of a being's sense organs. It is a filtered world.

World In Our Mind: A simplified, interpreted version of the perceived world using concepts that include causality and associative relationships.

Z

Zda: A generic name for a male HAI agent.

Appendix: Tutorial to Common Methods for Narrow AI

A: Overview of Modern Artificial Intelligence

A.1 Artificial Intelligence and Machine Learning

The term, artificial intelligence (AI), was coined by John McCarthy, Marvin Minsky, Nathaniel Rochester, and Claude Shannon in 1955 (Russell and Norvig, 2003). AI is tied to what we used to think of as what comprised a robot's brain, or to the function of such a brain. In a general sense, AI includes robotics. The term AI often emphasizes the software aspects, while the term robot includes a physical body as an important part.

AIs can be divided into two general categories, weak and strong AI. A weak AI (WAI) aims at carrying out specific tasks, while strong AI or artificial general intelligence (AGI) aims at creating a mechanical brain that is capable of what the human brain can do. We will spend most chapters considering WAI, as our major advancements so far are only in WAI.

In the areas referred to today as machine learning (ML), data mining, pattern recognition, and expert systems, progress may be said to have started around 1960. Samuel (1959) coined the term machine learning, reporting on programming a computer "so that it will learn to play a better game of checkers than can be played by the person who wrote the program." Though the terms AI and machine learning are often used interchangeably. ML emphasizes learning from data, whereas AI has a broader sense that can include ML and the implementation of software and hardware.

Bioinformatics involves ML studies in biology and drug discovery. As an interdisciplinary field of science, bioinformatics combines biology, computer science, and statistics to analyze biological data. An example would be an identification of candidate genes and single nucleotide polymorphisms (SNPs) for a better understanding of the genetic basis of disease, unique adaptations, desirable properties, and differences between populations. In the field of genetics and genomics, bioinformatics aids in sequencing and annotating genomes and their observed mutations. Since AI methods were introduced to biotech companies in the 1990s, different ML methods have contributed significantly to drug discovery.

In Part I, we discussed different types of machine learning approaches. Further classification of machine learning methods is summarized in Figure A.1. The discussions of different methods are provided in the following sections.

A.2 Artificial Neural Networks for Deep Learning

The recent great achievements in AI, mainly in supervised learning, are exemplified by *deep learning* (DL) for image processing, voice recognition, and natural language processing. An *Artificial Neural Network* (ANN), mimicking the mechanism of the human neural

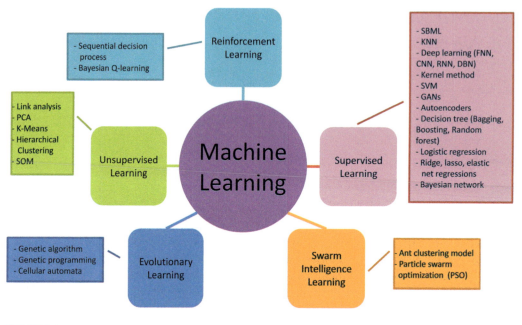

FIGURE A.1
Classification of machine learning methods.

network, uses adaptive weights between the layers in the network to model very complicated systems. The learning of the network is simply the adaptation (updating) of the weights.

To mimic the human neural network, an ANN consists of layers of nodes and weights (mimicking *synaptic connections*) that connect nodes in different layers. The part of an ANN within a single layer, mimicking a neuron, is called a perceptron (Figure A.2). A deep learning model is a multiple-layer ANN with as many as 1,000 hidden layers, modeling the cascade effects of neurons. Each layer takes the outputs from the previous layer as its inputs. The weighted sum of the inputs feeds the activation gate (function) to produce the output for the next layer until the last layer is reached. In such an ANN, the information

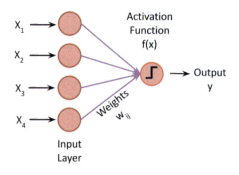

FIGURE A.2
A Perceptron mimicking a neuron.

is the weighted sum of information from the previous layer and forwarded from layer to layer. Thus, it is called a forward neural Network (FNN).

Learning in biological systems involves adjustments to the synaptic connections that exist between the neurons. The same is true for ANNs: learning for a DL network is essentially updating weights in the network using training data so that the output will match up closely with the true output.

Deep learning has various architectures, including (1) *Feedforward Neural Networks* (FNNs) for general classification and regression, (2) *Convolution Neural Networks* (CNNs) for image recognition, (3) *Recurrent Neural Networks* (RNNs) for speech recognition and natural language processing, and (4) *Deep Belief Networks* (DBNs) for disease diagnosis and prognosis. Of course, these are only examples of DL with different networks. Different problems can be solved using the same type of ANN, and different ANNs can be used to solve the same problem.

A.3 Data Structures and Fusion

AI and ML often rely heavily on data. The kinds of random variables considered here are binary, categorical (nominal and ordinal), time-to-event, vectors, matrices, sensors, sequences, trees, sets, shapes, manifolds, and functions.

Structured data refer to information with a high degree of organization. One such typical dataset is a relational database, such as a spreadsheet, where all data have the same format, same types, same variables, and often have a similar high quality. A relational database is seamless and readily searchable by simple, straightforward search engine algorithms or other search operations. In contrast, unstructured data, such as emails, medical records, and social media data, are essentially the opposite. They often have mixed formats (image, text, video, sound clips), different variables, and low quality. Traditionally, classical Statistics does handle structured data, but it is very difficult to handle massive unstructured data efficiently without manual interventions. Machine learning is expected to handle structured and unstructured data better. Since the pool of information generally available is so large, current data mining techniques often miss a substantial amount of the information that's out there, much of which could be game-changing data if efficiently analyzed. AI technology can be used to convert unstructured data into structured data or develop new AI systems that can directly handle unstructured data efficiently.

Data fusion is the process of integrating multiple data sources to produce more consistent, accurate, and useful information. A simple example will be combining data from various clinical trials and previously published clinical trial data. Such data usually are a mix of individual patient data and trial summary data (such as means, medians, confidence intervals, standard errors, sample sizes, and p-values). Interestingly, humans constantly use data fusion in comprehending the surrounding world. As humans, we rely heavily on our senses and physical movement. We rely on a fusion of smelling, tasting, and touching food to ensure that it is edible (or not). Similarly, we depend on our ability to see, hear, and control the movement of our body to walk or drive and to perform most of our daily tasks. Our brain performs fusional processing based on individual knowledge at instants in time, and we take the appropriate action. Such a level of data fusion is to be achieved by AI.

A.4 General Steps in Applying Machine Learning

In order to use ML methods, there are common steps involved, as outlined in the following:

1. Purpose: Elaborate the problem to be solved clearly and your purposes in using machine learning. This will help you narrow down a small set of machine learning methods for your target.

2. Data Source: Identify data source and data format (written on paper, recorded in text files, spreadsheets, or stored in an relational database), then process (convert, merge) them into one electronic format suitable for analysis. These data will serve as the learning material that an ML algorithm uses to generate actionable knowledge. The quality of any ML project is based largely on the quality of the data it uses.

3. Model Training: Unless your problem has been well studied and a trained model can be used as directed, you have to train the ML or determine the model parameters using your training data.

4. Performance Evaluation: Before you apply the ML algorithm, you need to evaluate its performance. Evaluation is usually done using the same training data because overfitting is a problem; another dataset, of so-called testing data, is needed to evaluate the model performance.

5. Model Optimization: Depending on model complexity, we often need to recursively use training data and test data to determine the optimal ML parameters and make comparisons among different ML algorithms to identify the optimal model among several ML methods. This parameter tuning process is often called *cross-validation*.

6. Apply the optimal model with trained parameters to the intended task.

In short, select your ML algorithm according to your clearly defined goal, use training data to determine training model parameters, test the trained model and retrain it if necessary, and apply the retrained model.

B: Similarity-Based AI

B.1 The Similarity Principle

To overcome the difficulties raised in Simpson's Paradox discussed in Part I, Section 3.4, we developed a similarity-based Machine Learning or SBML (Chang 2020).

Science aims to discover causal relationships and to predict future outcomes. So does learning (human or machine learning). All science, and learning itself, is based on a fundamental principle—the similarity principle (Chang, 2012, 2014). The principle can be stated as: similar things or individuals will likely behave similarly, and the more similar they are the more similarly they behave. For instance, people with the same (or a similar) disease, gender, and age will likely have similar responses to a particular drug or medical intervention. If they are similar in more aspects they will have more similar responses.

To qualify as a true scientific discovery, a finding must be verifiable. Otherwise, it cannot be called science. However, as history is unique, no two events are identical or repeat exactly, and even the same individual (especially a living being) will change constantly. For this reason, we have to group similar things together and, considering them as approximately the same, study their common or overall behaviors. In such a way we artificially construct recurrences of events. For example, studying a group of people with similar personalities, psychologists attempt to explain why those people behave the way they do. Pharmaceutical scientists treat people with the "same" disease to study the overall effect of a drug, even though individual responses to the drug may be different.

Indeed, similarity grouping is the basis for scientific discovery, and the similarity principle we believe in is the backbone of causality. The idea of a causal relationship is a way for human beings to handle the complex world in a simple form with a reasonable approximation because our brains are limited—we are not all-knowing!

The principle is unconsciously used at any moment in our daily life, at work, in all the sciences, in statistics, and even in mathematics. We will make the similarity principle operational (not just stopping at a conceptual level) so that it can be effectively used in the learning process.

B.2 Similarity Measures

A similarity measure or similarity function is a real-valued function that quantifies the similarity between two subjects (or two objects, two event sequences) in a simple form. Although no single definition of a similarity measure exists, usually such a measure is, in some sense, the inverse of the *dissimilarity* or distance (d) between two subjects. For instance, an exponential similarity function S is defined

$$S = \exp(-d)$$

We see that the similarity score reduces exponentially as the distance d increases. Here d ranges from zero to infinity, while the corresponding S ranges from 1 (two identical subjects) to 0 (completely different subjects).

Similarity scores can be used to build a network in which the nodes represent individuals (persons, objects, or events) and the links represent the associated similarities. We call this similarity network a *similarix*. A similarix is a weighted network with similarity scores as the weights of the links. Similarixes can be used in network analysis.

B.3 Similarity-Based Learning

According to the similarity principle, to predict the outcome Y of a new person with attributes X to a stimulus, we use the similarity-weighted outcomes $(Y_1, Y_2, \ldots, Y_N)$ of the N patients in the training set. That is,

$$Y = c \sum_j S_j Y_j$$

For a classification problem, rounding is applied to the predicted Y. The normalization constant $c = 1/\sum S_j$ and the similarity between the new person and the jth subject is

$$S_j = \exp(-d_j)$$

We define an attribute to be a value that measures whether, or to what extent, a certain property is held by a subject. An attribute vector is a sequence of attributes. Thus, the distance between attribute vector X of the new person and the attribute vector X_j for the jth subject is $d_j = |R(X - X_j)|$. Here R is a row vector. Most importantly, the attribute-scaling factor R we have introduced allows us to scale the distance according to the importance of each attribute to the outcome.

A subject is defined by the selected attributes. Therefore, for given paired subjects, a different selection of attributes can lead to a different similarity score. The similarity scores are also related to the outcome variable. For instance, gender difference has little effect on IQ outcome, but can be a great factor in the capability of bearing children! We use the attribute-scaling factors R to handle this at the training stage. In other words, learning in SBML is the updating of R using a training dataset.

Note that a regression model models the relationship between dependent and independent variables directly, while SBML models the relationship indirectly through modeling the relationship of the dependent attributes (outcomes) among different subjects by using similarity scores.

B.4 Training, Validation, and Testing

An ML model is generally in need of training to determine its parameters, such as the attribute-scaling factors, before it can be used in a real world problem. Moreover, the trained model often needs to be validated or tested for its performance. Cross-validation is often used in variable selection and tuning the model parameters, while testing is used to evaluate the performances of different ML methods. Training is usually performed on normalized datasets, making the attributes (features or predictors) range from 0 to 1 with standard deviation 1, as an example. Such standardization makes the model (parameters) easier to generalize to other applications as long as the attributes in the corresponding dataset are also normalized. The commonly used methods for validation and testing are:

1. Exhaustive cross-validation methods are cross-validation methods that learn and test using all possible ways to divide the original sample into a training and validation set.

2. Leave-p-out cross-validation involves using p observations as the validation set and the remaining observations as the training set. This is repeated for all ways to cut the original sample into a validation set of p observations and a training set.

3. Bootstrapping is the random selection, with replacement, of m samples of size p as training sets and n samples of size q as test sets. This method is more appreciated when the sample size is small.

In general, larger attribute-scaling factors R (as the number of epochs increases) will lead to a smaller training error. We can always reduce the training error to near zero when

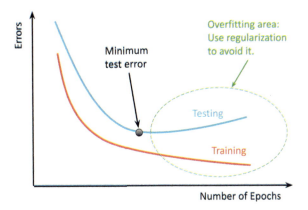

FIGURE A.3
Training error versus test error.

the R approaches infinity. However, this will lead to overfitting and increase test error (Figure A.3). The test error is our real concern, not the training error. Regularization is a commonly used technique used to overcome the overfitting problem.

Regularization

Regularization imposes a penalty on the complexity of a model in the form of a loss function based on the principle of Occam's razor (Chang, 2014). In learning, if we minimize the loss function instead of training error, the overfitting problem can largely be circumvented. If the prediction accuracy is measured by the mean squared error (MSE) between the predicted and observed outcomes, then *Tikhonov regularization* or a *ridge loss function* can be used and the optimization problem becomes one of finding a vector R that minimizes

$$L = MSE + \lambda |R|^2$$

Here $|R|$ is the norm or overall size of the scaling factors. By properly selecting the tuning parameter λ in the penalty term through cross-validation or predetermination, the training error MSE can be controlled to avoid overfitting.

Learning

Learning is essentially the updating of the model parameters R so as to minimize the loss, using the *Gradient Method Algorithm* with the training data. The gradient method makes the adjustment of R in the maximum slope direction (just as we go downhill following the steepest but shortest path). The scaling factor at iteration $t+1$ from iteration t is calculated using the formulation

$$R^{(t+1)} = R^{(t)} - \alpha \frac{\partial L}{\partial R}$$

If we view gradient $\frac{\partial L}{\partial R}$ as the direction of walking, then the constant learning rate α (e.g., 0.125) determines the stride length. The learning rate should be small enough to have sufficient precision, but large enough (e.g., 0.25) for computational efficiency.

Now we know how to use SBML to resolve the Simpson paradox and other statistical controversies discussed in Chapter 6. We first record the responses in all patients and collect all potential relevant attributes, such as baseline disease severity, vital signs, gender, age, genomics, and other demographics. Training data are then used to determine the attribute-scaling factors for the attributes. The learned scaling factors govern the relative importance of each attribute in the similarity score. After the scaling factors are determined, individual response is predicted using similarity-based weighting of the known responses. In short, to predict a patient's response, instead of basing the response (rate) in a predetermined category (e.g., all patients, male patients, or young female patients), we will weigh the responses of patients based on the similarity.

A Case Study

Consider, e.g., cystic fibrosis (CF)—a rare, inherited, and life-threatening disorder. CF damages multiple organs and systems in the body, including respiratory, gastrointestinal, and reproductive systems. In CF drug development, a clinical endpoint to evaluate a drug's efficacy is the absolute improvement in lung function (measured by the percent predicted forced expiratory volume in one second, or ppFEV1) compared to a baseline. The attributes of interest include treatment, age, sex, and baseline ppFEV1. In predicting ppFEV1 results from the trials, SBML shows a 22% improved precision over classic statistical optimal linear models, with only a small training dataset. SBML can be used in early clinical trials to predict later phase trial results in drug development for better trial design and planning. In precision medicine, SBML can also be used for predicting the treatment result for future individual patient results (rather than average results over all patients) to better inform the patient and doctors.

Nearest-Neighbors Method

As the scaling factors become very large the prediction using SBML will degenerate to the *K*-nearest neighbor (KNN) algorithm, but the relative scaling effects of different attributes are still there. When we buy a product or seek advice on some matter, we often seek out close neighbors or friends for their opinions, since they are similar to us (in many ways), and doing so is a convenient way to get helpful information. This is the basic idea behind the KNN. In a KNN, an object is classified by a majority vote of its neighbors, with the object being assigned to the class most common among its *K* nearest neighbors.

Despite its simplicity, KNN has been used in many classification problems, such as the deciphering of handwritten digits and satellite image scenes. In drug discovery and development, KNN is used for ECG Pattern Analysis and Classification (Thomas and Mathew, 2016) and for a three-dimensional QSAR (Nigsch et al., 2006).

There are many other similarity-based ML methods in drug development with prefixed similarities determined by field experts minus the attribute-scaling factors. From this perspective, more precisely, the SBML discussed in this book should be called *similarity-principle-based machine learning*.

B.5 Summary

The similarity principle is a fundamental principle that we constantly use in our daily lives, causality inferences, and scientific discoveries. The principle asserts that each attribute contains some information about the outcome of events and that similar things should have similar outcomes. This is virtually always true as long as the target population for the evaluation is also defined using the same set of attributes used in learning.

Similarity in SBML is context-dependent. That is, similarity is (1) outcome-dependent, (2) attribute-dependent, and (3) data-scope dependent.

SBML can help doctors to predict the drug effect in individuals to better prescribe medicines. It can also be used to build medical robots for personalized medicine.

SBML has a "shrinking effect" on the predicted outcome because the weighted average of outcomes is always between the minimum and maximum of the outcomes. However, if we use the derivatives of the outcome variable instead of the outcome variable, SBML can predict an outcome that is larger than observed outcome values.

In addition to the shrinking effect caused by the similarity weighting, the penalty term in SBML further shrinks the mean squared error (MSE). At the same time, the similarity normalization in the weights makes an unbiased adjustment in SBML. Most ML methods, such as ridge regression, have to make a tradeoff between biases and variance.

While most ML methods require big training data, the SBML works for small data too. Therefore, SBML can be used in drug development for rare diseases and for other problems even when only small amounts of data are available.

In almost all similarity-based ML methods, the similarities between subjects are usually determined subjectively by field experts. In SBML, the similarity scores are objectively determined by the training data through a limited number of scaling factors. An SBML R program is available from Chang's book (2020).

Training, validation, and testing are important steps when building an AI system. Only the trained model can be used in prediction in the real world. The validation processes are often used for tuning model parameters such as the learning rate, penalty parameters, and the number of epochs. The use of a penalty is an effective tool in dealing with overfitting problems.

Recursive learning resembles the natural human way of learning. It is an efficient way to learn from complicated data in which the differences are often difficult to precisely define. For instance, two trials conducted at different times or in different countries may differ in medical practice, or on account of race or other unknown characteristics. The recursive SBML can also be used for dimension reduction (Chang, 2020).

C: Artificial Neural Network For Deep Learning

C.1 Feedforward Networks

Types of Neural Networks

Artificial neural networks (ANNs) are computing systems inspired by the biological neural networks in animal brains. ANNs take input data and output desired outcomes after training. The learning in an ANN refers to its ability of outputting outcomes that, through training, are closer and closer to the right answer over time. The adjustments of weights in an ANN are what make the ANN learn.

An ANN model (Figure A.4) includes the input layer, one or more hidden layers, and the output layer. Each layer contains input and output nodes, weights, and activation functions. Deep learning ANN architectures include (1) *Feedforward Neural Networks* (FNNs) for general classification and regression, (2) *Convolution Neural Networks* (CNNs) for image recognition, (3) *Recurrent Neural Networks* (RNNs) for speech recognition and natural language processing, and (4) *Deep Belief Networks* (DBNs) for disease diagnosis and prognosis. Two other popular neural networks are *Generative Adversarial Networks* (GANs) for

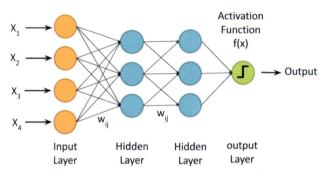

FIGURE A.4
Feedforward neural network.

classification problems and *Autoassociative Networks* (*Autoencoders*) for dimension reduction. Although an autoencoder will result in a dimension reduction in an unsupervised manner, the training process is supervised learning.

An FNN, also known as a multilayer perceptron, has input and output layers, and hidden layers in between. At each layer (except the input layer), an activation function f is applied to the weighted sum of input data from the previous layer. The resulting outputs at each layer serve the input data for the next layer. For example, the output Y_i for the ith node at the first layer is a function of input data x_i,

$$Y_i = f\left(\sum_j w_{ij} x_j \right).$$

The outputs Y_i will serve as the input for the (i+1)th layer, and so on. Different activation functions f can be used at different layers in an ANN, such as the *rectifier* (ReLU), *sigmoid*, and *tanh* functions used to mimic a biological mechanism. The neurons in the perceptron share the inputs, but not the weights and activation functions (Figure A.4).

Two layers in an ANN are usually fully connected by weights. As the number of layers increases, the number of weights will increase exponentially. Therefore, to reduce the computational burden, some links (weights) between layers can be dropped and the layers become more loosely connected.

Learning and Backpropagation Algorithms

The numbers of layers and nodes are usually fixed; the only things that can change are the weights in the network. The question is how to convert a person's way of learning into a set of rules for changing the weights so that the network outputs the right answer or appropriate response more often. In practice, the weight modifications are through training using the gradient method, more precisely, a *backpropagation algorithm* (BPA).

Backpropagation algorithms make deep learning ANNs computationally possible. In fact, a BPA for multilayer artificial neural networks was an important precursor contribution to the success of deep learning in the 2010s (Bryson and Ho, 1975), once big data became available and computing power was sufficiently advanced to accommodate the training of large networks. There are several AI software packages available in R for building ANNs, including *keras* and *kerasR*.

C.2 Convolutional Neural Networks

Ideas Behind CNN

A convolutional neural network (CNN) is actually a class of deep neural networks, mainly applied to image analysis. CNN architectures can also be used to detect very different lesions or pathologies in subjects without the need of manual feature design.

A CNN architecture consists of many layers (Figure A.5), each one playing a different role. (1) The *input layer* takes the input from the source images or objects and converts it to data or numbers. (2) A *convolution layer* identifies certain features of the images by inspecting the image's pieces and outputting a value dependent on the filter used. A filter is a powerful tool that makes it possible to discover a feature contained in the source images. To identify different elemental features we use filters at different convolution layers. (3) An *activation layer* decides whether the neuron fires ("spikes") for the current inputs. (4) A *pooling layer* converts the original higher resolution images to lower resolution images, in order to reduce the size of the images. (5) Although some weights connecting layers can be removed (dropped) to reduce the dimension for computational efficiency, the fully connected layers (*dense layers*) take the high-level filtered images and translate them into votes in classifying the source images.

Convolution Layers

The main idea of a CNN is seen at the convolution layers, where different filters are used. Each filter is used to identify or filter out particular features or image elements such as eyes, noses, lines, etc., just as when we search for particular objects from a complex picture.

The term convolution is from mathematics (calculus). It corresponds to an image inspection process through a small moving filter. A filter can be thought of as a piece of virtual glass with various transparencies at different locations according to the feature being investigated. Let's look into how convolutions work in CNN using Figure A.6.

Taking image X as an example, we code a value of 1 for the pixels where X is located and a value of –1 for all other places. The filter with a backslash is also coded using 1 and –1 implementing the same rule.

To filter the image, we place a filter over the image, starting from the left upper corner, do the calculation (filtering), and then move to the next position by a stride (one or more pixels to the left or down) and perform filtering again. We continue until the filter covers all possible positions. To calculate the convolution at a position, we simply (1) put the filter on top of the coded image, (2) count the numbers of matches (pixels with the same code, –1 or 1) and mismatches, and (3) compute the proportion of net matches:

$$\text{Convolution} = (\text{\# of matches} - \text{\# of mismatches})/(\text{size of filter in pixels})$$

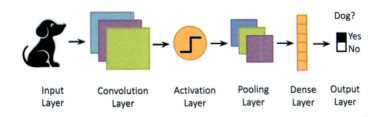

FIGURE A.5
A sketch of deep learning architecture (CNN).

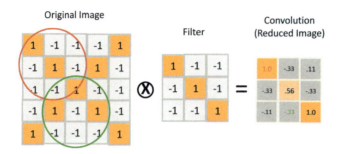

FIGURE A.6
Convolution produces a shrunken image.

Obviously, filtering will result in a shrunken image (fewer pixels), but, more importantly, the filtered image does show larger values on the diagonal of the filtered image, indicating that the original image has a backslash we were searching for using the filter. If there were no backslash in the original picture as the filter is looking for, the resulting picture would not have a backslash that is represented by higher values.

Pooling Layer

Pooling is a way to take large images and shrink them down while preserving the most important information in them. It consists of stepping a small window across an image and taking the maximum value from the window at each step. A window of 2 pixels on a side and steps of 2 pixels work well (Figure A.7). Other pooling methods exist, such as average pooling. A pooling layer performs pooling on a collection of images to help manage the computational load. The visual effect of pooling is somewhat as if one sees the image from a greater distance.

Hyperparameters

We now have a good picture of how a CNN works, but there is still a list of questions that need to be answered through training and validation:

1. How many layers of each type should there be, in what order? And how to deal with color images?

2. Some deep neural networks can have over a thousand layers; what is the trade-off among the number of layers, the size of each layer, and the complexity of filters or layers?

3. For convolution layers, what features or filters shall we use, and what size for each filter? How big should the stride be?

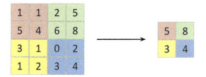

FIGURE A.7
Maximum pool with 2×2 filters and stride 2.

4. For each pooling layer, what window size and pooling algorithm should be used?

5. For each fully connected layer, how many hidden neurons or weights are needed?

These questions can be answered using ML software, but the topic is beyond the scope of this book.

CNNs for Medical Image Analysis

Medical image analysis is the science of analyzing or solving medical problems, using different image analysis techniques, for the effective and efficient extraction of information. Qayyuma et al. (2018) present a state-of-the-art review of medical image analysis using CNNs. The application area of CNNs covers the whole spectrum of medical image analysis including detection, segmentation, classification, and computer-aided diagnosis. Farooq (2017) presented a CNN-based method for the classification of Alzheimer's disease in MRI images having multiple classes and two networks.

Much other research has been done on CNNs for image analysis, including a multiscale CNN-based approach for automatic segmentation of MRI images for assigning voxels to brain tissue classes, a tri-planar CNN used for segmentation of tibial cartilage in knee MRI images, and segmentation of isointense brain tissue presented through a CNN using a multimodal MRI dataset by training the network on three patches extracted from the images. Other interesting studies include lung pattern classification for interstitial lung diseases using a deepCNN, predicting brain age with deep learning from raw imaging data results in a reliable and heritable biomarker, and dermatologist-level classification of skin cancer, again with deep neural networks.

CNNs can be used not just for images, but also to categorize other types of data. The key is to transform them and make them look like image data, in the form of a two-dimensional array or matrix. For instance, audio signals can be chopped into short time chunks, and then each chunk broken up into bass, midrange, treble, or finer frequency bands. This can be represented as a two-dimensional array where each column is a time chunk and each row is a frequency band. "Pixels" in this pretended picture that are close together are closely related. Researchers have also used CNNs to process text data for natural language processing and even to process chemical data for drug discovery. The rule of thumb is: if your data are just as useful after swapping any pair of columns, then you can't use a CNN. However, if you can make your problem look like finding patterns in an image, then CNNs may be exactly what you need (Rohrer, 2019).

C.3 Recurrent Neural Networks

Location invariance and local compositionality are two key ideas behind CNNs that do not always bear fruit. They make sense for computer vision applications but not for natural language processing or time-series events. The location where a word lies in the whole sentence is critical to the meaning of the sentence. Words that are not close to one another in a sentence may be more connected in terms of meaning, which is quite contrary to pixels in a specific region of an image that may be a part of a certain object. Therefore, it makes sense to look for a neural network that reflects the sequence of the tokens, whether they are words, events, or something else with a temporal axis. One such network is the *recurrent neural network* (RNN), which can have memories of its previous states.

The idea of the RNN came from the work of Ronald William and his colleagues in 1986. A RNN is a class of artificial neural networks for modeling temporal dynamic behavior. Unlike FNNs, RNNs can use their internal state as memory to process sequences of inputs. In other words, they often reuse the output or hidden outputs (internal states) as input again, hence their name. RNNs are useful for tasks such as unsegmented, connected handwriting recognition, and speech recognition. They have also been implemented for stock market prediction, sequence generation, test generation, voice recognition, image captioning, poem-writing (after being trained on Shakespeare's poetry), reading handwriting from left to right, and creating music.

A challenging issue with RNNs is the vanishing gradient problem when the RNN involves many layers. Traditional activation functions such as the hyperbolic tangent function have gradients in the range (0, 1), and backpropagation computes gradients by the chain rule. This has the effect of multiplying n of these small numbers to compute gradients of the "front" layers in an n-layer network, leading to the gradient (error signal) decreasing exponentially with n while the front layers train very slowly. The vanishing gradient will effectively prevent the weight from changing its value and can even completely stop the neural network from further training. A solution is to use a long chain of short-term memory units, called long short-term memory units (LSTMs) as shown in Figure A.8, as proposed by Hochreiter and Schmidhuber in 1997.

In 2009, a Connectionist Temporal Classification (CTC)-trained LSTM network was the first RNN to win pattern recognition contests for its successes in handwriting recognition. In 2014, the Chinese search giant Baidu used CTC-trained RNNs to break the Switchboard Hub 5′00 speech recognition benchmark. Google uses LSTMs for speech recognition on smartphones for the smart assistant Allo and Google Translate. Apple uses LSTM for the Quicktype function on the iPhone and for Siri. Amazon uses an LSTM for Amazon's

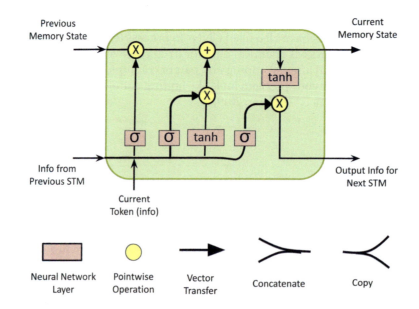

FIGURE A.8
Information flows in LSTMs.

Alexa. In 2017, Facebook performed some 4.5 billion automatic translations every day using LSTMs. Using LSTMs, Microsoft reported in 2017 reaching 95.1% recognition accuracy on the Switchboard corpus. In 2018, bots developed by OpenAI were able to beat humans in the game of Dota (Rodriguez, 2018). The bots have a 1,024-unit LSTM that sees the current game state and emits actions through several possible action heads. In 2019, DeepMind's program AlphaStar used a deep LSTM core to excel at the complex video game Starcraft. This was viewed as significant progress toward Artificial General Intelligence (Stanford, 2019).

Applications of LSTMs in Natural Language Processing

Here are some of the ways that LSTMs can be used for natural language processing (NLP):

1. Text Classification, including sentiment analysis, where class labels are used to represent the emotional tone of the text, usually as "positive" or "negative," spam filtering (classifying email text as spam), language identification (classifying the language of source text), and genre classification (classifying the genre of a fictional story).

2. Language Modeling, for predicting the probabilistic relationships between words, enabling one to predict the next word.

3. Speech Recognition, for understanding speech, to either generate text readable by humans or issue commands. Examples include transcribing a speech and creating text captions for a movie or TV show.

4. Caption Generation, to describe the contents of a digital image or video. This language model can be strategic, as it allows one to create searchable text for search engines.

5. Machine Translation, for translating source text from one particular language into another language.

6. Document Summarization, to create a short description about a document, such as creating a heading/abstract for a document or summarizing a news article.

7. Question Answering, to take a question posed in a natural language and provide an answer.

Applications of LSTMs in Molecular Design

In NLP, we essentially deal with sequences of words. Likewise, in drug discovery, we deal with gene sequences, proteins, and other molecular structures representable by a sequence of substructures. Therefore, LSTMs can be used for compound screening and molecular design. The basic ideas and how it works can be described as follows (Figure A.9).

To automatically produce a sentence or article, the key is to determine the conditional probability of the next word, s_{t+1}, given the previous words, s_1, s_2, and s_t. In a simple scenario where the aim is just to create grammatically correct sentences, we can train the RNN using a collection of grammatically correct sentences. The weights of the network will be adjusted to minimize error between the predicted words and the actual words in the training sentences.

In order to use RNN for De Novo Drug Design, 3D molecular structures of chemical compounds are rearranged into 1-D according to specific rules such as the *Simplified Molecular-Input Line-Entry System* (SMILES). After compounds are coded into 1-D sequences

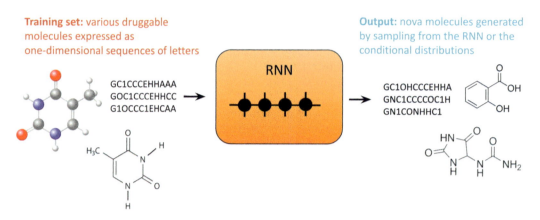

FIGURE A.9
Sampling Nova molecules from a trained RNN.

like English sentences, we can train the RNN with large 'druggable' ligands to design or generate new drug candidates. Likewise, researchers have created ChEMBL22 (www.ebi. ac.uk/chembl) with 677,044 SMILES strings for annotated nanomolar activities for training purposes. Gupta et al. (2018) trained their RNN on 541,555 SMILES strings, with lengths from 34 to 74 SMILES characters (tokens). RNN models can be used to generate sequences one token at a time, as these models can output a probability distribution over all possible tokens at each time step.

C.4 Deep Belief Networks

There are two major challenges in current high-throughput screening drug design: (1) the large number of descriptors which may also have autocorrelations, and (2) proper parameter initialization in model prediction so as to avoid an over-fitting problem. Deep architecture structures have been recommended to predict a compound's biological activity. Performance of deep neural networks is not always acceptable in quantitative structure-activity relationship (QSAR) studies (Ghasemi et al., 2018).

A *deep belief network* (DBN) consists of a sequence of restricted Boltzmann machines (RBMs). An RBM is an algorithm useful for dimensionality reduction. RBMs are shallow, two-layer neural nets that constitute the building blocks of deep-belief networks. The first layer of the RBM is called the visible, or input layer, and the second is the hidden layer.

The output of a hidden layer is used as the input for the next layer. Each DBN layer is trained independently during the unsupervised portion, and thus all can be trained concurrently. After the unsupervised portion is complete, the output from the layers is refined with supervised logistic regression. The top logistic regression layer predicts probabilistically the class to which the input belongs. The purpose of the unsupervised training is to select better features. Supervised learning is used for classification purposes. Therefore, a DBN combines unsupervised and supervised learning for the purpose of efficient learning.

Applications of Deep Belief Networks

Kim et al. (2017) compared DBNs with other methods in cardiovascular risk prediction. The authors proposed a cardiovascular disease prediction model using the sixth Korea National Health and Nutrition Examination Survey (KNHANES-VI) 2013 dataset to analyze cardiovascular-related health data. First, a statistical analysis was performed to find variables related to cardiovascular disease using health data related to cardiovascular disease. Then, a model of cardiovascular risk prediction by learning based on the DBN was developed. This statistical DBN-based prediction model has an accuracy of 83.9%.

Ghasemi et al. (2018) utilized a deep belief network to evaluate the DBN's performance using *Kaggle datasets* with fifteen targets containing more than 70k molecules. The results revealed that an optimization in parameter initialization could improve the ability of deep neural networks to provide high-quality model predictions. The mean and variance of the squared correlation for the proposed model and the deep neural network deployed are smaller than previous multilayer perceptron models.

C.5 Generative Adversarial Networks

Generative adversarial networks (GANs) are deep neural net architectures composed of two nets, pitting one adversarially against the other. GAN can be viewed as the combination of a counterfeiter and a policeman, where the counterfeiter is learning to pass false notes, and the cop is learning to detect them. Both are dynamic in the zero-sum game, and each side comes to learn the other's methods in a constant escalation. As the discriminator changes its behavior, so does the generator, and vice versa. Their losses push against each other.

In drug development, imaging markers can be used for monitoring disease progression with or without medical intervention. Models are typically based on large amounts of data with annotated examples of known markers aiming at automating detection. Doppler et al. (2017) developed a deep convolutional generative adversarial network that can learn a manifold of normal anatomical variability, accompanied by a novel anomaly scoring scheme based on the mapping from the image space to a latent space. Applied to new data such as images containing retinal fluid, the model labels anomalies and scores image patches indicating their fit into the learned distribution.

Deep GANs are an emerging technology in drug discovery and biomarker development. Kadurin et al. (2017) demonstrated a proof-of-concept in implementing a deep GAN to identify new molecular fingerprints with predefined anticancer properties. They also developed a new GAN model for molecular feature extraction problems, and showed that the model significantly enhances the capacity and efficiency of development of the new molecules with specific anticancer properties using the deep generative models.

Yahi et al. (2017) proposed a framework for exploring the value of GANs in the context of continuous laboratory time series data. The authors devised an unsupervised evaluation method that measures the predictive power of synthetic laboratory test time series and showed that when it comes to predicting the impact of drug exposure on laboratory test data, incorporating representation learning of the training cohorts prior to training the GAN models is beneficial.

Putin et al. (2018) proposed a Reinforced Adversarial Neural Computer (RANC) for the de novo design of novel small-molecule organic structures based on the GAN paradigm and reinforcement learning. The study shows RANCs can be reasonably regarded as a promising starting point from which to develop novel molecules with activity against different biological targets or pathways. This approach allows scientists to cover a broad chemical space populated with novel and diverse compounds.

C.6 Autoassociative Networks

An autoassociative network (autoencoder) is a type of artificial neural network used to learn efficient data coding in an unsupervised manner. Autoencoders encode input data as vectors. They create a hidden, or compressed, representation of the raw data (Figure A.10). Such networks are useful in dimensionality reduction; i.e., the vector serving as a hidden representation compresses the raw data into a smaller number of salient dimensions. Autoencoders can be paired with a so-called decoder, which allows one to reconstruct input data based on its hidden representation. Autoencoders are especially useful for dimension reduction, but the training method used is supervised learning, since the correct answer is known for each input. The training goal is to minimize the error between the output and the input.

An autoencoder learns to compress data from the input layer into a short code, and then decompresses that code into something that closely matches the original data. A simple autoassociative network can be a multiple-layer perceptron, where the output is identical to the input and the middle hidden layer is smaller. This means we can use the compressed middle layer to generate the original image.

Kadurin et al. (2017) presented the first application of generative adversarial autoencoders (AAEs) for generating novel molecular fingerprints with a defined set of parameters. In their model of a 7-layer AAE architecture with the latent middle layer serving as a discriminator, the input and output use a vector of binary fingerprints and concentration of the molecule. They introduce a neuron responsible for growth inhibition percentage to model the reduction in the number of tumor cells after the treatment. To train the AAE, the NCI-60 cell line assay data for 6,252 compounds, profiled on the MCF-7 cell line, are used.

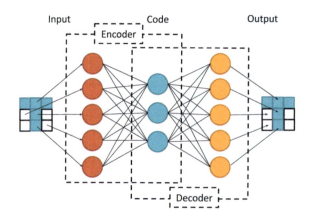

FIGURE A.10
Autoassociative network for data compression.

The output of the AAE was used to screen 72 million compounds in *PubChem* and select candidate molecules with potential anti-cancer properties.

C.7 Summary

We have discussed five different deep learning ANNs. In an FNN, the simplest type of ANN, weighted information is forwarded from layer to layer. At each layer, an activation function is applied.

Information in a CNN is also propagating from layer to layer. However, a convolution operation is applied between layers. Each filter tries to identify a particular image element.

CNNs are very effective in static image processing and have been used for disease diagnosis. However, in motion picture and language processing, there are not only the special attributes, but also temporal properties to be considered. For this reason, memoryless CNNs do not work efficiently for those problems and RNNs are developed to capture the temporal dimension. In RNNs, outputs at one layer are related to previous layers (not just the previous layer). The complex 3D structures of a chemical compound or protein are converted into a 1D sequence of symbols before the RNN is applied. LSTMs can effectively avoid the gradient-vanishing problem; they are often used for various tasks in drug development.

Due to the vast number of possible structures of chemical compounds and the extreme complexity of protein folding structures, dimension-processing using unsupervised learning will be beneficial to problem-solving. This is the key idea of deep-belief networks.

Two other special and very useful ANNs are GANs and autoencoders. A GAN can be viewed as the combination of a counterfeiter and a cop, where the counterfeiter is learning to pass false notes, and the cop is learning to detect them. Thus a GAN generates training data dynamically to effectively train the networks.

An autoencoder has a hidden layer that is smaller than the input layer, while the output is always the same (approximately) as the inputs. After extensive training, the smaller input at a hidden layer can securely generate (nearly) the same input image. Therefore, autoencoders can be used for compressing images or data.

D: More Supervised Learning Methods

D.1 Kernel Methods

In classical statistical models for regression and classification, the form of the mapping $y(x, w)$ from input x to output y is governed by a set of adaptive parameters w. During the learning phase, a set of training data is used either to obtain an estimate or *posterior distribution* of the parameters. The training data are then discarded, and predictions for new inputs are based purely on the learned parameters w. This approach is also used in non-linear parametric models such as neural networks, but SBML and Kernel methods (KMs) are memory-based approaches that involve storing an entire training set (dimension reduction is possible with modifications) in order to make future predictions. These methods are generally fast to train but slow at making predictions for test data points.

A typical kernel $k(x, x_j)$, defined as a *dot product*, can be viewed as a similarity between objects that are characterized by attributes x and x_j. Once the kernel is selected and weights w_j ($j = 1, \ldots N$) for the N training subjects are determined, the predicted outcome for the new subject with attributes x can be expressed as a weighted sum (linear combination) of the kernels (similarities).

$$Y = \sum_j w_j k(x, x_j).$$

Learning here is updating the weights based on the loss minimization in the same way as for SBML. This kernel method is extensively discussed by Schölkopf et al. (2004).

The KM appears to be similar to SBML, but they actually differ at least in two ways: (1) KMs use similarities to define subjects but do not apply the similarity principle as SBML does. (2) A KM is an over-parameterized model with N parameters, while SBML has only K attribute-scaling factors. (3) Similarities (kernels) in KMs are determined based on field-experts' judgments, while similarities in SBML are objectively determined through training the attribute-scaling factors.

Kernel methods are also used in other forms. For instance, there is the Nadaraya-Watson kernel-weighted method, in which the kernel is predetermined and the weight is the normalization factor. Therefore, this kernel method has no learning involved. The second example would be the local regression with a structured kernel, in which kernels are used as the weights in the error minimization process (Hastie et al., 2001).

The Kernel trick is intrinsic to the KM. It can be stated in this way: any algorithm for multidimensional data that can be expressed only in terms of dot products between vectors can be performed implicitly in the feature space associated with any kernel, by replacing each dot product by a kernel evaluation.

The kernel trick has huge practical implications since it is a very convenient way of transforming linear methods, such as *linear discriminant analysis*, into non-linear methods by simply replacing the classic dot product with a more general kernel, such as the *Gaussian RBF kernel*. Non-linearity via the new kernel is then obtained at no extra computational cost, as the algorithm remains exactly the same. Two advantages of Kernel methods are (Schölkopf et al., 2004):

1. The representation as a square matrix does not depend on the nature of the objects (images, persons, DNA sequences, molecules, protein sequences, languages) to be analyzed. Therefore, an algorithm developed for molecules can be used for image or language processing. This suggests a full modularity of analysis algorithms to cover various problems, while algorithm design and data processing can proceed independently.

2. The size of the kernel matrix used to represent a dataset of n objects is always $n{\times}n$, whatever the nature or the complexity or the number of attributes of the objects.

D.2 Support Vector Machines

Linear discriminant analysis (LDA) is based on the construction of the hyperplane that minimizes the misclassification error. Similarly, a *support vector machine* (SVM), developed in the mid-1960s, is a generalization of LDA for constructing hyperplanes that minimize the

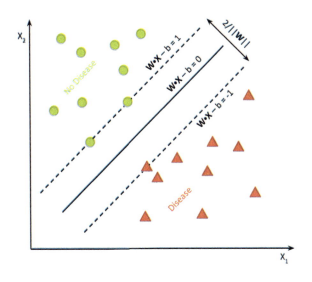

FIGURE A.11
Support vector machine in action.

misclassification or regression error. The SVM searches for a linear decision boundary that separates members of one class from the other (Figure A.11). In case such a hyperplane does not exist, SVM uses a non-linear mapping to transform the training data into a higher dimension before seeking the linear optimal separating hyperplane. With an appropriate non-linear mapping to a sufficiently high dimension, data from two classes can always be separated by a hyperplane. SVM has successfully been applied to handwritten digit recognition, text classification, speaker identification, etc., and it is less prone to overfitting. In the medical field, an SVM has been used in breast cancer diagnosis (Akay, 2009).

The question is that in the optimization, the max-margin hyperplane and classifier are solely determined by a few data points x_s that lie nearest to the hyperplane. These x_s are called *support vectors*. In the two-dimensional case as shown in Figure A.11, the support vectors are determined by the 3 data points on two dotted lines. The learning here is determining parameters w or the solid line (location and orientation) used to maximize the distance between the two dotted lines. To take all the data points (not just the support vectors) into consideration in a classifier, we can employ the soft-margin method, which imposes a penalty on misclassification.

Kernel methods and SVMs have been broadly used in bioinformatics (Schölkopf et al., 2004), including in the following studies: Inexact Matching String Kernels for Protein Classification, Fast Kernels for String and Tree Matching, Local Alignment Kernels for Biological Sequences, Kernels for Graphs, Diffusion Kernels, A Kernel for Protein Secondary Structure Prediction, Heterogeneous Data Comparison and Gene Selection with Kernel Canonical Correlation Analysis, Kernel-Based Integration of Genomic Data Using Semidefinite Programming, Protein Classification via Kernel Matrix Completion, Accurate Splice Site Detection for Caenorhabditis elegans, Gene Expression Analysis: Joint Feature Selection and Classifier Design, and Gene Selection for Microarray Data.

D.3 Decision Tree Methods

Classification and Regression Trees

Decision tree methods (DTMs), or simply *tree methods*, are among the most popular methods in statistical machine learning. They are intuitive, as well as easy to use and interpret. As an example, a physician could use a decision tree like the one shown in Figure A.12 for classifying a patient's risk of death within 30 days based on an initial 24 hours of data following a medical event or exam.

The decision rules might be something like this: the minimum systolic blood pressure within the initial 24 hours is checked, and if it's 90 or lower the patient is classified as high risk. Otherwise, check his age; if he is no more than 60 years old, classify the patient as low risk. If his age is more than 60 years old, then further check for sinus tachycardia; if it is present, classify him as a high-risk patient, but if not present he is low risk. In this example, given that the low and high risks are defined, one of the key questions is how to determine the threshold for each of the risk factors to minimize the error or the loss function.

There are two types of trees, based on the outcome: classification and regression trees (CARTs). In a regression tree, the outcome is a continuous variable, while in a classification tree the outcome is a discrete variable. For instance, in the classification tree shown in Figure A.12, each patient is characterized by K attributes or predictors. Each predictor x_i ($i = 1, \ldots, K$) is divided into two categories. Each end of the tree, called a leaf, has a value associated (e.g., 1 for high risk and 0 for low risk), presenting a classification of a patient. The goal of any tree method is to classify a subject based on their predictors to minimize the misclassification error rate. The construction of a classification tree involves three tasks.

1. Select the splits: one variable a time, $x_i < c_i$ versus $x_i \geq c_i$, where threshold c_i is to be optimized in terms of an *impurity* minimization.

2. Decide when to declare a node terminal without further splitting: stopping criteria tend to be myopic; instead, we can grow to a full tree and then prune it using cross-validation to prevent overfitting.

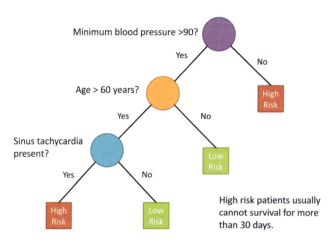

FIGURE A.12
Decision tree for hypertension patient classification.

3. Assign each terminal node to a class for classification trees or associated value for regression trees.

The common impurity measures for binary classifications are: misclassification rate, p, defined as proportion of misclassification of subjects, with Gini index defined as $GI = p \cdot (1-p)$, and gross-entropy or deviance defined as $GI = p \cdot \ln(p)$.

There are two competing factors in determining an optimal tree model: the accuracy of the tree method and computational efficacy.

For a given tree depth D, a commonly used approach in obtaining an optimal tree (minimizing ME, GI, or GE) is the greedy algorithm: for each parameter, try different thresholds. We can let the tree grow larger than what we need at the final state, then prune it.

Tree size is a tuning parameter governing the model's complexity and should be determined based on the data. An obvious idea is to split tree nodes only when the decrease in sum-of-squares due to the split exceeds some threshold. This strategy is too shortsighted, however, since a seemingly worthless split might lead to a very good split below it. The preferred strategy is to grow a large tree, stopping the splitting process only when some minimum node size or tree depth is reached. Then this large tree is pruned using *cost-complexity* pruning. The cost-complexity is a function error and the tree depth is based on a limited increase of the impurity allowed.

Unlike a classification tree, in a regression tree, the value V associated with each leaf is not predetermined, but is instead a parameter that needs to be determined (learned) in addition to the parameters of tree depth and split threshold c. The associated leaf value V_j serves as the predicted value at node j. All the parameters are learned through the minimization of the error (or loss function) between the predicted values and the observed values.

Committee Machine

A single big tree is not stable because a single error in classification can propagate to the leaves. To overcome this shortcoming, an ensemble method or committee Machine can be used. An *ensemble method* or *committee machine* involves using multiple learning algorithms in order to obtain better predictive performance than could be obtained from any of the constituent learning algorithms (experts) alone. The committee machine might use a variety of algorithms to assimilate expert input into a single output, such as a decision. A committee machine learns by integrating the learning of experts via predetermined rules or through second level training. Commonly used ensemble learning methods, such as *Bagging*, *Boosting*, or *Random Forests*, can be used to remedy the instability resulting from error propagation.

Bootstrap aggregating (*Bagging*) is simply forming an average of many different trees that are generated from multiple training sets drawn with replacement. We illustrate why bagging might be a good solution to the problem of error propagation. Suppose that A, B, C, D, and E are the five members of a trial jury. Guilt or innocence for the defendant is determined by simple majority rule. There is a 5% chance that A gives the wrong verdict; for B, C, and D it is 10%, and E is mistaken with a probability of 20%. When the five jurors vote independently, the probability of bringing the wrong verdict is about 1%. Paradoxically, this probability increases to 1.5% if E (who is most probably mistaken) abandons his own judgment and always votes the same as A (who is least likely to be mistaken). Even more surprisingly, if the four jurors B, C, D, and E all follow A's vote, then the probability of delivering the wrong verdict is 5%, five times more than that when they vote independently (Chang, 2012, 2014). From this example, we can conclude that a committee decision can be better than individual decision. Applying this idea to the decision tree method leads us to the tree-averaging method, Bagging.

Similar to Bagging is *Boosting*. Weak classifiers $G_i(x)$ with values of either 1 or –1 from n samples are those whose misclassification error rates are only slightly better than random guessing. The predictions from all of them are then combined through a weighted majority vote to produce the final prediction:

$$G(x) = \text{sgn}\left(\sum_{i=1}^{n} w_i G_i(x)\right).$$

Here *sgn* is the sign function. The key is that weights w_1, w_2 ..., wn are computed by the boosting algorithm in such a way that more accurate classifiers in the sequence will get larger weights.

A *Random forest* is an ensemble classifier that consists of many decision trees and outputs the class that is the mode of the class's output by individual trees. The method combines Breiman's bagging idea and the random selection of features. There are many versions of random forest algorithms. For example, for each node of the tree, randomly choose m (smaller than the number of predictors) variables, based on which decision at that node is made. Calculate the best split based on these m variables in the training set.

D.4 Bayesian Networks

Bayesian networks can be used for molecular similarity search. A Bayesian Network (BN) is a simple and popular way for making probabilistic inference based on Bayes' rule:

$$P(E) = \frac{P(E \mid H)P(H)}{P(E)}$$

A Bayesian Network is a kind of directed acyclic graph with some special properties. The nodes of the BN represent random variables, the parents of a node are those judged to be direct causes for it. The roots of the network are the nodes without parents. The links represent causal relationships between these variables, and the strengths of these causal influences are expressed by conditional probabilities.

Coronary Heart Disease with a Bayesian Network

The package *bnlearn* in R can be used for Bayesian Network Structure Learning, Parameter Learning, and Inference. This package implements constraint-based, pairwise, score-based, and hybrid structure learning algorithms for discrete, Gaussian, and conditional Gaussian networks, along with many score functions and conditional independence tests. The Naive Bayes and the Tree-Augmented Naive Bayes (TAN) classifiers are also implemented. In addition, some utility functions and support for parameter estimation (maximum likelihood and Bayesian) and inference, conditional probability queries, and cross-validation are included. Figure A.13 is a BN of coronary heart disease data, a simple example of using the package. The factors included in the analysis are Smoking: no or yes,

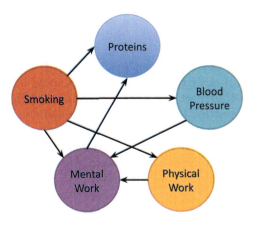

FIGURE A.13
Bayesian network for coronary disease.

Mental Work: strenuous or not, Physical Work: strenuous or not, Blood Pressure: Systolic BP <140 or not, and Proteins (Ratio of lipoproteins): < 3 or not. The conditional probabilities associated with the BN can be found elsewhere (Chang, 2020).

E: Unsupervised Learning

E.1 Basics of Unsupervised Learning

Unlike supervised learning, in unsupervised learning, there are no correct answers. The goal of unsupervised learning is to identify or simplify data structure. Unsupervised learning is of growing importance in a number of fields; examples are seen when a data scientist groups breast cancer patients by their genetic markers, shoppers by their browsing and purchase histories, or movie viewers by the ratings assigned by movie viewers. In so doing, one may want to organize documents into different mutually exclusive or overlapping categories, or one only might want to visualize the data.

Unsupervised learning problems can be further divided into clustering, association, and anomaly detection. A clustering problem occurs when we want to discover the inherent groupings in the data, such as grouping customers by purchasing behavior. An association-rule learning problem is one where we want to discover rules that describe connections in large portions of our data. An example would be when people who buy product *A* may also tend to buy product *B*. The third type of problem, anomaly detection or outlier detection, involves identifying items, events, or observations that do not conform to an expected pattern, such as instances of bank fraud, structural defects, medical problems, or errors in a text. Anomalies are also referred to as outliers, novelties, noise, deviations, and exceptions. In particular, in the context of abuse of computer networks and network intrusion detection, the interesting objects are often not rare objects, but unexpected bursts in activity. This pattern does not adhere to the common statistical definition of an outlier as a rare object. There are various outlier detection methods (Zimek and Schubert, 2017).

E.2 Association or Link Analysis

In many situations, finding causal relationships is the goal. When there are a larger number of variables, this task is not trivial. However, association is a necessary condition for a causal relationship. Finding a set of events that correlate with many others is often the focus point and springboard for further research. Link-analysis provides a way to find the event set with high probability density, bringing us closer to our ultimate goals. For example, finding sale items that are highly related (or frequently purchased together) can be very helpful for stocking shelves, cross-marketing in sales promotions, catalog design, and consumer segmentation based on buying patterns.

In network theory, link analysis is a data-analysis technique used to evaluate relationships (connections) between nodes. Relationships may be identified among various types of nodes (objects), including organizations, people, and transactions. Link analysis has been used in the investigation of criminal activity, computer security analysis, search engine optimization, market research, medical research, and even in understanding works of art.

Apriori, proposed by Agrawal and Srikant (1994), is an algorithm for finding frequently occurring sets of items in transactional databases. The algorithm proceeds by identifying the frequent individual items in the database and extending these to larger and larger sets of items as long as those item sets appear sufficiently often in the database. Apriori uses a bottom-up approach, where frequent subsets are extended one item at a time, and groups of candidates are tested against the data. The algorithm terminates when no further successful extensions are found.

Apriori uses *breadth-first search* and a *hash tree structure* to count candidate itemsets efficiently. It generates candidate itemsets of length k from item sets of length $k–1$, and then prunes those candidates that have an infrequent sub-pattern. According to the downward closure property, the candidate set contains all frequent k-length item sets.

Kuo et al. (2009) studied the suitability of the Apriori association analysis algorithm for the detection of adverse drug reactions (ADR) in healthcare data. The Apriori algorithm is used to perform association analysis on the characteristics of patients, the drugs they are taking, their primary diagnosis, comorbid conditions, and the ADRs they experience. The analysis produces association rules that indicate what combinations of medications and patient characteristics lead to ADRs.

E.3 Principal Component Analysis

Principal component analysis (PCA) is an important unsupervised learning tool for dimension reduction in drug design and discovery. Per Giuliani (2017), the reason that PCA is broadly used in the pharmaceutical industry is that it is a tool creating a statistical mechanics framework for biological systems modeling without the need for strong a priori theoretical assumptions. This makes PCA of the utmost importance, as it enables drug discovery from a systemic perspective, overcoming other too-narrow reductionist approaches.

As we discussed earlier in Section 3.9, attributes or predictors are generally correlated, making it difficult to interpret the effect of a predictor. Besides, the existence of associations indicates there are redundant predictors. That is, we can find a smaller set of predictors that can do the same job (prediction). The goal of PCA is to find such a smaller mutually independent (orthogonal) set of artificial predictors, one by one. The method is related to the eigenvalue and eigenvector of a matrix in linear algebra. The eigenvectors are artificial predictors, a set of linear combinations of the predictors that have maximal variance. PCA can be used as a tool for data pre-processing before supervised techniques are applied. PCA produces a low-dimensional representation of a dataset.

PCA, in a typical quantitative structure-activity relationship (QSAR) study in drug development, analyzes an original data matrix in which molecules are described by several correlated quantitative dependent variables (molecular descriptors). Although extensively applied, there is a disparity in the literature with respect to the applications of PCA in QSAR studies. Shahlaei (2017) investigated the different applications of PCA in QSAR studies using a dataset that included CCR5 inhibitors. The conclusion was that PCA is a powerful technique for exploring complex datasets in QSAR studies for the identification of outliers and can be easily applied to the pool of calculated structural descriptors.

A related method, principal component regression (PCR), is similar to a standard linear regression model but uses PCA for estimating the unknown regression coefficients in the model.

E.4 K-Means Clustering

Clustering refers to a very broad set of techniques for finding subgroups, or clusters, in a dataset. The goal of clustering is to find a partition of the data into distinct groups so that the observations within each group are quite similar to each other in some sense. Such a sense of similarity is often a domain-specific consideration that must be made based on knowledge of the data being studied. Earlier, when discussing SBML, we acknowledged that similarity is related to the purpose or outcome variable; therefore, the similarity must be related to some vague outcome or possible multiple outcomes/purposes. In libraries, we organize the books by different categories and sub-categories, although such selections of categories and sub-categories are based on customers' needs that are often not clearly defined. At home, we organize things into categories: clothes, shoes, kitchen utilities, and other categories, for convenience when we need to use them. Therefore, clustering must have some purposes that are difficult to clearly define.

A good clustering example in commerce would be clustering for market segmentation. Suppose we have access to big data (e.g., median household income, occupation, distance from the nearest urban area) for a large number of people who may or may not already be our customers. Our goal is to identify subgroups of people who might be more receptive to a particular form of advertising or to group them (in terms of data) according to the likelihood of purchasing a particular product.

Unlike PCA, which looks for a low-dimensional representation of the observations, clustering looks for homogeneous subgroups among the observations.

E.5 Hierarchical Clustering

Hierarchical clustering (HC) is another popular clustering method. In *K*-means clustering, we seek to partition the observations into a pre-specified number of clusters, while in hierarchical clustering we do not know in advance how many clusters we want. Instead,

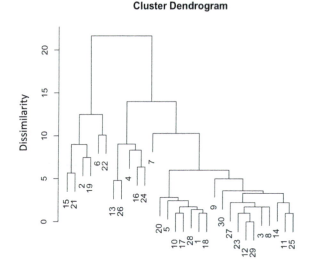

FIGURE A.14
Hierarchical clustering of 30 breast cancer patients.

hierarchical clustering will end up with a tree-like visual representation of the observations, called a *dendrogram*, that allows us to view at once the clustering obtained for each possible number of clusters (Figure A.14).

Hierarchical clustering seeks to build a hierarchy of clusters. Strategies for hierarchical clustering can be either *agglomerative* or *divisive*. An *agglomerative strategy* is a bottom-up approach, i.e., each observation starts in its own cluster, and pairs of clusters are merged as one moves up the hierarchy. A *divisive strategy* is a top-down approach, whereby all observations start in one cluster, and splits are performed recursively as one moves down the hierarchy.

Agglomerative Algorithm

1. Choose a dissimilarity measure between two subjects or clusters, e.g., the minimum Euclidian distance between subjects from two clusters.

2. In the set of n subjects, identify the most similar pair of subjects (with the minimum distance) and combine them into one cluster. Now there are $n-1$ clusters (a cluster can just have one subject).

3. Among the new set of $n-1$ clusters, identify the most similar pair of clusters with the smallest distance and combine them into one cluster.

4. Among the new set of $n-2$ clusters, identify the most similar pair of clusters based on the distance and combine them into one cluster.

5. This procedure continues until all n subjects have been combined into one cluster.

The R function *hclust*() implements hierarchical clustering in the Stats Package. In order to show a clear plot for the hierarchical clustering, only 30 patients from the *BreastCancer* dataset in *mlBench* package are used in the following analysis. The 9 different attributes included are cell thickness, size, shape, adhesion, etc. With the dendrogram, we can easily decide how many groups we want to divide patients into. For instance, if only 2 clusters are chosen, patients 15, 21, 2, 19, 6, and 22 will be in one cluster and the remaining patients will be in the other cluster. If 4 clusters are determined, patients 15, 21, 2, and 19 will be in cluster 1, patients 6 and 22 in cluster 2, patients 4, 13, 26, 16, and 24 in cluster 3, and the rest of the patients will be in cluster 4. The vertical axis presents dissimilarity between clusters. We can see that as the number of clusters increases, the dissimilarity decreases.

In the late 1990s, the United States National Cancer Institute conducted an anticancer drug discovery program in which, in successive years, approximately 10,000 compounds were screened in vitro against a panel of 60 human cancer cell lines from different organs (Shi et al., 1998). They tested approximately 62,000 compounds to collect information on activity patterns. Anticancer activity patterns of 112 ellipticine analogs were analyzed using a hierarchical clustering algorithm. A dramatic coherence between molecular structures and their activity patterns was discovered from the cluster tree: the first subgroup consisted principally of normal ellipticines, whereas the second subgroup consisted principally of N2-alkyl-substituted ellipticiniums. The ellipticiniums were more potent on average against p53 mutant cells than against p53 wild-type cells. This study, with its application of unsupervised learning, provided insights into the relationship between activity patterns of anticancer drugs and the molecular pharmacology of cancer.

The application of established drug compounds to new therapeutic indications, known as *drug repositioning*, offers several advantages over traditional drug development, including the reduction of both development time and costs. Sirota et al. (2011) used hierarchical clustering to predict novel therapeutic indications on the basis of comprehensive testing of molecular signatures in drug-disease pairs. Integrating gene expression measurements from 100 diseases and gene expression measurements on 164 drug compounds, the team rediscovered many known drug-disease relationships and predicted many new indications for these 164 drugs. They also experimentally validated some of the predictions.

Other applications include hierarchical clustering for large compound libraries (Böcker et al., 2005) and hierarchical cluster analysis in clinical research with a heterogeneous study population, focusing on visualization (Zhang et al., 2017).

E.6 Self-Organizing Maps

A *self-organizing map* (SOM) or self-organizing feature map (SOFM), is a type of artificial neural network (ANN) that is trained using unsupervised learning to produce a low-dimensional, discretized representation of the input space of the training samples, called a map. Here, dimension is not the feature dimension, but the number of data points.

Like most artificial neural networks, SOMs operate in two modes: training and mapping. Training builds the map using input examples, while mapping automatically classifies a new input vector. The output of an SOM can be visualized in the map space, which consists of components called nodes or neurons. The number of nodes (equivalent to clusters) is defined beforehand, usually in a finite two-dimensional region where nodes are arranged in a regular hexagonal or rectangular grid. The SOMs convert N data points in K-feature space to a collection of nodes (neurons) organized in a 2-dimensional space, called the map. Each node in the map has hidden K-features.

Yan (2006) applies self-organizing maps in compound pattern recognition and combinatorial library design. Schneider et al. (2009) used SOMs for compound library design, scaffold-hopping, and *repurposing*. Reker et al. (2014) used an SOM for identifying the macromolecular targets of de novo-designed chemical entities. Schneider and Schneider (2017) use an SOM for macromolecular target prediction. Researchers have also developed supervised SOMs for drug discovery (Xiao and Harris, 2006). Avram et al. (2014) used an SOM classifier for the prediction of inhibitors.

E.7 Remarks

Unsupervised learning is a critical foundation of supervised learning. Any application of supervised learning must involve some sort of unsupervised learning. We call this phenomenon *Entanglement of Supervised and Unsupervised Learning* (ESUL). For instance, when we decide which features need to be collected for our supervised learning model, we have already used implicitly unsupervised learning or clustering. That is, we perform simple clustering based on a certain set of features, instead of any other features, and assume that as long as two objects have identical values for these features their outcomes will be the same or similar, even though they might be different in other respects. Another example, where clustering is implicitly performed before any supervised learning, is when we decide the number of digits or decimal digits to keep in a set of measurements: we implicitly put objects with the same values into the same cluster, even though the rest of the decimal digits of their measurements might be different.

A clustering problem can be formulated as an unsupervised density problem. That is, find a subset (clusters) of data, such that the joint probability of data points belonging to the corresponding clusters is high (maximized). This optimization problem can be converted into a supervised problem (Chang, 2011; Hastie et al., 2001).

There are also ML problems situated between supervised and unsupervised learning, which can be solved via *Semi-Supervised Learning*. In semi-supervised learning problems, we have only parts of the input data labeled, and the rest are unlabeled. An example would be a photo archive where only some of the images (e.g., dogs, cats, persons) are labeled and a majority are not.

F: Reinforcement, Evolutionary, and SI Learning

F.1 Reinforcement Learning

The Concept of Reinforcement Learning

Reinforcement learning (RL) emphasizes learning through interaction with (real or virtual) environments. Feedback from one's environment is essential for learning. RL can be used when the correct answer is difficult to define or there are too many steps for the agent to take to complete the task. Taking a driverless car as an example, we cannot define the road conditions manually.

RL can be particularly useful in attacking problems that require strong interactions with different environments, such as self-cleaning vacuum cleaners and rescue robots. A rescue robot is a robot that has been designed for the purpose of rescuing people in mining accidents, urban disasters, hostage situations, and after explosions. The benefits of rescue robots to these operations include reduced personnel requirements, reduced fatigue, and access to otherwise unreachable areas. A well-known RL example is AlphaZero, a computer chess, shogi, and go player trained using RL. With just 24 hours of reinforcement learning, AlphaZero attained a truly amazing level of skill, defeating the three world-champion programs Stockfish Elmo, and AlphaGoZero.

Reinforcement learning can embody a model-based approach, such as a Markov decision process. The methods used to solve optimization problems include dynamic programming with either policy-based or value-based algorithms. Model-free RL techniques include Bayesian Q-learning, but there are also game-theory-based formulations. Chang (2010) discussed all of these approaches in the field of drug development. Czibula et al. (2015) proposed an RL model to solve the protein-folding problem, predicting the bidimensional structure of proteins in a hydrophobic-polar model.

The history of reinforcement learning has three threads. The first concerns learning by trial and error with roots in the psychology of animal learning. This thread runs through some of the earliest work in AI and led to the revival of reinforcement learning in the early 1980s. The second concerns the problem of optimal control and its solution using value functions and dynamic programming. For the most part, this thread did not involve learning. A third thread concerns temporal-difference methods such as used in the tic-tac-toe example (Sutton and Barto, 2018).

The origins of the first thread concerning temporal-difference learning are in part in animal learning psychology, in particular, in the notion of secondary reinforcers. A secondary reinforcer is a stimulus that has been paired with a primary reinforcer such as food or pain and, as a result, has come to take on similar reinforcing properties.

The second thread, an approach to optimal control problems in engineering, was developed in the mid-1950s by Richard Bellman and others through extending a nineteenth-century theory of Hamilton and Jacobi. The Bellman backward induction is a foundation for using Reinforcement Learning to solve a problem, known as dynamic programming (Bellman, 1957a, 1957b), and includes policy-iteration and value-iteration algorithms. In early AI, several researchers began to explore trial-and-error learning as an engineering principle. The earliest computational investigations of trial-and-error learning were perhaps by Minsky (1954, 1963) and by Farley and Clark (1954). RL is treated as a Markov decision problem that is similar to a Markov Chain, but with a reward and probability of moving to the next state, both associated with each action taken in the current state. However, in humanized agents, it is not a Markov Chain decision problem (MDP) because (1) the process is not a Markov chain due to the recursive patternization and because of hierarchical tokenization that involves more than two tokens, and (2) the environment involves not only non-living things, such as trees, cars, food, etc., but also humans or agents who have brains and can change behaviors according to Zda's actions. Therefore, an agent needs to determine the probability of taking each path (action) based on all parties involved, and those parties' actions and words.

As the third thread, Arthur Samuel (1959) was the first to propose and implement a learning method that included temporal-difference (TD) ideas as part of his celebrated checkers-playing program. TD learning is an unsupervised technique in which the learning agent learns to predict the expected value of a variable occurring at the end of a sequence of states. RL extends this technique by allowing the learned state-values to guide actions which subsequently change the state of the environment. Samuel's inspiration apparently came from Claude Shannon's (1950) suggestion that a computer could be programmed to use an evaluation function to play chess, and that it might be able to improve its play by modifying this function online. The temporal difference and optimal control threads were fully brought together in 1989 by Chris Watkins. In his work, Watkins extended and integrated prior work in all three threads of reinforcement learning research and developed Q-learning. Paul Werbos (1987) contributed to this integration by arguing for the convergence of trial-and-error learning and dynamic programming.

Beyond the agent and the environment, a reinforcement learning system usually involves four main sub-elements: a policy, a reward function, a value function, and, optionally, a model of the environment. A policy defines the learning agent's way of behaving at a given time. A policy is a mapping from perceived states of the environment to actions to be taken when in those states. It corresponds to what in psychology would be called a set of stimulus-response rules or associations.

A reward function in RL indicates what is good in an immediate sense, whereas a value function specifies what is good in the long run. The value of a state is the total amount of reward an agent can expect to accumulate over the future, starting from that state. Rewards determine the immediate, intrinsic desirability of environmental states, whereas values indicate the *long-term* desirability of states after taking into account the states that are likely to follow, and the rewards available in those states.

The reward function defines what are the good and bad events for the agent. For Zda, rewards can be a positive value (e.g., pleasure, energy boosting, appreciation by others) or a negative value (e.g., pain, augury). Zda has defined reward types; yet can add more reward types over his lifespan, which associate with the initial types of rewards.

Deep reinforcement learning (DRL) methods have driven impressive advances in AI in recent years. DRL is a combination of RL with deep learning neural networks. However, the concern has been raised that deep RL may simply be too slow to provide a plausible model of how humans learn. In the present review, Botvinick (2019) counters this critique by describing recently developed techniques that allow deep RL to operate more nimbly, solving problems much more quickly than previous methods.

F.2 Reinforcement Learning for Drug Development

Clinical Trial Phase Transition Probability

Clinical trials are often conducted in sequences in three phases. Sufficient positive results from a phase set off the next phase of the trial. Promising Phase 3 results will trigger the company's submission of a non-disclosure agreement to the regulatory agency for marketing approval. The results from earlier phases other than the immediate phase play only a minor role in the decision process. Such a transition process can be modeled by a Markov Chain (Figure A.15). The transitional probabilities (Table A.1) derived from a large database are valuable in RL for drug development (Chang, 2019). Among all 3583 Phase 1 trials for all disease indications, 63.2% successfully moved forward to Phase 2, and only 9.6% obtained regulatory approval for marketing. The transitional probability from one phase to another is simply the product of all the probabilities in between. These phase transitional probabilities are the probabilities of success on average. Different trial designs and many factors (actions) will change the probability of success. In fact, drug development is a sequence of decision processes. In each process, information and outcomes of an action are associated with uncertainties or probabilities. Therefore, a Markov chain is not sufficient; we have to use a sophisticated model that includes the action options. Stochastic modeling provides such a model.

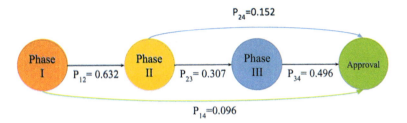

FIGURE A.15
Clinical trial phase transition probabilities.

A *Stochastic Decision Process* (SDP) is similar to a Markov chain, but there are also a decision (action) and cost associated at each state, a probability of reaching the next state, and the gain when the next state is successfully reached. Figure A.16 is an SDP for a typical clinical development program, which includes key design elements from Phase 1 and Phase 2 clinical trials. The actions here can be different clinical trial designs.

The success of a pharmaceutical company depends on integrating scientific, clinical, regulatory, and marketing approaches to the development and commercialization of therapies. Clinical development program (CDP) design offers several important benefits: (1) It eliminates unnecessary or redundant clinical trials used for internal decision-making; (2) It identifies and addresses critical path issues that could delay development timeliness; (3) It ensures that clinical programs focus quickly and unambiguously on key attributes of the compound.

The SDP provides a powerful AI framework for modeling the decision-making process in situations where outcomes are partly random and partly under the control of the decision-maker. Simulation-based RL is used to determine the set of actions or action rules (often called policy) that maximize the expected gain. A commonly used algorithm to

TABLE A.1

Phase Transition Probabilities of Clinical Trials

	No. of Test Drugs	Phase 1 to Phase 2	Phase 2 to Phase 3	Phase 3 to Approval
Hematology	86	73.3%	56.6%	63.0%
Infectious disease	247	69.5%	42.7%	64.5%
Ophthalmology	66	84.8%	44.6%	45.2%
Other	96	66.7%	39.7%	61.5%
Metabolic	95	61.1%	45.2%	55.5%
Gastroenterology	41	75.6%	35.7%	55.9%
Allergy	37	67.6%	32.5%	67.0%
Endocrine	299	58.9%	40.1%	55.9%
Respiratory	150	65.3%	29.1%	67.3%
Urology	21	57.1%	32.7%	61.2%
Autoimmune	297	65.7%	31.7%	53.5%
Neurology	462	59.1%	29.7%	47.8%
Cardiovascular	209	58.9%	24.1%	46.7%
Psychiatry	154	53.9%	23.7%	49.0%
Oncology	1222	62.8%	24.6%	33.0%
All Indications	**3582**	**63.2%**	**30.7%**	**49.6%**

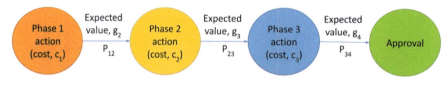

FIGURE A.16
Stochastic decision process for CDP.

find the optimal solution is the backward induction method, when the SDP is memoryless or a *Markov Decision Process*. The backward induction algorithm is derived from *Bellman's optimality principle*, and this is described elsewhere (Chang, 2010). Bellman's Optimality Principle can be stated thus: An optimal policy has the property that, whatever the initial state and initial decisions are, the remaining decisions must constitute an optimal policy with regard to the state resulting from the first decision.

RL with *Monte Carlo* simulations can provide a rational basis for decision-making and help in optimizing a compound's regulatory strategy and determining its position and value. Simulation of CDPs can increase the confidence in decision-making and help to define and track critical success factors and their uncertainties.

F.3 Genetic Algorithms and Genetic Programming

Genetic Algorithms

A genetic algorithm (GA), the name inspired by Darwin's theory of evolution, is an AI algorithm designed to solve an optimization problem. John Holland introduced genetic algorithms in 1960, and his student David Goldberg extended the GA idea in 1989. A typical genetic algorithm requires: (1) a genetic representation of the solution domain, (2) a fitness function to evaluate the solution domain, and (3) crossover and mutation operations.

Initialization: Generate an initial population, usually by random selection.

Natural Selection: During each successive generation, a portion of the existing population is selected to breed a new generation. Individual solutions are selected through a fitness-based random selection process. The fitness function is defined over the genetic representation and measures the quality of the represented solution. The fitness function is problem-dependent.

Genetic Operators: A genetic operator is an operator used in genetic algorithms to guide the algorithm toward a solution to a given problem. Crossover and mutation are the main types of genetic operators, but it is possible to use other operators, such as colonization-extinction and migration. The mutation probability is usually smaller than the crossover probability. A very small mutation rate may lead to genetic drift, whereas a mutation rate that is too high may lead to loss of good solutions. A recombination rate that is too high may lead to premature convergence of the genetic algorithm.

Termination: Termination can occur if one of the following conditions is met:

1. A good-enough solution is found.
2. The maximum number of generations is reached.
3. The highest-ranking solution's fitness has reached a plateau such that successive iterations cannot make significant improvements.

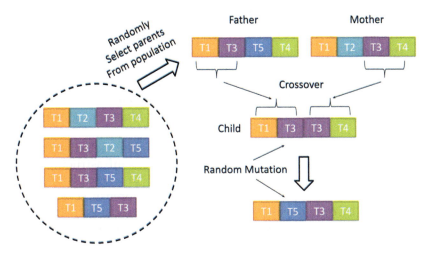

FIGURE A.17
Genetic algorithm for optimal treatment sequence search.

GAs can and have been used in medical fields. Infertility is a condition for which a GA can be applied to discover the most appropriate treatment. To treat infertility there are several options. The sequence of interventions is believed to be important, in addition to the demographic and baseline characteristics. There are many possible treatment courses, but randomly or exhaustively trying out the treatment sequences is inefficient or impossible. It is believed that if a long sequence of treatments is effective, then a partial sequence will likely retain partial effectiveness. If this assumption is true, then a GA might be a better way to search for the best treatment sequence. The basic idea is to view a treatment sequence composed of T1, T2, T2, T4, and T5 as a short DNA sequence in the GA (Figure A.17). A death (removal) of a treatment sequence can be defined by treatment failure. Through natural selection, better treatment sequences will survive long and dominate in the population, and thus have a better chance to be selected for multiplying than poor treatment sequences. The best treatment sequence(s) will survive in the end (Chang, 2020).

Ghaheri et al. (2015) introduced the genetic algorithm and its applications in medicine. They reviewed applications in disease screening, diagnosis, treatment planning, pharmacovigilance, prognosis, and health care management. Ghaheri et al. (2015) provided a comprehensive review of the applications of genetic algorithms in 14 areas of medicine: radiology, oncology, cardiology, endocrinology, obstetrics and gynecology, pediatrics, surgery, infectious diseases, pulmonology, radiotherapy, rehabilitation medicine, orthopedics, neurology, pharmacotherapy, and health-care management.

Genetic Programming

The term *genetic programming* was coined by Goldberg in 1983. Genetic programming (GP), like GA, is inspired by our understanding of biological evolution. It is an evolutionary computation (EC) technique that automatically solves problems without requiring the user to know or specify the form or structure of the solution in advance. At the most abstract level, GP is a systematic, domain-independent method for getting computers to solve problems automatically, starting from a high-level statement of what needs to be done (Poli et al., 2008). The idea of genetic programming is to evolve a population of computer programs. The aim is that, generation by generation, GP techniques will stochastically transform populations of programs into new populations of programs that will effectively solve problems under consideration. Like evolution in nature, GP has, in fact, been successful at developing novel and unexpected ways of solving problems. GP is similar to GA, but there are differences. The main difference is that individuals in GA are represented by one-dimensional strings, while individuals in GP are represented by tree structures.

GPs have proliferated, with applications in many fields, including: code-breaking, hardware bug detection, robotics, mobile communications infrastructure optimization, mechanical engineering, work scheduling, the design of water distribution systems, natural language processing (NLP), the construction in forensic science of facial composites of suspects by eyewitnesses, airlines revenue engagement, trading systems in the financial sector, software synthesis and repair, image processing, cellular encoding, *symbolic regression*, feature selection and classification, and sound synthesis in the audio industry (Langdon and Buxton, 2004). The series of 4 edited books on GP applications (Koza, 2010) collected 77 results where GP was human-competitive. GP has been successfully used as an automatic programming tool, a machine learning tool, and an automatic problem-solving engine. GP is especially useful in the domains where the exact form of the solution is not known in advance or when an approximate solution is acceptable.

In drug discovery, GP has been used for RNA structure prediction, molecular structure optimization, and for mining DNA chip data from cancer patients. Ghosh and Jain (2005) assembled articles across a broad range of topics on the applications of evolutionary AI in drug discovery. Barmpalex et al. (2011) used symbolic regression via genetic programming in the optimization of a controlled release pharmaceutical formulation and compared its predictive performance to artificial neural network (ANN) models. Their results showed that the predictive ability of GP on an external validation set was higher than that of the ANNs.

F.4 Cellular Automata

A *cellular automaton* (CA) is used to model both temporal and spatiotemporal processes. CAs normally consist of large numbers of identical cells that form a lattice (like a chessboard) with defined interaction rules.

Cellular automata, invented in the late 1940s by John von Neumann and Stanislaw Ulam, have been used to model a wide range of processes seen in image processing, virtual music creation, and physics (https://mathworld.wolfram.com/GameofLife.html). They also have a long history in biological modeling. Indeed, one of the first and most interesting CA simulations in biology is Conway's Game of Life (Berlekamp et al., 1982). The CA is simple but very capable. For example, in one application, there is a finite initial state such that any paragraph of English prose, when properly coded as a sequence of gliders (cell patterns that move across the lattice), will result in a "spell-checked" paragraph of English prose, again coded as a sequence of gliders.

The rules of CA can be defined in many ways. Here is a simple example (Chang, 2011): An occupant of a cell with fewer than two neighbors will, sadly, die of loneliness; with 2 or 3 neighbors, it will continue into the next generation; with 4 or more neighbors, it will die of over-excitement!

The objects (cells or proteins) in a CA simulation usually do not move: they only appear, change properties, or disappear. Thus, objects' properties and information are the only things that "move". In a variation on the CA model known as a dynamic cellular automaton (DCA), objects can exhibit motion (Wishart et al., 2005). We can apply random walks or other stochastic processes to DCAs. Depending on the implementation of the DCA algorithm, molecules can move one or more cells in a single time step. DCA models permit considerably more flexibility in simulating biological processes (Materi and Wishart, 2007).

Examples of CA applications in the pharmaceutical industry include drug release in bio-erodible microspheres (Zygourakis and Markenscoff, 1996), lipophilic drug diffusion and release (Fathi et al., 2013), drug-carrying micelle formation (Kier, 1996), the progression of HIV/AIDS, HIV treatment strategies (Santos and Coutinho, 2001), and the simulation of different drug therapies or combination therapies. Some CA models have the capacity to model extreme time scales (days to decades) efficiently and to simulate the spatial heterogeneity of viral infections.

F.5 Swarm Intelligence Learning

Concept of Swarm Intelligence

Systems in which organized behavior arises without a centralized controller or leader are often called *self-organized systems*, while the intelligence possessed by the system is called *swarm intelligence* (SI) or *collective intelligence*. Examples of swarm intelligence in nature include ant colonies, bird flocking, hawks hunting, animal herding, bacterial growth, fish schooling, and microbial intelligence.

Let's look into how ant colonies forage for food and find the shortest path leading to a food source quickly (Figure A.18). The process unfolds as follows. Several ants leave their nest to forage for food, randomly following different paths. Ants continue to release pheromones (a chemical produced by an organism that signals its presence to other members of the same species) during the food search process. Such pheromones on the path will

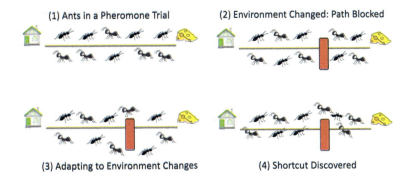

FIGURE A.18
Swarm Intelligence: ants adapt to environmental changes.

gradually disperse over time. Those ants reaching a food source along the shortest path are sooner to reinforce that path with pheromones, because they are sooner to come back to the nest with food; those that subsequently go out foraging find a higher concentration of pheromones on the shortest path, and therefore have a greater tendency (higher probability) to follow it. In this way, ants collectively build up and communicate information about locations, and this information adapts to changes in the environmental conditions! The SI emerges from the simple rule: follow the smell of pheromones. Mimicking the activity of ant colonies, the ant algorithm and other swarm intelligence algorithms have contributed to the advancement of AI technologies.

The SI characteristics of a human network integrate two correlated perspectives on human behavior: cognitive space and social space. In SI, we see the evolution of collective ideas, not the evolution of people who hold ideas. Evolutionary processes have costs: redundancy and futile exploration. Such processes are necessary to be adaptive and creative. The system parameters of SI determine the balance of exploration and exploitation.

An SI algorithm comprises a population of individuals that interact with one another according to simple rules in order to solve problems. Individuals in an SI system have mathematical intelligence (logical thought) and social intelligence (a common social mind). Social interaction thus provides a powerful problem-solving algorithm in SI.

An ant is simple and (arguably) dumb, while a colony of ants is complex and intelligent. Likewise, neurons are simple but brains are as complex as a swarm. Competition and collaboration among cells lead to human intelligence; competition and collaboration among humans form a social intelligence, or what we might call the global brain. Nevertheless, such intelligence is based on a human viewpoint, and thus it lies within the limits of human intelligence. Views of such intelligence held by other creatures with a different level of intelligence could be completely different!

SI has some similarities to *ensemble intelligence* (EI), but they are different in that each individual in SI has no intelligence, while each individual in EI is usually an expert. SI is necessarily the consequence of collective dumbness, a result of collaboration, while EI can be just the best opinion among or average opinion of the experts without any collaboration at all. Another difference is that SI requires a larger population of the same type of individuals, while a "population" in EI populations usually only involves a small set of individuals obtained by different methods.

SI is also different from reinforcement learning. In reinforcement learning, an individual can improve his level of intelligence over time since, in the learning process, adaptations occur. In contrast, SI is a collective intelligence from all individuals. It is a global or macro behavior of a system. In complex systems there are a huge number of individual components, each with relatively simple rules of behavior that never change. However, in reinforcement learning, there are not necessarily a large number of individuals; in fact, there can just be one individual with built-in complex algorithms or adaptation rules.

Ant Algorithm

An ant routing algorithm, introduced by Dorigo (1992), was inspired by the food-foraging behavior of ants hunting the shortest or fastest route. Its key algorithm can be described as follows:

1. Ants lay pheromones on the trail when they move food back to their nest.
2. Pheromones accumulate with multiple ants using the same path, evaporating when no ants pass by.

3. Each ant always tries to choose trails having higher pheromone concentrations.

4. In a fixed time period, ant agents are launched into a network, each agent going from a source to a destination node.

5. The ant agent maintains a list of visited nodes and the time elapsed in getting there. When an ant agent arrives at its destination, it will return to the source following the same path by which it arrived, updating the digital pheromone value on the links that it passes by. The slower the link, the lower the pheromone value will be.

6. At each node, the ant colony will use the digital pheromone value as the transitional probability for deciding the ant (data) transit route.

Particle Swarm Optimization

Particle swarm optimization (PSO), one of the bio-inspired algorithms, is a stylized representation of the movement of organisms in a bird flock to search for a problem's optimal solution. PSO is a metaheuristic, as it makes few or no assumptions about the problem being optimized and can search very large spaces of candidate solutions. PSO does not use the gradient of the problem being optimized. However, PSO does not guarantee an optimal solution is ever found. Each particle's movement is influenced by its local best known position, but is also guided toward the best known positions in the search-space. This is expected to move the swarm toward the best solutions.

A basic variant of the PSO algorithm works by having a population (called a swarm) of candidate solutions (called particles). These particles are moved around in the search-space in three possible directions: (1) the personal best direction, (2) the swarm's best-known direction, and (3) its current direction. We can randomly decide on one of the three directions or take a weighted three-directional vector. The process is repeated and by doing so it is hoped, but not guaranteed, that a satisfactory solution will eventually be discovered. Figure A.19 illustrates how a three-person team climbs to a mountaintop using the PSO search strategy.

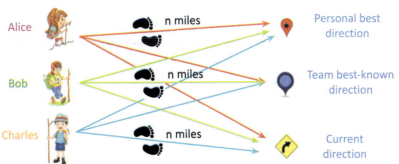

Goal: A team of Three to Find a Mountain's Summit

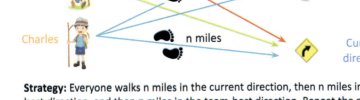

Strategy: Everyone walks n miles in the current direction, then n miles in the personal best direction, and then n miles in the team-best direction. Repeat the process

FIGURE A.19
A three-mountaineer team uses PSO.

F.6 Swarm Intelligence in Drug Discovery

If you were to construct an exhaustive list of swarm intelligence-based applications, your list would include complex interactive virtual environment generation in the movie industry, cargo arrangement in airline companies, route scheduling for delivery companies, packet routing in telecommunication networks, power grid optimization controls, data clustering and data routing in sensor networks, unmanned vehicle control in the U.S. military, and planetary mapping and micro-satellite control as used by NASA (Chang, 2020).

In the drug development process, a central feature is the prediction of the complex structure of a small ligand with a protein, the so-called *protein-ligand docking* problem, used in virtual screening of large databases and lead optimization. Korb et al. (2006) developed a new docking algorithm called PLANTS (Protein-Ligand ANTSystem), based on ant colony optimization, to facilitate structure-based drug design. An artificial ant colony is employed to find a minimum energy conformation of the ligand in the protein's binding site. The algorithm showed higher efficiency than a genetic algorithm.

Molecular docking is critically important for a ligand binding to the intended site, which is essential for a small molecular drug to take effect. Fu et al. (2015) studied a new approach for flexible molecular docking based on SI. They computed the interactions of 23 protein-ligand complexes. The experimental results show that their approach leads to substantially lower docking energy and higher docking precision in comparison to the Lamarckian genetic algorithm and the QPSO algorithm alone. This suggests that the novel algorithm may be used to dock a ligand with many rotatable bonds with high accuracy.

Protein essentiality is fundamental to comprehending the function and evolution of genes. The prediction of protein essentiality is pivotal in identifying disease genes and potential drug targets. Fang et al. (2018) presented a novel feature selection called the elite search mechanism-based flower pollination algorithm, used to determine protein essentiality. ESFPA uses an improved SI algorithm for feature selection and selects optimal features for protein essentiality prediction. The first step is to collect numerous features with the highly predictive characteristics of essentiality. The second step is to develop a feature selection strategy based on a SI algorithm to obtain an optimal feature subset. Then, an elite search mechanism is adopted to further improve the quality of the feature subset. The experimental results show that this SI method is competitive with some well-known feature selection methods.

Rajeshkumar and Kousalya (2017) presented a review of applications of SI algorithms in the pharmaceutical industry, including drug design, pharmacovigilance, and alignment of sequence. Soulami et al. (2017) used a particle swarm optimization (PSO) based algorithm for detection and classification of abnormalities in mammographic images by using texture features and support vector machine (SVM) classifiers.

G: Natural Language Processing

G.1 Syntax & Semantics of Language: Tokenization

Natural language processing (NLP) is an AI approach in dealing with the interactions between computers and human language, in particular, how one can program computers to process and analyze large amounts of natural language data. The applications of NLP include Chatbot, sentimental analysis, information extraction, spelling correction, speech recognition, machine translation, and predictive testing.

The Syntax and Semantics of Language involve structure and meaning of written text. For some languages, this may require preprocessing such as stemming, such as changing words, give, gave, gives, and given to give. Similarly, lemmatization is unifying the verb forms, e.g., changing words, gone, going, and went to go. Stop words are those words in the text which do not add any meaning to the sentence and whose removal will reduce the dimension of the feature set. Other preprocesses include Tokenization, Normalization, and tagging Parts of Speech.

Tokenization is breaking the raw text into small chunks, words or sentences, called tokens. These tokens help in understanding the context or developing the model for the NLP.

There are various tokenization techniques. Given a sentence or paragraph, White Space Tokenization tokenizes into words by splitting the input whenever a white space is encountered. This is the fastest tokenization technique. It will work for languages (e.g., English, but not Chinese) in which the white space breaks apart the sentence into meaningful words. Dictionary Based Tokenization is based on the tokens in the dictionary. If the token is not found, then special rules are used to tokenize it. Regular Expression Tokenizer uses regular expressions to control the tokenization of text into tokens. Penn TreeBank Tokenization is based on a tree corpus bank which gives the semantic and syntactic annotation of language. Penn Treebank is one of the largest treebanks.

G.2 Word Embeddings and Language Models

There are several different types of language models, each with their own strengths and weaknesses. Here are some examples of different language models:

N-gram models: These models are based on the frequency of sequences of words in a corpus of text. They work by counting the frequency of each n-gram (a sequence of n words or other units) in the corpus and using this information to predict the next word in a sentence.

A skip-gram model is a type of language model that is based on the idea of predicting context words, given a target word. It is often used in conjunction with n-gram models to improve the performance of language modeling.

Feedforward neural network models: These models use a feedforward neural network to predict the next word in a sentence based on the previous words. They work by encoding the previous words as a fixed-length vector and using this vector as input to the neural network.

Recurrent neural network (RNN) models: These models use a recurrent neural network to predict the next word in a sentence based on the previous words. They work by maintaining an internal state that represents the context of the sentence so far and using this state to generate the next word.

Convolutional neural network (CNN) models: These models use a convolutional neural network to predict the next word in a sentence based on the previous words. They work by treating the input sequence as an image and using convolutional filters to extract features from the sequence.

Transformer models: These models are based on the Transformer architecture, which uses a self-attention mechanism to process input sequences and capture long-range dependencies between their elements. Transformer models, such as GPT (Generative Pre-trained Transformer), have achieved state-of-the-art performance on a wide range of natural language processing tasks.

These are just a few examples of different types of language models, and there are many variations and hybrids of these models that have been developed. The choice of language model depends on the specific natural language processing task and the available data.

A distributional semantic model is a type of NLP model that represents the meaning of words based on their distributional properties. The underlying assumption is that words that appear in similar contexts tend to have similar meanings but they differ in a number of ways. CBOW, SkipGram, and GPT models all use word embeddings and are distributional semantic models.

Word embedding is a real-valued vector representation (encoding) of the meaning of words for text analysis, wherein words that are closer in the vector space are expected to be similar in meaning. Word embeddings can be obtained using a set of language modeling and feature learning techniques where words or phrases from the vocabulary are mapped to vectors of real numbers. Word embeddings are considered to be among a small number of successful applications of unsupervised learning at present. The fact that they do not require pricey annotation is probably their main benefit.

The term *word embeddings* was originally coined by Bengio et al. (2003) who trained them in neural language modeling. Collobert and Weston (2008) demonstrated that word embeddings trained on an adequately large dataset carry syntactic and semantic meaning and improve performance on downstream tasks. Mikolov et al. (2013) proposed the Continuous Bag-of-Words (CBOW), which brought word embedding to the fore through the creation of word2vec, and was based on a toolkit enabling the training and use of pre-trained embeddings. Unlike a language model that can only base its predictions on past words, as it is assessed based on its ability to predict each next word in the corpus, a model that only aims to produce accurate word embeddings is not subject to such a restriction. The word2vec algorithm uses a neural network model to learn word associations from a large corpus of text. Once trained, such a model can detect synonymous words or suggest additional words for a partial sentence. A year later, Pennington et al. (2014) introduced GloVe, a competitive set of pre-trained embeddings, suggesting that using word embeddings was suddenly among the mainstream. Rather than using the surrounding words to predict the center word as with CBOW, a skip-gram (Mikolov et al., 2013) uses the center word to predict the surrounding words.

Word embedding is a way to quantify the semantics. We want to represent words in such a manner that it captures its meaning in a way humans do—not the exact meaning of the word, but a contextual one. For example, when I say the word *run,* we know exactly what action, i.e., the context.

What are good quality word embeddings and how can we generate them? The simplest word embedding you can have is using one-hot vectors. If you have V = 10,000 words in your vocabulary, then you can represent each word as a $1 \times 10{,}000$ vector. In a simpler example, if we have 4 words, *apple, tiger, river,* and *train,* in our vocabulary then we can represent them as follows: *apple* = [1, 0, 0, 0], *tiger* = [0, 1, 0, 0], *river* = [0, 0, 1, 0], *train* = [0, 0, 0, 1]. If you have only 3 words (*tea, tiger, train*) in your vocabulary, then a one-hot coding system will be: *tea* = [1, 0, 0], *tiger* = [0, 1, 0], and *train* = [0, 0, 1]. However, such coding will miss the entire purpose of creating embeddings, i.e., to capture the contextual meaning of the words, because it fails to capture the correlation between words. There are various methods of learning correlations between words.

As we discussed in Part I Section 4.1, Connotation of Understanding, understanding text is mapping between symbols. Thus, which symbols (words) are used is not important, but the relative location of a word in the text determines the meaning of the word. Neighboring words determine a word's meaning. This is the notion of distributional semantics, a research area that develops and studies theories and methods for quantifying and categorizing semantic similarities between linguistic items based on their distributional properties in large samples of language data. This contextual text understanding in distributional semantic space turns out to be essential in natural language applications related to text understanding, knowing the other factors such as tone and physical environment may also play roles in determining meaning.

Both the CBOW and Skip-gram models can learn the underlying word representations for a word by using neural networks. In the CBOW model, the distributed representations of context (or surrounding words) are combined to predict the word in the middle. But in the Skip-gram model, the distributed representation of the input word is used to predict the context.

A prerequisite for any supervised neural network training is having labeled training data. Unlike the classification ANN to predict an object from an input image, the training goal in the Skip-gram model is to learn the weights of the hidden layer that are actually the "word vectors" that we're trying to determine. We'll define a neighboring word by the window size (hyperparameter).

Regarding the choice of the two models, Skip-gram works well with a small amount of the training data and represents well even for rare words or phrases, while CBOW will be several times faster to train than the skip-gram and have slightly better accuracy for frequently seen words (Figure A.20).

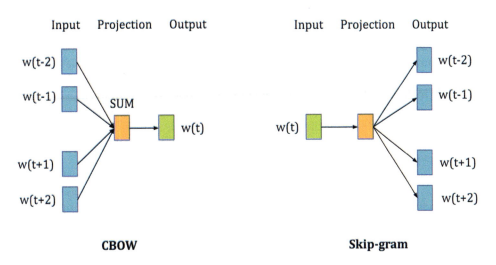

FIGURE A.20
CBOW and skip-gram models with window size of two.

G.3 ChatGPT and Relevant Architecture

ChatGPT is a state-of-the-art language model architecture developed by OpenAI. It was first introduced in a research paper titled "Language Models are Unsupervised Multitask Learners" by Alec Radford, Karthik Narasimhan, Tim Salimans, and Ilya Sutskever in 2018.

GPT models work on a principle called autoregressive which is similar to one used in RNN. It is a technique where the previous output becomes current input. The semi-supervised learning includes first performing unsupervised pre-training and then supervised fine-tuning. GPT model was based on Transformer architecture. It was made of decoders stacked on top of each other (12 decoders).

The architecture of ChatGPT is based on the Transformer, a neural network architecture that was introduced in a research paper titled "Attention is All You Need" by Ashish Vaswani and his colleagues in 2017. The Transformer uses a self-attention mechanism to process input sequences and capture long-range dependencies between their elements.

ChatGPT extends the Transformer architecture by pre-training a large neural network on vast amounts of text data, using a language modeling task. This pre-training enables the model to capture a wide range of language patterns and generate high-quality natural language output. The pre-training process involves training the model on large amounts of text data to learn to predict the next word in a sentence, given the previous words.

The final architecture of ChatGPT includes a stack of transformer blocks, each consisting of a multi-head self-attention mechanism, followed by a feedforward neural network. The output of the final block is then fed into a linear projection layer, which is used to predict the next word in a sentence or generate text. GPT-3 learning corpus consists of the dataset that includes 45TB of textual data or most of the internet. GPT-3 is 175 Billion parameter models as compared to 10–100 Trillion parameters in a human brain.

ChatGPT is a versatile architecture that has been fine-tuned for a wide range of natural language processing tasks, such as language translation, text summarization, question-answering, and conversational AI.

Generative ANNs differ from discriminative ANNs. Discriminative ANNs aim to classify an input into one of several predefined categories. The model is trained to find the boundary between the categories in the feature space and make predictions based on the closest boundary. Generative ANNs, on the other hand, aim to model the distribution of the data and generate new samples that are similar to the ones seen during training. These models are trained to estimate the probability of the input data given the class labels, and then generate new data based on this estimate. For instance, generative models can generate new data instances. They are used to generate new photos of animals that look like real animals, while a discriminative model could tell a dog from a cat. A generative language model is a probability distribution over sequences of words. It is used to generate new text that is similar to the training data. A discriminative model is used to classify input data into one of several categories.

The multi-head self-attention mechanism is a key component of the Transformer architecture, which is used in state-of-the-art natural language processing models such as GPT.

Self-attention is a way for the model to focus on different parts of the input sequence when processing it. In traditional recurrent neural networks (RNNs), information flows in one direction through a sequence of hidden states, and the model's attention is distributed evenly across all the previous states. In contrast, self-attention allows the model to look back at any position in the input sequence and weigh the importance of each position for the current prediction.

Multi-head self-attention extends the basic self-attention mechanism by allowing the model to attend to different subspaces of the input sequence simultaneously. The model projects the input sequence into multiple subspaces, and then computes self-attention for each subspace. This is achieved by splitting the input into multiple parallel representations, each with a different set of weights. The self-attention calculation is then performed separately on each representation, and the results are concatenated and fed through a linear layer to produce the final output.

The benefit of using multi-head self-attention is that it allows the model to attend to different aspects of the input sequence in parallel. This can help to capture complex and long-range relationships between different parts of the input and lead to improved performance on a wide range of natural language processing tasks. This is different from Humanized Architecture in this book, where the complex, long-range relationships are captured through recursions of hierarchical patterns

There are several key differences between the skip-gram model and GPT:

The word's context in the skip-gram model does not include the next word. The skip-gram model works by taking a single word as input and predicting the words that are likely to appear in its context. The context of a word is defined as the words that appear within a fixed-size window around the word in a sentence or text corpus.

In contrast, the GPT language model is pre-trained on a language modeling task that involves predicting the next word in a sequence of words, given the previous words. In this case, the context of a word does include the previous words in the sequence as well as any relevant information that might come from the larger context, such as the topic or genre of the text.

Training data: The skip-gram model is trained on a large corpus of text, but it only learns to predict the context words for a given target word. In contrast, GPT is pre-trained on a language modeling task, which involves predicting the next word in a sentence given the previous words. This task requires the model to capture a wide range of language patterns and contexts and to generate natural-sounding text.

Model architecture: The skip-gram model is based on a simple neural network architecture, whereas GPT is based on the more complex Transformer architecture, which uses a self-attention mechanism to capture long-range dependencies between elements of the input sequence.

Application: The skip-gram model is primarily used for learning word embeddings, which can be used in a wide range of natural language processing tasks. GPT, on the other hand, is a more general-purpose language model that can be fine-tuned on a variety of tasks, such as language translation, text summarization, and conversational AI.

GPT and Stable Diffusion are two different generative models that are used in natural language processing (NLP) and other fields, but they are different.

GPT is a language model that is based on the Transformer architecture and is pre-trained on a large corpus of text using a language modeling task, which involves predicting the next word in a sentence given the previous words. GPT uses a self-attention mechanism to capture long-range dependencies between elements of the input sequence, and it can be fine-tuned on a variety of NLP tasks.

Stable Diffusion, on the other hand, is a recently proposed generative model that is based on the concept of diffusion, a process that describes how particles spread out over time. In the Stable Diffusion model, each element of the input sequence is represented as a particle that diffuses over time, with the diffusion process controlled by a set of parameters that are learned during training. The model generates new samples by starting with a noise vector and gradually diffusing it over time to generate a sequence of words or other output.

Furthermore, there are several key differences between GPT and Stable Diffusion as elaborated below.

Model architecture: GPT is based on the Transformer architecture, which uses self-attention to capture long-range dependencies, while Stable Diffusion is based on a diffusion process that is controlled by learned parameters.

Training data: GPT is typically pre-trained on a large corpus of text, while Stable Diffusion can be trained on a variety of data types, including images and sound.

Performance: While both models are capable of generating high-quality text, Stable Diffusion has been shown to outperform GPT on some text generation tasks, particularly those that require generating longer sequences of text or more complex language structures.

Applicability: GPT is a more general-purpose language model that can be fine-tuned on a wide range of NLP tasks, while Stable Diffusion is a more flexible generative model that can be applied to a variety of data types beyond text, including image and audio generation.

When we code the language and events using parallel and sequential text strings, GPT can potentially be used for Humanized AI development.

References

Agrawal, R. and Srikant, R. (1994). Fast Algorithms for Mining Association Rules. Proceedings of the 20th VLDB Conference, Santiago, Chile.

Agrebi, S. and Larbi, A. (2020). Use of Artificial Intelligence in Infectious Diseases. Artificial Intelligence in Precision Health. https://doi.org/10.1016/B978-0-12-817133-2.00018-5

Afzal, N., Sohn, S., Abram, S. and Scott, C.G. (2017). Mining Peripheral Arterial Disease Cases from Narrative Clinical Notes Using Natural Language Processing. Journal of Vascular Surgery, 65: 1753–1756.

Akay, M.F. (2009). Support Vector Machines Combined with Feature Selection for Breast Cancer Diagnosis. Expert Systems with Applications, 36: 32403247.

Aleksander, I. and Morton, H. (2007). Depictive Architectures for Synthetic Phenomenology. In A. Chella & R. Manzotti (eds.), Artificial Consciousness. Exeter: Imprint Academic, pp. 67–81.

Anthimopoulos, M., et al. (2016). Lung Pattern Classification for Interstitial Lung Diseases Using a Deep Convolutional Neural Network. IEEE Transactions on Medical Imaging, 35(5): 1207–1216.

Arkin, R.C. (1998). Behavior-Based Robotics. Cambridge, MA: MIT Press.

Avram, S., et al. (2014). Self-Organizing Map Classification of MEK1 Inhibitors. Revue Roumaine de Chimie, 60(2–3): 167–173.

Bain, A. (1855). The Senses and the Intellect. London: John W. Parker and Son, West Strand.

Balogh, E.P., et al. (2015). Improving Diagnosis in Health Care. Washington, DC: The National Academies Press.

Baum, D. (2008). Reading a Phylogenetic Tree: The Meaning of Monophyletic Groups. Nature Education, 1(1): 190.

Burden, D. and Savin-Baden, M. (2020). Virtual Humans: Today and Tomorrow (Chapman & Hall/CRC Artificial Intelligence and Robotics Series) (1st ed.). Boca Raton, FL: Chapman and Hall/CRC.

Castro, V.M., et al. (2017). Large-Scale Identification of Patients with Cerebral Aneurysms Using Natural Language Processing. Neurology, 88: 164–168.

Barmpalex, P., et al. (2011). Symbolic Regression via Genetic Programming in the Optimization of a Controlled Release Pharmaceutical Formulation. Chemometrics and Intelligent Laboratory Systems, 107(1): 75–82.

Bellman, R. (1957a). A Markovian decision process. Journal of Mathematics and Mechanics 6.

Bellman, R. (1957b). Dynamic Programming. Princeton University Press, Princeton, NJ.

Bengio, Y., Ducharme, R., Vincent, P. and Janvin, C. (2003). A Neural Probabilistic Language Model. The Journal of Machine Learning Research, 3: 1137–1155.

Berlekamp, E., Conway, J. and Guy, R. (1982). Winning Ways for Your Mathematical Plays, Volume 1: Games in General. New York, NY: Academic Press.

Bermudez, L. (Feb 9, 2021). Overview of Embodied Artificial Intelligence. Machine Vision. Retrieved from https://medium.com/machinevision/overview-of-embodied-artificial-intelligence-b7f19d18022

Berruti, F., Nel, P. and Whiteman, R. (2020). An Executive Primer on Artificial General Intelligence. April 29, 2020. Mckinsey and Company. Retrieved from https://www.mckinsey.com/business-functions/operations/our-insights/an-executive-primer-on-artificial-general-intelligence

Blackmore, S. (2011). Consciousness – An Introduction. Oxford: Oxford University Press.

Botvinick, M. (May 2019). Reinforcement Learning, Fast and Slow. Trends in Cognitive Sciences, 23(5): 408–422.

Böcker, A., et al. (2005). A Hierarchical Clustering Approach for Large Compound Libraries. Journal of Chemical Information and Modeling, 45(4): 807–815.

Bradley, F.H. (1999). On Truth and Copying. In S. Blackburn & K. Simmons (eds.), Truth. Oxford: Oxford University Press, pp. 31–45.

Brooks, R. (1991). Intelligence without Representation. Artificial Intelligence, 47: 139–159, 389–401.

Bryson, A.E. and Ho, Y.-C. (1975). Applied Optimal Control: Optimization, Estimation and Control. Boca Raton, FL: CRC Press.

Carini, C., Menon, S. and Chang, M. (2014). Clinical and Statistical Considerations in Personalized Medicine. Taylor and Francis, CRC, Chapman & Hall.

Chabris, C.F. and Simons, D.J. (2010). The Invisible Gorilla and Other Ways Our Intuitions Deceive Us. New York, NY: Crown.

Chalmers, D.J. (1995) Facing Up to the Problem of Consciousness. Journal of Consciousness Studies, 2(3): 200–219.

Chang, M. (1996). WinGSAS – A Software Automatically Generates SAS Code (SAS Code Generator). Amherst, MA: University of Massachusetts.

Chang, M. (2007, 2014). Adaptive Design Theory and Implementation Using SAS and R. Boca Raton, FL: Chapman & Hall/CRC, Taylor & Francis.

Chang, M. (2010). Monte Carlo Simulation for the Pharmaceutical Industry. Boca Raton, FL: Chapman & Hall/CRC.

Chang, M. (2011). Modern Issues and Methods in Biostatistics. New York, NY: Springer.

Chang, M. (2012). Paradoxes in Scientific Inference. Boca Raton, FL: Taylor & Francis Group, LLC.

Chang, M. (2014). Principles of Scientific Methods. Boca Raton, FL: Mark Chang, Taylor & Francis Group, LLC.

Chang, M. (2015). Introductory Adaptive Design – A Practical Guide with R. Boca Raton, FL: Taylor and Francis/CRC/Chapman & Hall.

Chang, M. (2020). Artificial Intelligence for Drug Development, Precision Medicine and Healthcare. Boca Raton, FL: CRC/Taylor and Francis.

Chang, M. and Boral, A. (2008). ABC of Bayesian Approaches to Drug Development. Pharmaceutical Medicine, 22(3): 141–150. https://doi.org/10.1007/BF03256696

Chang, M. and Chang, M. (2017). iWordNet: A New Approach to Cognitive Science and Artificial Intelligence. Advances in Artificial Intelligence, 2017. https://doi.org/10.1155/2017/1948317

Chang, M., et al. (2019). Innovative Strategies, Statistical Solutions and Simulations for Modern Clinical Trials. Boca Raton, FL: Chapman & Hall/CRC, Taylor & Francis.

Chen, Y., et al. (2015). Cancer Adjuvant Chemotherapy Strategic Classification by Artificial Neural Network With Gene Expression Data: An Example for non-Small Cell Lung Cancer. Journal of Biomedical Informatics, 56: 1–7.

Chen, W., Grangier, D. and Auli, M. (2015). Strategies for Training Large Vocabulary Neural Language Models. Proceedings of the 54th Annual Meeting of the Association for Computational Linguistics, vol. 1, 1975–1985.

Chirgwin, R. (2014). What's That PARASITE Wriggling Inside My Browser? Nematode Fanciers Open Their Worm to a Kickstarter. The Register, p. 1.

Chisholm, H. (ed.) (1911). Association of Ideas. Encyclopedia Britannica 2 (11th ed.). Cambridge: Cambridge University Press, pp. 784–786.

Chow, S.C. and Chang, M. (2006, 2011). Adaptive Design Methods in Clinical Trials. Boca Raton, FL: Chapman & Hall/CRC.

Copeland, B.J. (2022). Encyclopædia Britannica. Retrieved November 13, 2022 from www.britannica.com/technology/connectionism-artificial-intelligence

Collobert, R. and Weston, J. (2008). A Unified Architecture for Natural Language Processing. Proceedings of the 25th International Conference on Machine Learning - ICML '08, 20(1): 160–167. http://doi.org/10.1145/1390156.1390177

Collobert, R., Weston, J., Bottou, L., Karlen, M., Kavukcuoglu, K. and Kuksa, P. (2011). Natural Language Processing (almost) from Scratch. Journal of Machine Learning Research, 12(Aug): 2493–2537. Retrieved from http://arxiv.org/abs/1103.0398

Corballis, M. (2007). The Uniqueness of Human Recursive Thinking. American Scientist, 95: 240–248.

Cowen, A.S. and Keltner, D. (2017). Self-report Captures 27 Distinct Categories of Emotion Bridged by Continuous Gradients. Proceedings of the National Academy of Sciences, 114(38): E7900–09.

Cuevas, E., Osuna-Enciso, V., Zaldivar, D., Perez-Cisneros, M. and Sossa, H. (2012). Multi-Threshold Segmentation Based on Artificial Immune Systems. Mathematical Problems in Engineering, 2015: 874761.

Curtis, V., Aunger, R. and deBarra, M. (2011). Disgust as an Adaptive System for Disease Avoidance Behaviour. Philosophical Transactions of the Royal Society B, 366(1563): 389–401.

Czibula, G., et al. (2015). A Reinforcement Learning Model for Solving the Folding Problem. International Journal of Computer Applications, 171–182.

Davis, R.L. and Zhong, Y. (Aug 2, 2017). The Biology of Forgetting – A Perspective. Neuron, 95(3): 490–503.

Dennett, D., (1987). True Believers. The Intentional Stance. Cambridge, MA: The MIT Press, pp. 212–216.

Doppler, C., et al. (2017). Unsupervised Anomaly Detection with Generative Adversarial Networks to Guide Marker Discovery. Ithaca, NY: Cornell University.

Dorigo, M. (1992). Optimization, Learning and Natural Algorithms. PhD thesis, Politecnico di Milano, Italy.

Drescher, G.L. (1991). Made-up Minds – A Constructivist Approach to Artificial Intelligence. Cambridge, MA: MIT Press.

Duffy, T.M. and Jonassen, D.H. (1992). Constructivism: New Implications for Instructional Technology. In T.M. Duffy & D.H. Jonassen (eds.), Constructivism and the Technology of Instruction – A Conversation. Hillsdale, NJ: Erlbaum, pp. 1–16.

Eichler, H.G. and Sweeney, F. (2008). The Evolution of Clinical Trials: Can We Address the Challenges of the Future? Clinical Trials, 15(S1): 27–32.

Esteva, A., et al. (2017). Dermatologist-Level Classification of Skin Cancer With Deep Neural Networks. Nature, 542(7639): 115–118.

Fairbanks, B. (2021). Five Educational Learning Theories and How to Apply Them. Retrieved from www.phoenix.edu/blog/educational-learning-theories.html

Fang, M., et al. (July 2018). Feature Selection via Swarm Intelligence for Determining Protein Essentiality. Molecules, 23(7): 1569.

Farley, B.G. and Clark, W.A. (1954). Simulation of Self-Organizing Systems by Digital Computer. IRE Transactions on Information Theory, 4: 76–84.

Farooq, S.M.A. (2017). A Deep CNN Based Multi-class Classification of Alzheimer's Disease Using MRI. Presented at the IST, 2017.

Fathi, M., et al. (November 2013). Cellular Automata Modeling of Hesperetin Release Phenomenon from Lipid Nanocarriers. Food and Bioprocess Technology. 6(11): 3134–3142.

Fechner, G.T. (1966) [First published. 1860]. In D.H. Howes & E.G. Boring (eds.), Elements of Psychophysics [Elemente *der* Psychophysik], vol. 1. (Translated by H. E. Adler). New York, NY: Holt, Rinehart and Winston, pp. 31–45.

von Foerster, E. (1973). On Constructing a Reality. In W. Preiser (ed.), Environmental Research Design, vol. 2. Stroudsburg: Dowden, Hutchinson and Ross, pp. 35–46.

Forsyth, R. (1981). BEAGLE: A Darwinian Approach to Pattern Recognition. Kybernetes, 10: 159–166.

Fox, R. (2001). Constructivism Examined. Oxford Review of Education, 27(1): 23–35.

Fu, Y., et al. (2015). A New Approach for Flexible Molecular Docking Based on Swarm Intelligence. Mathematical Problems in Engineering. 2015: 540186.

Garcia-Albea, J.E. and Lobina, D.J. (2009). Recursion and Cognitive Science: Data Structures and Mechanisms. Cognitive Science Society. Proceedings of the Annual Meeting of the Cognitive Science Society, 31: 1347–1352.

Georgeon, O.L., Casado, R.C. and Matignon, L.A. (2015). Modeling Biological Agents Beyond the Reinforcement-Learning Paradigm. Procedia Computer Science, 71: 17–22

Ghaheri, A., et al. (November 2015). The Applications of Genetic Algorithms in Medicine. Oman Medical Journal, 30(6): 406–416.

Ghasemi, F., et al. (2018a). Neural Network and Deep-Learning Algorithms Used in QSAR Studies: Merits and Drawbacks. Drug Discovery Today, 23(10): 1784–1790.

Ghasemi, F., et al. (2018b). Deep Neural Network in QSAR Studies Using Deep Belief Network. Applied Soft Computing, 62(2018): 251–258.

Ghosh, A. and Lakhmi, C.J. (eds.) (2005). Evolutionary Computation in Data Mining. Berlin/ Heidelberg: Springer-Verlag.

Giuliani, A. (July 2017). The Application of Principal Component Analysis to Drug Discovery and Biomedical Data. Drug Discovery Today, 22(7): 1069–1076.

Glasersfeld, E. (1995). Radical Constructivism: A Way of Knowing and Learning. London: The Falmer Press.

Gleitman, L. (2005). Language and thought (PDF). Cambridge Handbook of Thinking and Reasoning. Cambridge: Cambridge University Press.

Goertzel, B. (July 16, 2016). AGI Revolution: An Inside View of the Rise of Artificial General Intelligence. London: Humanity & Press.

Goertzel, B., et al. (eds.) (2020). Artificial General Intelligence. Proceedings of the 13th International Conference, AGI 2020. Berlin: Springer.

Goertzel, B. and Ikle, M. (2012). Introduction. International Journal of Machine Consciousness, 04: 1–3.

Goodfellow, I., et al. (2018). Deep Learning (Adaptive Computation and Machine Learning Series). Cambridge, MA: The MIT Press.

Gottlieb, S. (April, 2019). Statement from FDA Commissioner Scott Gottlieb, M.D. on Steps Toward a New, Tailored Review Framework for Artificial Intelligence-Based Medical Devices. Retrieved from https://www.fda.gov/NewsEvents/Newsroom/PressAnnouncements/ucm635083.htm

Guerin, F. (2008). Constructivism in AI: Prospects, Progress and Challenges. 34th Annual Convention of the Society for the Study of Artificial Intelligence and the Simulation of Behaviour (AISB 2008). Communication, Interaction and Social Intelligence, 1–4 April 2008, Aberdeen, United Kingdom.

Gulshan, V., et al. (2016). Development and Validation of a Deep Learning Algorithm for Detection of Diabetic Retinopathy in Retinal fundus Photographs. JAMA, 316: 2402–2410.

Guney, E., et al. (2016). Network-Based in Silico Drug Efficacy Screening. Natural Communications, 7: 10331.

Gupta, A., et al. (2018). Generative Recurrent Networks for De Novo Drug Design. Molecular Informatics, 37: 1700111.

Hastie, T., et al. (2001). The Elements of Statistical Learning: Data Mining, Inference, and Prediction (2nd ed.). New York, NY: Springer.

Haugeland, J. (1985). Artificial Intelligence: The Very Idea. Cambridge, MA: MIT Press.

Hauser, M.D., Fitch, W.T. and Chomsky, N. (2002). The Faculty of Language: What Is It, Who Has It, and How Did It Evolve? Science, 298: 1569–1579.

Haybron, D.M. (2000). The Causal and Explanatory Role of Information Stored in Connectionist Networks. Minds and Machines, 10(3): 361–380.

Hebb, D. (1949). The Organization of Behaviour. Hoboken, NJ: John Wiley & Sons.

Herbranson, W. T., & Schroeder, J. (2010). Are birds smarter than mathematicians? Pigeons (Columba livia) perform optimally on a version of the Monty Hall Dilemma. Journal of Comparative Psychology, 124(1): 1–13.

Herrnstein, R.J. (1972). Nature as Nurture: Behaviorism and the Instinct Doctrine. Behaviorism, 1(1): 23–52.

Hilbe, J. M. (1977). Fundamentals of Conceptual Analysis. Dubuque, IA: Kendall/Hunt Pub Co.

Hochreiter, S. and Schmidhuber, J. (1997). Long Short-Term Memory. Neural Computation, 9(8): 1735–1780.

Holyoak, K.J. and Thagard, P. (1989). Analogical Mapping by Constraint Satisfaction. Cognitive Science, 13: 295–355.

Holyoak, K.J. and Thagard, P. (1995). Mental Leaps: Analogy in Creative Thought. Cambridge, MA: MIT Press.

Huang, Z., Dong, W. and Duan, H. (2015). A Probabilistic Topic Model for Clinical Risk Stratification from Electronic Health Records. Journal of Biomedical Informatics, 58: 28–36.

Hussain, S.M.A. (2017). Brain Tumor Segmentation Using Cascaded Deep Convolutional Neural Network. Presented at the EMBC 2017.

Hutchins, J. (1999). Retrospect and Prospect in Computer-Based Translation. Proceedings of MT Summit VII, pp. 30–44.

Hwang, S. and Chang, M. (2022). Similarity-Principle-Based Machine Learning Method for Clinical Trials and Beyond. Statistics in Biopharmaceutical Research, 14(4): 511–522.

Izhikevich, E.M. and Edelman, G.M. (2008). Large-Scale Model of Mammalian Thalamocortical Systems. Proceedings of the National Academy Sciences, 105(9): 3593–3598.

Jackson, P.C. (2019). Toward Human-Level Artificial Intelligence: Representation and Computation of Meaning in Natural Language (Dover Books on Mathematics). Mineola, NY: Dover Publications.

Jaynes, E.T. (1957a). Information Theory and Statistical Mechanics. Physical Review, 106 (4): 620–630.

Jaynes, E.T. (1957b). Information Theory and Statistical Mechanics II. Physical Review, 108(2): 171–190.

Jozefowicz, R., Vinyals, O., Schuster, M., Shazeer, N. and Wu, Y. (2016). Exploring the Limits of Language Modeling. Retrieved from http://arxiv.org/abs/1602.02410

Kadurin, A., et al. (2017). The Cornucopia of Meaningful Leads: Applying Deep Adversarial Autoencoders for New Molecule Development in Oncology. Oncology, 8(7). https://doi.org/10.18632/oncotarget.14073

Kadurin, M., et al. (2017). druGAN: An Advanced Generative Adversarial Autoencoder Model for De Novo Generation of New Molecules with Desired Molecular Properties in Silico. Molecular Pharmaceutics, 14(9): 3098–3104.

Kahneman, D. (2011). Thinking, Fast and Slow (1st ed.). New York, NY: Farrar, Straus and Giroux.

Kier, L.B. (July 1996). A Cellular Automata Model of Enzyme Kinetics. Journal of Molecular Graphics, 14(4): 227–231.

Kim, Y., Jernite, Y., Sontag, D. and Rush, A.M. (2016). Character-Aware Neural Language Models. Proceedings of the AAAI Conference on Artificial Intelligence, 30(1). https://doi.org/10.1609/aaai.v30i1.10362

Kim, J.K., Kang, U. and Lee, Y. (June 2017). Statistics and Deep Belief Network-Based Cardiovascular Risk Prediction. Healthcare Informatics Research, 23(3): 169–175.

Klein, G. (2001). The Fiction of Optimization. In G. Gigerenzer & R. Selten (eds.), Bounded Rationality: The Adaptive Toolbox (1st ed.). London: MIT Press, pp. 111–112.

Koch, C. (2018). What Is Consciousness? Retrieved from https://www.scientificamerican.com/article/what-is-consciousness/

Kolmogorov, A. (1963). On Tables of Random Numbers. Sankhyā Ser. A. 25: 369–375. MR 0178484

Korb, O., et al. (2006). PLANTS: Application of Ant Colony Optimization to Structure-Based Drug Design. In Marco Dorigo (ed.) ANTS 2006: Ant Colony Optimization and Swarm Intelligence. Berlin: Springer, pp. 247–258.

Kosiński, W. and Zaczek-Chrzanowska, D. (2007). Pavlovian, Skinner, and Other Behaviourists Contributions to AI. NASA Technical Reports Server (NTRS) 20070038351

Koza, J. (1992). Genetic Programming: On the Programming of Computers by Means of Natural Selection (Complex Adaptive Systems) (1st ed.). Cambridge, MA: MIT Press.

Koza, J. (1994). Genetic Programming II: Automatic Discovery of Reusable Programs (Complex Adaptive Systems) (1st ed.). Cambridge, MA: MIT Press.

Koza, J., et al. (1999). Genetic Programming III: Darwinian Invention and Problem Solving (vol. 3, 1st ed.). Burlington, MA: Morgan Kaufmann.

Koza, J. (2010). Human-Competitive Results Produced by Genetic Programming. Genet Program Evolvable Mach, 11: 251–284.

Koza, J., et al. (2003). Genetic Programming IV: Routine Human-Competitive Machine Intelligence (1st ed.). Berlin: Springer.

Kuo, M.H., et al. (2009). Application of the A priori Algorithm for Adverse Drug Reaction Detection. Studies in Health Technology and Informatics, 148: 95–101.

Kwon, S. and Yoon, S. (2017). DeepCCI: End-to-End Deep Learning for Chemical Interaction Prediction. Preprint, arXiv1704.08432.

Langdon, W.B. and Buxton, B.F. (2004). Genetic Programming for Mining DNA Chip Data from Cancer Patients. Genetic Programming and Evolvable Machines, 5(3): 251–257.

Lutz, C. and White, G.M. (1986). The Anthropology of Emotions. Annual Review of Anthropology, 15: 405–436.

Mandal, S., Saha, G. and Pal, R.K. (2013). Reconstruction of Dominant Gene Regulatory Network from Microarray Data Using Rough Set and Bayesian Approach. Journal of Computer Science & Systems Biology, 6(5): 262–270.

Marsland, S. (2014). Machine Learning: An Algorithmic Perspective (2nd ed.). Boca Raton, FL: CRC Press Taylor & Francis Group.

Mandal, F.B. (2010). Textbook of Animal Behaviour. New Delhi: PHI Learning. p. 47.

Mao, J., Gan, C., Kohli, P., et al. (2019). The Neuro-Symbolic Concept Learner: Interpreting Scenes, Words, and Sentences from Natural Supervision. Presented as a Conference Paper at ICLR 2019. Retrieved from https://openreview.net/forum?id=rJgMlhRctm

Marques de, S.J.P. (2008). Chance, the Life of Games & the Game of Life. Berlin/Heidelberg: Springer-Verlag.

Maslow, A.H. (1954). Instinct Theory Reexamined. Motivation and Personality. New York, NY: Harper & Row.

Materi, W. and Wishart, D.S. (2007). Computational Systems Biology in Drug Discovery and Development: Methods and Applications. Drug Discovery Today, 12(7/8): 295–303.

Matlin, M.W. (2013). Cognition (Textbook) (8th ed.). Hoboken, NJ: Wiley.

McCarthy, J. (2006). The Philosophy of AI and the AI of Philosophy. Retrieved from http://www-formal.stanford.edu/jmc/ 25 June 2006

McCarthy, J. (2007). From Here to Human-Level AI. Artificial Intelligence, 171: 1174–1182.

McCarthy, J. (2008). The Well-Designed Child. Artificial Intelligence, 172: 2003–2014.

McCulloch, W.S. and Pitts, W. (1943). A Logical Calculus of the Ideas Immanent in Nervous Activity. The Bulletin of Mathematical Biophysics, 5: 115–133.

McDougall, W. (1928). An Introduction to Social Psychology (21st ed.). London: Methuen & Co. Ltd, p. xxii.

McGill, V.J. and Parry, W.T. (Fall 1948). The Unity of Opposites: A Dialectical Principle. Science & Society, 12(4): 418–444.

Menche, J., et al. (2015). Uncovering Disease-Disease Relationships Through the Incomplete Interactome. Science, 347, 1257601

Mikolov, T., Chen, K., Corrado, G. and Dean, J. (2013). Distributed Representations of Words and Phrases and Their Compositionality. Proceedings of the 26th International Conference on Neural Information Processing Systems, pp. 1–9. Ithaca, NY: Cornell University.

Mikolov, T., Corrado, G., Chen, K. and Dean, J. (2013). Efficient Estimation of Word Representations in Vector Space. Proceedings of the International Conference on Learning Representations (ICLR 2013), pp. 1–12.

Mill, J.S. (1865). Examination of Hamilton's Philosophy. Boston, MA: William V. Spencer, p. 134.

Miller, R.G., et al. (April 1993). The Fatigue of Rapid Repetitive Movements. Neurology, 43(4): 755–761.

Miller, T.P., et al. (2017). Using Electronic Medical Record Data to Report Laboratory Adverse Events. British Journal of Haematology, 177: 283–286.

Minsky, M.L. (1954). Theory of Neural-Analog Reinforcement Systems and Its Application to the Brain-Model Problem. PhD thesis, Princeton University.

Minsky, M.L. (1963). Steps toward artificial intelligence. Proceedings of the Institute of Radio Engineers, 49: 8–30. (Reprinted in E.A. Feigenbaum & J. Feldman (eds.), Computers and Thought. New York, NY: McGraw-Hill, pp. 406–450.)

Minsky, M. (1988). The Society of Mind (1st ed.). New York, NY: Simon & Schuster.

Minsky, M. (2007). The Emotion Machine: Commonsense Thinking, Artificial Intelligence, and the Future of the Human Mind. New York, NY: Simon & Schuster.

Mistry, P., et al. (2016). Using Random Forest and Decision Tree Models for a New Vehicle Prediction Approach in Computational Toxicology. Soft Computing, 20: 2967–2979

Murphy, P.A. (2020). Advocates of Artificial Intelligence as Behaviourists. Retrieved from https://becominghuman.ai/advocates-of-artificial-intelligence-as-behaviourists-1233b36b9f61

Nigsch, F., et al. (2006). Melting Point Prediction Employing k-Nearest Neighbor Algorithms and Genetic Parameter Optimization. Journal of Chemical Information and Modeling, 46(2006): 2412–2422

Panksepp, J. and Biven, L. (2012). The Archaeology of Mind: Neuroevolutionary Origins of Human Emotions (Norton Series on Interpersonal Neurobiology). New York, NY: W. W. Norton & Company.

Pennington, J., Socher, R. and Manning, C.D. (2014). Glove: Global Vectors for Word Representation. Proceedings of the 2014 Conference on Empirical Methods in Natural Language Processing, pp. 1532–1543. http://doi.org/10.3115/v1/D14-1162

Perez, C.E. (2021). Constructivism and Exponential AI Growth. Retrieved from https://medium.com/intuitionmachine/constructivism-and-exponential-growth-d00846c6c602

Piaget, J. (1936). The Origin of Intelligence in the Child. London: Routledge & Kegan Paul.

Piaget, J. (1945). Play, Dreams and Imitation in Childhood. London: Heinemann.

Piaget, J. (1954). Construction of Reality in the Child. London: Routledge & Kegan Paul.

Plutchik, R. (2002). Nature of Emotions. American Scientist, 89(4): 349.

Poli, R., et al. (2008). A Field Guide to Genetic Programming. Morrisville, NC: Lulu Enterprises.

Poorinmohammad, N., et al. (December 2014). Computational Prediction of Anti HIV-1 Peptides and in Vitro Evaluation of Anti HIV-1 Activity of HIV-1 P24-Derived Peptides. Journal of Peptide Science, 21(1): 10–16.

Putin, E., et al. (October 1, 2018). Adversarial Threshold Neural Computer for Molecular De Novo Design. Molecular Pharmacy, 15(10): 4386–4397.

Qayyuma, A., et al. (2018). Medical Image Analysis using Convolutional Neural Networks: A Review. Journal of Medical Systems, 42: 226.

Rajeshkumar, J. and Kousalya, K. (2017). Applications of Swarm Based Intelligence Algorithms in Pharmaceutical Industry: A Review. International Research Journal of Pharmacy, 8 (11): 24–27.

Ramsey, W. (1997). Do Connectionist Representations Earn Their Explanatory Keep? Mind & Language, 12(1): 34–66.

Rehme, A.K., et al. (2015). Identifying Neuroimaging Markers of Motor Disability in Acute Stroke by Machine Learning Techniques. Cereb Cortex 25: 3046–3056.

Reich, K. (2004). Konstruktivistische Didaktik. Lehren und Lernen aus interaktionistischer Sicht (2nd ed.). Munich: Luchterhan.

Reich, K. (2009). Constructivism: Diversity of Approaches and Connections with Pragmatism. In L.A. Hickman, S. Neubert, & K. Reich (eds.), John Dewey Between Pragmatism and Constructivism. New York, NY: Fordham University Press.

Reker, D., Rodrigues, T., Schneider, P. and Schneider, G. (March 18, 2014). Identifying the Macromolecular Targets of De Novo-Designed Chemical Entities Through Self-Organizing Map Consensus. Proceedings of the National Academy of Sciences, 111(11): 4067–4072.

Riegler, A. (1992). Constructivist Artificial Life and Beyond. Workshop on Autopoiesis and Perception. Dublin City University, August 1992.

Rodriguez, J. (July 2, 2018). The Science Behind OpenAI Five that just Produced One of the Greatest Breakthroughs in the History of AI. Towards Data Science Retrieved January 15, 2019.

Rohrer, B. (2019). How Convolutional Neural Networks Work. Retrieved from https://brohrer.github.io/how_convolutional_neural_networks_work.html

Rose, J. (2009). The Early Years: Some Comments on the Origins and Concepts of Cybernetics. Kybernetes, 38(1/2): 20–24.

Roth, M. (2005). Program Execution in Connectionist Networks. Mind & Language, 20(4): 448–467.

Russell, S. and Norvig, P. (2003). Artificial Intelligence: A Modern Approach (2nd ed.). Prentice Hall Series in Artificial Intelligence. Hoboken, NJ: Prentice Hall.

Saber Tehrani, A.S., Lee, H. and Mathews, S.C., et al. (2013). 25-Year Summary of US Malpractice Claims for Diagnostic Errors 1986-2010: An Analysis from the National Practitioner Data Bank. BMJ Quality and Safety, 22(8): 672–680.

Salmon, W.C. (1967). The Foundations of Scientific Inference. Pittsburgh, PA: University of Pittsburgh Press.

Samuel, A.L. (1959). Some Studies in Machine Learning Using the Game of Checkers. IBM Journal on Research and Development, 3(3): 210–229. (Reprinted in E.A. Feigenbaum & J. Feldman (eds.), Computers and Thought. New York, NY: McGraw-Hill, 1963, pp. 71–105.)

Sandberg, A. and Boström, N. (2008). Whole Brain Emulation: A Roadmap. Technical Report #2008-3. Oxford: Future of Humanity Institute, Oxford University.

Santos, R.M.Z. and Coutinho, S. (October 2001). Dynamics of HIV Infection: A Cellular Automata Approach. Physical Review Letters, 87(16): 168102.

Scarpelli, S. and Bartolacci, C., et al. (March 15, 2019). The Functional Role of Dreaming in Emotional Processes. Frontier Psychology, 10: 459.

Schacter, D.L. (2011). Psychology (2nd ed.). New York, NY: Worth Publishers.

Scheler, G. (2017). Logarithmic Distributions Prove That Intrinsic Learning Is Hebbian. F1000Research, 6: 1222.

Schmid, T. (2018). *Autom*atisierte Analyse von Impedanz-Spektren mittels konstruktivistischen maschinellen Lernens. PhD thesis, Leipzig.

Schmid, T. (2019). Deconstructing the Final Frontier of Artificial Intelligence: Five Theses for a Constructivist Machine Learning. In A. Martin, K. Hinkelmann, A. Gerber, D. Lenat, F. van Harmelen, & P. Clark (eds.), Proceedings of the AAAI 2019 Spring Symposium on Combining Machine Learning with Knowledge Engineering (AAAI-MAKE 2019). Stanford, CA: Stanford University.

Schmider, J., et al. (2019). Innovation in Pharmacovigilance: Use of Artificial Intelligence in Adverse Event Case Processing. Clinical Pharmacology & Therapeutics, 105(4): 954–961.

Schneider, G. and Schneider, P. (2017). Macromolecular Target Prediction by Self-Organizing Feature Maps. Expert Opinion on Drug Discovery, 12(3): 271–277.

Schneider, P., Tanrikulu, Y. and Schneider, G. (December 31, 2008). Self-Organizing Maps in Drug Discovery: Compound Library Design, Scaffold-Hopping, Repurposing. Current Medicinal Chemistry, 16(3): 258–266.

Schölkopf, E., et al. (2004). Kernel Methods in Computational Biology. Cambridge, MA: MIT Press.

Segev, I. (2019). Retrieved from https://www.youtube.com/watch?v=sEiDxti0opE

Segura-Bedmar, I. and Martinez, P. (2015). Pharmacovigilance Through the Development of Text Mining and Natural Language Processing Techniques. Journal of Biomedical Informatics, 58: 288–291.

Selvin, S. (1975). A Problem in Probability (Letter to the Editor). The American Statistician, 29(1): 67–71.

Shahlaei, C.Y.M. (2017). The Applications of PCA in QSAR Studies: A Case Study on CCR5 Antagonists. Chemical Biology and Drug Design, 91: 137–152

Shannon, C.E. (1950). Programming a Computer for Playing Chess. Philosophical Magazine, 41: 256–275

Shi, L.M., et al. (February 1998). Mining the National Cancer Institute Anticancer Drug Discovery Database: Cluster Analysis of Ellipticine Analogs With p53-Inverse and Central Nervous System-Selective Patterns of Activity. Molecular Pharmacology, 53(2): 241–51.

Shiota, M.N. (2016). Ekman's Theory of Basic Emotions. In H.L. Miller (ed.), The Sage Encyclopedia of Theory in Psychology. Thousand Oaks, CA: Sage Publications, pp. 248–250.

Sirota, M., et al. (2011). Discovery and Preclinical Validation of Drug Indications Using Compendia of Public Gene Expression Data. Science Translational Medicine, 3(96): 96ra77.

Sloman, A. (1978). The Computer Revolution in Philosophy: Philosophy Science and Models of Mind. Birmingham: University of Birmingham. Retrieved from http://www.cs.bham.ac.uk/research/projects/cogaff/crp/ https://www.cs.bham.ac.uk/research/projects/cogaff/crp/chap6.html

Smith, L. and Gasser, M. (2005). The Development of Embodied Cognition: Six Lessons from Babies. Artificial Life,11(1–2): 13–29. https://doi.org/10.1162/1064546053278973

Smolensky, P. (1999). Grammar-Based Connectionist Approaches to Language. Cognitive Science, 23(4): 589–613. https://doi.org/10.1207/s15516709cog2304_9

Swaminathan, N. (January–February 2011). Glia—the Other Brain Cells. Discover. Archived from the original on 8 February 2014. Retrieved January 24, 2014.

Soulami, K.S., et al. (2017). A CAD System for the Detection of Abnormalities in the Mammograms Using the Metaheuristic Algorithm Particle Swarm Optimization (PSO). In E. Sabir, H. Medromi, & M. Sadik (eds.), Advances in Ubiquitous Networking (2nd ed.). Berlin: Springer, pp. 505–517.

Stanford, S. (January 25, 2019). DeepMind's AI, AlphaStar Showcases Significant Progress Towards AGI. Medium ML Memoirs. Retrieved January 15, 2019

Stanford.edu (1993). Retrieved from https://news.stanford.edu/pr/93/931115Arc3062.html

Stanford.edu (2018). Retrieved from https://plato.stanford.edu/entries/social-norms/

Stanford.edu (2019a). Retrieved from https://plato.stanford.edu/entries/language-thought/

Stanford.edu (2019b). Retrieved from https://plato.stanford.edu/entries/connectionism/

Sun, G., Matsui, T., Hakozaki, Y. and Abe, S. (2015). An Infectious Disease/Fever Screening Radar System Which Stratifies Higher-Risk Patients Within Ten Seconds Using a Neural Network and the Fuzzy Grouping Method. Journal of Infection, 70(3): 230–236.

Sutton, R.S. and Barto, A.G. (2018). Reinforcement Learning: An Introduction (2nd ed.). Denver, CO: Bradford Books.

Tarantola, A. (2022). MIT Solved a Century-Old Differential Equation to Break 'Liquid' AI's Computational Bottleneck — The Discovery Could Usher in a New Generation of Weather Forecasting and Autonomous Vehicle Driving Virtual Agents. Engadget. Retrieved from https://www.engadget.com

Thomas, N. and Mathew, D. (2016). KNN Based ECG Pattern Analysis and Classification. International Journal of Science, Engineering and Technology Research (IJSETR), 5(5).

Tzezana, R. (2017). Artificial Intelligence Tech Will Arrive in Three Waves. Futurism. 3. 28. 17. Retrieved from https://futurism.com/artificial-intelligence-tech-will-arrive-in-three-waves

Vanhaelen, Q., Aliper, A.M. and Zhavoronkov, A. (2017). A Comparative Review of Computational Methods for Pathway Perturbation Analysis: Dynamical and Topological Perspectives. Molecular Biosystems, 13: 1692–1704.

Veldhuyzen, W. and Stassen, H.G. (1977). The Internal Model Concept: an Application to Modeling Human Control of Large Ships. Human Factors: The Journal of the Human Factors and Ergonomics Society, 19(4): 367–380.

Von Eckardt, B. (2003). The Explanatory Need for Mental Representations in Cognitive Science. Mind & Language, 18(4): 427–439.

Wallace, M. and Dunlop, G. (1999). Retrieved from http://psych.fullerton.edu/mbirnbaum/psych101/eliza.htm

Wang, L., Zang, J., Zhang, Q., et al. (2018). Action Recognition by an Attention-Aware Temporal Weighted Convolutional Neural Network (PDF). Sensors, 18(7): 1979.

Warren, H.C. (1921). A History of the Association Psychology. New York, NY: Charles Scribner's Sons.

Watkins, C.J.C.H. (1989). Learning from Delayed Rewards. PhD thesis, Cambridge University.

Weidlich, I.E., et al. (2013). Inhibitors for the Hepatitis C Virus RNA Polymerase Explored by SAR with Advanced Machine Learning Methods. Bioorganic and Medicinal Chemistry, 21, 3127–3137.

Weizenbaum, J. (1966). ELIZA–A Computer Program for the Study of Natural Language Communication Between Man and Machine. Communications of the ACM. 9: 36–35.

Werbos, P.J. (1987). Building and Understanding Adaptive Systems: A statistical/numerical Approach to Factory Automation and Brain Research. IEEE Transactions on Systems, Man, and Cybernetics, 17: 7–20.

Williams, R.J., Hinton, G.E. and Rumelhart, D.E. (October 1986). Learning Representations by Back-Propagating Errors. Nature, 323(6088): 533–536.

Wishart, D.S., et al. (2005). Dynamic Cellular Automata: An Alternative Approach to Cellular Simulation. Silico Biology, 5:139–161.

Xiao, Y. and Harris, R. (2006). Supervised Self-Organizing Maps in Drug Discovery. 2. Improvements in Descriptor Selection and Model Validation. Journal of Chemical Information and Modeling, 46: 137–144.

Yahi, A., et al. (2017). Generative Adversarial Networks for Electronic Health Records: A Framework for Exploring and Evaluating Methods for Predicting Drug-Induced Laboratory Test Trajectories. In U. Von Luxburg and I. Guyon (eds.), Proceeding of 31st Conference on Neural Information Processing Systems (NIPS 2017), Curran Associates Inc. Long Beach, CA, USA

Yan, A. (July 2006). Application of Self-Organizing Maps in Compounds Pattern Recognition and Combinatorial Library Design. Combinatorial Chemistry and High Throughput Screening, 9(6): 473–480.

Yang, M., Kiang, M. and Shang, W. (2015). Filtering Big Data from Social Media: Building an Early Warning System for Adverse Drug Reactions. Journal of Biomedical Informatics, 54: 230–240.

Yonelinas, A.P., Aly, M., Wang, W.C. and Koen, J.D. (November 2010). Recollection and Familiarity: Examining Controversial Assumptions and New Directions. Hippocampus, 20(11): 1178–1194.

Zang, J., Wang, L., Liu, Z., et al. (2018). Attention-Based Temporal Weighted Convolutional Neural Network for Action Recognition. In Lazaros Iliadis, Ilias Maglogiannis, Vassilis Plagianakos (eds.) AIAI 2018: Artificial Intelligence Applications and Innovations. IFIP Advances in Information and Communication Technology. Cham: Springer International Publishing, pp. 97–108.

Zhang, W., et al. (2015). Deep Convolutional Neural Networks for Multi-Modality Isointense Infant Brain Image Segmentation. NeuroImage, 108: 214–224.

Zhang, Z., et al. (February 2017). Hierarchical Cluster Analysis in Clinical Research With Heterogeneous Study Population: Highlighting Its Visualization With R. Annals of Translational Medicine, 5(4): 75.

Zimek, A., Schubert, E. (2017). Outlier Detection. In L. Liu & M.T. Özsu (eds.) Encyclopedia of Database Systems. Berlin: Springer, pp. 1–5.

Zhou, T., et al. (2010). Solving the Apparent Diversity-Accuracy Dilemma of Recommender Systems. Proceedings of the National Academy of Sciences, 107: 4511–4515.

Zygourakis, P.K. and Markenscoff, A. (1996). Computer-Aided Design of Bioerodible Devices with Optimal Release Characteristics: A Cellular Automata Approach. Biomaterials, 17(2): 125–135.

Index

Note: Locators in *italics* represent figures and **bold** indicate tables in the text.

9781032491578